# Introduction to the Use of Computers in Libraries

# Introduction to the Use of Computers in Libraries
## A Textbook for the Non-Technical Student

By Harold C. Ogg

**Information Today, Inc.**
Medford, NJ
1997

Special thanks to:
Lucinda J. Angell, Information Specialist,
for her research and assistance.

Printed in the United States of America.

**Library of Congress Cataloging-in-Publication Data**

Ogg, Harold C.
       Introduction to the use of computers in libraries  / Harold C. Ogg
       p.      cm.
       Includes bibliographical references and index.
       ISBN 0-938734-99-7
       1. Libraries—Data processing.   I. Title.
   Z678.9.O28   1997
   025'.00285—dc21                                          96-45414
                                                                CIP

Price: $42.50

Editors: Lauree Padgett, Diane Zelley
Cover Design: Jeanne Wachter

# Contents

# Preface

This is a therapy book about desktop computers. Its aim is to heal one malady—technophobia—by prescribing a regimen of pragmatic applications for users and potential users of such hardware. It is at the same time a book on library automation bent on serving as a good explanation rather than a purveyance of theory. This intent will probably offend the purists and theoreticians, but PCs are costly and there is work to be done.

The text was also created on the assumption that librarians and educators took vows of poverty upon receiving their MLS, AMLS, M.Ed., or other similar professional degrees. Since it appears that the well-funded armed services will not be holding bake sales to purchase new tanks and bombers, thereby not yielding their shares of revenues to libraries and schools, we in the book business are stuck sometimes with the necessity of invoking such fundraising vehicles and must make do with resources at hand. But we *do* derive a bit of ironic satisfaction from being able to perform our duties cheaper *and* better, and that's what this book is all about—how to do it good and on a shoestring budget.

Unfortunately, a few librarians, both young and old, have an aversion to anything that plugs into a 115 volt socket, save for a reading light. The sense is that only the technically minded can make a personal computer perform efficiently or with any degree of payback. To soothe that particular mental affliction, this book takes a different approach to teaching the users of computers in libraries, by providing an inundation of examples. If the reader picks up a bit of the theory of computer science along the way, so be it. Such knowledge will make for good conversation at the next trustees' social.

Much of the material herein relates to classroom assignments given the last few years to graduate students who have had little or no training on the use of PCs. The attempt is to relate a familiar activity to an applications software program and let the student manipulate the program with his or her own data. This hands-on approach takes some of the chill out of the air and gives the student a motivation for acquiring further uses of "the box." Thus the practical aspects provide foundations for more abstract concepts in later studies, and the new knowledge impresses the students' department heads and boards of directors immeasurably.

I have found that the concepts of basic computer science are best learned when taught (sometimes by rote) as vocabulary words. As such, these are **boldfaced** in the text and cross-referenced in the index. Sources of programs are given as appropriate, with prices and ordering information. Since no library science text would be respectable without one, there is a bibliography at the end of the chapters, with an annotated list of library/computer science periodicals suggested for first purchase thrown in for good measure.

This text was born of a need for a classroom resource to supplement lectures in computer science for practicing librarians. It is the result of ten years of teaching Introduction to the Information Sciences at Indiana University and the track Introduction to the Use of Computers in Libraries and Library Information Retrieval Systems at Chicago State University. The book is arranged, in fact, such that a two-semester (or two-quarter) sequence of introductory/advanced coursework can be presented following the topical sequence of the chapters. A sample curriculum is presented in Appendix B.

Many years of teaching introductory computer science to librarians have presented to me several common denominators. I have noticed that many of the students who have registered for my classes, although having reached graduate school, have never laid hands on a computer keyboard. While many library schools are mandating that an introductory computer course or two be completed prior to matriculation in an MLS program, I often sense an underlying yet subtle air of technophobia in each new crop of students. I have also found that library school students learn computer technology better if the abstract matters are tied to practical examples. Therefore, this book will stress "library applications" as a central theme as a motivation to learn the nuts and bolts of computer technology.

Many of my students are, or have been, public school teachers. Another frequent occurrence is that their respective institutions tend to have only meager appropriations for computer terminals and workstations. To address this commonality, I have emphasized those machines and utilities which can be had for not much money. The area of so-called high-end computing is not ignored, however, and the final chapters deal with more elaborate setups, including multistation environments.

While the concepts presented throughout the text are generically applicable to all types of computers, the specific emphases are on IBM and compatible personal computers (PCs) and Apple Macintoshes. Minicomputers will be discussed only as they pertain to automated circulation systems. Mainframe and larger computers are included in the discussions for recognition purposes, in the sense that a knowledgeable librarian should be able to deliver good reference service and appropriate literature on the subject. But the examples and illustrations will emphasize the desktop environment because of its widespread popularity and relatively low cost.

Not intending to be encyclopedic, the text nonetheless places a considerable emphasis on terminology. Computer science, like any information science or library science, is keyword and acronym heavy. In addition to being essential for learning the more abstract principles of computer science, I have found that terminology acts as a sort of judo when dealing with patrons and other information scientists. It's rather like speaking Tex-Mex; if you forget the Spanish, just throw in a little English and your listener thinks you have a great command of the south-of-the-border language!

Finally, the bibliography and source lists are intended to be as representative as possible. After all, this is a library science textbook, and reading lists are assumed. One of the intents of this book is that it makes the reader a proficient collection developer and software consumer. It should also be useful for classroom teachers who wish to develop teaching units and media setups.

I was advised some twenty years ago that the best approach to information technology is KISS or Keep it Simple, Stupid! This is perhaps an appropriate acronym with which to introduce the book, and a reasonable credo with which I can claim to have written it. Just don't expect KISS to appear in the index.

For the obligatory technical note: the draft for this text was created using WordPerfect version 5.2 for Windows version 3.1. This word processing software was selected for its ability to handle an elaborate indexing process and multiple on-screen typefaces. The latter, aided by the TrueType technology, added enough variety to the screen to keep me going many nights after normal sleep was past the point of recall.

Harold C. Ogg
Chicago, Illinois

# Chapter 1

# Fundamental Concepts

This text is going to present computer science from the point of view of needs. That is to say, the book will outline computing and information science from a perspective of what librarians and educators need to do with the technology and how it can help them perform their jobs more efficiently. There will, indeed, be a considerable amount of theory interspersed in the readings, but the technospeak will be liberally mingled with practical examples and illustrations. It is the latter, hopefully, that will provide enough motivation for students, librarians, and teachers to enjoy the subject and "take something back to the job" that will enrich this idea we call "information science."

The book begins with an introduction to the hardware—the "stuff" of computers. The next chapters will introduce and detail the programs that can run on various configurations of equipment, working forward through the permutations and intricacies of more advanced computing processes. Initially, however, the text starts with a rigorous overview of hardware from a standpoint that should be familiar to reference librarians: a focus in the manner of *Consumer Reports*, to make readers cognizant of the best plan of attack for obtaining value and quality in the equipment needed for getting started.

## A VERY BRIEF HISTORY OF COMPUTING

This isn't a history book so it will touch only briefly on the developments in computer and information science merely to place modern times in proper perspective. Given the popular statistic that cumulative knowledge doubles at least every ten years, and that scientific knowledge is

*1*

doubling possibly even faster, it would help to look—at least in passing—at the events and milestones that spawned all this machinery and tools that help keep track of mountains of data.

The word "computer" is a relative term. Further, the term "data processing" does not necessarily imply that one is going to use an electronic device to complete a task. A modern day anecdote tells of a newspaper advertisement promoting a "mechanically-reliable, user-friendly, all-languages word processor for only $99.95." Subscribers to this incredible bargain receive a number two lead pencil instead of the assumed keyboard-and-screen hardware!

Humankind began to count things about 25,000 years ago. The concept of "many" was too relative, however, because important items—children, seasons, the enemy—had to be accurately quantified. Thus, numbers were invented about 5,000 years later. The **decimal system** was generally popular because most normally constructed humans had 10 fingers, thereby possessing a convenient counting device in their hands. **Base 10 arithmetic** was thus born. The decimal system was not universal, however, as some Aboriginal tribes developed a numbering system using base 4. A few isolated tribes even developed a number system of **base 2**, a **binary system**. Digital computers, too, use base 2 arithmetic, which is discussed in detail later in this chapter.

Counting was not the only activity which demanded a kind of **data processing**. In modern day parlance, **number crunching** describes the various mathematical processes which electronic computers handle and manipulate. But ancient humans, like their contemporaries, often found a need to keep track of large amounts of non-numeric data. History is full of examples of ingenious devices invented for this purpose: the Babylonians had the clay tablet, Egyptians the papyrus, and the Sumerians the cuneiform writing system. The Babylonians arranged their tablets into jars and, in a crude manner, "invented" the first card catalog. Their bookkeeping system even featured billing statements in which a symmetrically engraved tablet could be split down the middle, with one half surrendered as a receipt. In Greco-Roman times, wax tablet books (codices or codex) were used, and later, parchment was employed upon which writing was applied with a split reed pen.

History is full of counting devices. The **abacus**, a beads-on-wires device introduced in the Orient about 3000 B.C., is still in use today. Stonehenge, the Mayan temples, and the Aztec pyramids also exemplify varieties of counting devices, all of which computed variously the seasons, dates, harvests, and other matters on which there can only be speculation. In a more contemporary time, French mathematician Blaise Pascal invented the mechanical adder in 1642 for gambling! And in 1694 Gottfried Wilhelm von Leibniz introduced his toothed-wheel calculating machine that, for the first time, demonstrated the process of multiplication by repeated additions. All these inventions were, in their own way, forerunners of devices introduced in the computer age. The principles behind such contraptions were the same as for electromechanical computers—they just didn't plug into the wall!

Two devices are noteworthy for their pioneer attributes. In 1801, Joseph Marie Jacquard invented a loom that would weave cloth while guided by instructions from punched cards. In 1886, Herman Hollerith presented a machine to calculate U.S. census data by repeated arithmetic on numbers represented by holes in punched cards. The **Hollerith card** was the forerunner of the so named IBM card which was commonplace in the 1950s and 1960s and is still in use today. These two similar media are significant for their incorporations into so many of the activities we collectively call **data processing**. The principles they represent are simple yet fundamental to the evolution of automation.

As is often the case, the development of the modern day computer was accelerated by a war. In this instance, it was World War II, with its many demands for quick reports of weapons trajectories, secret code decryptions, and so-called "superweapon" and guided missile development. Inventors and researchers had considerably more than the "sticks and bearskins" building blocks of their forerunners with which to experiment. The vacuum tube and electromechanical relay were already perfected to a high degree, and paper-tape and wire-wrapped instruction boards were making appearances. These components would lay the foundation for solving the most difficult of barriers to high-speed, automated computing: how to cope with heat and mechanical failures, how to prevent loss of data when the power is turned off, and how to store a program to be run or modified at later times.

It was during and immediately after the war years that the first generation computers, whose acronyms still surface from time to time in scientific footnotes, appeared. **ENIAC**, the **Electronic Numerical Integrator and Computer**, was introduced at the University of Pennsylvania by a team of scientists led by John W. Mauchly and J. Presper Eckert. The device weighed 30 tons, housed 18,000 vacuum tubes, and required 1,500 square feet of floor space. It was a thousand times faster than machines which used electromechanical relays, but could nonetheless accept program instructions only one at a time. **EDSAC**, the **Electronic Delayed Storage Automatic Computer**, introduced at Cambridge University in 1949, featured a mercury acoustic delay line that could hold one or two instructions in reserve. And **ACE**, the **Automatic Calculating Engine,** developed between 1945 and 1950 by the National Physical Laboratory in London, used punched cards for input but also included the concept of addressing. **Addressing** is the principle in computer science which allows manipulation of data by location rather than by value. It is a concept which works in a manner not unlike the ordering and accessing of post office boxes to organize the mails.

**Figure 1.1** Vectra 386/25N desktop computer (photo courtesy of Hewlett-Packard Company)

**UNIVAC**, or **Univ**ersal **A**utomatic **C**omputer, was developed by Mauchly and Eckert and used from 1951 to 1963. This was the first machine to use magnetic tape for input and output and was also significant because it could handle **string** (character) **data**. The decade for the perfection of storage techniques was the 1950s. Magnetic drums evolved into magnetic cores, and **core memory**, collections of these electrically alterable magnetic cores, became commonplace. Magnetic disk storage also gained prominence. International Business Machines (IBM), Sperry (now UNISYS), Digital, Wang, and Xerox became household words. In the late 1970s the microcomputer age was launched, and in 1981 the IBM corporation introduced its version of the now standard **personal computer** (**PC**). Much of what we now take for granted was unknown thirty and even twenty years ago. A 1993 journal advertisement claimed, "A person who uses computers as a tool on the job will earn about 15 percent more salary than a person who doesn't." Clearly, the person who desires workplace advantages will avail him/herself of the technology that was developed, it seems, only yesterday.

## A BRIEF INTRODUCTION TO THE THEORY OF COMPUTER SCIENCE

To recapitulate the previous sections, data processing encompasses the following four components:

- Input or data collection
- Numeric or character manipulation
- Storage
- Retrieval

To reiterate, data processing does not necessarily imply that a computer will be used. In fact, mechanical computing may not enter into the picture. If it does, there is the more specific term **electronic data processing** (**EDP**), which specifies that some type of electromechanical device is used.

While there are many architectural variations, computers are configured one of two ways, either as **analog** or **digital** devices. An analog computer measures and manipulates continuously varying quantities. The automobile speedometer, if it is the type that uses a needle pointer, is such a device. A mercury thermometer is another analog computing device. The distinction is that there is never an exact (i.e., perfectly finite) quantity stated with an analog computer; the data are constantly changing, although very precise measurements can be taken. Such computers have widespread applications in scientific laboratories.

A digital computer is the type with which the average person interacts, and such devices will be the focus of this text. The time/temperature display on a bank building is a digital device because the output displayed is always a whole number. The temperature given is either 75 degrees or 76 degrees, never 75.5 degrees or some temperature in between. These digits leave little doubt as to exactly how hot or cold it is, at least superficially. There is an implied precision, however, but one which is generally accepted. It is this universal acceptance that opens the door for widespread use of digital computers, including a multitude of library applications which will be discussed in the rest of this book.

"Digital" implies that a computer handles data in precise chunks. However, a computer doesn't know what is a five or a 10 or any other number until we define that number for the machine. In fact, a digital computer can handle only ones and zeroes, in a **binary** counting scheme. In computerese, this methodology is best illustrated in the following discussion:

Inside any computer, be it Jacquard's loom, ENIAC, an IBM 370, a hand calculator, or any of thousands of other computing devices, is an arrangement of **switches**. A switch can be mechanical, like a light switch, or **electromechanical relay**, or it can be a **solid state** device, like a transistor or integrated circuit. But there is a common denominator: all of these switches are capable of representing the condition of "on" or "off." If a light switch is "up," it is "on," and the attached bulb burns; if the switch is "down," no current flows, and the bulb is dark or "off." In the most elementary sense, this is a representation of information: if a bulb is "on," the room is bright; otherwise, the "off" switch represents a dark room.

Taking the concept of "on" and "off" a step further, then mathematically on = 1 and off = 0. This arrangement is acceptable to a digital computer because its circuits can sense the flow or absence of electricity. A presence of 5 volts = "on" = 1, and 0 volts = "off" = 0. With this arrangement, we have information capable of being quantified and computed. The punched cards for Jacquard's loom can have holes or no holes in specified areas; the presence of a hole might equal 1, meaning "weave a stitch," and the absence of a hole might equal 0, meaning "do not weave a stitch." With a sufficient collection of holes/no holes on a card, there is enough information to create a specific pattern in a piece of cloth. And when these punches are rearranged and placed on different cards to be interpreted by the loom, they produce variations in patterns for the cloth being manufactured. In fact, the cards can be retained and used again another day. In computer parlance, this is the idea of a **stored program**, a concept which was introduced as one of the four components of data processing (i.e., storage) in the preceding section.

Each generation of computers handles the ones and zeroes differently, but the underlying theories remain the same. In the computers of the 1930s, where relays and vacuum tubes were used, considerable amounts of energy and material were required to manipulate the binary data. Relays used magnetic coils to hold their contacts in an "on" state, and vacuum tubes, similar to the ones on older radio and television sets, used filaments to regulate the passage (= 1) or no passage (= 0) of electricity. Relays made a considerable amount of noise when being accessed; both relays and vacuum tubes were bulky and radiated excess heat. A large room was required to house enough relays or tubes to represent even a few thousand "1 or 0" data elements.

One breakthrough in speed and efficiency was the introduction of the **magnetic (ferrite) core**. Such a device works on the principle of magnetic polarity. A core is arranged so that wires are passed through the center of its toroid-shaped body. If an electric current flows through a wire in one direction, the core is magnetized in a clockwise direction. If the current is switched to flow in the opposite direction, the core is magnetized in a counterclockwise direction. A set of sensing wires "reads" the magnetic polarity—clockwise or counterclockwise—and reports the condition of the core (along with many others) to the computer's central processing unit. Clockwise can = 1 and counterclockwise can = 0. Magnetic cores can be made quite small: several thousand can fit in a thimble. An advantage of core memory is that it can retain its information (i.e., magnetism) even when the power is shut off. Such memory is said to be **non-volatile**. This was a very popular information storage medium for many years and can be found in large computers through the mid-1960s, for example, in the IBM 360.

Transistors were invented in Bell Laboratories in 1948 and represented a breakthrough in computing possibilities. Transistors take up relatively little space, are noiseless, and give off little heat. These devices, however, still represented a technology of **discrete components**; that is, one transistor was required to represent one 1 or 0. In order to miniaturize further the subcomponents to build more sophisticated computers, arrays of transistors had to be combined into single packages. This achievement was realized in the late 1960s and introduced as **integrated circuit (IC)** technology. Modern ICs can hold thousands of transistors and are characterized as **large scale integrated (LSI)** or **very large scale integrated (VLSI)** devices. The availability of these packages makes handheld calculators and laptop/notebook computers possible and affordable.

With all this compactness came higher processing speeds. Computer speed is measured internally by the number of operations or **machine language instructions** performed in one second. Speed is also measured in terms of the amount of time required to access a piece of data. Mechanically, speed is a function of the computer's internal clock, a very precise crystal similar to the one in your quartz wristwatch, which is usually measured in millions of cycles per second, or megahertz (MHz); this speed is typically appended as a suffix to the microprocessor designation, as "80486-50" to designate an Intel 80486 processor with a 50 MHz clock. Early computers could retrieve stored information in a matter of milliseconds (ms), or thousandths of a second; "faster and faster" became the order of the day, and speeds moved from milliseconds to microseconds (µs) to nanoseconds (ns). There is currently under development an access speed of a few picoseconds (ps) of data in **cache memory**, an auxiliary storage space on the computer's mainboard. "Pico-" is an expression of *trillionths* of a second! Cache memory (and regular computer memory, for that matter) is nowadays usually placed on plug-in circuit components called **single inline memory modules (SIMMs)** to allow further compactness and modularity of computer machinery.

What about all these ones and zeroes, then, and how do they relate to present-day computing? This is where all those who suffered through the so-called New Math of the 1970s receive their just dues. Digital computers, because they so readily handle ones and zeroes in their circuitry, are perfect candidates for the binary number system. Also known as **base 2 arithmetic**, the binary system supports the computations and calculations of the PCs, mainframes, minicomputers, hand calculators, and other data processing devices that are in common use today. With some variations and allowances for differences in computer models, base 2 arithmetic works as follows:

A single one or zero to a computer is a **bit**, or **binary digit**. For convenience, a computer groups these bits into clusters of eight, to equal one **byte**. Larger computers also group the bytes into **words**, where (depending on the computer model) two bytes equal one word, four bytes equal one doubleword, and so on. Personal computers typically set one byte = one word. Although not used often, one half of a byte is a nibble, sometimes spelled nibl. And for programmers, the leftmost bit is the **most significant bit (MSB)**, and the rightmost is the **least significant bit (LSB)**.

This use of mathematics can give the computer a number system with which to work. In the decimal number system, every number is a power of 10; in the binary system, all the numbers are powers of 2. The binary system has its own set of advantages and problems, but for the sake of not getting too technical, suffice to say that base 2 arithmetic is quite acceptable for computational purposes; it just takes more room with all those ones and zeroes to represent any given quantity! In shorthand, binary numbers are sometimes represented as $1001\ 0110_2$ (read one zero zero one zero one one zero sub two). The preceding number equals 150 in the decimal number system, and the appropriate shorthand would be $1001\ 0110_2$ = $150_{10}$. The **hexadecimal** (base 16) **number system** is sometimes used as a shorthand notation by computer programmers to represent clusters of four bits, but for brevity, hex math will be omitted from this text.

Bytes can also represent characters and symbols. This is accomplished by standard agreement that $0110\ 0001_2$ = "a," and so on. For personal computers, the **American Standard Code for Information Interchange (ASCII)** table is used to set numeric equivalents for non-numeric characters. For larger machines, the **Extended Binary Code for Decimal Interchange (EBCDIC)** of IBM is used. There are a number of other codes for specific machines, but the preceding are two of the most popular. In the remainder of this text, the terms ASCII file and text file will be used interchangeably. The two are not exactly equivalent, but for the sake of simplicity, they will be treated as if they were.

# CATEGORIZING THE COMPUTERS

For a better perspective on the computer, it can be classified into its various forms. After a discussion of the types and sizes of computers, the various models can be presented from an applications standpoint with emphasis on functionality and adaptability to task.

For the sake of clarity, computers are grouped into three categories: **mainframes**, **minicomputers** (or "minis") and **microcomputers** (or "micros"). The latter is sometimes given the interchangeable term **personal computers** (or **PCs**). The terms can be swapped in this text because the categorization is not always absolute. Labeling computers by size is not always accurate, either—there are micros that act like minis, minis that have the power of mainframes, etc. It isn't a cut-and-dried process, and there must be agreed-upon criteria before beginning a discussion of one category or another.

## Mainframe Computers

Most persons conjure a vision of huge, floor model boxes with thousands of blinking lights when asked to define a mainframe. In a sense, at least historically, this is a true picture. "Big," until very recently, was a legitimate adjective when discussing mainframe computers. These were (and are) heavyweight machines which demanded a concurrent heavyweight budget to maintain. One punchline often used to close discussions of "What's a mainframe?" was "Companies have them and libraries don't."

It is easy to define a mainframe by its demands. Usually necessary for a mainframe computer's well-being is an environmentally controlled room, properly air conditioned to a temperature at a constant 68-70° Fahrenheit. To limit damage by building vibration and to accommodate a seemingly endless array of connector cables, a raised floor is desirable. Air filters are often part of the environmental controls, although mainframe computers are no longer operated in a so-called "clean room." And, more often than not, the mainframe will be placed on a separate, isolated electrical circuit so that its power source can be free of interference of other electrical activity in the surrounding physical plant.

But it is no longer possible to call a computer a mainframe in terms of its bulk. Several manufacturers have redesigned their high-end processors to be off-the-floor, **rack-mounted** machines. This design allows the main component, the **central processing unit** (**CPU**) to be integrated with other support devices, usually in the same metal frame. This **modularity** provides an extremely compact arrangement and further allows free interchange and substitution of components should service or replacement be indicated.

## Mini- and Microcomputers

In the late 1970s and early 1980s, it was relatively easy to distinguish minicomputers from micros. For one thing, there simply weren't that many microcomputers around. Micros tended to include hobbyist machines and smaller desktop models with no more than 16 to 64 kilobits of random access memory. Minis were viewed as the "serious" computers, ones that cost many thousands of dollars and were purchased mainly by businesses and industry. The purpose of these minicomputers was to perform work, and a lot of it. Minis supported high capacity tape drives and disk drives and were capable of handling rather sophisticated task management schemes. One popular example was the DEC PDP/11, which found its way into several library automation systems.

In the 1990s, the distinction between minicomputers and microcomputers is difficult, if not impossible, to define. There are microcomputers available which are of sufficient size and speed to eclipse and outrank the performance specifications of some minicomputers. And, these "super micros" can handle high volumes of data and are capable of computational management duties such as multitasking (see chapter 6) which were possible only on mini- and mainframe computers even a few years ago. The trend is to lump minis and micros into one arena and categorize them according to specific, physical characteristics.

It is perhaps easier to define a minicomputer by listing the general characteristics of a microcomputer, and then declaring that, if the machine is "bigger and faster" and is outside the definition of a micro, then it must be a mini. This is probably not a highly scientific method of classification, but it is certainly simple enough and reasonably accurate. Also for simplicity's sake, the terms "microcomputer" and "personal computer" can be used more or less interchangeably. While the term "personal computer" sometimes connotes a machine from the IBM arena, Apple Macintoshes and the Macs can be considered as PCs.

Microcomputers can be defined by the types of processor chip they contain. When personal computers were still the fancy of hobbyists, the processor chip most commonly found inside was the Intel 8008. This evolved into the 8080 of the same company and was later supplanted by the Zilog Z80 microprocessor. The first IBM PC contained an Intel 8088 chip, and the later IBM XT model used a slightly more sophisticated Intel 8086. Apple computers used Motorola 6502 processors, and the subsequent Macintosh line employed chips from the more advanced Motorola 68000 series.

The mid-1980s IBM AT computers advanced to the newer Intel 80286 microprocessor, and subsequently to the 80386, 80386SX, and 80486DX and 80486SX chips. Macintosh progressed in turn, using the Motorola 68020 and 68030 processors. Intel made available an 80586 chip in 1993 under the trade name Pentium, and the company announced the release of an 80686 chip as the P6 for sometime late in 1995. Intel's chip series, along with Motorola's, will no doubt progress to higher numbers. For now, it is necessary only to "know" the chips for recognition purposes— these numbers appear repeatedly in both technical and nontechnical literature, and in consumer-oriented publications. Larger numbers typically translate into capabilities for more complicated task handling and the ability to access greater volumes of data more efficiently and swiftly.

The other significant characteristic that distinguishes microcomputers is the bus configuration. The **bus** is the computer's set of internal lines (or wires, if you prefer) that allows the various circuits in the machine to communicate with one another. A bus is sometimes referred to as the plug or plugs into which the various circuits are inserted, but more accurately, these plugs should be called bus *slots*. Early personal computers were manufactured with proprietary buses, such that circuit boards (cards) from one manufacturer's machines would not fit into the machines of other companies. One of the first attempts at standardization was the **S100 bus**, which made circuit cards from a number of manufacturers usable in a relatively large permutation of microcomputers. However, the first widely accepted slot arrangement was the **industry standard architecture (ISA)** bus, a configuration existing in the majority of PCs manufactured through the present day. IBM also introduced the **microchannel (MC) architecture** which is prevalent in the company's PS/2 line of microcomputers. Other variations have appeared, for example, the **extended industry standard architecture (EISA)** bus, which is evident in many high-end, larger personal computers, and the **Local Bus**, which is actually an auxiliary bus that provides an exclusive, high-speed pathway for some video and disk drive signals. Apple Macintosh has its own **NuBus architecture**, and a number of third party vendors (including Apple itself) make available plug-in circuits to expand the capabilities of Macintosh computers.

There are a number of other subtle characteristics which can be used to proclaim that any given machine "is a mini or is a micro," but for the purposes of this text, these other subtleties are relatively unimportant. After a discussion of what's inside the box, it's time to proceed to what makes them tick.

## A *VERY* SHORT INTRODUCTION TO DOS

The purpose of this chapter is to give the reader enough of an overview to be able to understand the basic computing (i.e., applications programming) concepts of chapter 2. There will be a more detailed discussion of the disk operating system (**DOS**) in chapter 6. While Macintosh owners will have an advantage in being able to skip this section, it is essential for understanding the use of IBM and compatible computers.

All computers have built-in circuits which handle chores common to all brands of computers in their particular group of machines (e.g., IBMs, Macintoshes, AS/400s, Suns, etc.). These tasks consist of housekeeping routines and system services. **Housekeeping routines** monitor the computer's internals and set up the machine when it is turned on so that it is in a ready state, with no electrical problems, to accept commands and load programs to perform useful work. It is necessary for each machine to organize itself into a **default condition**, a group of setups in the electrical circuits which the housekeeping routines place in order before releasing the machine to the user. **System services** are a set of callable routines found in a **basic input/output system** (**BIOS**) circuit, which usually consists of a single or pair of microchips that can be accessed by the disk operating system to accept keystrokes, write files to disks, display characters on the computer's screen, and perform similar duties. All these routines can be accessed by computer programmers, but for the purpose of turning the machine on, loading a program, and performing a computing task, they are incidental. In fact, this is exactly the purpose of a disk operating system—to make knowledge of these low-level services unnecessary to the end user. What is important here is to absorb just enough DOS to get started—a few commands to load the programs of the next few chapters in order to interact with them. There are just a couple of conventions of DOS to get "up and running," before proceeding.

When you first boot a machine, a **prompt** such as C:\> or A:\> or similar will appear on the screen. The computer is said to be in **command mode**, ready to accept your instructions. The letter (here, "A" or "C") is indicative of the **current drive** on which you are working; if you change to another disk drive, the one to which you switch becomes your new current drive. The **default drive** is the one whose letter first appears on the screen when you power on. Armed with this information, you are able to run any program loaded on your hard disk drive (usually C:) or on a floppy disk (here, the A: drive) by typing its name. For example, if you wanted to run the PC-Type program described in the next chapter, you would simply type the boldface letters shown below, as

C:\> **PCT**, if the program is on the hard disk drive, or
A:\> **PCT**, if the program is on a floppy disk in the A: drive

and follow the instructions printed on the screen. Similarly, if there were programs called "123" (Lotus 1-2-3 described in chapter 4) and "DBASE" (dBase IV, described in chapter 5) on the hard disk (C:) drive, you would invoke them by typing the boldface letters after the C:\> prompt, as

C:\> **123** (for Lotus), or
C:\> **DBASE** (for dBase IV)

and the programs would load and ready themselves for your commands. Note that it doesn't matter whether you type "**pct**" or "**PCT**"; DOS does not distinguish between upper- and lowercase letters at the command level.

That's all there is to it! The important point to remember is that once the program is loaded, watch the screen closely and follow specific directions. Present day software, especially for personal computers, is highly intuitive and somewhat self directing and requires only that you move carefully through unfamiliar territory. Many programs, such as PC-File (chapter 5) are menu-driven in order that the end user need only type the first letter of a command (such as "S" for "search the file") to invoke a desired result. And, perhaps the most important advice of all is *read the user manual!* With a minimum of effort, you can be up and running almost immediately with most programs. The intricacies of DOS and advanced features of other "power" programs can be learned later. That's why this text has delayed the introduction of operating systems until a foundation in applications programs has been outlined. The next four chapters endeavor to build that foundation and give a somewhat comprehensive overview of the kinds of software activities that are happening in computer-oriented libraries of the 1990s.

# Chapter 2

# Applications Programs and Public Domain Software

Teachers of composition and rhetoric tell their pupils that before they place pen to paper, they must have something to say. So it is also with computers, with a variation on the theme: before users can make the machine work, they must have something to do. This is the reason that when a support technician is queried with, "What kind of computer should I purchase?" the most logical reply should be, "What are you going to do with it?" That sentiment is the thrust behind this chapter: before a variety of activities possible with computing machines is considered, readers need a feel for the realm of possible tasks such machines can handle.

This chapter is going to further introduce microcomputers and computer technology by demonstrating the work a computer can perform. There will be an attempt at a learning motivation using the medium of shareware and public domain software—public domain has the same meaning whether it is attributed to a print medium or a computer program—giving numerous examples of the kinds of library activities that can be addressed through this relatively inexpensive medium. Building on the elementary mechanical principles illustrated in chapter 1, this chapter puts hardware and software together to conclude a basis for understanding specific technical matters discussed in the later chapters.

Public domain software—the phenomenon which exploded onto the market in the 1980s—has been chosen as an introductory medium into the principles of computer programs for libraries because of its (now) universal availability, low cost, and simplicity of use. This area of software particularly appeals to libraries because of its affordability—programs initially introduced in the public domain can typically be licensed for a $10 to $75 registration fee. Additionally, there is user group support for many of the popular software programs which rivals the technical service of the "commercial" software houses. Some of the programs in the public domain are actually better than the retail, heavily advertised counterparts, and there are literally hundreds (if not thousands) of different programs and utilities from which to choose.[1]

The majority of programs mentioned in this chapter are for IBMs and compatible (also known as **clone**) computers. Should you decide to experiment with or examine one or more of the titles below, you should first allow yourself a working knowledge of the DOS operating system outlined in chapter 6. With the rudiments of the Disk Operating System in mind, you should then be able to load and execute any of the utilities and applications grouped under this general heading of shareware and public domain software.

## CATEGORIES OF SOFTWARE

Regardless of the sizes of the machines upon which they are run, computer programs, or **software**, can be categorized into a few basic groups. Classified according to function, they are as follows:

1. **Word processors**. These programs turn a computer into very sophisticated typewriters. With them, you can edit, revise, format for printing, check spelling and grammar, and find synonyms and antonyms for virtually any kind of document you can imagine. Letters, memoranda, publicity flyers, and book length publications are all possible creations from a word processor.

2. **Spreadsheets**. With this software, you perform "what if?" and financial planning operations with budgets, cost analyses, tabular calculations, and row X column (read "row by column") setups. You use these programs for number-intensive tasks.

3. **Databases**. These programs create and maintain fact files, mailing lists, bibliographies and book catalogs. Database software places large amounts of information into an orderly, retrievable and searchable recordkeeping system. Some vendors incorporate word processors, spreadsheets, and database management programs into one bundle, called an **integrated software package**. The purpose of these all-in-one bundles is to allow compatibility of data such that a file created in the word processor area, for example, is usable in the database component without the necessity of converting or retyping the file.

4. **Operating systems (O/S)**. This software acts as the liaison, or interface, between the humans and the machines. The O/S

interprets user input and output and provides the computer with resources to run programs, print documents, and store information within the larger expanse of the machine environment.

5. **Languages**. This software provides the "building blocks" for creating other programs. With their own grammars, syntaxes, verbs and operators, computer languages allow program developers to create and maintain applications such as the word processors, spreadsheets and databases mentioned immediately above.

6. **Graphics packages**. These programs allow users to draw pictures, diagrams, and images for incorporation into other programs. The graphics thus created might include forms, charts, **screen dumps** for "slide" shows and visual presentations, or cartoons for inclusion in publication quality documents.

7. **Desktop publishing programs**. More than just sophisticated word processors, these pro-

**Figure 2.1** Line art graphic

grams allow creation, at the computer terminal, of presentation quality publications such as books, newsletters, pamphlets, and publicity documents. Desktop publishing programs usually also permit incorporation of output from graphics packages (as with the example in Figure 2.1) and provide copy for printing on a wide range of sophisticated, high-resolution printers.

8. **Games**. Last but not least, games can be of the arcade variety (action-oriented) or of a more intellectual nature to include word quizzes, mathematical puzzles, interactive fiction, and creative writing activities.

## LEVELS OF SOPHISTICATION IN SOFTWARE AND USER GROUPS

Not all software programs are created to be equal; they vary in complexity and number of features. For the sake of categorization, they are grouped into three levels as follows:

1. **Commercial and developer grade**. The software from this group is fully documented, fully supported by the vendor, and offers frequent updates and revisions to the base product. It is usually **turnkey**; that is, it works as purported as soon as you take it out of the box and load it onto the disk drive. And it is generally transportable to other computers of the same class. This grade of software has usually taken many hours to write and develop, but it is typically mass-produced and nationally advertised in order to keep costs to a minimum.

2. **Generic**. This level of software is generally produced by outsiders and third-party vendors for particular machines. These are usually applications programs that perform one or two tasks which are sometimes issued as **proprietary** software for a specific computer. These programs are moderately expensive and may or may not include the source code listings for end users to modify. Often the user manuals can be purchased separately, but there may be little or no support after the sale.

3. **Flea market software**. These programs are obtained through clubs, user groups, and electronic bulletin boards. Such software may have been written as authors' contributions to a pool of programs and are usually obtainable for the price of the diskette upon which they are distributed. Flea market software comes with no guarantees and may not be documented. It is a relatively inexpensive way to start a personal software collection, but you run the risk of frustrations and the possible spread of computer viruses. More about viruses will be discussed in chapter 12.

User groups are not a bad way to get involved with software, either as an end user or as a developer/programmer. User groups are also not limited to the users of flea market software; in fact, there are user groups for major software programs such as Oracle (database), OCLC (library bibliographic utility), GEAC (library automation software), and MUSIC (academic computing system). It is the involvement by and the users of the various programs that garner the attention of the developers, and ideas for new features in subsequent releases of programs many times emanate from user group caucuses.

Depending on the membership constituencies, user groups provide a variety of activities. They hold meetings and sometimes annual conventions to swap ideas and to discuss problems and solutions. Many times, the meetings are at the vendors' headquarters or corporate offices, with the vendor picking up the tab for travel and lodging. User groups can often negotiate discounts on software, and many groups are offered access to private sales given by the vendors on overstock or discontinued items. Vendors sometimes offer free continuing education courses and seminars on their products that may be available only to members of their user groups. Finally, the user groups themselves may maintain mailing lists and newsletters of official and unofficial information about software products, including complaints, hints, advice on use, advertisements, sources, trends, new equipment specifications, and instruction. Regardless of the level of sophistication of software you are using (or intend to use), it is good practice to investigate, and perhaps participate in, the user group for your targeted product, if you intend to make any significant investment of time in using and maintaining it.

Public domain software is sometimes defined in terms of subcategories. A term that is frequently used to define "public domain software" is **shareware**, which is more accurately an activity than a legal concept. Often called "bannerware" and sometimes erroneously "freeware," the shareware practice is widely used to introduce and market new programs. The mechanism typically works as follows: a software author, who has written a program he or she believes is marketable, makes demonstration copies of the program and distributes them on floppy disks, sometimes free of charge, to potential customers. These demonstration copies are often full-fledged versions of the entire program, although some programs may be abridged in the demo versions. Some companies, a list of which appears in the Bibliography, redistribute the shareware disks at a small profit and with the full consent and blessing of the original authors. The authors also sometimes distribute their demo disks to managers of electronic bulletin boards in order that the users of such boards have access to the software.

It is at this point that shareware marketing departs radically from commercial software marketing. Shareware authors typically spend little or no money on advertising, their approach resulting in a distribution system that relies heavily on word of mouth. The demonstration versions of their programs usually carry a message that the unabridged version (or updated version) of their programs must be licensed; in other words, a fee must be paid for continued use of the software. Many times, the responsibility for payments for usage are placed solely on the honor system. The authors state, "If you find this program to be of value and would like to have the latest version, I request that you pay $XX.XX." Authors often promise that registration brings a few months of telephone support, a printed manual, or free updates for a given period of time. Shareware is a very popular concept and judging from the number of titles that have appeared in shareware catalogs in the past five years, it is a successful concept as well.

## COPYRIGHT

Copyright provisions for computer software have had to play "catch-up" with the sections of the copyright law for print and audiovisual media. The problem has been that of recognizing authorship of computer programs as an intellectual pursuit worthy of protection against plagiarism and illegal copying. Once it was possible to place a monetary value on information, the determination of the severity of copyright violations pertaining to software was finally decided. The paradox that had to be resolved in the courts was whether data files on disks were worth more, in an abstract sense, than the magnetic media upon which they were inscribed!

Copyright, as it applies to computer programs, isn't difficult to understand. The principle is very similar to the conditions by which you purchase a book: you "own" the book in the sense that the paper, binding and jacket are your property, but the ideas or stories contained in the book are not. You may not make a copy of the book for resale, nor may you extract portions of the work for your own purposes, unless you have the author's permission or pay a royalty. It is the same with a computer program, except that we generally speak of the purchase of software as a licensing process. In other words, you "own" the diskette(s) upon which the program was furnished to you, but the actual program—the intellectual endeavor of the programmer who wrote it—remains the property of that programmer or the company for whom he or she works. Unlike a book, however, you must register your copy of the software (unless you bought it from a purchase order or from a company representative, in which case the program may have been preregistered for you). This may impose further restrictions, and you might have to seek the vendor's permission if you wish to resell or transfer the license to another party. In any case, you must destroy all copies of the original program before you pass it on to the new "owner."

Software copyright is covered by federal law, but most states add their own extensions to the basic copyright provisions. Generally in force is that you license a program for use on one machine. You may transport the program from one computer to another, but you must guarantee, as a condition of your license privileges, not to use the program simultaneously on two or more computers. There are provisions for multiple copy use, typically sold as **site licenses**, or, in the case of educational institutions, as **laboratory packs**, and often at a discount for multiple purchases of the same program. The programs contained in lab pack multiples are usually priced at a fraction of the cost of separate, individual copies of the same program, but multiple copies of user documentation are often not included, as a cost-cutting factor.

One common extension to copyright is the so-called **shrinkwrap law**. In this instance, the magnetic media upon which the software is shipped are wrapped and sealed in plastic. There is typically an adhesive seal covering the opening, which variously states that by opening the package, you agree to the terms of the software license included with the program documentation. Another extension is the **look and feel doctrine**. The latter is a very difficult area for the courts to agree upon. There are only a few basic categories of software, and one spreadsheet may well resemble all others. What is left for the courts to decide is whether one program, when described by its authors to be functionally equivalent to that of another vendor, is close enough in appearance to the other to constitute copyright violation. The look and feel challenge has heretofore been applied primarily to infringement of musical copyright; software houses seem to have taken over the spotlight from the entertainment industry!

Licensing arrangements also vary depending on the type of computer you are using. Mainframe software licenses, for example, sometimes allow you to run a given program only on a single CPU, but without regard to the number of terminals that will be accessing the program. Other mainframe software vendors have different levels of licensing, the price increasing with the level of sophistication and size of the central processor. And still others set fees to reflect the number of simultaneous users who access the system. The most restrictive vendors limit the use of their programs to one CPU and to one specific serial number of processor. But the agreements all have one thing in common: you cannot do what the license does not allow you to do; otherwise, the vendor has grounds for legal recourse and also, in most cases, has the right to withhold use of the program from you.

To further complicate the situation, technology changes much more rapidly than the legal responses to it. A **local area network** (see chapter 15) is essentially one computer with many others connected to it, sharing its programs and resources. However, software vendors take the position that, if their programs are used over such a network, this constitutes multiple usage and can be in violation of a single-user license provision. For that reason, many vendors license two versions of their software: single-user and network. In libraries, an extension of this situation exists where there are databases on CD-ROM discs, configured in a manner that multiple computers can access the information over a networked arrangement. Some vendors take a "don't care" attitude, and others are adamant that multi-user subscriptions must be purchased. There is no pattern to the enforcement of such charges, and library materials selection departments and committees would be prudent to ascertain licensing arrangements before deciding on subscriptions based on the CD-ROM media format.

Software copyright makes for interesting dilemmas in the distribution of programs. Circulating collections of software have caused a particular controversy, especially where the doctrine of fair use has been challenged. It is a similar situation that arises from time to time in public libraries as to whether a royalty fee, payable to the author, ought to be collected each time a book is charged to a borrower. The debate regarding software continues, further complicated by the fact that there are numerous categories of software (public domain, shareware, freeware, etc.) which have slightly differing levels of protection under copyright. It is prudent for any library to keep an accurate set of records of software under its purveyance, both of the serial numbers of licenses used in-house (both by staff and by patrons and users), and of the purchases and number of copies of any programs that circulate. Item for item, computer programs are more expensive than books, and this and the fact that the law is not as definitive on software as on more traditional media are two reasons that good documentation of software holdings is essential to protect the agency against frivolous claims of copyright violations. As with any preventive measure, a library's best protection against such claims is the maintenance of good audit and purchase records.[2]

Copying of software is allowed for the purpose of making **archival copies**. The program you license is usually distributed on one or two sets of magnetic media. For a mainframe computer, you will ordinarily receive licensed programs on magnetic tape, either in a **reel-to-reel** format or in **data cartridges**. With minicomputer setups, such as those that are UNIX-based, your program is probably also provided in a tape cartridge. For Macintosh computers and PCs, the shipping media are either 3-1/2" or 5-1/4" floppy diskettes. In any case, these media constitute the **distribution disks** or tapes, the **master copies** from which the program(s) are launched. It is a good rule of thumb never to install the software from the master copies. You should make a **backup copy** of the media, and the installation and configuration of the program should be performed from the backups, not the masters. Such backup copies constitute archival copies and, as long as you do not use the program on more than one machine (i.e., if the software is licensed for "single user only"), you may make a reasonable number of archival copies for the purpose of guarding against damage to or loss of the masters. Copyright provisions allow you to do this, and the law recognizes that loss of programs and data through mechanical failures underscores the need for keeping backup copies of valuable software.

## CATALOGS AND OTHER SOURCES OF PROGRAMS

Mail-order purchases of software and hardware are not to be avoided. Even for libraries in larger cities, mail order can be a time- and money-saving alternative to door-to-door shopping for automation paraphernalia. Naturally, as in any transaction, you must be careful with whom you deal. From time to time you can find lists of mail-order vendors, with performance ratings, in such journals as *PC Magazine*. Talk to other librarians in your area for additional, word-of-mouth recommendations.

A list of catalogs of popular mail-order resellers is given in the Bibliography at the end of this book. Note that many of these catalogs are annotated. Although cover prices for the catalogs are given (generally two or three dollars per copy), it is almost always possible to get on a vendor's mailing list for a year or two of free catalogs simply by making a minimum purchase. The entries of programs available by mail order can be redundant from catalog to catalog, particularly in the shareware arena, but this fact allows for even better comparison shopping.

A number of retail establishments rely on customer brand loyalties for repeat business. Such business courting of the end-user market counts heavily on trademarks (and not necessarily machine performances) to sell computers, thereby keeping the selling price at nearly full retail. A number of mail-order houses employ the same tactic, but with a twist: they "talk" the product to death in print. Their catalogs have a familiar theme; seemingly innocuous products merit one to three pages of description. Sometimes there are indeed bargains to be found, but many times the "technical descriptions" are little more than glad tidings.

Such catalogs can, however, be used advantageously. Librarians are trained to make critical reviews of books and literature, and it should be no different in the evaluation of computer programs and software. Many times, even the most verbose of catalogs will, between the lines, offer a wealth of information about products which appear (usually less expensive) in other promotional literature. The value of information about software that buyers are interested in can be amplified even with material from the "chatty" brochures. And eventually, with intelligent consumers, the prices in catalogs aiming for brand-loyal customers will follow market trends. Perhaps it is up to the librarians to be the pacesetters.

There is a growing trend for mail-order resellers to offer detailed product information by telefacsimile (fax) machine. The process is straightforward: you need a fax machine with a built-in telephone, or one which can have a telephone connected to it. A vendor offering this service will provide coded numbers next to product entries. You enter the telephone number of the vendor's fax machine (usually requiring a toll call to do so) and, when prompted (usually with a tone or beep), you enter the product code. The vendor's fax will transmit one or more pages of information detailing the program or product about which you inquired. While you, the consumer, are typically paying for the call, you don't have to wait days for a response, and there is usually enough information upon which to base a purchase decision. Vendors offering this service are also noted with their entries in the Bibliography.

Further along in this text, chapter 10 will consider in more detail the process of evaluating and selecting computer software and hardware. For now, some general programs and those with brand name recognition will be considered. Keep in mind, though, that brand loyalty isn't all bad, and there is much quality software to be had in the trademarked arena. The purpose of this final section is to provide a motivation for exploration into the many areas of computer software available for library task management.

## APPLICATION: PUBLIC DOMAIN SOFTWARE AND INEXPENSIVE SOFTWARE PROGRAMS TO SUPPORT LIBRARY PROCESSES

Among the myriad of titles to be found in shareware catalogs, many offerings are directly applicable to library processes. Registration for these programs generally falls in the $50.00 and under range, and one or more of the utilities mentioned in this section might be perfect solutions for PC-based tasks. In fact, there is even a Shareware Authors Kit[3] for librarians who aspire to write and sell their own programs but don't have a large budget for advertising and marketing.

Automated circulation systems will be discussed in chapter 13. However, Paragon Systems' The Home Software Series includes a PC-based program called the Home Library Books Program[4] which allows an abridged bibliographic entry of materials to be keyed onto a workscreen and categorizes items by title, author or subject. A subject catalog can be maintained, and paper printouts are possible. A companion module to the program allows maintenance of a database of Books on Loan, and the two modules effectively constitute a desktop cataloging and circulation system. A cataloging-only system is also available from KN Associates; called the Reference Cataloging System[5]; it is a database program for the organization of books, journals, movies and other reference materials and is aimed at the person who wants to organize research on a PC rather than on note cards. For the cataloging of documents, Business Librarian[6] handles a database of nonbook items and allows the classification of materials by sets, locations within the library, subjects, and user-defined keywords. The program is indexable, menu-driven, and allows output of printed reports.

LIBCARD and ACCPRINT are two programs designed for librarians who have but a fundamental knowledge of IBM and compatible computers.[7] Although the title implies that the LIBCARD is a program for keeping track of borrowers' registrations, it is actually a program for printing out the multiple filecards and spine and pocket labels required when a new book or VHS cassette is cataloged for circulation. There is an optional MAGAZINE module which makes filecards for periodicals and prints a compiled listing of titles, acquisition codes, and subscription prices of periodicals. There is also a MAGLIST stand-alone program which prints a simplified list for distribution to other libraries of all periodicals held by any given library. With entry into the program of the same basic information, LIBCARD prints the multiple cards required for a new accession and creates the file, ACCESS.DAT, used by ACCPRINT to print accession records. Because the programs can run on PCs with dual floppy disk drives (i.e., with no hard disk drive present in the machine), ACCPRINT requires that the utilities COMMAND.COM and SORT.EXE (see MS-DOS section in chapter 6) reside on the program disk and in the same subdirectory; in other words, the floppy disks must be **bootable** (capable of setting up the PC in a command mode). LIBCARD and ACCPRINT were written in GW-BASIC (chapter 8) and compiled with Microsoft QuickBASIC version 4.5. As such, the files LIBCARD.BAS and ACCPRINT.BAS require a separate purchase of the GW-BASIC interpreter. It is this same author PATRON program that actually handles borrowers' cards. This module was also written with QuickBASIC version 4.5 and its menu-driven interface supports the following functions:

1. Entering new patron data
2. Printing overdue mailing labels
3. Listing expired library cards
4. Printing an alphabetic list of patrons
5. Printing a numeric list of patron cards
6. Printing bulk mailing labels

Reference Management System[8] is a dBase III (see chapter 5) and Wordtech dBXL file compatible program for managing entry, search, and report of bibliographic data. It provides a self-explanatory, menu-driven system for handling many important data entry, viewing, editing, sorting, searching, and reporting operations. Reference material in files is managed as records which contain data fields. There are fields for single or multiple authors, titles, sources (publication, volume, pages, year), keywords, sponsors, comments, special codes, and abstracts. It is fully indexable and allows for output to printers. This is a particularly useful database tool for cataloging and classifying pamphlets and vertical file material when it is inconvenient or too expensive to use one of the commercial bibliographic databases to do so. For those who prefer to work from the Windows platform, the Document Management System[9] is a system of book and pamphlet cataloging which allows input, editing and retrieval from data entry fields within the Windows interface. The program will allow the detailing of chapters within documents, and the materials and their contents are fully indexable and can be cross-referenced. The author has built in a feature of online help, even though navigation around the program is highly intuitive, with a "document" window at the top of the screen and an "article" window at the bottom.

Even some standard library reference books are appearing as shareware. For those who wish an alternative to the American Library Association's annual *American Library Directory*, there is the *Bates Directory of U.S. Public Libraries*,[10] a floppy-disk-based compendium which can be viewed, edited and printed out. It is possible to search by state and ZIP code, and libraries needing such a capability can request that the program print mailing labels. Other reference books are fast becoming available on CD-ROM, and several notable titles will be detailed later in this text. And specialty shareware programs, for collection management of specific subjects, will be outlined at the end of chapter 10.

## NOTES

Where either "PBS" or "TSL" is noted following addresses of program vendors, shareware versions of the programs noted can be obtained from Public Brand Software or The Software Labs respectively; PBS and TSL catalogs are annotated in the Bibliography.

1. Beiser, Karl. "Microcomputing." *Wilson Library Bulletin*, February, 1987, pp. 42-45.
2. Valauskas, Edward J. "Copyright: Know Your Electronic Rights!" *Library Journal*, August, 1992, pp. 40-43.
3. Shareware Authors Kit (SAK), published by GroupWare, P.O. Box 300, Dupont, WA 98327-0300. $45.00, standard edition; $99.00 professional edition (TSL disk #9605).
4. The Home Library Books Program, published by Paragon Systems, Inc., Dept. PDHL-B, 20016 Roscommon Street, Harper Woods, MI 48225. $12.50 (incl. s/h) plus $5.00 for a printed manual (PBS disk #CR6.0).
5. The Reference Cataloging System, published by KN Associates, 114 Eighth Street, Ann Arbor, MI 48103. $35.00 (PBS disk #CR18.1).
6. Business Librarian, published by Pitlak Corporation, 1639 Valecroft Avenue, Westlake Village, CA 91361. $14.95 (PBS disk #CR18.1).
7. LIBCARD, ACCPRINT, and PATRON, published by Jesse F. Adams, P.O. Box 126, Olga, WA 98279. $30.00; additional $20.00 fee for use of the MAGAZINE and MAGLIST modules (PBS disks #CR1a.0 and #CR1b.0).
8. Reference Management System, published by Paul Douglas Goodell, 234 Mulberry Place, Ridgewood, NJ 07450. $45.00; additional $5.00 for updated version of shareware disk (PBS disks #CR4a.1 and #CR4b.1).
9. Document Management System, published by Edward B. Toupen, P.O. Box 44231, Denver, CO 80201. $25.00, plus additional fees if telephone or mail support is desired (PBS disk #CR11.0).
10. *Bates Directory of U.S. Public Libraries*, published by International Features, P.O. Box 1349, Lake Worth, FL 33460. $25.00 (PBS disks #RD51a.0 and #51b.0).

# Chapter 3

# Word Processors and Printed Output Data Representation

There is an anecdote that uses (skewed) principles of data representation to make its point. There once appeared an advertisement offering a "portrait of a U.S. president, machine-engraved, and certified by an agency of the federal government, for $5.00 including shipping and handling." All subscribers to this solicitation received, for their trouble and money, a U.S. postage stamp in a cellophane envelope. Another story, to which allusion was already made in chapter 1, is more contemporary. To elaborate further: the advertisement offered "a full-functioning word processor, with no moving parts, able to handle multi-language lexicons and an expanded number of typefaces, with an undo facility, for $99.95." Of course, mail-order purchasers of this item were greeted with a shipment of a number 2 graphite pencil!

The point to be made here is that people are becoming too accustomed to graphic images and documents being handled by a computer or some other form of machine. "Information processing" and "data processing" do not inherently imply that mechanical or electrical devices will be used in the procedures. To expand on knowledge of the principles of information science and before the subject of word processing is considered, the principles of data representation will be discussed. This will put the next three chapters in their proper perspective and provide a foundation for understanding how "information science" evolved into a synonym for "computerized automation."

The most common way to represent data is to place it in print. There are numerous other ways to display information; here are some of the more common media:

- **Punched cards**. The **Hollerith card**, or so-called "IBM card," uses rectangular holes punched in stiff paper to store both numeric and text data. This is analogous to the binary representation techniques described in chapter 1. In any specified area (zone) of a card, if a hole is punched, a 1 is represented. If there is no hole, a 0 is indicated. As cards are passed along a metal roller, contact "fingers" sense the presence or absence of a punch. If a finger passes through a hole, electric current can flow to an underlying metal plate or drum, and a 1 is sensed. In the absence of a hole, the paper acts as an insulator and no current flows, hence a 0. A variation on the Hollerith card is the **aperture card**, which is merely a Hollerith card with a small piece of microfilm imbedded in the center. To retrieve such a card through a sort process is to retrieve the contents of the film simultaneously. Incidentally, Herman Hollerith arbitrarily chose eighty columns for the width of his card, and this is why most video terminals and line printers default to eighty columns for printing text.
- **Punched paper tape**. Synonymous with teletype machines, punched paper tape represents data in a manner similar to that of punched cards, except that the data stream is relatively endless. Tape can be rolled and stored for playback into a tape reader. Because decks of punched cards can inadvertently be mixed or shuffled, tape is more advantageous where the arrangement and order of data are important to program integrity.
- **Toothed wheels**. These are the foundation of automobile odometers and some mechanical adding machines. The numbers displayed depend on the position of the cogs on the gearwheels inside the counting device. Blaise Pascal is generally credited with the invention of the toothed-wheel mechanical adder, which he invented to compute odds and keep track of his gambling wagers.
- **Light bulbs**. In the simplest sense, a bulb is either on or it is off. If on, it can represent a "1"; if off, it may represent a "0." If you juxtapose many bulbs in rows, a binary number set can be established. For example, eight bulbs illuminated as in Figure 3.1 could represent the binary number 1010 1101, which is 173 in decimal.

**Figure 3.1** Light bulbs representing binary number $1010\ 1101_2$

- **Light emitting diodes (LEDs)** and **liquid crystal displays (LCDs).** When used as devices to represent raw data, LEDs and LCDs are an extension of the "lights on, lights off" technology. An LED is a device that, when a current of electricity is passed through it in one direction, produces a bright glow. If the current is reversed, the LED ceases to glow. If forward current = 1 and backward current = 0, it is readily obvious that binary circuits inside a computer can be used to drive a display made of patterns of LEDs in a manner similar to that of the row of light bulbs in Figure 3.1.

  An LED can also be manufactured to be linear as well as spherical. From a proper physical arrangement of such linear LEDs, a **segmented display** can be created. Consider the pattern in Figure 3.2:

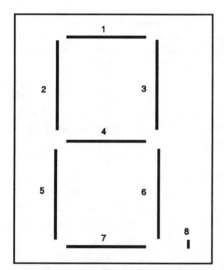

**Figure 3.2** Digit created with LED segments

Note that each LED segment is numbered and that there is a decimal point segment numbered "8." If a data byte was assigned to "drive" this display, each of the eight bits of that byte could have a value of "1" or "0" to represent "on" or "off." Remember that each segment of the display is an individual LED; the arrangement is just such that, by varying the values of the data bits, a byte can represent a decimal number in a format more easily recognized by humans who are more accustomed to dealing with base 10 numbers.

In other words, if there is a byte of data in which the bit values "1" and "0" represent the direction of flow of current and the leftmost bit is segment number 1 and the rightmost position represents segment number 8 (the decimal point), the LED array can be "lighted" to variously show the decimal numbers 0 through 9. If these values are applied simultaneously to the segments in the display pattern, a recognizable decimal number can be represented. Allowing the display to "read" this byte, where the bits turn to ON OFF ON ON OFF ON ON OFF etc., the display's readout (Figure 3.3) will show: The byte $1011\ 0110_2$ stands for "turn on a number 3 with no decimal point."

- **Neon tubes** have been used as an alternative to LED displays. Neon gas is placed in glass tubes similar to, but much smaller than,

the bright, glowing advertisements so popular in store
windows. These straight
tubes can be arranged in
patterns inside a larger, protective glass tube, such that
by varying which segments
are on or off at any given
time, patterns of letters and
numbers can be formed
from numbers inside a computer or other driver device.
The principle is exactly the
same as with segmented LED
displays.

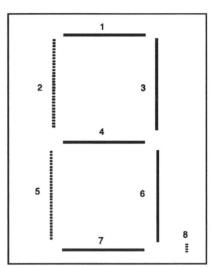

**Figure 3.3** LED display representing the decimal number "3"

- **Liquid crystal displays
  (LCDs).** LCDs function in a
  manner similar to that of
  LEDs, except that in an LCD
  a segment of crystal is excited by an electric current to appear light
  or dark in response to the voltage applied, rather than glowing.
  Liquid crystal displays have been refined to a degree of resolution
  where they are usable in **laptop** and **notebook** computer screens.
  The low-power consumption of LCD screen panels makes them
  particularly attractive for computing situations in which the power
  source is batteries. This allows a user to derive a considerable
  amount of computing time between recharges, which can be
  advantageous when a portable computer is being used, for example, at long board meetings and seminars.
- **Cathode ray tubes** (**CRTs**). CRTs are also known as video and
  "TV" tubes, and represent the ultimate example of using a "lights
  on, lights off" technique to represent data. Using electron beams
  aimed at a glass face, CRT assemblies can paint letters and numbers very rapidly across an electronic "page." The beams hit and
  excite various colored **phosphors** on the inside of the glass, and
  by lighting enough dots (**pixels**) on the screen, create lines of
  data. The use of CRTs for graphics representations will be discussed in more detail in chapter 9.

## WORD PROCESSING SOFTWARE

To get back to the basic intention of this chapter, it is assumed that, for
the most part, your library computing needs will involve the production of

some kind of **hard copy**, or paper-based printout. Word processing software programs, as with other categories of computer programs for PCs and Macintosh computers, run the gamut of features and prices. It is as much a matter of how much you are willing to learn, i.e., how much to invest in time to practice the program, as how much you are willing to spend. "Most expensive" does not always translate to mean "best."

On the low end of the price spectrum, Buttonware's PC-Type[1] for the IBM and compatibles is an excellent entry-level word processing program. Originally introduced as shareware, PC-Type is capable of typing letters, reports, manuscripts, and longer documents. The program can also support right and left justification of text as well as **word wrap** (or **wraparound**), which is the ability of a typed word to jump to the beginning of the next line of text if it cannot fit on the first one. The original versions of PC-Type evidenced a transition phase where word processors were used to create ASCII (text only) files as source code for program language compilers. Even in its earlier versions, PC-Type provided a spelling checker (although not a spelling corrector) and a line draw graphics facility. Its text documents could be interfaced with the spreadsheet program PC-Calc and database manager PC-File.

PC-Write[2] is another fully functional word processor available at a fraction of the cost of "commercial" programs. PC-Write supports a variety of printers, including LaserJets and PostScript models; printer control is available via a simple menu-driven setup program. The program supports outline and hanging indent margins, cut and paste, automatic page numbering and pagination, and maintenance of footnotes. A word count feature and 50,000 word spell checker are included. Like PC-Type, PC-Write is an excellent program for editing ASCII files, a feature which makes both programs advantageous for persons writing compiler source code. The program can also work on WordStar formatted files as well as its own proprietary ones. PC-Write also supports mail merge and can handle comma delimited files as well as **discrete line data** (lists with one data element per line, with a carriage return at the end of each line). PC-Write has attracted a respectable amount of third party support in the literature, and has, in fact, branched into two separate products. PC-Write Standard Level is still the de facto shareware product, while PC-Write Advanced Level is typically available in stores as a shrinkwrapped product. The Advanced Level program incorporates all the features of Standard Level and additionally includes a built-in *Roget's Thesaurus*, an index and table of contents generator, support for generation of page headers and footers, context-sensitive help screens, and mouse support. "Advanced" does not mean "expensive," and both versions of PC-Write are economical alternatives for libraries that need sophisticated word processing on a tight budget.

Several of the so-called "high-end" programs have a considerable history. WordStar[3] had its beginnings on pre-PC machines, in the late 1970s when the Intel 8080 microprocessor, 64 kilobytes of memory, and the CP/M operating system all reigned supreme. WordStar functioned splendidly within the current limitations of the time, and, because everything is relative, outperformed most of its competitors' products in terms of speed, ease of use, and size of files it could handle. WordStar leaped into popularity when it was offered as part of the Osborne I computer package, a bundle deal of a portable computer that resembled a sewing machine when closed, dual floppy disk drives, and the SuperCalc spreadsheet and CP/M operating system for the pay-one-price deal of $1,500. WordStar is still around (Osborne is not), its current (1995) release sold as version 7. The latest version is also available to run under the Windows interface, and WordStar has shed many of its original, cryptic, two-key commands that related little to the word processing services they were to invoke. The on-screen representation of a document under creation is very faithful to the appearance of the resultant hard copy printout, and font manipulations with WordStar (including PostScript and TrueType technology) are easily handled.

Microsoft Corporation's entry is MS Word, or Microsoft Word for Windows[4] in its latest incarnation. The release for Windows version 2 was what launched Word into heavy contention for marketshare, and there is, of course, a package which runs with Windows 95, the latest Windows version at the time of this writing. Because it is a Windows product, Word allows a smooth mixing of graphics with text, and it has a powerful preview mode. The program allows tabulation of numeric data before they are incorporated into the text, and it provides for templates and model text formats to be established so that documents have a uniform appearance. There is also an annotation mode so that reviewers and editors can imbed comments and suggestions without causing these notes to output when the document is sent to the printer. Word also allows storage of standard pieces of formatted text (**boilerplate**) and graphics in files so that they can be retrieved into whatever documents might require them. The Academic Edition of Word for Windows includes two templates for formatting term papers and dissertations according to the specifications in Turabian's *A Manual for Writers of Term Papers, Theses, and Dissertations.*[5]

WordPerfect[6] is perhaps the most popular PC- and Macintosh-based word processor in use in North America. At the time of the writing of this text, WordPerfect's most generally available versions were 6.1 for DOS and Windows and 3.0 for Macintosh. There is also a version for the UNIX operating system. If run under Windows 3.1 or Windows 95, WordPerfect takes advantage of all the Windows graphical user interface facilities, including the TrueType font manager. The latter makes WordPerfect extremely attractive for use with laser printers.

The setup and draft copy for this text were accomplished using WordPerfect 5.2 for Windows. The selection was made for several reasons: WordPerfect allows WYSIWYG (what-you-see-is-what-you-get) display of a document, and because a specific typeface could be used while the draft was being composed, the author could view the book almost exactly as the published copy would appear. Thus, nuances of typography, which otherwise might not surface until after general distribution of the text, would appear immediately and corrections could be made "on the fly."

WordPerfect has another facility which was useful in compiling the various chapters of this book. This author, when teaching courses in information science, relies heavily on terminology. His class handouts often consist merely of lists of terms with which students should be familiar to master the course material. WordPerfect allows creation of an index or **concordance** outside the mainstream of a document, thus allowing an author to write a search list of terms to be referenced. Using such a process, this author created a list of index terms from various class handouts. The list was run through a sort routine to alphabetize the terms and then passed to WordPerfect to search the various chapters; the index was thus created without having to tag each occurrence of a word in chapter proper. Thus, no occurrences of words were missed, and additionally, terms not covered in chapter discussions were identified so that text enhancements could be made in cases of "forgotten" concepts.

## PRINTERS

Even in the midst of all the various ways to manipulate words and text by electronic means, the printed page will never become obsolete. Library schools of the 1960s and even 1970s were proclaiming that cans of magnetic tape would replace vast archives of books and manuscripts. The age of the paperless office was imminent, so claimed the prophets, and interoffice communications would be accomplished either via pocket-sized diskettes or electronic mail. And by the year 2000, the various computer-based electronic media would replace print in the overnight manner that compact discs replaced vinyl phonograph records.

The problem is that somebody forgot to relate the aforesaid prophecy to the end users. "Paperless" was a term that proved totally unacceptable, not only to librarians, but to other print-oriented workers as well. The computer was a victim of its own success: the automation technology of the 1970s and 1980s proved wonderfully applicable to traditional crafts such as typesetting, page composition, graphics representation, and even touch typing. What were once highly skilled but painstaking endeavors were suddenly rendered many times faster and more presentable than the same jobs accomplished with manual methods. Users with PCs and even low-end equipment could output professional-looking documents. Instead of eliminating paper, the computer actually created new requirements for it. And many of the resultant publications have been delightful.

For librarians and end users to be cognizant of the many possible things that can be created with a word processor and printer, it is necessary to discuss the various options of output peripherals. This section will outline the classes of printers and the jobs and products of which each type is capable.

The earliest printers for computers were based on teletype (TTY) machines, which used an impact head against a fabric ribbon to create characters and numbers, one at a time. Appropriately called **impact printers**, such devices were satisfactory where "quick and dirty," draft quality output was all that was required. Such printers were little more than electric typewriters modified for computer output. As devices to produce a printed copy of information, they got the job done. As to aesthetics, they left much to be desired.

**Dot matrix** printers represented a breakthrough in quality printed output at low cost. First offered in six-pin and then in nine-pin and later 24-pin models, these printers output to paper through a simple technique—the creation of letters and numbers in a grid, using dot patterns. It was soon discovered that graphics images could be output using dot matrix printheads, by printing pictures and images one line at a time in a manner not unlike the rendering of pictures in newspapers. With various mechanical manipulations of the printhead by computer software, different styles of typefaces could be output, and publications which approximated those output by discrete (single letter) printheads were realized on **near-letter-quality (NLQ)** dot matrix printers. For software to give proper instructions for output to a variety of printer brands, there had to be an agreed standard. Because it became the most popularly selling brand of dot matrix printers, the Epson line of printers became the de facto standard for software print protocols, and most major printer manufacturers will, somewhere in the technical specifications for their particular brand, state whether their product follows the **Epson protocol** for computer printer output.

Computer printers enjoyed a rapid evolution in the 1980s. Before NLQ dot matrix printers could provide a more refined output, **daisy wheel** printers made an appearance on the market. These printers were essentially electric typewriters without keyboards which used an impact element whose "fingers" resembled the petals of a flower. Such printers were advantageous in applications where it was desired to have numerous typefaces in publications; wheels were easily changed, and wheel elements were relatively inexpensive. The only drawback was that daisy wheel printers were also relatively slow, their best average output being about 20 or 30 characters per second, compared to dot matrix printers' top speeds, in draft mode, of about 240 characters per second.

In the second half of the 1980s, technology and ink science developed to the point where it was practical to manufacture ink cartridges capable of extremely fine, pinpoint output. **Inkjet** and ink cartridge printers thus became popular peripherals for IBM and compatible PCs and Macintosh computers. Because of their relatively low cost, such printers have captured the desktop market and are ideal for libraries which need a source of precise output for publications. Capable of printed output of two to four pages per minute, inkjet printers have many uses where production (i.e., high volume) output is not necessary. They are compact, and have the output graphics quality of many of the high-end, dry-process printers.

In the 1990s, **laser** printers have become the machines of choice for those shops that can afford them. The cost has dropped considerably since laser printers were first introduced, and the street price for a midrange, office grade laser printer is about $1,300 to $1,500 (1995 prices). The Hewlett Packard Corporation's laser printers have become the de facto standard, and, as with Epson for dot matrix printers, the **Hewlett-Packard protocol** is the point of reference to which manufacturers of other brands declare their software compatibility. "Laser" printers employ an electrostatic process for causing the image to adhere to paper not unlike that found in photocopy machines; the term "laser" refers to the beam that places the electrical charge on the printer drum to affix the proper amounts of toner to the various points on the output medium. Most laser printers employ a dry toner process to deposit "ink" on the page, and disposable (or refillable) toner cartridges are the norm for this type of equipment.

Because they output data a page at a time, laser printers don't "type" characters across a platen as do impact printers. Rather, laser printers' logic circuits fashion **pages** of data as **bitmap images** and store these images in memory for setup and arrangement before being sent to the print drum. Laser printers typically have internal memory circuits separate from those of the computer. Also, such printers almost always have expansion slots which can accept the additional banks of memory necessary to handle complex or lengthy documents. When images are loaded into the printer and taken away from the computer's main memory, they can be more quickly processed and printed because the main (i.e., computer) processor is not tied up with a lengthy input/output task.

A laser printer's circuits typically respond to a **page control language** (**PCL**), a set of instructions permanently encoded into the printer's logic circuitry that determine how data are to be received from the computer

**Figure 3.4** Laser printer (photo courtesy Hewlett-Packard Corporation)

(input) and how they are to be displayed on paper (output). A page control language handles such information as appearances and styles of type fonts, page orientation, descriptions of alternate character sets (e.g., mathematical or foreign), margin settings, and page breaks. Most laser printers also provide expansion slots that will accept plug-in cartridges to accommodate a wider variety of type fonts, different printer emulations, and alternate page control languages such as PostScript. The PostScript language will be discussed as it applies to desktop publishing in chapter 9.

When PostScript was first introduced on printers intended for use in a PC environment, the PostScript language was imbedded in the logic circuitry of the printer itself. In other words, the PostScript interpreter was an integral, unremovable part of the hardware. For laser printers first manufactured in the early 1980s, a choice had to be made between the cheaper bitmapped models and the those in the PostScript class. If you wanted to upgrade to PostScript at a later date, it was necessary to purchase a new printer. At the very least, you had to return your printer to the manufacturer to have the logic board swapped, a process that could tie up the printer for several weeks and cost more than a thousand dollars!

Apple Computer Corporation entered the printer business with its LaserWriter and LaserWriter NT. The latter was a PostScript printer, but Apple made a significant impact on the market by offering its standard LaserWriter with upgrade capabilities. For approximately the price difference between the LaserWriter and the LaserWriter NT, a person desiring conversion to the PostScript model could purchase a kit, which an Apple representative had to install (but usually in a dealer's store), to achieve the capabilities of the more powerful PostScript (NT) printer. This privilege was highly attractive to organizations on tight budgets, and an individual or a small library could gradually approach the business of high-end document processing.

In order for printers to function, they must be connected properly to the computer. Any device which is physically connected to a computer via a cable is said to be **hard wired**. Most computers will have at least one **serial port** and one **parallel port**; these are designated **COM1:** and **LPT1:**, respectively. If there is a second serial or parallel port, these will be noted as **COM2:** and/or **LPT2:**. "COM:" is shorthand for "communications"; early computers connected more often to other computers than to individual printers, and it was logical at the time of the introduction of personal printers to hook them to the communications port. **Parallel transmission** of data over short distances is faster than **serial transmission**, and later computer models included an "LPT" or "line printer" port intended for printer attachments. The COM: port is still typically used for mouse connections and modem hookups (see chapter 16), but LPT: predominates for printers. The shorthand acronyms "COM:" and "LPT:" are widely used in hardware documentation and in word processor setups, and even a casual user should well note the differences.

Parallel transmission of data involves the sending of data bits (usually in groups of eight) over wires which are, as the name implies, side by side or parallel to one another. Serial transmission of data involves the arrangement of data bits (also usually in groups of eight) one after the other and sent down a single wire. Serial data must first be translated from these groups of eight bits into a one-after-another arrangement when transmitted, and rearranged into groups of eight when received at the other end of the wire. This process obviously takes more time than parallel transmission, which requires no such ordering and dismantling at either end of a wire. However, the transmission of data bits over parallel wires, especially long ones, can result in some bits arriving at the receiving end early and some late. The result is garbage data resulting in unusable information. Parallel transmission is thus preferred over short distances, and serial transmission is reserved for longer runs, since the data bits cannot "leapfrog" in the wire when output in a serial fashion. The speed of serial transmissions must be carefully monitored, however, and units of transmission called **baud rates** are imposed to prevent garbling of data either by the sending or the receiving computer. Data transmissions will be discussed again in chapter 16.

## USES OF WORD PROCESSORS

Thus far in this chapter, much space has been devoted to describing how word processors work, what kinds of features they offer, and how they represent text in an intelligent, sophisticated manner. The remainder of this chapter will focus on the types of activities that are possible for libraries to exploit from word processors, along with an example project which marries PCs with word processing software.

A few years after the introduction of personal computers, word processors became much more sophisticated and offered "spinoff" utility programs to perform related tasks. Such utility programs included **spelling checkers**, **thesauri**, **grammar and style checkers**, and **online dictionaries**. Sometimes these utility programs operate within the word processors they support; at other times they function independently, as separately running entities. Often, such utilities run as **terminate and stay resident (TSR) programs**, dormant while the word processor is running and activated by pressing a **hot key** combination. For example, WordStar allows the loading of the software version of the *American Heritage Dictionary* in the background. If a user wishes to check the definition of a word, he/she presses the key combination "Alt-D," and the word designated by the cursor in WordStar's edit screen is defined in a pop-up window.

One interesting, if not amusing story told about thesaurus usage on a computer predates PC-based word processors by about fifteen years. In the early 1960s when the post-Sputnik frenzy to absorb anything technical was in full swing, scientists endeavored to computerize the translation of Russian language documents into English. Because scientific documents usually contain few idiomatic expressions, they are the easiest writings to which to apply word-for-word lookup techniques for synonym translations. A group of scientists loaded a computer with a lookup table of Russian vocabulary words, and ran a collection of scientific papers against it. The printer dutifully output several pages of information about "water goats," a concept which reappeared in the printout every three lines or so. Baffled, the scientists halted the process and looked up the Russian words in a standard Russian/English dictionary. The concept that the computer was attempting so desperately to translate was the phrase "hydraulic rams!"

**Mail merge** is a common activity in word processing environments, and most good word processors will have some facility for handling it. The most common applications of mail merge are the creation of mailing lists and generation of "form" letters for advertisements and solicitations. Two files are maintained by the word processor: a database of names and addresses of correspondents, and a template file of boilerplate letters, into which the names and addresses are merged. From these two files, duplicate yet personalized mailings can be output, and each recipient gets an "individualized" letter. Mail merge has many applications for libraries, and the final section of this chapter illustrates one such activity.

## APPLICATION: MAIL MERGE TO CREATE BROADCAST LETTERS

The mail merge facility of most word processors is commonly used in libraries to generate publicity letters, solicitations, announcements, legal notices, and a variety of correspondences requiring personalized letters. Combining the power of word processing software with the typeset quality output of laser and near-letter-quality dot matrix printers, several hundred letters can be generated in a short time, with a minimal outlay of human resources. Once a mailing list is created, it is easily modified and updated as a database file, using only a stand-alone PC or Macintosh computer.

In word processing, **merging** refers to the process of combining information from at least two sources to produce an entirely new file or document. Mail merging is a good example in which an address file (of customers, patrons, or students) and a document file, also known as a **boilerplate** or **template file**, which contains the skeleton form of the desired output letter, are created. The result of a merging will be a third file containing a separate letter for every name and address.

The following example uses the popular WordPerfect IBM version 6.0 for DOS to create a primary file (the template of the letter for the merge) and a secondary file (the list of names and addresses to appear in the output letters). The exercise will assume that you have WordPerfect loaded on the computer's C: drive and that the work files and output files will exist in the same subdirectory (WP60) as the word processing program. The program is loaded by typing WP at the C:\WP60> prompt, and the following steps are taken to complete the task:

1. Create a file called ADDRESS.WKB. Type the names and addresses provided at the end of this section, following the instructions given below. Note that you can view the codes mentioned in each of the steps by toggling the "reveal codes" function (Alt-F3 or F11).
   a. Type **name** and then press Merge R (F9) to create the first field. Notice that the ^R merge code and Hard Return are inserted for you when you press Merge R.
   b. Type the **address** (either two or three lines) and press F9 to end the field.
   c. Type the **first name** and press F9.
   d. Type the **telephone number** and press F9.

　　　e. Now that the record information has been typed, you are
　　　　ready to insert an ^E to end the record. Press Merge Codes
　　　　(Shift-F9) and then type "e" to select ^E. Note that an ^E and
　　　　a page break are inserted for you when you use Merge Codes
　　　　to end a record.
　　　f. Save your document. Press F7, and type ADDRESS.WKB. Do
　　　　not exit WordPerfect.
　2. Create a file called LETTER.WKB. Type the template letter pro-
　　vided, following the instructions given below:
　　　a. Press Merge Codes (Shift-F9), type "f" to select ^F, and then
　　　　enter "1" to insert field one into the "To" **name** during a
　　　　merge.
　　　b. Press Merge Codes (Shift-F9), type "f" to select ^F, and then
　　　　enter "2" to insert field two into the "To **address** during a
　　　　merge.
　　　c. Press "Enter" four times. At the new line, type "Dear" and one
　　　　space, press Shift-F9, type "f" to select ^F, and then enter "3"
　　　　to insert field three into the "Dear ," during a merge.
　　　d. Type the body of the letter and following the phrase ". . . the
　　　　name of. . .," press Shift-F9, type "f" to select ^F, and then
　　　　enter "1" to insert the F1 field.
　　　e. Save the document. Press F7 and type "LETTER.WKB." Do
　　　　not exit WordPerfect.
　3. At the blank screen, you should press Merge/Sort (Ctrl-F9) and
　select merge (1).
　　　a. Enter "LETTER.WKB" for the name of the primary file, and
　　　　then enter "ADDRESS.WKB" for the name of the secondary
　　　　file. When the merging is completed, the last letter in the
　　　　merged document should be on your screen. Press Ctrl-
　　　　Home and then the UP arrow to scroll to the top of the last
　　　　letter. Once the merging is completed, the letters are ready to
　　　　send to the printer. However, most people never save the
　　　　merged letters because they can always be created again by
　　　　simply merging the primary and secondary files.
　　　b. Print the merged file and exit from the document.
　　　c. Retrieve (Shift-F10) and enter "LETTER.WKB" to retrieve the
　　　　primary file.
　　　d. Press "Home" twice and then the UP arrow to move the cur-
　　　　sor to the beginning of the letter. Press Merge Codes (Shift-
　　　　F9) and then type "m" and select "Date" option to insert a ^D
　　　　merge code.
　　　e. Press "Enter" four times to add extra spacing. Note: the ^D
　　　　merge code performs the same task as WordPerfect's "Date"

text feature. Whenever you merge the primary file,
WordPerfect automatically inserts the current date at the position of the ^D.

f. Press Exit (F7) and type "y" to save the edited letter.

g. Press Merge/Sort (Ctrl-F9) and select Merge (1).

h. Print your final draft. The letter is now ready for mass mailing.

Here is the mailing list; you can use any names you wish, but the following are furnished as examples:

Samuel Spade                                    Howard Massey-Ferguson
Marginal Computer Components, Inc.   Precision Silverware, Inc.
1234 Shady Lane                               Thirteen Tractor Pull Road
Woeis, ME 02258                             Manhattan, KS 55449
Sam                                                   Howie
(999) 432-8498                                 (401) 865-3985

Bette Davis                                        Bolivar Shagnasty
The Eyes Have It PCs, Inc.                Terribly Expensive Parts,Ltd.
397 Hill and Dale Road                     9635 Farfetched Blvd.
Farout, CA 94802                             Hurricane, FL 33086
Bette                                                 Bolivar
(707) 327-5500                                 (718) 555-9436

and so forth, using the same format for additional entries.

The following template letter can be used to complete the application
exercise:

^F1^

^F2^

Dear ^F3:

This year, as you know, has been a difficult time for the budgets of
public agencies. Your public library is not immune to recessionary
times, and we have suffered considerably from the cutbacks in funding and the gradual erosion of our tax base. We regret that, once again
in such a short period of time, we must appeal to you for financial
help.

Our goal is to raise $50,000 to restore to its former level our books and
materials budget. Unless we raise this amount from donations and
from the private sector, we will be unable to place new materials on
our shelves in the coming year. With the final budget handed us by
the county commission, we will be able to do little else but maintain
our physical plant and attempt to keep our facilities open regular
hours for the entire calendar year.

A donation of $25, $35, $50, or whatever you could give would be greatly appreciated. In addition, the names of those who pledge $100 or more will be inscribed on the library's signature wall now under construction in the lobby atrium. Imagine showing your friends the name of ^F1 inscribed permanently on firebrick in the main library. Remember that this is *your* public library, and a prompt response from you would be most welcome.

Sincerely,

Leslie P. Johnson, Director

Mid-Sized Public Library District

After the merge, all the letters output should resemble the following:

Samuel Spade

Marginal Computer Components, Inc.

1234 Shady Lane

Woeis, ME 02258

Dear Sam:

This year, as you know, has been a difficult time for the budgets of public agencies. Your public library is not immune to recessionary times, and we have suffered considerably from the cutbacks in funding and the gradual erosion of our tax base. We regret that, once again in such a short period of time, we must appeal to you for financial help.

Our goal is to raise $50,000 to restore to its former level our books and materials budget. Unless we raise this amount from donations and from the private sector, we will be unable to place new materials on our shelves in the coming year. With the final budget handed us by the county commission, we will be able to do little else but maintain our physical plant and attempt to keep our facilities open regular hours for the entire calendar year.

A donation of $25, $35, $50, or whatever you could give would be greatly appreciated. In addition, the names of those who pledge $100 or more will be inscribed on the library's signature wall now under construction in the lobby atrium. Imagine showing your friends the name of Samuel Spade inscribed permanently on firebrick in the main library. Remember that this is *your* public library, and a prompt response from you would be most welcome.

Sincerely,

Leslie P. Johnson, Director

Mid-Sized Public Library District

Library applications of mail merge projects are numerous. Reports to the Board of Trustees, for example, where each member receives duplicate information, can be customized with each member's name inserted at appropriate locations in the correspondence. A children's librarian can create a short story which contain a few merge codes, into which children's names can be inserted, to personalize an illustrated storytime to reflect the names of the children anticipated to be in the audience. And longer documents, such as newsletters, can contain merge codes so that mailing labels can be output at the same time the final page of the newsletter is created, printed directly on the outside page.

## NOTES

1. PC-Type, published by Buttonware, Inc., P.O. Box 96058, Bellvue, WA 98009. (800) 528-8866. PC-Type+, $69.95.
2. PC Write, published by Quicksoft, Inc., 219 First Ave. N #224, Seattle, WA 98109. Standard Level, $59.00; Advanced Level, $89.00. (Shareware versions are available from Public Brand Software as disks #WP2 and #WP32; see Bibliography for address.)
3. WordStar, published by WordStar International, Inc., P.O. Box 2030, Cameron Park, CA 95682. $495.00.
4. Microsoft Word for Windows, published by Microsoft Corporation, One Microsoft Way, Redmond, WA 98052-6399. $495.00.
5. Turabian, Kate L. *A Manual for Writers of Term Papers, Theses, and Dissertations.* Fifth edition. University of Chicago Press, 1987. 300 pp.
6. WordPerfect, published by Novell, Inc., 122 E. 1700 S, Provo, UT 84606. $395.00 (Windows version); $495.00 (DOS version); $189.00 (Macintosh version).

# Chapter 4

# Spreadsheets

Spreadsheet programs are one of the older types of software created for microcomputers. Since computers were initially designed to handle numeric manipulations, it was natural for an application to be created that would handle financial data. One of the first such spreadsheet programs was VisiCalc for the Apple II computer. Present-day spreadsheet programs are many times more elaborate, but they all exhibit the same basic look and feel of that original Apple II program.

Spreadsheet anatomy is really quite simple. All spreadsheet programs consist of X/Y grids of **cells**, into which constants, variables, formulas, text, and labels are entered. Mathematical operations can be performed on the data which are placed in the cells. The grid is arranged in two lettered **columns** and numbered **rows**. Depending on the sophistication of the program and the memory capacity of the computer, it is possible to have several hundred columns (a typical number is 256) and several thousand rows (typical is 8,192). But there are usually displayed about seven or eight columns and twenty-four rows on a computer screen at any given moment. Obviously, then, it is possible to manipulate a spreadsheet containing a very large budget, accounting ledger, or financial program only if there is a way to maintain data and references offscreen. And indeed, this is exactly the way spreadsheets function.

Think of a spreadsheet as a very large piece of paper, spread out on a tabletop several feet wide and perhaps twice that many feet long. If you write data onto the sheet very precisely, taking care to align the rows and columns so that the budgetary decision makers and auditors can read exactly the numbers you intend to convey, you might require a magnifying glass to interpret various parts of the task. This is precisely what the computer does with a spreadsheet: it uses the rectangular video screen as a very large magnifying glass, and, with the aid of the arrow keys and Home/PgUp/End/PgDn keys, moves that glass to the precise locations on the sheet to which you need to refer. What you must keep in mind is the issue of **cell references**. Cells are typically referenced by column and row, e.g., the upper left cell is A1, the one immediately to its right is B1, the one immediately below A1 is A2, and, if the spreadsheet is capable of displaying perhaps fifty-two columns and 256 rows, the last cell, i.e., the one on the lower right, would be ZZ256 (using two alphabets and 256 numbers). It is important to remember that in order for spreadsheets to keep track of calculations of many numbers which are interdependent, these cell references must be heeded. Figure 4.1 illustrates the need for such vigilance, because the "Sum of All Columns," a sum of sums, is completely dependent on the "Sums of Individual Columns."

| | A | B | C | D | E | F | G | H | I | J |
|---|---|---|---|---|---|---|---|---|---|---|
| 1 | | | | | | | | | | |
| 2 | | | Use of Cell References and Ranges | | | | | | | |
| 3 | | | In Spreadsheet Programs | | | | | | | |
| 4 | | | | | | | | | | |
| 5 | | 123 | 246 | 987 | ◀--- | These are | | | | |
| 6 | | 456 | 468 | 654 | ◀--- | Constants | | | | |
| 7 | | 789 | 680 | 321 | ◀--- | (Hard-Coded Data) | | | | |
| 8 | | | | | | | | | | |
| 9 | | 1368 | 1394 | 1962 | ◀--- | Sums of Individual Colums | | | | |
| 10 | | | | | | | | | | |
| 11 | | | | 4724 | ◀--- | Sum of All Columns | | | | |
| 12 | | | | | | | | | | |
| 13 | | | | | | | | | | |

**Figure 4.1** Sample spreadsheet

Depending on its relative level of sophistication, a spreadsheet may have a repertoire of several hundred formulas. A **spreadsheet formula** is a built-in function of the program to return a value passed to it as an argument. An **argument** is the datum or data which are typically passed to the formula through its parentheses, as in the following example from Lotus 1-2-3:

Formula: @SUM( ) Formula with argument: @SUM(3+4+5)

It should be readily apparent that the @SUM( ) formula takes the numbers 3, 4, and 5 and totals them.

A more efficient way to use formulas is to pass arguments in terms of cell ranges. A **cell range** is a shorthand reference to a row, column, or rectangle of two or more cells in a common group. For example, if it is desired to total the contents of data in cells A1, A2, A3, B1, B2, B3, C1, C2, and C3 (nine cells), rather than passing the argument of nine cells to the @SUM( ) formula as @SUM(A1+A2+A3+B1+B2+B3+C1+C2+C3), a considerable amount of typing, Lotus 1-2-3 allows the passing of arguments as ranges. Thus, the same formula becomes @SUM(A1..C3), picking up the upper left and lower right cell references, which Lotus 1-2-3 recognizes as a range because of the ellipsis separating the first and last cell references.

Figure 4.2 shows the same spreadsheet as in Figure 4.1, except that the cells containing sums are marked to show the actual formulas. This example uses Microsoft Excel, whose formula formats differ slightly from those of Lotus 1-2-3. Note that the =SUM( ) formulas contain ranges of numbers reflecting the three values in each column, namely, B5:B7, C5:C7, and D5:D7. Note, however, the formula in cell D11, which sums the range B9:D9—a sum of three =SUM( ) formulas! This is an example of a backward reference to cells, in which previous computations affect other ones (here, the =SUM(B9:D9) ) in cell D11. Any changes that modify the totals in the three column totalling =SUM( )s thus will have a cascade effect on

| | A | B | C | D | E | F | G | H | I |
|---|---|---|---|---|---|---|---|---|---|
| 1 | | | | | | | | | |
| 2 | | | Use of Cell References and Ranges | | | | | | |
| 3 | | | In Spreadsheet Programs | | | | | | |
| 4 | | | | | | | | | |
| 5 | | 123 | 246 | 987 | ◀--- | These are | | | |
| 6 | | 456 | 468 | 654 | ◀--- | Constants | | | |
| 7 | | 789 | 680 | 321 | ◀--- | (Hard-Coded Data) | | | |
| 8 | | | | | | | | | |
| 9 | | =SUM(B5:B7) | =SUM(C5:C7) | =SUM(D5:D7) | ◀--- | Sums of Individual Columns | | | |
| 10 | | | | | | | | | |
| 11 | | | | =SUM(B9:D9) | ◀--- | Sum of All Columns | | | |
| 12 | | | | | | | | | |
| 13 | | | | | | | | | |

**Figure 4.2** Spreadsheet with cells displaying formula

another part of the sheet. For this reason, it cannot be emphasized enough that the creator of a spreadsheet-based financial document should maintain an accurate record of all cell references.

## SPREADSHEET SOFTWARE

Spreadsheets vary widely in complexity and in price. PC-Calc,[1] a spreadsheet program for the IBM PC and compatibles, provides many of the basic functions described above and is compatible with the other Buttonware programs PC-Type and PC-File described in chapters 3 and 5. PC-Calc evolved into the Lotus 1-2-3 compatible AS-EASY-AS[2] program and has many capabilities of the more sophisticated, "commercial" spreadsheets, including chartmaking, spreadsheet linking, importation of dBase database files, and macro recording. It is useful not only as a financial and budget planning program, but also as an inexpensive teaching tool.

There are several spreadsheet programs which are considered "high end" software. SuperCalc[3] has been around nearly as long as VisiCalc and is one of the "old guard" of spreadsheets. While not currently as popular as some others, SuperCalc nonetheless has its niche. SuperCalc had its beginnings as a CP/M based program (see chapter 6) and for awhile was packaged gratis with Osborne I and similar 8-bit computers. It evolved into a sophisticated program and was one of the first spreadsheets to support color, graphics and charting capabilities, and a number of atypical (for the time) peripheral devices such as pen plotters. Its most recent incarnation is SuperCalc 5, available for IBM and compatible computers.

Lotus 1-2-3[4] is available for both the IBM and Macintosh computers and is the standard by which all others are measured. While Lotus 1-2-3 does not have the high percentage of marketshare it once enjoyed, the program nonetheless has a wide following, along with a vast body of third party support literature. Lotus 1-2-3 is available in both DOS and Windows versions, and, of course, in a version for Macintosh System 6.X and System 7. The DOS version has some variations, and many users are staying with version 2.2 because that release operates exclusively within the IBM's lower 640-kilobyte memory range. Versions 3.X and 4.X are more sophisticated and provide more features, but they require extra (extended or expanded) memory beyond the basic 640K—a feature not found on the original IBM PCs or XTs. Lotus 1-2-3 also provides for linked spreadsheets, a feature which allows users to cross reference cells in separate sheets with one another for more complex data analyses.

MS Works[5] is a Microsoft product and is well-suited for shops and environments where there are not many other programs available. In fact, MS Works is an **integrated software** package, which consists of the basic spreadsheet, a word processor, and a database manager. Files from any one section can be read and manipulated by either of the other two. Because Works must maintain numerous cross references from one application to another, it tends to be a simpler program, although no less powerful, than others of its kind. As such, it is also a useful teaching tool and provides the foundation for curricula in introductory computer applications in many business and data processing courses.

Microsoft Corporation has another well-placed entry in the spreadsheet arena, namely, Excel 5.0 for Windows.[6] This latest version exploits all the features of Microsoft's other flagship product, Windows 3 (detailed in chapter 7). The result is a blend of tools that makes Excel useful for a broad range of financial, statistical, and graphical tasks. And, despite its ability to handle intricate and complex formulas and reports, Excel is comprehendible even to a novice user. It is presented here in more detail than the ones mentioned above because it incorporates all the standard

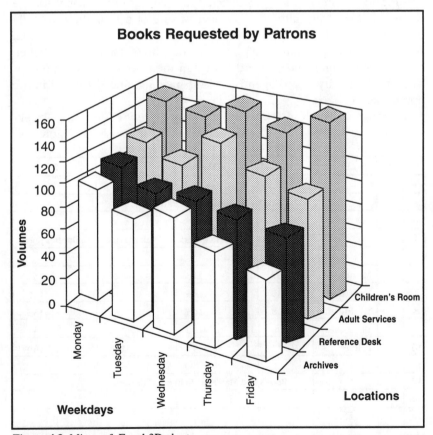

**Figure 4.3** Microsoft Excel 3D chart

features of modern spreadsheets and lends itself nicely to the presentation of a library example.

There are versions of Excel for both the PC and the Macintosh (the Mac version is 2.0 as of this writing). Except for the nuances of difference between the Mac and IBM (Windows) platforms, the two versions appear remarkably similar on the screen. This is partly by design, and users who switch between platforms will find the familiar mouse support with point-and-shoot capabilities in both versions. Because of its power in displaying presentation graphics, the Mac has traditionally had an advantage for showing graphical results of spreadsheet data. But the newer IBM versions of the software have made choice of platform a matter of personal preference.

The example in Figure 4.3 is a simplified rendition of a hypothetical survey on library usage. The investigator has tallied requests for card catalog lookups at service desks, using perhaps the count of paper call slips as support documents. Having selected the 3D bar chart facility for the representation of the study data, a clear picture of user traffic can easily be displayed. This chart can be reproduced either as a direct print from within the Excel program itself, or it can be photocopied from a screen dump of the original chart. Hard copy can then be distributed, perhaps as part of a library board agenda or staff meeting, and discussed in the appropriate context.

The chart in Figure 4.3 was, in fact, created very easily using Excel's built-in facility called the ChartWizard. A simple spreadsheet (Figure 4.4)

| | A | B | C | D | E | F |
|---|---|---|---|---|---|---|
| 1 | | | | | | |
| 2 | | | Books Requested by Patrons | | | |
| 3 | | | | | | |
| 4 | | | Archives | Reference Desk | Adult Services | Children's Room |
| 5 | | | | | | |
| 6 | | Monday | 102 | 113 | 124 | 150 |
| 7 | | Tuesday | 89 | 104 | 118 | 145 |
| 8 | | Wednesday | 108 | 105 | 135 | 155 |
| 9 | | Thursday | 88 | 100 | 110 | 144 |
| 10 | | Friday | 79 | 97 | 105 | 160 |
| 11 | | | | | | |
| 12 | | | Books and Materials Requested (Volumes) | | | |
| 13 | | | | | | |
| 14 | | | | | | |

**Figure 4.4** Spreadsheet data for chart in Figure 4.3

was created from data collected from the call slip count. Excel, incidentally, allows a simultaneous print of spreadsheets and charts on the same page if desired. The chart in Figure 4.3 was actually created using the default settings in Excel for this type of graphic. In other words, the placements of text labels, appearance of type fonts, axis numeric ratios, and shading of the vertical bars were left to Excel's charting subroutines. For most users, this plain and neat appearance is adequate for general presentations.

There are many times, however, when it is desirable to vary from the norm and create custom presentations. With Excel (and most other high-end spreadsheet programs), a wide range of variations can be accomplished. If the printout is to be magnified many times, for example, to be distributed as a poster, the crosshatch patterns on the value bars can be varied. Typefaces for labels and captions can also be varied, and Excel takes advantage of the Windows TrueType technology (see chapter 9) for screens and printouts. For output as **slide presentations**, i.e., the showing of multiple graphics directly on the computer's screen, Excel provides a palette so that color can be used in the graphics for best emphasis. The program can also take a 3D chart and rotate it so that alternate viewing perspectives can be demonstrated. Different kinds of charts, e.g., pie, line, 2D bar, scatterplot, and others, are also possible using the same basic spreadsheet.

A good textbook on statistics will tell you what is the most appropriate type of chart for the data you wish to present. Excel makes experimentation easy, and one or two clicks of the mouse pointer allow you to switch between chart models. The chart in Figure 4.5 is made from the data in the spreadsheet of Figure 4.4, the only presentational difference being the manner in which the values are drawn. The individual library will have to determine which presentation is most appropriate for its particular needs on any given occasion.

## APPLICATION: THE ANNUAL BUDGET PROCESS

Libraries vary widely in the timing of their budgetary cycles. This is an area of library administration where it makes little difference whether the agency is tax-supported or private, academic, corporate, or public. There are specific criteria which are common to all libraries, and it doesn't matter whether the mandates of fiscal accounting are set by a governing board, public law, or corporate auditors. The budget is a responsibility which has been made many times easier by using a spreadsheet tool to consider the "what ifs" of line items and make possible the meeting of deadlines to balance the books.

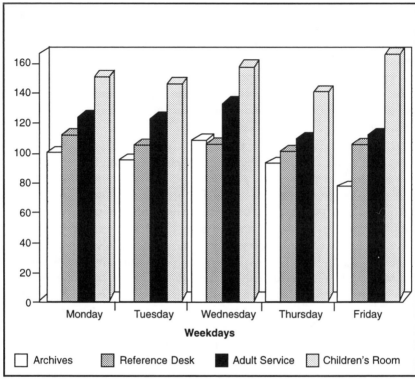

**Figure 4.5** Bar chart, presenting same data as in Figure 4.4

Few library schools require intensive accounting courses as part of the MLS curriculum. It is recommended that if library administration is the intended major of your studies, you should include a course in financial or managerial accounting and one in fund accounting (some schools list the latter as not-for-profit accounting). This text does not purport to teach you library accounting principles, but this section assumes you have either studied some accounting or would use your reference skills to read a few case studies on library budgeting. The remainder of this chapter will present a detailed example of how spreadsheets can be used to make intelligent money decisions to keep the auditors and library governing board happy.

There are several common denominators that can be labeled "problem areas" which pertain to library budgetmaking. These are

1. Distributions (collections) of revenue are often made at the last possible minute.
2. A library typically cannot legally be in debt (except for outstanding bond issues) at the beginning of a new fiscal period.

3. A proposed budget for an incoming fiscal period is usually considered over several months' time. Issues beyond the finance committee's control (e.g., a change in library law regarding financial regulations) can occur while the budget process is pending.

4. Unexpected revenue conversions (e.g., losses from lawsuits, reassessment of taxable property, receipt of gifts or endowments) can significantly alter the operating fund's cash base.

The following application example is based on actual circumstances regarding the finalizing of an operating budget for a public library. Based on events in the state of Indiana, it exhibits many of the features of other jurisdictions, including elements of the list above, mandated during a budget cycle. For the purpose of showing how these criteria can be applied to a spreadsheet process, the elements are summarized as follows:

1. The budgetary process in Indiana starts around the beginning of June and concludes anytime from the middle of October to the middle of December. Hearings progress from a local level (board meeting) to the state level (final approval by the State Board of Tax Commissioners).

2. The fiscal year for most libraries is January 1 through December 31. A library's ledgers must be balanced at the close of business on December 31, and all outstanding obligations must be met at that time. No debt, except for bonded indebtedness, can be carried from one fiscal year to another. (However, in actual practice, encumbrances such as book purchases are carried into a new fiscal year.)

3. Property tax distributions, from which a library derives the bulk of its operating capital, are typically held until the last statutorily allowable moment. In other words, a library can expect that the final collection of its tax revenues will not be released until the morning of December 31.

4. Indiana has a ceiling on tax levies of no more than a five percent increase over the previous year. This legislation imposes the following formula on municipal corporations:
   assessed value of property in current fiscal year X 1.05 = maximum tax collection in incoming fiscal year
   However, the assessed *valuation* of property within the taxing district may increase more than five percent; this increase is at the discretion of the county assessor.

5. It is possible for property tax collections to be over the five percent statutory ceiling; property owners sometimes pay their taxes in advance as a hedge against recessionary times (or in anticipation of low crop yields, in some of the more rural counties). By

law, a library must place these additional monies into a so-called excess levy fund. The proceeds are used to reduce a future year's levy and cannot be spent by a library as a windfall resource.

All these factors cause numerous permutations in the life of the budget cycle. The process is actually one of intelligent "guesstimating," and until spreadsheet software arrived on the market, the activity generated a considerable amount of eraser crumbs and adding machine tape—with a fair amount of midnight oil and mathematical errors thrown in for good measure!

The following illustration is a condensed version of a library's operating fund budget. The example is simplified to keep the figure to one page (screen) as in Figure 4.6, but the principles are nonetheless the same.

There are six major categories in the operating budget. In the category marked Requested, the planning committee has entered what it thinks

|    | A | B | C | D | E | F |
|----|---|---|---|---|---|---|
| 1  |   |   |   |   |   |   |
| 2  |   |   | Hillsboro Public Library | | | |
| 3  |   |   | Trial Budget for Calendar 1995 | | | |
| 4  |   |   |   |   |   |   |
| 5  |   |   | Requested | Received | Difference | |
| 6  |   |   |   |   |   |   |
| 7  |   | Salaries | $250,000 | $250,000 | $0 | |
| 8  |   | Books | $75,000 | $75,000 | $0 | |
| 9  |   | Equipment | $50,000 | $50,000 | $0 | |
| 10 |   | Cleaning | $7,500 | $7,500 | $0 | |
| 11 |   | Repairs | $15,000 | $15,000 | $0 | |
| 12 |   | Postage | $2,500 | $2,500 | $0 | |
| 13 |   |   |   |   |   |   |
| 14 |   | Totals | $400,000 | $400,000 | $0 | |
| 15 |   |   |   |   |   |   |
| 16 |   | Revenue Percentage Received | | | 100.00% | |
| 17 |   | Budget Requested | | | $400,000 | |
| 18 |   | Tax Draw Actually Received 12/31/94 | | | $400,000 | |
| 19 |   |   |   |   |   |   |
| 20 |   |   |   |   |   |   |

**Figure 4.6** Initially proposed operating fund budget

the final line amounts will be. The total of this column is simply the sum of the six line item figures above. All the figures in the Received column are multiples of the Requested amounts. Each figure is computed on the basis of the percent figure in the Revenue Percentage Received cell. In other words, the amount Received for Salaries is computed by converting the 100.00% to a whole number, 1.00, and multiplying the Requested amount for salaries. The Difference is merely the computation of each of the Received amounts minus the Requested amounts. Since Figure 4.6 assumes that calendar 1996 has not yet occurred, the Requested and Received amounts are the same.

Figure 4.7 is the same spreadsheet as in Figure 4.6, but this time showing cell formulas and cell designations. Assuming that the 1996 budget goes into effect on January 1 of that year, the bulk of the budget can be established any time prior to 1/1/96. The key here is the

| | A | B | C | D | E | F |
|---|---|---|---|---|---|---|
| 1 | | | | | | |
| 2 | | | Hillsboro Public Library | | | |
| 3 | | | Trial Budget for Calendar 1995 | | | |
| 4 | | | | | | |
| 5 | | | Requested | Received | Difference | |
| 6 | | | | | | |
| 7 | | Salaries | $250,000 | =+C7*E16 | =+D7-C7 | |
| 8 | | Books | $75,000 | =+C8*E16 | =+D8-C8 | |
| 9 | | Equipment | $50,000 | =+C9*E16 | =+D9-C9 | |
| 10 | | Cleaning | $7,500 | =+C10*E16 | =+D10-C10 | |
| 11 | | Repairs | $15,000 | =+C11*E16 | =+D11-C11 | |
| 12 | | Postage | $2,500 | =+C12*E16 | =+D12-C12 | |
| 13 | | | | | | |
| 14 | | Totals | =SUM(C7:C12) | =SUM(D7:D12) | =SUM(E7:E12) | |
| 15 | | | | | | |
| 16 | | Revenue Percentage Received | | | =+E18/E17 | |
| 17 | | Budget Requested | | | =+C14 | |
| 18 | | Tax Draw Actually Received 12/31/94 | | | $400,000 | |
| 19 | | | | | | |
| 20 | | | | | | |

**Figure 4.7** Initially proposed operating fund budget with cell formulas revealed

amount of operating money that the library receives on December 31, 1995, in this illustration, $420,000. Assuming also that the budget committee has decided to allocate excess revenues (or shortfalls) uniformly across all line items, the Received amounts need only be proportional to the money taken on the last day of the outgoing year. In other words, the only action that the budget officer needs to take is to enter an amount in Tax Draw Actually Received 12/31/95, and the rest of the budget computes automatically. Notice that the Revenue Percentage Received is just the calculation of the Tax Draw/Budget Requested. And, as shown above, the multiplication factor for the Received column takes its information from the Percentage cell. The Total under the Received column makes a handy cross-check of the Tax Draw, since both figures are independent of one another.

Figure 4.8 shows the revised budget, after the actual Tax Draw has been recorded, and with cells displaying dollar amounts instead of formulas.

|    | A | B | C | D | E | F |
|----|---|---|---|---|---|---|
| 1  |   |   |   |   |   |   |
| 2  |   |   | Hillsboro Public Library | | | |
| 3  |   |   | Trial Budget for Calendar 1995 | | | |
| 4  |   |   |   |   |   |   |
| 5  |   |   | Requested | Received | Difference | |
| 6  |   |   |   |   |   |   |
| 7  |   | Salaries | $250,000 | $252,500 | $12,500 | |
| 8  |   | Books | $75,000 | $78,750 | $3,750 | |
| 9  |   | Equipment | $50,000 | $52,500 | $2,500 | |
| 10 |   | Cleaning | $7,500 | $7,875 | $375 | |
| 11 |   | Repairs | $15,000 | $15,750 | $750 | |
| 12 |   | Postage | $2,500 | $2,625 | $125 | |
| 13 |   |   |   |   |   |   |
| 14 |   | Totals | $400,000 | $420,000 | $20,000 | |
| 15 |   |   |   |   |   |   |
| 16 |   | Revenue Percentage Received | | | 105.00% | |
| 17 |   | Budget Requested | | | $400,000 | |
| 18 |   | Tax Draw Actually Received 12/31/94 | | | $420,000 | |
| 19 |   |   |   |   |   |   |
| 20 |   |   |   |   |   |   |

**Figure 4.8** Revised operating fund budget, after tax draw

This would be the final form presented to the budget committee or other financial governing body, subject to its final revisions. The point is that a statutory requirement has been met—the budget has been balanced at the end-of-year closeout, without a "burning of the midnight oil." Obviously, this process could be applied to individual departments as well as to a library as a single entity.

## NOTES

1. PC-Calc, published by Buttonware, Inc., P.O. Box 96058, Bellevue, WA 98009. (800) 528-8866. PC-Calc+, $69.95.
2. AS-EASY-AS, published by TRIUS, Inc., 231 Sutton, P.O. Box 240, N. Andover, MA. $69.00. (A shareware version is available as Public Brand Software disk #SP7; see Bibliography for address.)
3. SuperCalc 5, published by Computer Associates International, One Computer Associates Plaza, Islandia, NY 11788-7000. $249.00.
4. Lotus 1-2-3, published by Lotus Development Corporation, 55 Cambridge Parkway, Cambridge, MA 02142. $495.00 (DOS version); $495.00 (Windows version); $495.00 (Macintosh version).
5. MS-Works, published by Microsoft Corporation, One Microsoft Way, Redmond, WA 98052-6399. $149.00 (DOS version); $249.00 (Macintosh version).
6. Microsoft Excel, published by Microsoft Corporation, One Microsoft Way, Redmond, WA 98052-6399. $495.00 (Windows version); $495.00 (Macintosh version).

# Chapter 5

# Databases

Society lives and breathes on its information. In a list of reasons for existence of libraries, undoubtedly one of the first is "to disseminate information." This thing called **information** is defined as "a specific form of literature which records problems and solutions to problems; facts." Many will argue that there are other definitions of information, and that the preceding is too trite. But it can generally be agreed that information is a commodity, and, as such, it exhibits three characteristics: it does not exist to entertain; it is generally not common knowledge; and it is usually found in discrete parcels somewhat narrower than the field of interest.

**Knowledge**, on the other hand, is usually derived from reading, observation, or experimentation.

Certain parameters are applicable to the measurement of information:

1. **Quantity**, where information is defined as a specific number of pages, words, or data bits
2. **Content**, which is the semantic meaning of the information and its related value which is determined by expert analysis
3. **Structure**, the format or organization and relationship between statements
4. **Language**, the symbols, alphabets, codes, and syntax in which ideas are expressed
5. **Quality**, the completeness, accuracy, relevance and timeliness of the information
6. **Life**, the time span over which value can be derived from the information.

There are three general types of information: alphabetic, numeric, and graphic. **Alphabetic information** is given the attribute "long life" and is typically seen in instructional and educational situations. **Numeric information** has a relatively short life and is used often as raw data, to describe "how much" in research and development and engineering circumstances. **Graphic information** has a longer life than numeric information, but a shorter life than alphabetic information, and is often used in business in pictorials to give visual displays of commercial concepts. Although the scope of the three types of information has been rather narrowly defined, this text will nonetheless use their few attributes to move into the next consideration of information handling—storage and retrieval.

## INFORMATION STORAGE AND RETRIEVAL

The phrase "database techniques" implies that a computer and appropriate software will be used to administer files of information and the various records contained therein. However, databases were maintained for years before it became practical to install them into some electromechanical device. With acknowledgement that the processes below were developed before the advent of commonplace (read electronic) computing, the following list defines the fundamental operations of information storage and retrieval:

1. **Indexing**. Here are the methods of recognizing, selecting, identifying and arranging information to facilitate organized storage and searching. Techniques for accomplishing this task include the coordination of words (so that any individually selected word accurately represents each document or record), classification (as with subject headings, e.g., as found in a Sears or Library of Congress subject list), and permutation (so that every word in a title, subject heading, etc., has some degree of significance).
2. **Storage**. This includes the methods of maintaining indexes to facilitate searches. Indexes themselves must conform to a storage medium, e.g., card catalogs, printed lists, paper tape, and photographic or magnetic memory devices. Documents and records, too, must be placed in a medium suitable for long- and short-term dormancy; a suitable medium might be as simple as a paperbound or spiral notebook, and also a microfilm, ROM chip, or magnetic tape or disk.
3. **Retrieval**. This includes the methods of extracting the required identifications of documents and records from the index and the ways of extracting documents and records from storage. Such methods might include serial searching, selective (random)

searching, batch searching, logical (Boolean and keyword) searching, or simply browsing.

## THE COLLECTION AND PROCESSING OF INFORMATION

Information retrieval schemes, as they apply to database construction, must adhere to eleven general elements. There is some redundancy from concepts presented in the previous section, but the following is intended to give a more abstract and comprehensive summary of database construction before a more machine-oriented, concrete view is considered:

1. **Organization** is the element that first instigates deposit of information into the system. Such organization may arise intellectually or spontaneously.
2. **Transmission** arises from a geographical gap, the process of bringing together separate but related pieces of information.
3. **Evaluation** reduces transmission errors and decreases subjectivity. Information should be recorded to be as error-free as possible.
4. **Selection** is the direction of information to the correct recipients, or, the decision of what to keep and what to discard.
5. **Analysis** is inspection by experts for the potential value of the information. Except for mathematical models, this element stands the least chance of becoming a fully automated process. Artificial intelligence methods don't seem to handle this type of database analysis efficiently.
6. **Indexing** is the task of structuring information so that succeeding manipulations can be accomplished.
7. **Storage** is an accumulation or capacity function; a type of "delay line" or a "hold" until the information is needed again.
8. **Retrieval** obtains responses from storage based on criteria which can be stated intellectually. Indexing is input; retrieval is output.
9. **Correlation** is the actual manipulation of information according to mathematical, logical, or statistical rules which change to conform to levels of abstraction of information while preparing it for dissemination. This action is taken more by programmers and database designers than by end users.
10. **Dissemination** is the distribution of information for use, to direct most efficiently to points of utilization.
11. **Utilization** is the prime motive for information storage and retrieval and the gathering of information to fit viewpoints of those who would use it.

## COMPUTER TECHNIQUES FOR MAINTAINING DATABASES

Shortly after it was discovered that computers could manipulate and compute large amounts of data rapidly, the fact that these machines could also store vast quantities of data upon which work was to be performed also became evident. The advantage of using a programmable computing device was that it would allow **stored programs** and data to be loaded and unloaded repeatedly, without the necessity of an operator or typist having to manually key all the numbers into the machine anew every time a subsequent calculation was to take place.

Recall from chapter 1 that the four basic functions of data processing are (1) Input or data collection, (2) Numeric or character manipulation, (3) Storage, and (4) Retrieval. The concept of databases focuses more on items (3) and (4), although some input and manipulation also takes place in the maintenance of databases. And, this chapter is looking at databases for the sake of understanding how such entities as online bibliographies, automated book circulation and patron files, and information retrieval services coordinate and maintain their accumulations of data. As such, this chapter examines database software, and chapter 17 discusses specific, named databases.

All databases, regardless of size, exhibit a **hierarchy** or rank order of data contained therein. From the specific to the general, database hierarchy is constructed as follows:

- **characters**, or individual letters or numbers in the database
- data elements, or **fields**, which contain one specific piece of information such as a name, quantity, or label
- **records**, or collections of data elements (cf. unit record, a term used in the early days of database maintenance); for example, the name and address of a patron in an automated circulation system file
- **files**, or sets of related records, such as a mailing list
- the **database** itself, a set of related records such as the aggregate of patron files, circulation files, and bibliographic records which constitute an automated circulation system.

Individual files can assume one of two attributes, that of a **master file** or of a **detail file**. A master file is generally thought of as a **transaction file** in which data seldom change, for example, as in a file of MARC records into which entries are appended but infrequently altered. A detail file is more transient, for example, as in a patron file in which established records are often accessed for address or name changes.

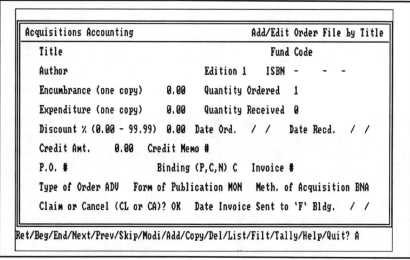

```
┌──────────────────────────────────────────────────────────────────────┐
│ ┌──────────────────────────────────────────────────────────────────┐ │
│ │ Acquisitions Accounting                     Add/Edit Order File by Title │ │
│ │   Title                                 Fund Code                   │ │
│ │   Author                       Edition 1    ISBN  -     -    -      │ │
│ │   Encumbrance (one copy)    0.00   Quantity Ordered   1            │ │
│ │   Expenditure (one copy)    0.00   Quantity Received  0            │ │
│ │   Discount % (0.00 - 99.99)  0.00  Date Ord.   / /   Date Recd.  / / │ │
│ │   Credit Amt.    0.00   Credit Memo #                              │ │
│ │   P.O. #                    Binding (P,C,N) C   Invoice #          │ │
│ │   Type of Order ADV   Form of Publication MON   Meth. of Acquisition BNA │ │
│ │   Claim or Cancel (CL or CA)? OK   Date Invoice Sent to 'F' Bldg.  / / │ │
│ └──────────────────────────────────────────────────────────────────┘ │
│ Ret/Beg/End/Next/Prev/Skip/Modi/Add/Copy/Del/List/Filt/Tally/Help/Quit? A │
└──────────────────────────────────────────────────────────────────────┘
```

**Figure 5.1** Title search screen in an accounting program

The hierarchy of databases directly addresses the first (i.e., inputting) function of the four basic functions of data processing. An inputter may enter data one character at a time, a field or line at a time, or an entire record at once using an input or **template** screen. The input environment depends on how the database programmer originally coded the input section of the database software, and, of course, the appearance and function will vary from program to program. A typical input screen appears in Figure 5.1.

Data storage has evolved over the years in a very sophisticated manner. The trend has been toward denser, more compact storage, and data compression has been uppermost in the minds of systems engineers when designing hardware capable of supporting high density devices. The evolution in providing more efficient storage has progressed as follows (in roughly chronological order):

1. Placing data in core memory, inside the computer itself. This technique was employed with first generation computers, but with the accompanying problem that, when data reside in the computer, no other program or routine can occupy the space. This is all right for transient data but not for data that must be put aside for future manipulation or retrieval.

2. Use of paper tape. This medium was taken from tape reader/punches on teletype machines and proved to be a cheap, reliable method of storage.

3. Use of punched cards. This was an adaptation of the **Hollerith card** used in the 1890 census and proved to be as reliable as paper tape. An added advantage: card decks can be altered by adding and deleting specific cards, and by rearranging (**collating**) cards to attain a specific, desired sort order. Note that paper tape, once punched, cannot be altered in specific sections or spliced to rearrange the data.

4. Development of **magnetic tape**. In the 1940s, engineers who placed magnetic tape recorders on the consumer electronics market coincidentally provided a medium for data storage on similarly constructed machines. Magnetic tape is still in widespread use today, typically in 1,600 bpi (bits per inch) and 6,250 bpi formats on mainframe tape drives. With the advent of personal computers, off-the-shelf cassette tape recorders were used as input/output storage devices and provided a cheap, although relatively slow mechanism for storing large amounts of data. Present-day tape devices in all ranges of computers from micros to mainframes generally use cartridges instead of reel-to-reel systems.

5. Introduction of **disk packs** and **hard disk drives**. Magnetic media need not be in tape format; in fact, the magnetic particles necessary to record data bits can be packed into a denser array if rigid base media are employed. Removable disk packs are usually associated with mainframe computers, and hard disk drives can be found on virtually any size and brand of computer. Hard disk drives can be manufactured to reside in sealed containers, and, with virtually no chance of contamination by airborne particles, can be produced as models with capacities of more than a gigabyte (one billion bytes) that will fit in a desktop personal computer.

6. Development of **floppy disks** (diskettes). These media work on the same principle as magnetic tape, with the obvious geometrical difference in format. Floppy disks originally appeared in 8" format, with 5-1/4" format soon following. Currently popular both for IBM compatible machines and Macintosh computers are 3-1/2" diskettes, nicknamed "stiffies." Other size formats have appeared on the market, but the predominate sizes are the 5-1/4" and 3-1/2" versions. DOS versions 5.0 and later will support a floppy disk capacity of up to 2.88 megabytes. Diskette surfaces must be prepared into tracks and sectors (see Figure 5.2) before they are usable. Floppy diskettes were originally offered as hard-sectored (with ten index holes cut into the diskette material, to notify the computer where to physically

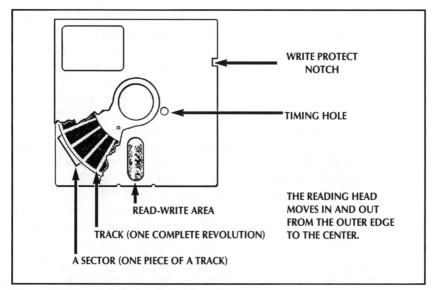

**Figure 5.2**  Floppy disk, showing tracks and sectors

locate the sectors), although nowadays most diskettes have only one index hole and are considered soft sectored.

Iomega Corporation offers a high-density, floppy disklike medium under the trademark of Bernoulli, which can be configured for storage capacities of up to 90 megabytes. The latter can be used only in the company's proprietary drives called, appropriately enough, **Bernoulli Boxes**.

7. Burning data into **PROMs** (**programmable read only memory** chips), integrated circuits placed directly into the computer itself. With the advent of high-density chips, this technique became more feasible than using the computer's main memory for long-term storage as in the early days of computers, but still is a more expensive solution than the use of erasable media. The disadvantage is that, once data are burned into such circuits, no alterations are possible without replacing the entire chip. There is a variant **PROM** called an **EPROM**, or **erasable programmable read only memory**) and an **EEPROM** (**electrically erasable programmable read only memory**), but these chips are typically used in industrial settings and specialty applications and are not generally found handling database tasks.

8. Using optical drives as data retrieval devices. **CD-ROMs** (**compact disk/read only memory**) are becoming popular as database

media, and the number of titles available on CD-ROMs is increasing. This medium will be discussed in greater detail in chapter 11. CD-ROMs have one drawback: although a typical CD-ROM disk can hold about 650 megabytes of data, the medium, as the name implies, is a read-only device. Technology is currently evolving into a phase where optical disks can both be written to and erased with off-the-shelf hardware. The greatest roadblock to this technology is presently the cost; such devices are still in the $800 to $1,500 price range (1995 dollars). In the meantime, the market offers at lower cost several **WORM (write once, read many)** devices which can accept user input data, but cannot be erased once inscribed. **Document imaging** is a currently popular trend for storing large databases of graphics and nontext images on CD-ROM formatted discs; this topic will be covered more in chapter 11.

Database programs are more dependent on the hardware and storage media upon which they are used than are other categories of software. For the reasons behind this dependency, the two elementary types of data files—sequential and random—need to be examined.

**Sequential access files** are constructed like sets of encyclopedias. The basic set consists of a fixed number of volumes. Once the set is published, if the authors wish to add articles or update entries, such rewrites must be printed in the form of supplements or yearbooks. The new information is available at the end of the modified set, but further information must forever be appended past the last supplement. Also, to delete information, it is necessary to remove volumes (or pages) from the interior of the set. The latter action leaves obvious gaps on the shelf, and, if aesthetics are to be maintained, an entirely new set of encyclopedias (with updates and corrections included) must be printed.

**Random access files** contain the same information as sequential files, but the data are not necessarily placed in the files in any orderly fashion. It would be as though an encyclopedia were published in a looseleaf format. Adding or removing pages at any point in the set could be done; however, doing so would alter the pagination. Nonetheless, sequential access and random access methods both have their advantages and disadvantages, and the choice of either methodology depends on the application in which the processed are invoked.

A sequential file must have a separate index, just as with a hardbound set of encyclopedias. A database program must first determine the "page," or record number of the data desired, and then perform its seek based on the information in the index. A random file's records usually have an additional field called a **key**, upon which inquiries can be made directly and without going through a separate index. This method can be compared to our looseleaf encyclopedia, where individual articles have an index tab at the sides of the pages for direct access by the reader. Thus, in the case of print encyclopedias, each method has obvious uses in terms of speed versus flexibility. It is so with databases written in computer software as well; based on the need for speed over accessibility or vice versa, a programmer will construct a database program accordingly. For an end user, the choice is usually invisible.

From this discussion, is should be clear why database programs are machine dependent. A magnetic tape, since it is physically a ribbon of data, prefers sequential files over random. To rearrange a sequential file on a tape requires a complete rewrite of the data contained thereon. However, a tape can store a relatively huge amount of data at low cost, and tape is desirable where access methods are not critical. Magnetic disks have an advantage in storing random files. Because the data tracks on disk media are usually concentric, the addition or deletion of records is easily accomplished. Again, the medium and method selected depend on the application.

Library circulation systems are good examples of the evolution of databases from pencil and paper processes to computerized environments. Circulation databases involve the input, storage, manipulation, and retrieval of vast quantities of data involving patron names, book titles, and borrowing records. Automated library systems will be discussed in more detail in chapter 13.

## CODES AND CODING SCHEMES

One attribute of database programs and their ensuing files that immediately strikes even a first-time user is the enormity of space that is required to store information. The key factor to successful database construction and maintenance is the efficient, economical use of the space available for the data. Storage of information in an unabridged, raw form is uneconomical, both in terms of the expense necessary to purchase and maintain the hardware storage medium and in terms of access time necessary to search and retrieve information from haphazardly indexed files. In this section are some techniques and shorthand for compressing and labeling the data to be manipulated.

Chapter 1 noted the existence of two popular codes, ASCII and EBCDIC, which are used for representation of letters, numbers, and control characters inside the computer's memory. When standardized, codes can be quite useful by enabling easier retrieval of data and communication from one information system to another by allowing data to be handled in the same fashion in each system. A **code** is a group of characters used to identify an item of data and to show its relationship to other items in the same set. Two examples are ZIP codes in the United States and postal codes in Canada and Great Britain. The common attribute of these codes is geography, and when properly used on pieces of mail, ZIP and postal codes make delivery swifter and more efficient. The advantages of codes are obvious, and the usefulness of codes predates the widespread availability of computers.

As with everything in data processing, the existence of a process or tool does not automatically mean that it must be used. Before a code is employed, one simple question must be honestly answered: is a code really needed in the particular process to be streamlined? The answer to this question might be a simple "yes" or "no," or it might require an extensive systems analysis to determine. The latter will be discussed in more detail in chapter 14. For now, this chapter leaves the question with the caveat, "Don't use numbers just for the sake of having numbers." The following are a few considerations that should be posed before taking the plunge into a coding scheme with which you might have to live for several years:

1. Who will use the items or data to be coded? In any coding scheme, survey your audience. Is the code you're proposing inappropriate or too complicated for the intended users?

2. How often will the items to be coded be retrieved or used? In other words, in database parlance, what is the anticipated frequency of **hits** in a search of the database? An example here is the ready reference collection that most libraries keep behind the public service desk. Is it necessary to assign a catalog number nine or 10 digits in length to a guide such as the *Physicians' Desk Reference* that you might use as frequently as once per hour?

3. What are the coded items used for? A code should relate to the use of the coded item. Tire size codes, for example, contain wheel diameters as well as rim measurements. Not only does the tire code allow for classification of inventory in a database program, it allows the installer to read directly, from the code, the information necessary for proper fit on the intended automobile.

4. How much data should the code contain? Don't overkill the code by making it too long; many manufacturers create lengthy codes to persuade a customer that the company's product line is extensive. They often forget that a "PS/2 model 30" computer is easier to remember than a "model XJ330SX/PDQ" residing on the same shelf.

5. How many items are to be coded? If there are few items in the database, a code just adds an extra field to the record and takes up more space than it saves.

6. How often will the codes be used in a search process? It is super-fluous to use a coding scheme for infrequently used items. You could be engaging in a project that requires a 100-plus hours to code data items so rarely accessed that you end up saving only five or 10 seconds of retrieval time.

7. How will expansion of the database affect the coded items, and how will extraordinary growth of the information reflect on the coding scheme? Well into the 1950s, many states used an all-number scheme for automobile license plates. Six numbers were adequate for many years, as long as any given state had fewer than a million registered cars. When the number of autos grew, many states didn't know how to handle the plate codes and had to resort to (sometimes strange) combinations of letters, numbers, and add-on stickers.

8. If the code is to be handled by a computer program, are there any system characteristics to which the code must adhere? In early releases of PC database programs, there were limits on the numbers (and numbering) of records within available database software. Some programs, for example, would not allow a numeric field larger than 4,194,304, due to a language limitation in the database's executable file. The latter has an obvious dis-advantage if the data you're organizing has many thousands of elements.

All arguments, pro and con, aside, there are nonetheless many reasons in favor of using codes to simplify the handling of data and information. The message in the previous section is not that codes are to be avoided if possible, but that great care should be exercised to ascertain that improper code design does not create *more* work or inefficiency. There are several attributes of a good coding scheme, and these considerations should be noted when planning or evaluating codes for a particular data processing or information management environment:

1. The code should be expandable, allowing for additional entries. If possible, some overload should be anticipated. (The Dewey Decimal System is a good example; the cataloging of non-Western materials usually requires five or more places beyond the decimal to properly categorize any given non-Western title.)

2. The code should be precise; it must identify the specific item.

3. The code should be concise; it should be as brief as possible, yet fully describe the item.

4. The code should be convenient; it should be easy to encode and decode.

5. The code should be meaningful; it should be useful to people dealing with it, and it should contain some characteristics of the item described (e.g., as with the example of tire sizes above, there should be a "human readable" element).

6. The code should be operable; it should be compatible with present and future methods of manual or machine-based data processing.

Code design is not complicated. In fact, there are only a few basic types of codes, with others just being variations on the seven listed below:

1. **Simple sequence code**. This is basically an ascending (or descending) count such as

    1, 2, 3, 4, or A, B, C, D, or A1, A2, A3, A4

2. **Block sequence code**. This is a hierarchical code similar to the outline form, with some zero padding, of publications and books. This type of code appears as

    | | |
    |---|---|
    | A.0.0 | furniture |
    | A.1.0 | chairs |
    | A.1.1 | dining room chairs |
    | A.1.2 | kitchen chairs |
    | A.1.3 | rocking chairs |
    | A.2.0 | tables |
    | A.2.1 | dining room tables |

    and the like. Dots, or other **delimiters**, are optional.

3. **Group classification code**. Similar to the block sequence code, the group classification code establishes major, intermediate, and sometimes minor classes in a freestyle manner. The Internet uses such a scheme to establish user addresses:

    hcogg@ix.netcom.com

    where "hcogg" is the user's name (or alias), "ix.netcom" is the institutional locator name, and "com" is the extension designating commercial enterprises. "@" and "." are field delimiters.

4. **Significant digit code**. In such a code, the place value has meaning, although the position of a number letter within the string might not indicate relative importance or rank within the entire code. Again, using the tire size code as an example, the size G78-15 is broken down into

    | G | 78 | 15 |
    |---|---|---|
    | tire profile | ratio of height:width | load capacity |

5. **Mnemonic code**. The code contains one or more abbreviations or acronyms germane to the item being coded. In clothing, a code might appear as

SHM32COT for shirt, man's, size 32, cotton

SHW34SIL for shirt, woman's, size 34, silk

6. **Alphabetic derivation code**. Similar to the mnemonic code, this code uses a piece of one or more of the information fields in the database to establish a code relationship. From the mailing label of a periodical, this might appear as

SMI902107032AP95

where SMI is Smith, the name of the subscriber; 90210 is the five-digit ZIP code; 7032 is the four-digit street address; and AP95 is April 1995, the month of expiration of the subscription.

7. **Self-checking code**. In this code, mathematics ascertains that the code was entered correctly at the keyboard or at a point-of-sale terminal. A simple data checking rule might be programmed into the computer code that accepts input from a terminal. This is true of codes such as ISBN numbers and works as follows: suppose that the code field consists entirely of six numbers, of which the sixth must be such that the sum of it and the other five are evenly divisible by ten. If a data entry operator were to key the following code

864255, where

$8 + 6 + 4 + 2 + 5 + 5 = 30$,

the entry would be accepted by the system because $30 \div 10$ creates no remainder. However, if the data entry operator entered 864355, where

$8 + 6 + 4 + 3 + 5 + 5 = 31$,

the entry would not be accepted because $31 \div 10$ leaves a remainder of 1. The rightmost 5 is a **checksum digit**, which is not actually a part of the code, but merely a number interjected to "make things come out even." This is another way of saying that 864255 is a valid code, while 864355 is not. Compare this technique to that of **parity checking** in chapter 16.

The above principles were used to create codes familiar to catalogers and other library personnel in the classification and retrieval of materials in the library. The Dewey Decimal Classification, Universal Decimal Classification, and Library of Congress Classification are but three such codes that are here to stay—and they keep on growing! They also are prime examples of why codes should be carefully planned before implementation. A generally accepted principle is that once a code is established and used a few years, it is virtually impossible to abolish it or convert it to a new system of codification.

## DATABASE PROGRAMS

Database software runs the gamut in price, from low-end, economy programs to high-end software that can cost thousands of dollars. In the PC and Macintosh arenas, database management software has been around nearly as long as the machines themselves. The forerunners were, of course, mainframe-based. There are still many mainframe programs written and yet being developed under database languages such as DB2 and CICS. For experienced database programmers, the transition to desktop environments was not difficult.

Database management programs that can be classed as inexpensive include PFS:File, PC-File[1] and PC-File:dB+. PC-File was initially offered as shareware, and the current version, compatible with dBase files (as is PC-File:dB+), retails for $129.00. PC-File is used in the example, "The Electronic Rolodex," demonstrated at the end of this chapter. PC-File is an example of a **flat file** database, in which records are grouped together, perhaps sequentially, but may not have a relationship from one to the others. PC-File will also allow the incorporation of **memo fields**, comments not actually part of the database records, a feature found in many of the higher end programs. More costly, and somewhat more complex and fully featured, are dBase III+, dBase IV, dBase 5.0 for Windows, R:Base, FoxBase, Clarion, and Clipper, to name a few. These "high-end" programs are usually combinations of database management systems and programming languages, and it is possible to use them as both the control programs for data handling and as developers' tools to create proprietary software for in-house use or for sale to PC user clients. dBase IV will be featured in the discussion of database software for the remainder of this chapter because it has evolved as a de facto standard among PC database programs and it exhibits all the attributes necessary to explain database program software.

dBase IV,[2] or "dBase," as it is commonly known, has been around since the days of the CP/M operating system. It was the first database program targeted specifically for small computers, and its advocates will also swear to dBase still being the biggest and the best. dBase certainly is a standard, both of measure and of convention, and its niche in the marketplace is established. What makes the program a standard are the conventions applied to its database **file header**; that is, the first 512 bytes of the database file adhere to entry conditions that can be emulated by other database program formats so that databases can be shared among compatible programs. dBase is an example of a **hierarchical database**, in which each record has some element of relationship to all other records in the same file. In 1992, dBase's parent company, Ashton-Tate, was acquired by Borland Corporation, which continues to offer dBase IV along with its own previously released Paradox database product. Borland's dBase IV ultimately evolved into dBase 5.0. However, the active installations of dBase III and dBase IV have remained widespread, and many third-party utility programs still exist for each version. Thus, many users still matter-of-factly specify III, IV or 5.0 when speaking of the version of dBase supported in their particular computing shops.

dBase began life as dBase II (there never was a commercial "dBase I") and would run in the limited 64 kilobytes of memory imposed by the desktop computers of the early 1980s. Originally, dBase was an **interpretive language**, requiring that the basic (executable) dBase file be present in the computer's memory for the database commands to execute. Later versions (dBase III and dBase IV) provided **runtime modules** so that the full dBase .EXE component would not have to be loaded into memory (or even purchased) to run dBase programs. Ultimately, dBase developed a **compiler** version of its program so that dBase language modules could run completely on their own. Third-party vendors had been filling the gap, notably WordTech Systems, whose Arago Quicksilver[3] compiler product took dBase code and produced standalone .EXE files which will run completely independent of other .EXE or database command modules. Interpreters, compilers and runtime modules will be discussed in more detail in chapter 8.

Despite these minor drawbacks, dBase is a powerful language. It can be programmed with source code, as with any language, or it can query and modify database files from its own command line, i.e., from the famous "dot prompt" (simply a "." at the left of the screen, waiting for instructions). dBase IV also includes the standard **structured query language** (**SQL**, see chapter 17) ability for database searches in addition to its own native commands. dBase will handle long and complicated programs if required, source codes for which can take many hours to develop if written from scratch. dBase IV provides a **template language** facility in which the programmer merely specifies how the input screens are to appear, what kinds of data are to be stored, the number and sizes of the fields, etc., typing this information into the Applications Generator. dBase then takes over, "writing" the source code for the programmer. Other vendors have provided code generators for dBase, the Genifer[4] product being a typical example. The following is a sample of a Genifer-generated dBase code used to maintain the budget files for a library acquisitions department[5]:

```
procedure chkfil
* Verify that all the database files accessed by the
* program exist. If a database file is missing, set
* files_ok to .F. and display a message. If they all
* exist, check their index files, and create any that
```

```
* are missing
close databases
if .not. file ('BOOKS.DBF')
   do disp_msg with 'File BOOKS.DBF not found'
   files_ok = .F.
endif
if .not. file ('ACCOUNTS.DBF')
   do disp_msg with 'File ACCOUNTS.DBF not found'
   files_ok = .F.
endif
* Index if index file missing
if files_ok
   if .not. file ('FUNDCODE.NDX')
      @ 23,00
      @ 23,00 say 'Creating index FUNDCODE'
      use BOOKS
      index on fund code to FUNDCODE
      use
   endif
   if .not. file ('ISBN.NDX')
      @ 23,00
      @ 23,00 say 'Creating index ISBN'
      use BOOKS
      index on isbn to ISBN
      use
   endif
   if .not. file ('TITLES.NDX')
      @ 23,00
      @ 23,00 say 'Creating index TITLES'
      use BOOKS
      index on title to TITLES
      use
   endif
   if .not. file ('ACCOUNTS.NDX')
      @ 23,00
      @ 23,00 say 'Creating index ACCOUNTS'
      use dCCOUNTS
      index on fund code to ACCOUNTS
      use
   endif
endif return
```

None of the above program segment was hand-coded by a program-mer; rather, the routine was derived from the template language accessed from the database definition section of the code generator. Genifer requires only that a programmer "paint" the input/output screens, define the composition of the database and its fields, create text files containing any online help facilities, and optionally define the formats for any on-screen or hard copy printouts. Genifer provides an in-depth tutorial which, once a person has mastered the fundamentals, allows an end user to create a functional database system in an hour or two. The publisher also provides the source code for the template language, and advanced programmers can customize the generated code at will.

Database language compilers also lend themselves to development from third-party programmers. For example, dBase III has become such a standard that **function code libraries** have been developed for it. For example, programmers who code in the C language (see chapter 8) can access dBase III .DBF files using a utility from Lattice, Inc., known as dBC III+.[6] Because C language compilers can produce true binary (executable) code, the programs run faster and without the overhead code (i.e., additional program runtime modules) that the basic dBase interpreter imposes. Such library functions are **callable** by the program application into which they are incorporated and add a high degree of efficiency and speed to applications such as the accounting program and electronic Rolodex utility mentioned in this chapter.

Database programs are also the targets for an all-inclusive programming scheme known as **cross-platform computing**. Typically, when proprietary database programs are written, i.e., coded, for a particular function required as a special application (such as the maintenance of automated circulation system patron databases), they are intended for only one machine or group of similar machines. Some vendors, such as the Oracle Corporation, however, write their programming tools and function libraries in such a manner that the source code generated is transparent to the type of computer upon which the code is run, hence, cross-platformed. In other words, an Oracle database program written on an IBM PC running MS-DOS could, with a simple recompilation, function on a machine running UNIX or on a Macintosh running System 7. Cross platforming also applies to operating system software, and will be discussed further in chapter 7.

Library applications of database programs are many and varied. Small libraries in particular can use PC and Macintosh database software on individual workstations for utilities such as disk-based shelflists and community fact files. Used in conjunction with word processors, database programs can assist the library in maintaining mailing lists of friends of the library, potential donors/benefactors, staff, and members of community organizations. As illustrated above, database software can be used to manage library budgets and appropriations accounts and provide printouts for book selection committees to gauge the rates of spending in various subject categories. Even in larger environments of multistation automated circulation systems, satellite departments can maintain individual databases of local files, for example, of books and materials charged from a reserve book room.

## APPLICATION: THE ELECTRONIC ROLODEX

The purpose of this exercise is to demonstrate how databases are created and programmed, and how data and information can be manipulated, stored, and retrieved in a simple yet useful example. The exercise is an example of a **relational database**, one in which one or more fields hold a relationship to all similar fields in the other records of that database. The Electronic Rolodex is also an example of an **information retrieval system** so prevalent in modern libraries. Whether it is for the storage of facts, names and addresses, or new book titles, a database installed on an individual workstation at a reference desk can be invaluable for quick retrieval of up-to-date information. The names and addresses in the Electronic Rolodex might be those of Friends of the Library, community leaders, elected officials, organizational members, or any entity where the principals are in constant flux.

This application specifically requires a copy of PC-File or PC-File:dB. The Rolodex database was originally designed to run on the shareware versions of PC-File, and it should be upwardly compatible to the now commercial version of PC-File:dB available at retail stores. The exercise assumes that you are using a dual floppy system, with PCF.EXE in the A: drive and a blank, formatted floppy diskette in the B: drive. It doesn't matter whether the drives are of dissimilar sizes or if they are reversed (i.e., dual 5-1/4" and 3-1/2" drives or vice versa). If you wish, you can run the program exclusively from a hard disk drive by substituting the appropriate disk references (e.g., C: for A: and B:) in the instructions.

In cookbook fashion, perform the following:

- Boot (load) the computer with DOS (at least version 3.0).
- Place the diskette containing PCF.EXE in the A: drive.
- Place a blank, formatted diskette in the B: drive.
- Open PC-File by typing PCF at the A> prompt.

When prompted, select "B" as the working drive (i.e., the drive to hold the database files) and "root directory" (the "\" character) as the directory in which to place the files.

The initial screen is shown in Figure 5.3. PC-File is now prepared to design the database.

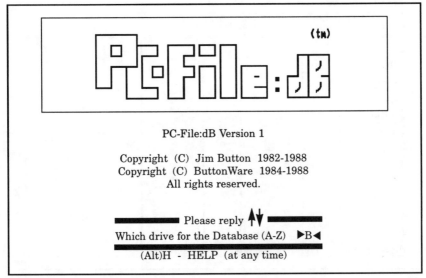

**Figure 5.3** PC-File:dB signon screen

If the floppy diskette in the B: drive is newly formatted, there will be no database files thereon; therefore, when PC-File asks if you want to define a file, answer "Y(es)." PC-File will ask whether you want to create a database using its "fast" or "paint" method; "fast" is quicker and allows use of program defaults, so choose "F(ast)." Note that, to "accept" many of the choices in PC-File, the user must press the F10 special function key instead of merely pressing "Enter." Be aware of the differences and read the directions given on the screens to ascertain which method is required.

The design screen is shown in Figure 5.4. Using the Tab key to move through the screen, enter the following input screen design:

- at column 1, row 3, enter NAME
- at column 1, row 5, enter ADDRESS
- at column 1, row 7, enter CITY
- at column 1, row 8, enter STATE (or PROVINCE)
- at column 1, row 10, enter PHONE
- at column 3, row 8, enter ZIP (Canadians, POSTCODE)

Note here that you are entering not specific names, etc., but merely **field labels** for the database to use to accept input information. When finished, press F10 to accept the screen design.

The next screen asks for field lengths. The term "length" is somewhat confusing here, since what is really desired are the field *widths*. Enter these values: NAME, 20 characters; ADDRESS, 25 characters; CITY, 15 characters; STATE (PROVINCE), 2 characters (Post Office abbreviation

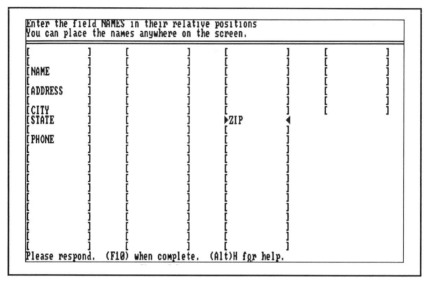

**Figure 5.4** PC-File:dB design screen

codes for states and provinces will be used); PHONE, 12 characters (3 for area code, 1 for a hyphen, 3 for the exchange, 1 for another hyphen, and 4 for the rest of the number); and ZIP, 5 characters or POSTCODE, 7 characters (3 characters, 1 space, and 3 more characters). Once again, enter F10 to terminate the activity.

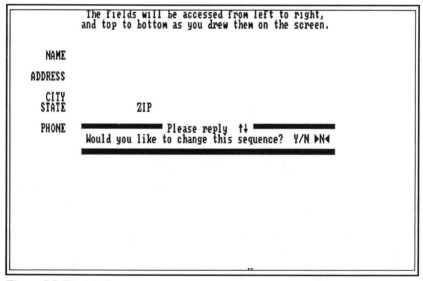

**Figure 5.5** Final design screen

You will be shown a screen similar to that of Figure 5.5 as an example of what your designed input screen will look like. The final design screen will ask, "Any windows?" Answer "N(o)." When asked "Any changes?" answer "N(o)" as well, unless you need to start over to correct something.

You will now create the Electronic Rolodex name and address file. A prompt screen will appear, asking for your choice(s) of activities. Select F1 to "Add records." Of your own choosing, make up names and addresses (or use real ones, if you like) for at least six persons. Be certain that at least three of them are from one single state or province; this is for the purpose of demonstrating PC-File's sort capabilities at the end of the exercise. The first time you enter a record, you will be asked "Save? Y(es), N(o), or X (don't ask)." Select "X" if you want PC-File to cease the cajoling for accurate data. A sample input screen appears as Figure 5.6. When you are finished entering data, press F10 on a blank screen (with no data entered) to get back to the selection menu. Press "Q" twice to quit back to the DOS prompt.

We will now open the database as an existing file. Again, type "PCF" at the A> prompt and repeat the appropriate cookbook steps above (type "B" for the data drive, "\" for the path, etc.), but when PC-File requests a filename, tab to "Rolodex" and press F10 to choose it. Again at the selection menu, press F2 then "S" (simple search) to initiate a database inquiry. Search on the ZIP (or POSTCODE) field, for example, and search for any code you know that you entered when you created the database.

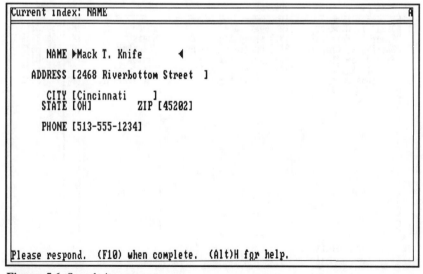

**Figure. 5.6** Sample input screen

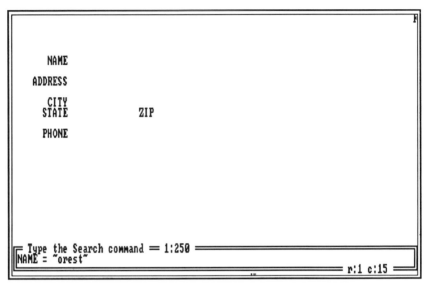

```
        NAME

     ADDRESS

        CITY
       STATE              ZIP

       PHONE












  ┌ Type the Search command = 1:250 ═══════════
  ║NAME = "orest"
                                          ═══ r:1 c:15 ═══
```

**Figure 5.7**  Complex search screen

Perform some searches on NAME and CITY as well; note that PC-File is
**case sensitive**, i.e., you must enter upper and lower case letters exactly
as they were originally input, or you'll get "not found" messages. When
finished searching, enter "Q" for "Q(uit) finding."

```
    NAME              ADDRESS              CITY          ST PHONE

[ ] Diana F. Windsor   10 Royal Lane        Queen City    MD 555-2394
[ ] Arbor T. Forestt   6913 Shady Lane      Woeis         ME 555-2356
[ ] Charles A. Chaplin 9373 Humoresque Court Columbus     OH 555-0088
[ ] John J. Smith      369 Taylor Mill Road Dayton        OH 555-0333
[ ] Mack T. Knife      2468 Riverbottom Street Cincinnati OH 555-1234
[ ] Charlene Johnson   9753 First Street    Philadelphia  PA 555-3456
         ─── End of File











► ◄ Select a record, or give another command
  Use (Tab) and (Shift)(Tab) to position the fields
  Please respond.  (F10) when complete.  (Alt)H for help.
```

**Figure 5.8**  Printout resulting from sort

Now a complex ("C") search will be executed. When you are prompted, enter a formula like NAME = ~orest~ to perform the search. Note that this search will work for persons whose names are F<u>orest</u> or F<u>orest</u>t; you don't have to remember the exact spellings. The tildes ("~") are **delimiters** for the purpose of establishing the exact letters and spacings (if any) of this, a **substring** search. The setup screen for a complex search in PC-File is in Figure 5.7. The advantage of a search by formula is that you can usually find what you're looking for, even if you know only a portion of the entry in the database. Complex searches will be covered in more detail in chapter 17.

You will now perform a sort. Press F7 from the selection screen to begin the sort routine. A sort is performed as follows: select a field, either by choosing a field number and pressing F10, or by tabbing to the field and then pressing F10. You will be asked "ascending ("A") or descending ("D")?" For strictly alphabetical order, choose "A." Had you chosen the "D" option, the field would have been sorted in reverse (Z to A) alphabetical order. "Descending" is more often used for sorting numbers when you want the largest number to appear first. In our Electronic Rolodex, we'll sort on STATE and NAME.

When the sort is complete, press F2 and "+" to browse the file. This results in a screen with column separators as in Figure 5.8. Press F6 if you want a printed copy of the report. When prompted, enter a title and follow the prompts for the default settings. When finished, quit to DOS (press "Q" twice).

The structure of the Electronic Rolodex can be modified for other purposes. For example, the NAME field could be ORGANIZATION, the ADDRESS field could be longer or have two lines, etc.; the possibilities are endless. Even on a floppy diskette, it is possible to add several thousand records to the six created in this exercise, and, of course, modifications to existing records are possible. Since older versions of PC-File are in the public domain, several departments in the library could have copies on various workstations at no cost. Departments could exchange data files on floppy diskettes, making dissemination of up-to-date database information as easy as making duplicate copies of the diskettes. Again, the possibilities are many, and the Electronic Rolodex acts as a springboard to further database creativity.

## NOTES

1. PC-File and PC-File:dB+, published by Buttonware, Inc., P.O. Box 96058, Bellevue, WA 98009. $129.95.
2. dBase, published by Borland Corporation, 1800 Green Hills Road, P.O. Box 660005, Scotts Valley, CA 95067-9985. $795.00 (DOS version); $495.00 (Windows version); $495.00 (compiler version).

3. Arago Quicksilver, published by WordTech Systems, Inc., 21 Altarinda Road, Orinda, CA 94563. $250.00.
4. Genifer, published by Bytel Corporation, 1029 Solano Avenue, Berkeley, CA 94706. $295.00.
5. Ogg, Harold C. "Writing Your Own Accounting Programs." *Computers in Libraries*, December, 1989, pp. 34-38.
6. dBC III+, published by Lattice, Inc., 3010 Woodcreek Drive, Suite A, Downers Grove, IL 60515 (mailing address P.O. Box 3072, Glen Ellyn, IL 60138). $395.00.

# Chapter 6

# Operating Systems

Regardless of size, every computer possesses an **operating system**. An operating system is analogous to the voltage regulator in an automobile. A car has many wires and electrical systems and subsystems. However, some mechanism has to interpret the various signals from the driver as to how much voltage and current are required to initiate and sustain the various operations and responses desired of the vehicle. A computer's operating system functions in a similar manner, letting the central processor know what its user is attempting to derive from the machine's internals. A piece of software acts as an intermediary between the CPU and the human operator, channeling the various electrical impulses to the proper targets to accomplish the job. Chapter 1 already presented a brief introduction to the popular MS-DOS (disk operating system) widely used in IBM and compatible PCs, and this chapter will elaborate on DOS and detail a number of other operating systems commonly found in library and educational settings.

For most machines, the operating system is loaded at bootup time. **Bootup** (also know as bootstrapping) occurs when the machine is powered on by closing the on/off power switch. From an "off" state (no power applied), a machine is said to be **cold booted** when it is turned on; if a machine is merely restarted or reloaded without completely turning off the electrical power, it is said to be **warm booted**. An IBM compatible computer can be warm booted by simultaneously pressing the Ctrl, Alt and Del keys—the so-called "three-finger salute." "Ctrl-Alt-Del," incidentally, is a preferred method for restarting the computer if it should become unresponsive to input from the keyboard. In any case, the operating system must be the first program loaded. Without an operating system, a computer runs in a manner similar to an automobile without a driver—the machine can idle and perhaps make a bit of progress, but it will usually crash and become useless and immobile.

It *is* possible to build a computer that is devoid of an operating system, but such an arrangement makes the job of computing quite difficult for the user. One of the few computing environments that does not use a discrete operating system in the hardware is the area of industrial controls. The computers in this type of situation use **dedicated microprocessors** which are built to execute one specific task or group of tasks. These chips have instructions "burned" into them such that they contain **dedicated programs**, i.e., software routines that are unchangeable except through electrical processes. Such a setup has advantages in terms of speed and efficiency but is of little consequence for libraries and offices that must support a variety of software applications programs.

At boot up time, the DOS operating system may load some other programs necessary for the operation of the computer. Typical of such programs are special files called **device drivers**, small units of computer code which attach peripheral devices such as printers, scanners, or plotters to the operating system and allow communications between such hardware and the CPU. Device drivers are necessary to tell the system how to access a given accessory peripheral, how to send data to or receive data from the device, and how to determine the settings of the electrical connections (**protocols**) between the computer and the device in question. In DOS, device drivers are usually placed in a CONFIG.SYS file, which can be modified as needed with a text editor. It is also possible to load **terminate and stay resident** (**TSR**) **programs** at boot time. TSRs are programs which remain dormant, loaded in computer memory until called upon, at which time they may "pop up" or temporarily take over the computer screen. Examples of this type of program are electronic calendars (schedulers), help boxes, and fax transmission programs. Because device drivers and TSRs make considerable demands on memory, the DOS operating system, in versions 5 and later, has internal facilities for managing device drivers and TSR programs so that there is minimal disruption to other, larger programs that must be loaded.

An operating system's "front end" is not complicated. Through use of software code called a **shell**, an operating system passes information to a CPU to inform the computer which keyboard key was just pressed, where the printer port is located, what kinds of peripheral equipment and accessories are connected to the processor board, how fast information is to be passed out from or received into the computer from a distant source, which files are to be accessed, and what programs are to be added or deleted. While the syntax and forms of shell commands vary from one operating system to another, the basic functions of the various operating systems are all similar.

Most operating systems are **proprietary**, that is, they are machine specific. In other words, an operating system written for an IBM AS/400 minicomputer will not run on, nor can it be loaded on, a Macintosh LC. This is because the architectures of the various brands of computers differ, and the operating systems address the internal circuitries directly. Moreover, different computers have different kinds of external and internal equipment attached. For example, there is no such thing as a mouse for a mainframe computer; therefore, an IBM 370's operating system would have no use for a subroutine that includes a mouse driver. Personal computers do not access tape drives by means of data channels, so DOS has no need for channel drivers to operate tape backup accessories. Typically, when you study an operating system, you study its target family of computers as well. The mastery of an operating system is much the same as learning a programming language, and many of the same rules apply.

For the sake of order, the text will look at operating systems from smaller to larger, and from older to newer. There are many operating systems in current use, and many which are defunct. The purist will note that many which are now or once were popular, are omitted. The purpose of this chapter is to present a representative sample and discuss the ones which are judged, in the author's opinion, most likely to be of value to librarians.

## PROPRIETARY SYSTEMS: CP/M AND MP/M

Arbitrarily, the first part of the discussion will center on the "middle years" of computer evolution, coinciding with the introduction of personal computers in the late 1970s. From that milestone it will switch in a sort of end-of-one-era-beginning-of-another fashion. As there were computers before PCs, so were there operating systems which predate CP/M. This is a good beginning point because the explosion of popular literature in the computer field began roughly in the mid-1970s, and there is a wealth of both journal and book-length material appearing on the market in the decade of the '80s.

Until the late 1970s, operating systems were either bundled with their respective machines or were written exclusively by the machines' manufacturers. There wasn't much operating system (O/S) software written by so-called "third party" authors, and any particular brand of computer was only as useful as the quality of the operating system written by the engineers who designed the hardware. As often as not, the O/S was billed as an "extra cost option" with the computer. This was absurd, because the computer was only so much wire and steel without its operating system. But the market was ripe for a cottage industry, needing an entire field of system programmers who could offer computer users an alternative to the sometimes high-priced operating systems forced upon them by the computer manufacturers.

The Heath Company is a good example of a case study of the metamorphosis of operating systems. Heath was, for many years, known for its line of high quality radios and stereos offered in kit form. In 1977, the Heath Company became one of the first vendors to offer a hobbyist computer, the model H-8. The computer was designed around the 8080 processor chip and was later improved to operate on the Zilog Z-80 processor. An entry level computer kit, containing a central processing unit, terminal/keyboard and cassette tape interface, could be purchased for about $1,500.00 (1977 dollars). Heath immediately expanded its line to the more powerful model H-11, another hobbyist machine based on the PDP-11 microprocessor. Many librarians might remember the PDP-11 chip as being in the first minicomputers operating automated circulation systems.

Initially, Heath's engineers built their computers' operating systems into the computers' hardware. For the H-8, the operating system was coded into system **firmware**, that is, burned into a **read only memory chip (ROM)**. The operating system was known as PAM-8, for Panel Monitor 8, and was programmed via a keypad on the front of the computer. Many system functions such as program load, memory access, and system reboot were one- and two-button key combinations entered via a front panel keypad and were simple to execute. Therefore, by entering instructions directly from the keypad, a user communicated directly with the ROM and memory circuits of the computer. Programs were stored on high quality cassette tapes and were loaded directly from a cassette recorder/player. A user would ready the tape deck, press the "load" button on the keypad, and after a few minutes, a program would be available at the console keyboard. It was a relatively slow process but greatly simplified from the input processes common to mainframe computers of the first half of the decade.

Eventually, the use of cassettes became too cumbersome and it was necessary to use a newer, faster medium for data and program input. Heath's engineers introduced a peripheral **floppy disk** system, in which programs and utilities were loaded from and saved to magnetic disks contained in protective envelopes (see Figure 6.1). However, the invocation of the operating system from the front panel keypad was too awkward to accommodate the various services required by the disk drives, and a software-based operating system had to be devised. The H-8/H-11's engineers had to follow the trend of the time and write their own operating systems in-house. The H-8 operating system was the more popular and actually possessed many of the commands and features of subsequent

**Figure 6.1** Floppy disk drives and diskettes

O/S software. The company called this operating system H-DOS, an acronym for Heath Disk Operating System.

While H-DOS was being acclaimed by Heathkit afficionados, an embryonic, soon-to-be-standard operating system was evolving. **CP/M**, or Control Program for Microprocessors, was being introduced by Digital Research for several brands of hobbyist microcomputers. In appearance, CP/M looked very similar to H-DOS and exhibited many of the same functions. While CP/M commands could be executed in the same manner on the different brands of computers it supported, one manufacturer's version of CP/M wouldn't necessarily work on a competitor's machine. The commands were becoming standard, but there were as many hardware versions of CP/M as there were brands of computers. It was a progressive step that operating system command language was standardizing, but O/S software was still proprietary to each company's particular machine.

CP/M became so popular that it established some standards which are still in evidence today. For example, the **eight-and-three rule** of file naming is still prevalent in MS-DOS and PC-DOS (see below). For executable programs and text or document files stored on disk, this means that a name of such a file can have one to eight letters, and a one- to three-letter extension. The following are examples of CP/M filenames:

MYFILE.DOC, a document file
CHECKERS.BAS, a checker game written in the BASIC language

WS.COM, the WordStar word processor program
MY_STORY.TXT, a text file
RECIPES, another document file

CP/M introduced some conventions that persist into present day operating systems. Notable is the set of resident commands available in the system's **basic disk operating system** (**BDOS**) that provides fundamental, immediate services of the operating system:

DIR, to obtain a listing of files on a floppy disk
ERA, to delete or erase a file or files
REN, to rename a file
TYPE, to list the contents of a file on the screen or on a printer; and
SAVE, to write the contents of memory to a disk file

CP/M in its original issue had only the five aforementioned resident commands, sometimes referred to as "built-ins." A **resident command** is one that is always available at the operating system level, regardless of whether there is a floppy disk in a drive or not. That is to say, if the user is at the system prompt (usually designated by A: or A> or a similar notation on the screen), a resident command typed at the console is instantly executed because it is already loaded into the computer's memory. This is analogous to the command shell which will be discussed below with MS-DOS and UNIX. Compare this with **transient command**, one which is part of the operating system's repertoire but must be present on disk to be executed. Examples of the latter in CP/M were STAT, a command for listing files and sizes of files on a disk, and PIP, a utility for copying files from one disk to another.

Because CP/M was such a relatively simple operating system in terms of space constraints, it lent itself nicely to illustrating a computer memory map. A **memory map** is a picture of the contents and purposes of the various areas in random access memory, with entry point addresses for programmers who would alter and enhance the operating system software. Such a memory map is shown in Figure 6.2, which illustrates the **transient program area** and compartments for various utilities which run while the computer is in operation. In this illustration, the Microsoft BASIC interpreter program (see chapter 8) is loaded into the transient program area, on address boundaries 2K to 25K and requiring 23 kilobytes of memory. A "scratchpad" area is available from 25K to 54K to give BASIC adequate space for performing calculations and storing the results of computations for use at various times while the program is running. The other, smaller areas in memory contain the operating system services necessary for running the screen display, accepting keystrokes (entry/exit area), and reading and writing to and from the disk drives. It is the responsibility of the operating system to "remember" the relationships between these areas and to keep the various components in proper, accessible order.

While its ghosts still linger in closets full of "older" computer equipment and in the minds of some of the earlier hobbyists, CP/M is not dead. In fact, the system still thrives in parts of Asia and is still widely used in Japan.

A spinoff of CP/M, MP/M was slightly ahead of its time. **MP/M**, or **m**ulti-**p**rogram for **m**icroprocessors, was an attempt to create the first **local area network** of several microcomputers connected together for the purpose of **resource sharing**. MP/M was an extension of CP/M with

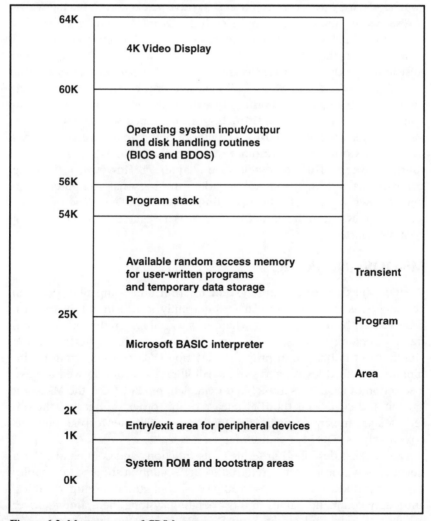

**Figure 6.2** Memory map of CP/M computer

additional commands to read files on a remote computer, share messages, and access equipment not connected to a local workstation. There was not widespread acceptance of MP/M because it was too difficult to hook up, and it required a person with considerable knowledge of the hardware to maintain the system. Also, its capabilities were limited: CP/M machines, and, by extension, MP/M computers, were limited to a physical maximum of 64 kilobytes of random access memory. Once the resident portion of the MP/M operating system was loaded, in many setups there remained insufficient room to accommodate resource sharing, let alone run other programs in the same available memory space. And the commands were too cryptic for the average user. Local area networks (**LANs**) would surface again in the early 1980s amid much controversy as to their usefulness. LANs will be discussed in detail in chapter 15.

Soon after the IBM personal computer was introduced, Digital Research introduced a 16-bit version of CP/M designed to run on this new 16-bit "PC." **CP/M-86** was all-inclusive of the features of the original CP/M release, with a number of extensions and new, special commands. USER allowed a **partitioning** of disk space so that several persons could share the same disk(s), without being able to read or access each other's private files. Another new command, SUBMIT, was a forerunner of **batch file** processing (see chapter 7). However, a fledgling company named Microsoft was invading the personal computer scene with its own version of a PC operating system, MS-DOS. The battle for supremacy was fought, and CP/M-86 was relegated to the annals of computer history.

## MS-DOS AND PC-DOS

**DOS**, the **disk operating system** for IBM and compatible personal computers, is the most popular O/S currently in use in North America. DOS has evolved to the point where it is as full-featured as many mainframe operating systems, and it can be every bit as complicated to use. Hundreds of books are in print that describe DOS concepts from beginning to advanced levels, and even small libraries would do well to have a selection of DOS titles available for circulation. MS-DOS is the Microsoft version and PC-DOS is the IBM release of this program. Because the differences are mostly cosmetic, this text simply will refer to both versions collectively as "DOS."

DOS is best described in terms of its functions and commands. For a quick review, the reader is referred to the section at the end of chapter 1. If you include the list of reserved words, configuration setup variables, and utility command names in this operating system, there are well over a hundred verbs and modifiers in DOS. However, the average user can make DOS perform splendidly with an abbreviated list of commands. The following set of commands is recommended for basic knowledge:

- ASSIGN swaps letter assignments of disk drives. Use this command if you must "fool" a particular drive into acting like a differently lettered one, e.g., to make the computer read drive B: as though it were drive A:. It is useful for running older programs that must have specific drive assignments.
- ATTRIB hides or write protects a file or group of files. For example, if you issue the command ATTRIB +R MYFILE.DOC, the file MYFILE.DOC is set to read only (R/O) status, i.e., it cannot be erased.
- BACKUP, in conjunction with RESTORE (below), allows you to make and retrieve archival copies of files or an entire disk or set of disks.
- BREAK, when set to "ON," extends the number of instances that Ctrl-C (which can cause a program to terminate) will intervene in a running program.
- CHDIR (CD) allows movement between divisions where a disk has been divided into directories and subdirectories. For example, by invoking A:\> CD LETTERS, you will find yourself in the LETTERS subdirectory of the disk in drive A:.
- CHKDSK reports on statistics of disk usage and tells how much total space in bytes is available, how many bytes are used by all the files, and how much room remains on the disk. It also performs some error checking of and reporting on fragmented disk files.
- CLS clears the screen of the video display.
- COMP compares contents of two files, byte by byte. It is useful for identifying and eliminating duplicate files.
- COPY copies an entire file or group of files to a different disk or directory.
- DATE reads the computer's internal clock and allows you to change the date if necessary.
- DEL (ERASE) deletes one file or a group of files on disk.
- DIR returns a catalog of files on disk, listing file sizes and dates and times of creation. The use of **wildcards** ("*" and "?" to specify entire filenames or individual letters in the filename) is permitted in conjunction with this command.
- DISKCOMP compares the contents of two floppy disks, track by track. See also COMP.
- DISKCOPY copies the contents of an entire floppy disk to another, track by track.

- FORMAT physically prepares the surface of a floppy disk to receive data and programs.
- HELP is used with other MS-DOS commands, as in HELP COPY, and provides online explanations of the various DOS utilities. It is similar to the MAN facility in UNIX, although not as extensive.
- LABEL "names" an entire disk (see VOLUME).
- MEM returns statistics on current use of RAM (random access memory).
- MKDIR (MD) creates a directory or subdirectory on disk.
- MODE sets the attributes of devices such as printers, display terminals, for specific configurations.
- MORE allows the display of files and directory entries one screen at a time.
- PATH, when set, allows programs to be accessed and run from within other directories and subdirectories.
- PRINT displays a file on the printer.
- PROMPT alters the appearance of the DOS level command prompt on the video screen.
- QBASIC is an extension and refinement of the BASIC language interpreter.
- RENAME (REN) changes the name of a program or file.
- RESTORE, in conjunction with BACKUP (above), allows you to make and retrieve archival copies of files or an entire disk or set of disks.
- RMDIR (RD) erases an empty directory or subdirectory from disk.
- SORT alphabetizes a text or ASCII file.
- SYS places system tracks on a formatted disk.
- TIME sets the system clock.
- TREE displays the disk directory as a tree with branches to represent subdirectories.
- TYPE, similar to PRINT, displays a file on the screen or printer.
- UNDELETE recovers a previously erased file.
- UNFORMAT reverses the FORMAT command; used to recover accidentally deleted data as a result of erasing files with the FORMAT command.
- VER returns the DOS version number on the screen.
- VERIFY checks the integrity of a disk after using the FORMAT command.
- VOL or VOLUME returns the "name" of the disk assigned by the LABEL command.
- XCOPY makes a copy of all or selected files and subdirectories on a disk, checking for disk integrity during the process.

There are a few DOS commands which are actually small software programs. These utility programs are similar to the transient commands described with CP/M. Beginning with DOS version 5, a text editor called EDIT was furnished with the O/S package. This replaced the long-standing line editor, EDLIN, which nonprogrammers often found difficult to use. QBASIC, an interpreter version the BASIC language (see chapter 8), is also included in the DOS package. The DEBUG program, a utility of interest primarily to assembly language programmers, is also still included with the standard release of DOS. The latter is useful for detecting program errors at a machine level, stepping through memory locations and examining individual machine instructions one at a time.

## OS/2

**OS/2**, or Operating System/2, is a spinoff from DOS. It was first developed by Microsoft Corporation, the developer of DOS, with the rights subsequently sold to the IBM corporation. However, OS/2 is a powerful enhancement of the Disk Operating System, and it performs many tasks of which DOS is not capable. OS/2's outstanding feature is its ability to multitask, that is, to run several programs simultaneously. OS/2 is fully compatible with DOS, and, in fact, will run DOS (as well as Windows) programs if required. OS/2 may be found in larger libraries and certainly in academic computing facilities, and its popularity warrants some discussion in detail.

**Multitasking** has found applications in both technical and nontechnical environments. Any time a computing task is currently being accessed, for example, as in the editing of a file with a word processor, it is said to be running in the **foreground**. There may be other tasks that run simultaneously which are not visible to the user. These tasks are said to be in the **background**; UNIX (which is discussed later) calls these background tasks **daemons**, and other operating systems have similar special names for background tasks. An example of a daemon might be a program that polls the telephone line for an incoming document file via fax transmission. The concept is that a user of a highly trafficked PC cannot tie up the PC's **system resources** for one job that may be accessed only occasionally. A library application for multitasking might be an automated circulation system that prints overdue book notices in the background while book discharges are taking place at the check-in desk. OS/2 could be the operating system of choice for a programmer of such application software.

A simple example of multitasking is that of an academic computing laboratory where a number of very detailed mathematical formulas are executing simultaneously. Operations which tie up the CPU for long periods of time are said to be **compute bound**. Consider, for instance, an algorithm to compute to 100 places the value of pi ($\pi$). Theoretically, pi (22/7) can never be computed to an exact number, and as it computes to many places to the right of the decimal point, the resolution of the fraction takes up more and more time in the CPU's arithmetic registers. Under OS/2, the computation is started in the foreground and allowed to run. Invoking the program manager, the user closes the screen which is running the program that computes pi, but he/she does not terminate the program itself. The user is then free to load and run other programs; the pi program is still actively running somewhere in the computer's memory. The user may, from time to time, "check in" with the task to monitor its progress; if the pi program completes while still assigned to background mode, the results are simply placed on a screen for inspection when the user wishes to call them up. Depending on memory size, several such background jobs can be similarly run on the same computer.

One specialized area of computing that depends on a computer system's ability to multitask is **real-time programming**. Programs written to operate in real time require a **timeshare language**, of which C and Pascal are two possible examples. In this area of computing, many terminals have access to common files, such as those which comprise large databases. Each terminal has the ability to modify the various files on a continuous, immediate basis; thus the attribute "real time." An example is the circulation desk of a library where books are charged and discharged. As the codes of the borrowers' cards along with the catalog numbers of the books are keyed or wanded into the machines, the bibliographic and patron databases are updated to indicate which books each given borrower has charged or returned. Real-time updates are necessary because there may be reserve book lists on which the next person waiting for a particular title wants his/her book as soon as it becomes available. And, because there may be several terminals connected to the same bibliographic and patron databases but performing different jobs (e.g., one terminal charging books, one inputting new book titles, etc.), the process of multitasking continues in this real-time mode.

Multitasking should not be confused with multiwindowing or **task management**. Programs such as DesqView and Windows allow the user to open multiple programs simultaneously, in a multiprocessing mode. However, these program managers handle multiple programs in a sort of "juggling" act. While one program is being invoked, the others which have been designated as "open" are actually dormant in the background. The background, "open" programs are waiting in a state of readiness that is more quickly accessed than invocation from a command prompt, but no computing is occurring in such "background" processes. In a true multitasking environment, a program does not shut down when relegated to the background; in task management environments, the background programs are merely "placed on hold." This is not to say that task management programs are not of value; more accurately, they are versions of multitasking operating systems which require far less of the system's resources to execute. Which manner of process management to choose depends primarily on the complexities and speed required of your computing setup.

OS/2 requires a PC with at least an 80286 or higher numbered processor. The reason is that OS/2 must be loaded on a machine capable of running in **protected mode**, which is a hardware function originally designed into Intel 80286 CPU chips. Protected mode is OS/2's way of managing programs that are running in the foreground and background as multitasked objects. If a program is placed in a certain location in the computer's memory (RAM), it is said to be protected by OS/2 from intrusions by other programs that might compete for the same space. If a machine running OS/2 runs out of available memory when program requests exceed available RAM space, OS/2 uses the free space on the hard disk drive as **virtual memory**. That is, any program running in the background might be temporarily **spooled** onto the hard disk until sufficient RAM is available to contain it. For this reason, computing shops that plan to use OS/2 as their operating system of choice must ascertain that the individual PCs are of sufficient capacity to support it. Computers with eight megabytes of RAM or more and hard disk drives of at least 100 megabytes or larger are not unrealistic for entry level OS/2 systems. OS/2 versions 2.0 and higher will require an 80386sx or greater numbered chip to run the 32-bit addressing system inherent in the software. The "32 bits" refers to the fact that 80386 and 80486 chips can handle a memory address four bytes wide, making it possible (theoretically) to place binary information anywhere within a four gigabyte address space.

The opposite of protected mode is **real mode**, which describes the majority of DOS-based programs. OS/2 runs real mode programs in its **compatibility box** and, in so doing, functions in a manner nearly identical to that of standard DOS. If necessary, some language compilers can output programs in **bound** versions, whereby they are able to run either in DOS's real mode or OS/2's protected mode. Some **OEM (original equipment manufacturer)** versions of OS/2 allow a dual boot setup whereby a user can have both OS/2 and DOS loaded on the same machine. Zenith Data Systems' OEM version of OS/2 allows the user to choose the desired system at bootup time merely by holding down the Alt key until the system prompt appears on the screen. OS/2 includes a Windows-like platform called the Workplace Shell (called the Presentation Manager in versions prior to 2.0), and many Windows-based programs can be run without modification from the Workplace Shell desktop. OS/2 as a graphical user interface similar to Windows will be discussed further in the next chapter.

## UNIX AND XENIX

UNIX is a child of Bell Laboratories and was first introduced in 1969. Its initial purpose was to support the C programming language (see chapter 8) developed by Kernigan and Ritchie in 1978.[1] However, the UNIX operating system (and the C language) gained a rapid popularity in universities and in many corporations. UNIX developed its own following and niche with user groups and third-party support spread over a wide range of programming environments. A battle currently wages over which PC operating system will ultimately predominate—DOS, OS/2 or the PC version of UNIX—but the current statistics reflecting installed versions of UNIX point to the fact that UNIX is growing and will claim a significant part of the upper level computing market for years to come.[2]

UNIX initially appeared on minicomputers and on some mainframes, but it ultimately became available for larger PCs as well. UNIX offers much versatility in **distributed processing** environments, that is, in situations where tasks are performed on separate (and usually smaller) computers rather than en masse on one centralized computer. It is an operating system capable of multitasking and of handling multiple users through a system of user **accounts** and user **privileges**. An account gives a user a specified amount of time and program resources on the system, and privileges (or privilege levels) dictate how much freedom a given user is allowed in his/her or others' accounts and directories. Because of its ability to handle user accounts and multiples of workstations, UNIX is particularly adaptable for use in networked environments.[3]

Multiuser systems such as UNIX and Novell NetWare (see chapter 15) require the services of a **system administrator**. This person maintains software, diagnoses trouble situations, handles user accounts, and keeps a record of system hardware configurations. The system administrator must have an intimate knowledge of the hardware upon which UNIX is run, because many of the facilities of UNIX are machine dependent. Further, many end users will typically be programming at a relatively high level of sophistication and will need exact details of the hardware setup. It is the responsibility of the system administrator to maintain detailed records about users and user clusters. If a change or upgrade to a system is to be made, the decision to do so must be considered very carefully, because a seemingly innocuous modification might affect the efforts of dozens of UNIX users.

UNIX is available in a number of configurations. The IBM mainframe version is known as AIX; the Apple Macintosh version is A/UX; the PC versions are available as **Xenix** and UNIX, the former being a slightly abridged version of its larger partner. While there are several versions of UNIX that run on personal computers, the Santa Cruz Organization (SCO) version enjoys a widespread popularity.

Apple A/UX requires at least a Mac II with 5 megabytes of memory (RAM) and an 80-megabyte hard disk drive to run. The Mac II's disk drive(s) can be **partitioned** in such a way that the computer can run both A/UX and Mac O/S selectively, but this dual identity is usually cumbersome and requires a larger computer to perform effectively. However, connectivity on the A/UX system is very straightforward. The system administrator can opt either to run A/UX over standard AppleTalk cabling (see chapter 15), or via a setup of multiple serial (communications) ports allowed by various add-in circuit boards. DigiBoard is a popular manufacturer of such boards, and that company's products allow connections of non-Macintosh terminals to the A/UX system.

A/UX, in addition to presenting a high quality standalone UNIX environment, also provides an efficient teaching tool. Where DOS provides utilities for **batch file programming** (see chapter 7), UNIX includes a similar facility called **shell programming**. A more complex facility than that of DOS, shell programming employs a C language-like script repertoire of commands to automate various operating system procedures and sets of procedures. However, it is not the easiest process to learn and requires some prerequisite knowledge. A/UX makes available the Macintosh's graphics interface to allow the procedures to be run from pulldown menus, as with standard Macintosh applications programs. However, an added feature is that the invocation of a procedure triggers a writing of the shell script in the background. A learner can switch to the background script to view the accompanying UNIX program code, and, from an examination of the A/UX generated code, study the process or modify the command(s) to suit a particular set of circumstances.

Access to a UNIX system requires a login and a password. The system administrator, in monitoring system use and account activity, maintains a list of valid passwords and user IDs. Upon successful login, a user will note some background activity while the system readies a new user area. After a few moments, the screen reports a system prompt (as "[1]" or "$" or "%" or the like, depending on the version of UNIX installed), in a manner similar to that of DOS, and the system is ready to accept commands.

UNIX employs a **hierarchial file structure** which is also similar to that of DOS. That is to say, files can be stored at different levels of the file system structure. Each level of the hierarchy consists of files and directories and pointers to other levels. Since UNIX presents such a logical directory structure, files that are related to one another (e.g., document files that correspond to a particular word processor) can be placed in separate directories. As such, a user can view and access the various directories' contents by specifying the appropriate directory names.

As an account holder in a UNIX system, each user is assigned a personal directory in which to store files and create logical subdirectories. The personal, or **unique directory**, is called the **home directory** for any particular user. These directories, as topmost levels of access for any particular person, are analogous to the root directory in DOS. Because DOS is a single-user operating system, the root represents the highest overview of all the directories and subdirectories on any particular disk. In UNIX, a user might employ his/her first name for the home directory and further subdivide home into logical storage areas for various documents. For example, Lisa might prefer a separation of files into word processed documents, ASCII text, and C language programs. Graphically, Lisa's user area of UNIX might appear as follows:

```
                          /lisa
        ┌───────────────────┼───────────────────┐
  /lisa/wordproc        /lisa/textfil        /lisa/source
        |                   |                   |
   letter1.ltr          report1.txt         cprogram.c
   letter2.ltr          report2.txt         secrets.c
```

Note that UNIX by convention prefers lowercase letters. This is because of UNIX's close ties to the original issue of the C programming language (see chapter 8), which, at its inception, used no uppercase letters for reserved words and variables.

Of course, many users would be enrolled on any given UNIX system and each user would have a home directory. It becomes self-evident that these home directories are actually subdirectories of a larger whole. UNIX does have a designated root directory, but it is usually inaccessible to general users and is "invisible" to all but the system administrator. However, if privileges are set appropriately for various account holders, users can access files and programs in directories in areas other than under their homes.

Note that UNIX differs from DOS in that the path and directory separator is the "/" character (DOS uses the "\"). Also, in UNIX the full path name begins with a "/," so that secrets.c in Lisa's user area would be properly described as /users/lisa/source/secrets.c.

MS-DOS, as shipped, offers one shell, the COMMAND.COM file. As mentioned above, this command shell contains all the resident commands immediately available at the DOS prompt. UNIX and XENIX offer similar conventions, except that there are three shells indigenous to the operating system, namely, the Korn Shell, the Bourne Shell and the C

Shell. Each shell offers similar facilities, and it is mostly a matter of personal preference which shell a user will invoke.

Some typical UNIX commands follow. A comparison with the DOS commands in the section above will exemplify many similarities of use and syntax between the two systems.

- cat—concatenate file(s) and print
- cd—change directory
- cmp—compare two files
- date—show date and time
- ex—invoke the EX line editor
- grep—search a file for a particular pattern
- ls—list contents of a directory
- mail—invoke the mail facility
- man—find manual information by keyword; MAN is an online documentation facility
- mkdir—make a directory
- mv—move or rename a file
- pg—display a file on the screen, one page at a time
- sort—sort and merge files
- vi—invoke the VI screen-oriented text editor
- wc—count the number of words in a file

UNIX is a multitasking operating system like OS/2. The UNIX system is written so that processes can be run in the background, behind the scenes so to speak, while other computing jobs are actively being executed from the console. In UNIX, these background processes are called **daemons** (described above) and are fundamental for making UNIX perform successfully as a multiuser operating system. As a microcomputer-based operating system, it is accurate to describe UNIX as "DOS and more"; that is, UNIX has several command shells compared to only one for DOS; standard UNIX has several text editors comparable to DOS's EDLIN utility, and UNIX gives users several levels of access to the computer's architecture and services. It is reasonable to assert that a knowledge of CP/M or DOS or similar command-based operating systems should be prerequisite learning to to a study of UNIX in order to derive the full power and capabilities from the latter.

## JOB CONTROL LANGUAGE

Over the years, IBM has generically called its several proprietary operating systems **JCL (job control language)**, and the label has stuck. Actually, several mainframe manufacturers unofficially call the command languages of their operating systems "JCL," and the use of the term has become popularized, somewhat like Kleenex and Xerox. JCL programs have their own command syntaxes. For example, the REXX language is used for creating JCL in some IBM mainframe systems. The term **control cards**, named for the Hollerith cards that were loaded into the card readers ahead of programs and data in computers of the 1960s, is still to be found around mainframe shops. In fact, some JCL commands still address the logical punch and card reader devices, where, in reality, the "punch" is merely a read or write process to tape or disk. Typical mainframe operating systems include CMS, VMS, DOS/VSE, VM, VM/ESA, and dozens of others. The choice of operating system depends largely on the brand of mainframe computer chosen and the processes it will run. **VARs (value added resellers)** may also provide operating system utility programs such as IBM's PROFS[4] (the Professional Office System) for VM/System Product, which allows for electronic mail and message forwarding in addition to the basic set of VM functions.

## MUSIC

**MUSIC**, or Multi-User System for Interactive Computing, is commonly found in colleges and universities in academic computer facilities. A mainframe-based operating system, it serves as a platform for computer instruction and local area communication, the latter providing a system of **electronic mail (e-mail)** and the potential for connection to systems outside a mainframe proper. MUSIC has a powerful accounting system, and it is relatively easy to maintain a system of use charges and user privileges at the administrative level. MUSIC is developed and maintained by McGill University in Montreal, Quebec.

MUSIC is actually "an operating system within an operating system." It typically works "under" the VM operating system, and, as such, has access to many of the IBM mainframe's VM facilities. MUSIC features a system of personal scheduling and editing called TODO and a proprietary SCRIPT language leading into MUSIC's text editor, all of which comprise MUSIC's Office User's System. MUSIC has evolved to such a point that DOS and personal computer users will find many similarities. This was a deliberate action by MUSIC engineers in an attempt to make the operating system of mainframe computers and PCs equally familiar to both groups of persons. Users of DOS (and UNIX) will find many common denominators in MUSIC's command system, and the following short list of MUSIC commands should be intuitively familiar to persons whose initial exposure to operating systems was on a PC workstation:

- BASIC invokes the MUSIC BASIC compiler.
- /CANCEL aborts whatever activity is currently in progress.
- COMPARE file1 file2 compares the contents of two named files.

- COPY copies the contents of one file to another.
- /DEFINE PFn defines the keyboard's PF keys to represent a macro string.
- EDIT filename invokes the MUSIC text editor.
- HELP topic invokes the MUSIC help facility.
- LIBRARY lists the files in a user's account directory.
- MAIL invokes the MUSIC mail facility.
- PRINT filename outputs a file to the printer.
- RENAME oldfile newfile renames a user file.
- SORT filename sorts or alphabetizes field items in a user file.
- /TIME displays the time of day.

In MUSIC, commands that begin with the "/" character can be imbedded in a JCL script language. In comparing the short lists of commands in CP/M, DOS, UNIX, and MUSIC, it should now be obvious that all operating systems have common denominators of commands. Depending on the architecture of the machines upon which they are run, all operating systems are performing basically the same tasks—it is only the syntax that varies. For example, to obtain a listing of files on a user's working directory, CP/M uses the command DIR as does DOS; UNIX uses LS; and MUSIC uses LIB or LIBRARY. These **immediate commands** (i.e., ones in which the results are posted immediately to the computer screen) will all result in the same action—a columnar listing of user files on the screen. Some commands obviously do not translate from one operating system to another because of the nature of the hardware upon which they are run. For example, DOS has no command to "read card" because there never was a card reader device designed for PCs.

## NOTES

1. Kernigan, Brian and Dennis M. Ritchie. *The C Programming Language*. Second edition, 288 pp.
2. Yager, Tom and Ben Smith. "Is UNIX Dead?" *BYTE*, September 1992, pp. 134-146.
3. Brandt, D. Scott. *Unix-Based Network Communications*. 175 pp.
4. *Introducing the Professional Office System*. International Business Machines Corporation, 1983, 38 pp.

# Chapter 7

# Computing Platforms and Graphical User Interfaces

Up to this point in the text, the discussions have centered around computing from the **command prompt**. That is, the preceding chapters have outlined a number of activities that can be launched by typing a single word or phrase on the computer's screen or from a console. If you have been interspersing some hands-on training with the reading of this text, the A> or C> prompts should be quite familiar to you.

Interacting with a computer from a prompt is known as **text-based computing**. It isn't necessary to have a video terminal attached to the computer to communicate with a CPU; in fact, as was noted in chapter 1, early computers were set up with banks of toggle switches, with outputs read from punched tape. It wasn't until about the 1930s that scientists realized that the familiar **teletype machine**, or **TTY**, could be used as an input/output device. This coupling of typewriter keyboard and computer paved the way for the user friendliness taken for granted in modern day computing.

Because it is such a popular medium, this chapter will consider in depth the matter of **graphics user interfaces**, or **GUIs**. GUIs act as stepping stones between high-level computing projects and neophyte computer users. Sometimes called **intelligent front ends**, graphical user interfaces eliminate the need for end users to program the setup dialogues and job control statements from which word processors, spreadsheets, tutorials, and the like are run. GUIs take much of the trepidation from computing and make work at a computer terminal appear in familiar settings. As with any computing task, someone has to pioneer the setups and administer the workstation environments. This chapter gives an insight into the backroom tasks that shape such interfaces.

## BATCH FILE PROGRAMS

In the last chapter, reference was made to script file programming. Often, when operating systems are used at the **command level**, i.e., invoking operating system services from a prompt ( "A>," "C>," or "%" or similar), it may be desirable to issue several commands at one time. To execute these commands repeatedly, it is necessary to retype the commands anew, one at a time. However, using script files, or, in the case of DOS, batch files, a series of commands can be issued as a unit. It becomes necessary only to type the name of a **batch file**, which is merely an ASCII (text) file of a list of the commands to be executed. These files can be created with any word processor or line editor or just from DOS's EDIT utility. Batch and script files can be simple or elaborate, and their importance is sufficiently significant that they may be classed as "platforms" when the subject of graphics user interfaces is considered.

In the next chapter, batch *processing* will be discussed. This should not be confused with batch *file execution*, which is the task of running separate computer programs, one after another, in a **batch mode** as opposed to an **interactive mode**. In interactive mode, feedback and results of a computation are usually available immediately on the screen or printer; in batch mode, there may be a delay of results if batches are scheduled for some specific time period during the computing day. In DOS, batch files have the extension .BAT. If there is a file on disk called ACCOUNTS.BAT, and if an operator types ACCOUNTS at the prompt, all the commands in the ACCOUNTS.BAT file are executed, one after the other. The following is a code example of a simple batch file called SWAPSYS.BAT:

```
ECHO OFF
REM begin with root directory
C:
CD \
REM swap CONFIG.SYS files
REM CONFIG.TMP is a placeholder
COPY CONFIG.SYS CONFIG.TMP
ERASE CONFIG.SYS
RENAME CONFIG.BAK CONFIG.SYS
RENAME CONFIG.TMP CONFIG.BAK
CD \
```

The purpose of this batch process is to vary the DOS environment according to the needs of equipment attached to the system. PC setups often require that .SYS (system) files be installed at powerup time, to act as **device drivers** for certain types of peripheral accessories, such as scanners, in order that DOS be able to recognize the existence of such hardware. However, some device drivers set up conflicts within DOS and cannot be installed simultaneously with others. Thus, there must be a way to establish an "either/or" setup for the computing environment at boot-up time. SWAPSYS.BAT allows this variation and, by having the DOS command statements placed in a batch file, only one command—SWAP-SYS—needs to be typed to consummate the setup. The REM statements are merely comments to document the lines of text and do not execute along with the other statements.

Many other types of batch files are possible, and ones with several hundred lines of code are not unknown. The Norton Utilities, a software disk and system management program, features a section called the Batch Enhancer that adds features to the basic set of batch-oriented commands of DOS. In DOS itself, a special file known as AUTOEXEC.BAT can optionally be present on disk. At bootup time, the operating system checks for the presence of this batch file, and, if found, its contents are immediately executed before the computer is turned over to the user for input. AUTOEXEC.BAT, an <u>auto</u>matic <u>exec</u>ution script, performs house-keeping chores for DOS so that a PC is able to perform in a customized manner for the user. For example, the AUTOEXEC.BAT file can contain the setup for the appearance of the system prompt—it may be desired that the prompt appear with the name of the subdirectory as "C:\PRO-GRAMS>" rather than the generic "C>"; also, the DATE and TIME can be set; temporary work areas or "scratchpad" areas can be established for certain programs that will access them; a PATH, or subdirectory search formula, can be created; and input/output modes for establishing printer types and screen definitions can be modified. A more detailed listing of batch file commands is in the DOS users' manual.

## MENU PROGRAMS

A desirable feature of computer programs is that they be **menu-dri-ven**. This feature means that, once a program is started from a command line, or from a picture icon, a user need only highlight a program func-tion with the arrow keys and hit "Enter" to access that function, or, in the case of graphics interfaces, point to the program selection with a mouse pointer and click a button. A **menu** on a computer screen is not unlike one found in a restaurant—it is a list of choices from which a user selects one or more options that will satisfy his/her computing needs in a given situation. In its simplest form, a menu can appear at the terminal as the following:

**PROGRAM SELECTION MENU**
**SELECT BY NUMBER:**
1. WordStar
2. WordPerfect
3. dBase IV
4. SuperCalc
5. Lotus 1-2-3
6. Return to DOS
**Your choice (1 through 6)?—**

This screen, and the actions that must be taken to invoke the five programs in the list, can be programmed as a batch file as described in the previous section. The file could be called MENU.BAT, and, if desired to have the menu immediately available whenever the computer is turned on, the command MENU could be placed somewhere in the AUTOEX-EC.BAT file as well. In fact, the AUTOEXEC.BAT file can be written to load any executable program, or other batch file, in order that the PC be powered up to a ready state for performing a particular task.

Several types of menus are possible on a PC or Macintosh screen. With the availability of computer video systems that are more graphics oriented, menus do not have to be line oriented as in the MENU.BAT example above. Applications programmers have several choices of menu types: **pulldown menus**, in which a selection box rolls down from the top of the video screen, like a window shade; **drop down menus**, which fall from a line at the top of the screen called a **status bar**; and **popup menus**, which appear as boxes or windows at preselected locations on the screen. Whatever type is invoked, there appears a list of selections of which each choice usually appears as highlighted text, or **reverse video**, whenever it is selected. Such graphics devices are useful for laypersons and end users of applications programs in general office environments, when it is necessary to keep command line typing and interaction with the operating system at a minimum.

## MACINTOSH SYSTEM 6.0.X AND SYSTEM 7

Arguably, the Macintosh user interfaces, System 6 and successor System 7, may have been the foundation of all current GUIs. Because the Macintosh interface is used on Apple's computers as the front end for users, the Systems 6.0.X and System 7 might properly be considered with operating systems (see chapter 6). However, because of appearances and icon-based functionality, the Macintosh System 6 and System 7 interfaces will be considered in context with the GUIs that are used predominately on Intel processor-based machines.

What Apple did with the Macintosh from the beginning, that is, virtually eliminate the **command line prompt**, is not without mimicry. Microsoft Corporation, and then IBM Corporation, have attempted to replace the command line with icon-based, program-launching facilities with OS/2's Workplace Shell which is discussed later. Also, Windows authors have proclaimed that Windows 95, the issue after Windows version 3.1, may eliminate the need for DOS altogether. These actions may ultimately create a dichotomy, with a command line platform becoming the exclusive domain of programmers and developers, and the graphics interface collecting all the end users. Admittedly, there will remain ambidextrous persons who will switch back and forth between the two, but the polarization may become a reality within the next couple of years.

But as a graphics user interface, the Apple Macintosh exhibits features which are still considered to be pioneering. Systems 6 and 7 present a disk's file structure as pictures of folders, suitcases, stacks of cards, and papers. What would appear as a named directory in DOS appears as a manila file folder on a Macintosh. Collections of related files, e.g., type font descriptor files, appear as suitcases on a Macintosh screen to indicate that such files are to be installed on a hard disk as a package. Individual documents, such as word processed documents, appear as sheets of paper on the Mac's workspace. Indeed, the Macintosh will allow you to toggle between small and large icons and named files if you wish, but a screenful of filenames in place of pictures seems to be the exception instead of the rule. Indeed, the operating of a Macintosh computer from a command line and filenames is rather a defeat of the philosophy of the Macintosh GUI—to take away the complexities of getting a job done by using a computer.

## WINDOWS

Few PC-based computer programs have been the subject of as many articles and discussions as Microsoft Windows. The product has launched a large-scale revolution in the way people work with computers, and it has commanded a following that could accurately be termed evangelical. There is much support literature as well as numerous major programs designed to work with it. Coursework to teach Windows has appeared in college curricula, and there are countless third-party, noncredit continuing education seminars to present Windows' intricacies. Thousands upon thousands of dollars are being spent on learning and developing the powers of this innocuous program which retails for $149.95 and can be had at discount for about $50.00.

What is this Windows and what does it look like? Windows began life as simply "Windows" for IBM PCs (Intel 8088- and 8086-microprocessor-based machines), evolving into Windows/286 and Windows/386 (the so-called "versions 2") to take advantage of Intel's more sophisticated CPUs. The next Windows is 3.1, which runs *under* MS-DOS; that is to say, the DOS operating system is loaded into the PC before Windows is launched. To start Windows 3.1, a user simply types "WIN" at the command prompt, or even simpler, allows a batch file to start Windows automatically at bootup time. Such an action can be programmed into the AUTOEXEC.BAT file (see batch files, page 105), in which case the user needs do nothing except turn on the computer.

The latest incarnation of Windows is Windows 95. Long awaited and much touted by the media, Windows 95 is supposed to be an operating system in the truest sense of the word. That is, Windows 95 no longer considers itself an interface; the product loads into a computer without the necessity of running DOS as a support platform. However, Windows 95 features a compatibility box that will run DOS programs from a desktop environment—a sort of "reverse" way to continue to take advantage of the many thousands of DOS-based programs still extant. Windows 95's intent is to exploit the hardware capabilities of the newer Intel microprocessor CPUs and to make computing more intuitive to casual and nontechnical users. There was considerable media hype for months before Windows 95 was released, and much editorializing was made of the new operating system. Out of fear that publisher Microsoft Corporation would overwhelmingly dominate the PC software industry, several antitrust lawsuits were threatened to block the release of Windows 95. There was also doom predicted that Windows 95 would render the Apple Macintosh an insignificant player in the personal computer arena. Whatever unfolds in the marketplace, it is certain that Windows 95 will play a major role in the way personal computer paradigms are formed for the remainder of this century.

Windows works in a manner similar to that of other GUIs, inasmuch as it permits the running of several programs simultaneously. While Windows does not allow true multitasking as do OS/2 and UNIX, it does allow **program swapping** in which programs which have been started but are not immediately needed can be placed in the background. In such an environment, a user might start WordStar to write a memorandum and decide halfway through the writing that some figures in the Excel spreadsheet need to be consulted. WordStar is then **minimized**; Excel is started, and, when the needed figures are obtained, Excel is minimized and WordStar once again is brought to the foreground. The advantage of having several programs "on call" in this manner is that the loading/unloading/running of the various software programs is faster than calling up the programs completely from scratch each time they are needed. A user does not "lose his/her place" in the task—the process is somewhat akin to leaving bookmarks in several novels that one is perusing.

Microsoft Corporation has released a version of the Windows program it is calling Windows NT. It eliminates the need for DOS, or any other operating system, since Windows NT acts as its own self-contained operating system in the same manner as OS/2. At its initial invocation, Windows begins at the Desktop, presenting a window (or frame, if you prefer) containing several **icons** (picture representations) of setup tasks on a **wallpaper** background which lead to the running of other programs. From that point, the running of any program to be loaded by Windows is simply a matter of pointing the mouse arrow at the appropriate program icon and clicking the mouse button once or twice. Although this action makes the running of any program quite simple, to achieve this simplicity, someone must provide the setups from which Windows derives its information. This is where the complications arise: there are script files variously called WIN.INI, SYSTEM.INI and numerous .PIF (program information) files that contain system level code for screen configurations, directory information, printer codes, font specifications, and so forth, and these files must be programmed in order that casual users don't have to worry about them. In a typical office environment, end users such as planners and administrators usually don't program their own Windows setups; this task is delegated to the data processing department. In larger organizations, programmers may also develop in-house applications using the Microsoft Windows Development Kit, or one of the newer tools such as Asymetrix' ToolBook or Visual Basic (see below). Whatever the case, the Windows "front end" is the same for everyone, and there are common denominators of which users will take advantage.

It is this set of commonalities that makes Windows so attractive for software developers and end users alike. A scan of the literature and bookstores will evidence that many popular, commercial software programs which were once "DOS-only," such as WordStar, Lotus 1-2-3, WordPerfect and Ventura Publisher (to name but a very few), now have Windows versions—or are available to run under Windows exclusively! There is a very powerful reason for this new loyalty: Windows consists of a core of utility functions and **dynamic link libraries (DLLs)**. These functions are available as **system calls** to any program that would use them. For example, a vendor of a word processing program (e.g., WordPerfect) might want to make available a font management program within the word processor, in order that typefaces and styles could be manipulated from within the program. Such a facility is already "programmed into" Windows, and the author of WordPerfect need not write a proprietary module to handle fonts—Windows already makes it available for the calling! Putting this action into the vernacular, it is the old adage of "why buy a cow when milk is so cheap?" Vendors thus save hundreds of programmer hours of coding time, and Microsoft expands its customer base. The symbiosis has created a following of almost religious proportions.

The attraction works with equal strength on the side of users as well. Most end users will have more than one applications program on their PCs; typically, there will be at least one word processor, one spreadsheet, and quite likely a database manager and various utility programs. These programs will exhibit commonalities, e.g., the need for printer drivers, file library management, backup copying, screen definition resolution, and the like. The Windows repertoire can handle all these things. Through its Control Panel, Windows can manage printer port assignments, output communications speeds, font cataloging and sizing, sharing of program files and graphics between applications, screen colors, and multimedia responses such as sounds and animations. Typically, for one person's workstation, that user will expect the same printer setup for his/her word processor as for the spreadsheet, etc., and the same environmental setups for all applications on the PC. The question arises, "Why have each individual applications program maintain hardware setups when one utility program could consolidate all the settings into one file?" The answer to this question is precisely the raison d'être of Windows: with a graphical user interface as powerful as Windows, you don't need to "buy the same real estate twice" and maintain a disassociated collection of software packages. Windows also supports the convention of **object linking and embedding (OLE)**, a facility which allows the contents (and sometimes the graphics) of one program to be imported and shared by another. With OLE, if changes to the original data are made in the calling program, these changes will be recorded in the creating program as well.

Windows ships with several utility programs which, in themselves, are highly useful computing tools. Windows Write is a handy word processing program with many features, and it can offer well-formatted output compatible with more than a dozen popular word processing file specifications. Windows Paintbrush allows a user to create graphics and drawings (in color, if desired) which can be exported into other programs in either bitmap or PC-Paintbrush (.PCX) file format, or printed directly from Windows. Windows Terminal is a communications program which, if the PC has a modem attached, can control dialup sessions (see chapter 16) and manage the user's directory of remote computers and bulletin boards frequently accessed. There is also a Notepad editor, a hand calculator, a Rolodex-like Cardfile database manager, and a Calendar program for keeping track of appointments and meetings. Many of these tools are callable by other Windows-based programs and comprise an accessory set of relative sophistication. There are other "little" accessories available from third-party vendors for such tasks as icon drawing, font management, program launching, and batch file management, many of which are to be found as shareware or in the public domain.

DOS, UNIX and other operating systems that run programs from the command prompt are far from dead. Windows and GUIs have begun a trend which will capture a significant portion of the desktop computing market for some time to come, and perhaps permanently. But there will always be a need for both graphics computing platforms and line-oriented interfaces—the need depends on the end user. As popular as Windows has become, there will certainly arise competition to the product. The remainder of this section will focus on a few aspiring GUIs that could give Windows some incentives to evolve into an even more sophisticated and attractive product.

## DOS AND OS/2

For those who don't need the complexities of Windows or don't care to lay out the cost of an additional facility for their desktops, DOS, beginning with version 5.0, offers an alternative. If a DOS user purchases the 5.0 upgrade kit, or chooses to install his/her own DOS on a hard disk drive using the on-disk installation utility, a desktop shell called the DOSSHELL will be placed on the hard drive by default. The DOSSHELL is then loaded at each subsequent bootup of the computer, unless the user eliminates the command line invoking DOSSHELL from the AUTOEXEC.BAT file. DOSSHELL is actually a useful alternative to the Windows GUI, as the DOSSHELL presents a similar interface to the File Manager section of Windows. It is not at all unlike some menu programs described above and allows a user to select and run various programs by the "point-and-click method"; that is, by placing the mouse pointer on the name of a program the user wishes to run and clicking the left mouse button. The list of available selections can be modified easily, and the DOSSHELL can be used to invoke file management commands (e.g., rename, delete, copy to subdirectory, etc.) as well.

OS/2 presents its own version of a graphics user interface. As described in chapter 6, the OS/2 operating system was developed by Microsoft Corporation, with the rights later sold to IBM. As such, there is a friendly(?) battle between the two companies to make one or the other graphics user interfaces of OS/2 or Windows predominate the end-user market. OS/2 uses as its ammunition the Workplace Shell, which, in appearance and function, is not unlike the Desktop in Windows. In reality, the Workplace Shell resembles the Macintosh interface more than other PC-based graphics user interfaces. Users of OS/2 who are accustomed to the Presentation Manager will have to do a bit of relearning, but the Shell, Presentation

Manager and Windows all have common actions and attributes so that users should have little difficulty navigating among any of the three. OS/2, like other GUIs, uses a system of folders and icons to organize and run the various programs in its charge. Users who require a true 32-bit operating system should consider OS/2 and its Workplace Shell.[1]

## CURSES AND X WINDOWS

As mentioned previously, early business-oriented, and then consumer-oriented computers borrowed their input/output interfaces from teletype (TTY) technology. This was all right as long as data were entered a line at a time, typewriter style, and retrieved in the same fashion. But more sophisticated applications required graphics and non-alphanumeric characters on the screens to make output look more professional and attractive. There needed to be a method for establishing a standard of full screen addressing.

You have used full screen addressing every time you have used a word processor. **Full screen addressing** simply means that the computer's video display memory keeps track of information wherever it is typed on the screen; the information does not have to be typed exactly after the prompt, or at a specific line and column location. The program which is loaded keeps track of screen locations and reacts accordingly whenever additional information is requested, or required, to be stored. DOS, by comparison, is not full screen addressable; it will allow for a few spaces to be typed preceding a command, but the command itself must be entered on the same line as the C> prompt. A synonym for full screen addressing is **cursor addressing**, and there are many utility programs and language libraries to accomplish the technique.

The UNIX operating system first developed a product called Curses (a.k.a. cursor addressing) which would allow manipulation of various points on a teletype-based CRT using **relative cursor addressing**. The technique is simple: video memory is set up as an X/Y grid, with intersections on the grid corresponding to the pixels on the screen. A library of system calls (usually written in C language) allows such invocations as line draw, box draw, field placement, and graphics manipulation (using the special, non-alphanumeric characters) which are atypical of typing straight copy. Using these system calls, a programmer can create work zones on the screen and draw elementary graphics, making the display more attractive to the end user.

Curses was a forerunner of Windows, although not its ancestor. Versions of Curses have been developed for DOS, notably, by Lattice,[2] but except among language developers, the system never gained widespread acceptance. Part of the reason is that Curses is not always machine independent;

that is, a slightly different version of Curses may have been necessary to address screen attributes of CRTs in Compaq and IBM PCs, and the version of Curses may have had to be modified to accommodate differences in Microsoft C, Borland C, and Lattice C compilers, among others. In short, there were just too many variations of the C language and video specifications to allow Curses to become a universal standard.

Curses and other similar products made obvious the need for a more uniform standard of full screen addressing. Some vendors authored more advanced products, taking advantage of the evolution in standardization of the C language by ANSI (American National Standards Institute), and of evolving, uniform hardware standards by PC manufactures and companies striving for "100 percent IBM compatibility." The Window Boss[3] was a significant intermediate product for its ability to create frames and windows using C language calls of a higher level than basic Curses, and, to its credit, it was first issued as shareware. Window Boss can still be seen in demonstration format on many electronic bulletin boards, and it remains a solid utility, both for its low cost and ability to teach windowing techniques from the included source code.

X Windows is the current evolutionary step in full screen addressing for UNIX systems, and it has developed to such a degree as a GUI that it is often indistinguishable from Windows. It is a **cross platform** product, inasmuch as X Windows code written for a Sun Sparc workstation should run, without being rewritten or modified, on any Intel 80486-based machine which also runs UNIX. Both Windows and X Windows are sold in developers' packages with tools for creating computing platforms for end users. The next section will consider two relatively high-end utility programs for developing interfaces and platforms for the Windows GUI. These are available at the retail store level and have a significant body of third-party literature available for further reference.

## ASYMETRIX TOOLBOOK AND VISUAL BASIC

Although Windows is a very user-friendly interface, it, as any program, must have intelligent development behind it. Windows, as a **front end product**, has countless hours of human resources behind its invention and refinement. Although commercial products such as Excel for Windows and WordPerfect for Windows require research and development teams to ensure the sophistication required by such complicated spreadsheet and word processing programs, lesser (and more specific) applications should not require as much development time. Such items as slide presentations, electronic Rolodexes, font managers, and learning games should not require teams of engineers to create. Thus, the Asymetrix Toolbook[4] and Visual BASIC[5] have been developed as **code**

**generating engines** to allow nontechnical users to create professional-looking, end-user utility programs to run under the Windows GUI.

There are other Windows application generators on the market, but the Asymetrix ToolBook and Visual BASIC predominate. These programs were introduced soon after the Microsoft Windows Software Developer's Kit (SDK), a library of functions which requires that Windows applications be programmed in the C and Pascal languages, insisting on programmers with a knowledge of system calls and link libraries to achieve the desired screens and interfaces. Third-party Windows applications generators filled a need in the market, that is, for a set of tools that would allow persons other than power programmers to make use of Windows resources and create intelligent, visually pleasing software applications. Visual Basic actually caused a momentary resurrection in the popularity of the BASIC language (described in the next chapter) as a development tool. The Visual Basic engine exploits the graphics capabilities of GW-BASIC and QBASIC, both of which have been matter-of-factly included with MS-DOS versions 5.0 and later.

There are also a number of developmental tools for Windows which are less complicated than the Asymetrix ToolBook and Visual BASIC; many of these perform only one or two functions such as screen representations of printer output and picture **tiling** (i.e., a layout of samples of graphics in a grid pattern); however, these "little" utilities are usually very inexpensive, and some are free or available in the public domain.[6]

## NOTES

1. Salemi, Joe. "OS/2 2.0: Does It Fulfill the Promise?" *PC Magazine*, April 28, 1992, pp. 165-192.
2. Lattice Curses, published by Lattice, Inc., 3010 Woodcreek Drive, Suite A, Downers Grove, IL 60515 (mailing address P.O. Box 3072, Glen Ellyn, IL 60138). $129.00.
3. Window Boss, published by Star Guidance Consulting, 273 Windy Drive, Waterbury, CT 06705. $69.95.
4. Asymetrix ToolBook, published by Asymetrix Corporation, 110-110th Avenue N.E., Suite 717, Bellevue, WA 98004. $395.00.
5. Visual Basic, published by Microsoft Corporation, One Microsoft Way, Redmond, WA 98052-6399. $199.00 (Standard Edition); $495.00 (Professional Edition).
6. Ogg, Harold C. "Developing Applications Programs for Windows 3." *REMark*, December 1991, pp. 26-30.

# Chapter 8

# Programming Languages

It was never the intent of this text to teach computer programming. For most librarians, writing a program or software utility from scratch would be a highly inefficient use of time. As seen in chapter 2, there are many free and/or inexpensive programs to perform a multitude of tasks. In the context of the discussions that follow, a **computer program** is a set of language statements that follow a rigid syntax and format, written for the purpose of generating one or more files of executable machine code. These language statements are also known as **program statements**, the aggregate of which comprise the **source code**, which can be modified and refined as circumstances dictate. The machine code is to be used by a target computer for performing work and specific jobs called **applications**, which consist of word processors, spreadsheets, databases, and the like.

So why mention languages at all, let alone devote an entire chapter to the subject? The motivation here is the same as for learning the other; concepts of computing and information science: to gain a familiarity with the terminology of the field. This is particularly important in performing reference and book selection in the field of computer languages. There are many of them, some (obviously) are more important than others; each one has a specific application or applications, and a considerable number are exotic or even obsolete. To become familiar with a computer language is a process similar to learning a foreign language: there are syntax, grammar, vocabulary, etc. You merely need to know what words to use when, and why.

The generally accepted honor of "World's First Programmer" goes to Lady Augusta Ada Lovelace (1816-52). She was the daughter of Lord

Byron, and for eight years a mentor to Charles Babbage. She wrote a translation of Babbage's paper on the Analytic Engine, including insights, that grew to three times the original work. In addition to correcting Babbage, Lovelace introduced the concept of the loop and subroutine in computer programs. Babbage and Lovelace were about 100 years ahead of their time—these ideas were not studied again seriously until the 1930s. The United States Department of Defense, along with several other federal agencies, uses a standard programming language called Ada, named as a tribute to Lovelace's contributions.

## BATCH PROCESSING: HOW IT USED TO (AND MAY STILL) BE

Hollerith cards allowed the storage of programs and data in eighty-column formats at a time. In other words, each card represented one line of program code or information. Since programs and data punched onto cards had to be produced as decks, they were said to be run in **batch mode**. There is an old joke that there are two kinds of card decks—those that have been dropped, and those that are about to be dropped. The humor, nonetheless, serves to illustrate the considerations (and problems) that are attributable to punched card decks.

Programming with punched cards is traditional, and the activity follows a set format. A programmer creates program statements on a **coding sheet**, which is usually printed with separators for programming languages which must follow a rigid columnar structure. The collection of sheets become a **source document**, which is typically given to a keypunch operator to code onto the Hollerith cards. The collection of cards is a **source deck**. The keypunch operator may also be given instructions to punch the cards in a very specific manner, as with **left justification**, where all statements and data begin in column one, or to pad out the card with zeroes in a **zero fill** operation. This deck may be further **collated**, or sorted, if it contains data which must be read into the program in a specific order.

The source deck is fed into the computer's card reader and processed by a language **compiler** program. In turn, the computer's **card punch** outputs an **object deck**, which is fed back into the machine for **linking** with subroutines the computer may have available for specific computations. Upon execution, the computer's printer may output a **hard copy** printout, typically on the familiar green and white **greenbar paper** so often associated with data processing shops. The information imprinted on this paper may follow a rigid style or format, dictated by a **layout sheet** or **format sheet** which the programmer may have included with the coding sheets he/she has submitted.

Batch processing is still in use in the 1990s, although usually not with Hollerith cards as the input medium. Many computer systems still refer to the **logical reader** and the **logical punch** as input and output, where such I/O is actually from and to an on-disk text file. The days of rack upon rack of punched cards in the computer room are long past, as are the misfilings and tearings of the stiff paper card medium once so necessary for most computing operations. It is said that the origin of the term **bug**, which represents any malfunction in a computer program, is based on the actions of a rather healthy insect having crawled into a deck of Hollerith cards and wreaked havoc when the cards were passed through the reader. Such legends abound even though the concept of "computer science" is relatively new; a folk tradition is building.

Programming languages are categorized into a three-level hierarchy:

1. **Machine language**. The computer understands a repertoire of ones and zeroes.
2. **Assembly language**. This is a "bridge" between machine and natural language.
3. **Natural language**. Also called a "**high level language**," included here are the "name brands" such as COBOL, Pascal, and BASIC described below.

Computer programming in the 1990s takes on a look much different from that of the early days. Most programming is accomplished directly at a terminal keyboard, from source files on disk, and with a seemingly endless variety of languages from which to choose. The next sections will explore a few of those options.

## BASIC PROGRAMMING

When the breakthrough in "personal" computing occurred, there appeared immediately a need for a simple, universal computer language with which to write programs. As described in chapter 1, the first PCs were actually hobbyist computers, used primarily by experimenters and scientists. The low cost of these machines made them attractive to the general computing public. And this public didn't want to write programs in the manner with which the experimenters were content, i.e., by flipping binary switches or feeding the CPU rows and rows of base 2 numbers. The consumers and potential consumers wanted to communicate with PCs in plain English.

**BASIC**, or **b**eginners' **a**ll-purpose **s**ymbolic **c**ode (the "I" is stretching the acronym a bit!), fits the "plain English" criterion nicely. The language was created in such a manner that a user or programmer could "talk" to it; that is, anyone making an inquiry at the keyboard need only type a statement such as "PRINT 4 + 3" to obtain the immediate response of "7"; such a program is called an **interpreter**. A BASIC interpreter, then, is one of many examples of **interactive programs** (others mentioned in this book include dBase IV and MINITAB) which can provide the user with immediate feedback from keyboard entries. Heretofore it was necessary, in most cases, to imprint program statements on decks of punched cards or on paper tape, subsequently loading these media into the computer in batch fashion (refer to the previous discussion) and waiting for the answer. Interpreted BASIC gave the user a form of immediate gratification. The interpreter could handle longer, stored programs as well, or another format of basic, a **compiler**, could transform the BASIC language statements into **binary**, or **executable code**, resulting in .COM files or .EXE files that the computer could run even if the interpreter program were not in place in the computer's memory.

The IBM corporation jumped onto the bandwagon in 1981, and when the company introduced its IBM PC, a copy of interpreted BASIC was included with the hardware package—burned into a ROM chip inside the computer! IBM (and a number of other manufacturers) had decided that BASIC was going to be the predominate personal computer language of the 1980s and beyond, and, making it an internal feature of the hardware, made it immediately available to the user. In fact, with the earlier PCs, if the user didn't place a bootable floppy diskette in the A: drive immediately after powering up, BASIC would automatically be loaded, ready to run. The fact that IBM's BASIC was in **firmware**, i.e., wired into the computer's circuits instead of disk-based, caused some compatibility problems. Many software programs written by IBM in BASIC wouldn't run on other brands of PCs whose BASIC was loaded from disks and constructed of a slightly different syntax. For the first few years, there wasn't a consensus as to language standards, and variations such as Dartmouth BASIC, Benton Harbor BASIC and others, abounded. After a couple of years, IBM abandoned the idea of ROM-based BASIC and distributed the language on disks. It happened as well that BASIC found its niche as a teaching tool, having been surpassed by the more powerful Pascal and C languages (discussed in a later section) for high-level programming. BASIC is still in use, the predominate syntaxes today being GW-BASIC (for "gee whiz") and QBASIC.

CBASIC was introduced by Digital Research to run under the CP/M operating system as a **pseudocompiler**, much in the same manner as code generated with dBase IV's Developers' Edition. With such an arrangement, a **runtime module** must be in the same disk directory as the main program (or at least accessible to it). Such a program, when it makes **function calls**, such as SQRT(X) to compute the square root of a variable X, will search the runtime module to ascertain that the square root code is present; if so, the function executes and the proper number is (hopefully) returned. Programs written to access pseudocompiled languages usually execute faster than those run under interpreted languages, but there must always be a runtime module present for successful execution of pseudocompiled programs. For persons developing code for sale, there might be a royalty to pay each time a program is sold with a copy of a runtime module, unless the pseudocompiler is marked with "royalty free distribution" on the software license. The concept of a pseudocompiler has always been commonplace in mainframe environments, but not as typically in the PC arena; PC users demand stand-alone, executable (.EXE and .COM) files that are completely portable from one machine to another. Curiously, the OS/2 and Windows environments (chapters 6 and 7, respectively) have resurrected the idea of runtime modules for PCs with their **dynamic link libraries** (**DLL**s) necessary for the running of some OS/2- and Windows-specific code—and the concept comes around full circle!

BASIC can be used in libraries for applications that are not too involved with multiple processes, and the BASIC language is quite adept at organizing files on individual workstations and at public desks. The following example illustrates a short BASIC program used to maintain a new books list at a readers' services desk:

```
10 REM ELECTRONIC BOOK CATALOG
20 REM THIS PROGRAM WILL INPUT ANY NUMBER OF BOOKS
30 REM THIS SAMPLE CODE ACCEPTS A MAXIMUM OF 50 TITLES
35 '
40 OPTION BASE 1: REM DON'T WANT THE FIRST TITLE TO BE #0
50 DIM T$(50): REM AN ARRAY FOR 50 TITLES
60 INPUT "HOW MANY TITLES? "; N
70 FOR C = 1 TO N
80 LINE INPUT "TITLE OF BOOK—"; T$(C)
90 PRINT
100 NEXT C
110 PRINT
120 '
130 REM THIS PART OF PROGRAM RETRIEVES THE TITLES INPUT
135 REM IN THE TOP HALF OF THE CODE
140 INPUT "BOOK NUMBER? "; C
150 LPRINT
160 LPRINT "BOOK NUMBER "; C: "'IS"; T$(C)
170 PRINT
180 LINE INPUT "ANOTHER BOOK NUMBER <Y/N>? " R$
190 IF R$ = "Y" THEN GOTO 140
200 PRINT
```

210 LPRINT "RUN COMPLETED"
220 END

By typing "RUN" at the "ok" prompt, the user would see the following screen output of the BASIC Program:

ok
RUN
HOW MANY TITLES? 5 (number is input by user)

TITLE OF BOOK? GONE WITH THE WIND (also input by user)
(repeats 5 times)

.

.

BOOK NUMBER? 1 (number input by user)

BOOK NUMBER 1 IS GONE WITH THE WIND (output to printer)

ANOTHER BOOK NUMBER <Y/N>? N (input by user)

RUN COMPLETED

ok

In a practical situation, the preceding program would be split into two parts, one for data input and the other for data retrieval. The LPRINT statements could be changed to PRINT or "?" if output to a screen and not a printer were desired. Also, a user would probably not be expected to query by book number; the person writing the program would modify the code so that string (character) data were input at the input prompts.

The example shows principles of data file programming that can be used in BASIC for small applications. BASIC, however, is not well-suited for large databases because of the limits it places on the number of storable records and the relatively cumbersome manner in which it must be coded. File buffers must be set, decisions must be made of sequential vs. random file programming, and planning must be accurate so that the initial file structure does not have to be modified at later intervals.[1]

All computer programs are based on the principle of algorithm construction. An **algorithm** is a fixed, step-by-step procedure for accomplishing a given result, or, a defined process or set of rules that leads to and assures development of a desired output from a given input. Computer programming terminology is universal from language to language, and algorithmic principles that work with BASIC should work similarly with Pascal, C, Fortran, or with any of dozens of other languages. A recipe for chocolate cake is an algorithm, and if a baker is careful, a recipe should cook the same (more or less) from kitchen to kitchen. Before this section on BASIC ends, a discussion of a few of the fundamental constructs of the BASIC language that apply to the other languages described in this chapter is necessary. These constructs are the building blocks that allow the development of program algorithms, and, in turn, of complete programs. This list is not comprehensive, but it will serve as a "recognition level" summary of programmers' tools. The BASIC language consists of the following:

1. **Constants**. These can be alphabetic or numeric, as

    10                7.15                "Smith"

    Note that alphabetic constants in BASIC are **delimited** with quotation marks.

2. **Variables**. Similar to algebra, letters can represent changing numeric quantities, and, in BASIC, when appended to a dollar sign ("$") can signify **string** data, such as

    X          A2          X$          INTEREST          NAME$

    where X or A2 might = 2, 4, 6, etc., INTEREST might = .05, 075, etc., and X$ or NAME$ might = "Jones," "Ohio," or any other string (character) data.

3. **Operators**. As in arithmetic; +, -, / (divide), and * (multiply); also (depending on the program or dialect of BASIC), ^ or ** can mean exponentiation (e.g., 4 ^ 3 and 4 ** 3 both mean $4^3$). Additionally, the signs < (less than), > (greater than), = (equal to), <= (less than or equal to), >= (greater than or equal to), and <> (not equal to) are used in programming statements of comparison, both for mathematical expressions and string manipulations. Also, BASIC allows for the use of **logical operators** such as AND, OR, and NOT; a detailed discussion in the use of logical statements is given in chapter 17.

4. **Statements**. These are more accurately, verbs and separators and their accompanying targets. Every programming language has its own list of reserved words which includes action inducers and directors. In BASIC, such statements include PRINT, GOTO, READ, INPUT, and END. Because BASIC is somewhat self-documenting, the statement

    100 PRINT "My name is Mudd"

    will do exactly what you would expect—output "My name is Mudd" to the video screen.

Interpreted BASIC requires that each statement be preceded by line number. Compiled BASIC is a **top down language** where statements are executed (i.e., compiled) in the order in which they are written, with line numbers used only where forward and backward references are expected. A hybrid of both, CBASIC requires no line numbers except for GOTO and label references but allows line numbers if the original source code featured them.

5. **Remarks and comments**. A desired facility of any language is its ability to allow programmers to insert documentation sentences between sections of code. This is done in order that subsequent users of the source code be able to follow the logic of the original programmer. In BASIC, the remark operator is REM (or an apostrophe) and the statements

    100 REM This line of code does nothing
    200 '      This line doesn't do anything, either

are not compiled or executed. They do exactly what the REMarks say—nothing!

6. **Input.** It can be either numeric or alphabetic. BASIC distinguishes between the two, as do most languages, and the statements

    100 INPUT A_NUMBER:      REM typist inputs a number
    200 LINE INPUT A_NAME$:   REM typist inputs a name

accept a numeric quantity and a data string respectively.

7. **Output.** It can be directed to the screen, to a printer, or to any other peripheral device. The statements

    100 PRINT "This is an output test."
    200 LPRINT "This is another output test."

will direct the string "This is an output test." to the CRT and the string "This is another output test." to whatever printer is currently connected to the system. In BASIC, the "?" character can be used as a shorthand for PRINT, and line 100 could be written as

    100 ? "This is an output test."

to save a few seconds' typing time.

8. **Transfer directives**. The two types of transfers, or **jumps**, are unconditional and conditional. An **unconditional transfer directive** requires an immediate action, such as

    100 GOTO 200: REM This statement jumps to line 200

A **conditional transfer directive** requires a bit more setup effort. Such a directive allows a jump to another place in the program only when a certain condition or conditions are met. Conditional transfer directives take the forms

    IF . . . THEN
    IF . . . THEN . . . ELSE
    DO . . . WHILE

DO . . . UNTIL

FOR . . . NEXT

In BASIC, the IF . . . THEN . . . ELSE statement might be coded as

100 IF FLAG = 1 THEN GOTO 200 ELSE END

which simply means that, if some quantity FLAG is equal to 1, then proceed to line 200 and do whatever is in that statement; otherwise, terminate the program. The DO directives do not have a direct translation into BASIC, but the FOR ... NEXT statement is similar. It is presented like

100 FOR X = 1 to 100

110 PRINT X

120 NEXT X

which sets up a counter X initially to equal 1; the counter increments by 1 while looping from 100 to 110 to 120 and back, until the counter equals 101, at which time the statement following 120 is then executed.

9. **Functions**. Also called **function calls**, these constructs may be provided by the vendor (so-called "canned" features), or they may be created by the programmer. In the latter case, they are termed **user-defined functions**. BASIC has many functions common to other high level languages, and the following

100 LET X = 45

110 PRINT SIN(X)

120 PRINT TAN(X)

would, quite obviously, print to the screen the values of the SIN and TANgent of some angle X which, in this example, happens to equal 45.

One further application of BASIC as it applies to library situations is given in its entirety in Appendix A. Because of its length, it has been separated from the body of this chapter. Having gained a familiarity with the elements of BASIC, the reader should be able to identify (or modify!) most of the constructs in the résumé generator code that follows the narrative body of this text.

# FORTRAN

**FORTRAN** (**for**mula **tran**slation language) is an old standard used widely by members of the scientific community. Because of its ability to handle complex mathematical equations and return computations to many decimal places of accuracy, it is the language of choice in laboratories and organizations where heavy "number crunching" is performed. Unfortunately, FORTRAN has few applications in library settings because of its relative weakness in handling string (character) data. But it is important in light of its widespread use, and, for that reason, is included here for recognition purposes.

FORTRAN is not a difficult high level language to learn, and, for a person versed in basic computer logic and algorithms, about twenty to twenty-five hours of study would result in a reasonable fluency in the writing of FORTRAN code. FORTRAN is position specific; that is, it matters to the compiler in which column the lines of code are placed. For example, line numbers must be in columns 1 through 6. FORTRAN code is easy to document and comments or remarks are merely preceded with the letter "C." The following is a sample of FORTRAN code written to perform a simple inventory, followed by the output of a short run of the program:

```
        C A SAMPLE FORTRAN PROGRAM
        C THIS PROGRAM COMPUTES THE VALUE OF
        C AN INVENTORY

000001          KOUNT = 0
000002          TOTALV = 0.0

        C STATEMENTS 1 AND 2 SET UP AREAS FOR
        C ACCUMULATIONS

000003          WRITE(3,1)
000004        1 FORMAT(1H1, 15X,'INVENTORY STATUS,
                  XYZ CORPORATION., JANUARY, 1994')
000005          WRITE(3,2)
000006        2 FORMAT(1H0,15X,'INV.QUANTITY
        PRICE          VALUE          DATE DESCRIPTION')
000007        6 READ(1,3)INV,NQUAN,UPRICE,IDATE,D1,D2,D3
000008        3 FORMAT(13,12,F4.2,2,16,3A4)
000009          IF(INV-999)4,99,4
000010        4 KOUNT = KOUNT + 1

        C STATEMENT 10 WILL COUNT THE NUMBER OF
        C INVENTORY ITEMS

000011          QUAN = NQUAN

        C STATEMENT 11 CONVERTS AN INTEGER
        TO A DECIMAL

000012          VALUE = QUAN * UPRICE

        C STATEMENT 12 COMPUTES THE VALUE OF EACH
```

```
                 C INVENTORY ITEM
000013                WRITE(3,5)INV,NQUAN,UPRICE,VALUE,IDATE,
                         D1,D2,D3
000014                5 FORMAT(1H0,6X,14,7X,13,2X,F5.2,4X,F7.2,2X,
                         19,2X,3A4)
000015                   TOTALV = TOTALV + VALUE

                 C STATEMENT 15 ACCUMULATES THE TOTAL VALUE
                 C OF ALL INVENTORY ITEMS

000016                   GO TO 6
000017                99 WRITE(3,7)TOTALV,KOUNT
000018                7 FORMAT(1H0,' TOTAL INVENTORY VALUE'
                         F9,2,7X,'COUNT IS ',I12)

                 C STATEMENTS 17 AND 18 WILL CAUSE THE TOTAL
                 C VALUE OF INVENTORY AND ITEM COUNT TO
                 C BE PRINTED

000019                   CALL EXIT
000020                   END
```

The resulting printout reads as follows:

INVENTORY STATUS, XYZ CORPORATION, JANUARY 1994

| INV. | QUANTITY | PRICE | VALUE | DATE | DESCRIPTION |
|------|----------|-------|-------|------|-------------|
| 1 | 10 | 25.00 | 250.00 | 2/28/94 | METERS |
| 2 | 15 | 10.00 | 150.00 | 1/31/94 | SOCKETS |
| 3 | 25 | 20.00 | 500.00 | 2/15/94 | TRANSFORMERS |

TOTAL INVENTORY VALUE          900.00          COUNT IS 3

# COBOL

Grace Murray Hopper can perhaps be honored with the title "World's Second Programmer" (after Lady Augusta Ada Lovelace) for her invention of **COBOL** (**Co**mmon **B**usiness **O**riented **L**anguage). Admiral Hopper developed COBOL while serving in the U.S. Navy in World War II. Her philosophy of computer programming was, "Why start from scratch with every program you write?"

While Hopper's COBOL has undergone many revisions and is much expanded from the original version introduced almost half a century ago, it has remained a standard for authors of accounting, database, financial, and report generating code in many countries. It is used also to teach file structures in advanced programming classes in colleges and universities.

A significant feature of COBOL is that it is **self-documenting**. COBOL is written in English sentences, using easily recognizable verbs and operators, and the language allows the programmer to define variables which state exactly what their quantities represent. In other words, variables like TRIAL-BALANCE and TOTAL-PARTS-ORDERED can be used for mathematical computations in COBOL programs.

COBOL is not a difficult language to learn, but it is extensive. Depending on the release, COBOL exhibits a repertoire of nearly 300 **reserved words**, i.e., vocabulary elements that must be coded exactly and cannot be employed as user-defined variables, along with a host of subtleties in the language. To take advantage of the self-documenting feature, a COBOL programmer must write syntactically precise code (with periods, commas, modifiers, etc.) in exact locations. A subroutine in the procedure division to write sales reports might appear as follows:

```
00100     OUTPUT-FILE-LISTING.
00110     MOVE NAME TO NAME-OUT.
00120     MOVE SALES-AMT TO SALES-OUT.
00130     MOVE COMMISSION TO COMM-OUT.
00140     WRITE REPORT-LINE FROM DETAIL-LINE
          AFTER ADVANCING 2 LINES.
00150     READ SALES-FILE
00160     AT END MOVE 'YES' TO CARDS-AT-END.
```

COBOL and other high-level languages championed the idea of **structured programming**, or, as it is sometimes called, **top down programming**. In such a format, the main body of the code, i.e., the logic area, appears at the beginning of the program. Everything else in the program is coded as subroutines, and the main body executes the program functions by making repeated calls to the subroutine structures. It is a clean, orderly way of writing code and lends itself to easy comprehension by persons who would perform **patch programming**, also known as **maintenance programming**—updates, enhancements, and fixes to the original source code of any program. A newer trend in the writing of program code is to use **object oriented programming** (**OOP**) techniques, in which functions and routines are written as objects, with rules, syntax, and parameters making those routines callable by other programs.

COBOL is usually transformed into a usable program through a compiler. A **compiler** is a software program that takes properly written COBOL (or any appropriate language) statements and transforms them into **object code**. Object code is then link-edited with one or more libraries of function routines and output in a final form, an executable program file. The resultant program might be able to run by itself, as a **stand-alone program**, or it may require the presence of a runtime module. Runtime modules, as introduced above, are files of routines that are called by an executable program but for some reason (usually space considerations) were not permanently linked with the object code at compile time. There is little difference in terms of efficiency or speed of execution, and stand-alone programs and those with accompanying runtime modules are often found side by side, residing on the same computer system. COBOL and other languages are said to be **portable** if generic language code can be compiled on a number of different computers with no alteration of the original source program. As such, COBOL is given the attribute of being **multiplatformed** because its resultant executable files can operate under a variety of operating systems.

## PASCAL AND THE C PROGRAMMING LANGUAGE

Pascal and C are lumped together because of their similarities of purpose. These languages are the best known of a group of so-called **pointer-based languages**. The name is derived from the abilities of such languages to manipulate or point to specific addresses in the computer's memory to process and store data.

Of the two, Pascal is the older, although C is the more widely used. In fact, it has been estimated that over 75 percent of all microcomputer programs are written in the C language. Pascal was named for the French mathematician Blaise Pascal and has very little to do with his computational techniques. C was just the logical growth of the B language and not named for anybody. C was the invention of Bell Laboratories engineers Brian Kernighan and Dennis Ritchie who needed a specialty compiler for some in-house processes. The language was published[2]; the rest of the programming world liked what it saw and the power of this new code, and the rest is computing history.

Pascal and C are important to libraries for two reasons: there is a large body of literature in print on these languages, and many colleges and universities use one or the other as the language of choice in teaching computer science algorithms and concepts. There is also a considerable amount of function libraries which feature callable code for C language and Pascal. A notable example is dBASE TOOLS FOR C,[3] a code library which allows dBase III+ programs to incorporate routines for finance, statistics, and various mathematical processes not included in the standard dBase interpreter program. Below is a sample Pascal Program:

```
PROGRAM Averages (Input, Output);
(* The following program reads 50 numbers from an *)
(* input file and prints their average to an *)
(* output file.        *)
```

```
VAR    Num,(* placeholder for number read *)
       Total,(* accumulator for numbers read *)
       Average : Real;(* calculated average *)
       Counter : Integer; (* the FOR loop index *)
BEGIN
       Total := 0.0;
       FOR Counter := 1 to 50 DO BEGIN
              Read (Input, Num);
              Total := Total + Num;
       END;
       Average := Total / 50.0;
       Writeln (Output, 'The average of 50 numbers is', Average);
END.
```

Just for a brief comparison of several of the languages above, the following code segments would increment a counter within a larger program. Note the syntactical differences; each piece of code is handling exactly the same computation.

| | |
|---|---|
| **Machine language**: | 58 40 D7 F8 |
| | 41404001 |
| | 50 40 D7 F8 |
| **Assembly language**: | L    4,ECOUNT |
| | LA    4,1(4) |
| | ST    4,ECOUNT |
| **BASIC**: | CT% = CT% + 1 |
| **FORTRAN**: | ECOUNT = ECOUNT + 1 |
| **COBOL**: | ADD 1 TO EMPLOYEE-COUNT. |
| **C language**: | ecount += ecount |
| **Pascal**: | Ecount := Ecount + 1; |

Remember that the machine and assembly language statements would differ depending on which machine they were run. The remainder, however, are considered portable and would change little, if any, if run on a variety of computers.

There are literally hundreds of computer languages which are, or have been, in common use. Many of the names are not household words because of their exclusivity or limited applications, and many are defunct. Ada (used by U.S. federal agencies) and WATBOL are still around; SNOBOL and PL/1 (programming language 1) have more or less fallen by the wayside. Some, such as RPG (report program generator), a popular high level language for output oriented business programs, do not categorize well. There is a saying among programmers that "the most popular language is the one in which I'm writing all my code." Whatever the case, a well-stocked technical library will want to have a representative selection of the "popular" languages in its service area. The final determination of "popularity" is left to the discretion of the book selection committee.

## NOTES

1. Finkel, LeRoy and Jerald R. Brown. *Data File Programming in BASIC: A Self-Teaching Guide.* 338 pp.
2. Kernigan, Brian and Dennis M. Ritchie. *The C Programming Language.* Second edition, 288 pp.
3. dBASE TOOLS FOR C, published by J.T. Cooper & Company for Ashton-Tate Publishing Group (now Borland Corporation), 20101 Hamilton Avenue, Torrance, CA 90502-1319. $39.95.

# Chapter 9

# Desktop Publishing and Optical Character Recognition

After the personal computer was introduced in the early 1980s, the technology "settled in" to a routine of improving and enhancing the basic PCs and Macintosh computers. The focal points were on both the hardware and software. On the hardware side, "faster and more sophisticated" was the order of the day, in which CPUs with larger and larger instruction sets were developed. Software sometimes had to play catch-up with the microcircuits which appeared, it seemed, as new models almost daily. A considerable amount of research and development was lavished on the appearance of the video screen, and, subsequently, on the applications programs that could take advantage of the higher resolutions and expanded color variations of the displays. A significant result of technological developments was desktop publishing software.

Until the advent of personal (read desktop) computers, professional typesetting was just that—the domain of professionals with elaborate, expensive equipment that required a considerable amount of special training to operate. Moreover, desktop publishing was never developed for mainframe, or even minicomputer environments; the cost would have been just too prohibitive. Even microcomputers had to wait for the right moment; desktop publishing, because of the amount of computations and recordkeeping involved in managing a document, requires a relatively powerful and speedy processor to support the activity. The breakthrough is rightly attributable to the Macintosh computer, because Apple's entry in the desktop computing market was already graphics oriented. The IBM sector did not lag behind, however, and the 80286-based

AT-class personal computer provided the speed and sophistication needed for desktop publishing activities.

Thus, the stage was set in the mid-1980s for a launching of desktop publishing software. There were two flagship entries at the time—Aldus PageMaker and Xerox Ventura Publisher (both described later in this chapter)—which offered utilities and facilities for document creation where word processors left off. This code for **desktop publishing**, or **DTP**, placed on a workstation, gave a user the ability to create publications on a PC which, while being edited and manipulated, appeared on the screen in a format nearly identical to the final copy which would be output to the printer. With some practice, persons who theretofore knew only basic editing through word processors could become semiprofessional typesetters. And, as a bonus, those users could include pictures and graphics images in a considerable range of newsletters, publicity fliers, handbooks, posters, and even books. Even the smallest libraries could create in-house the forms and publications they needed, instead of having to rely on commercial artists or printing houses—and the finished products could usually be had in a day or so rather than weeks into the future!

Before the intricacies of desktop publishin are discussed, it is important to understand the advances in technology that made the activity possible. The spotlight will be on the video display, the computer screen, for an understanding of what makes computer reproduction of a document so faithful with desktop publishing software.

## CRT PHYSICS

In chapter 3, we introduced the notion of using the computer's screen (the cathode ray tube, or CRT) as a video display for a variety of outputs to support various word processors. The screen is of particular importance in desktop publishing because the desired effect is a **WYSIWYG** (what you see is what you get) representation of the final document. The output is of such significance that a detailed summary of video options will be given before the intricacies of desktop publishing are discussed.

Bluntly stated, desktop publishing on a PC could have never been possible if video technology had not advanced rapidly through the early 1980s. It was already mentioned in the previous chapter that CRTs attached to computers of the 1950s through 1970s were primarily text based. Graphics, if any were included in text documents, were simple and primitive. When IBM introduced the IBM PC in 1981, the accompanying monitor was of **monochrome** design—usually with either white, green or yellow **phosphors** to illuminate the screen—and was still text based! A few months thereafter, a "color" monitor was introduced and given the nomenclature **CGA** for **color graphics adapter**. By today's standards, this display was considered to be of **low resolution**; the CGA monitor was capable of displaying eight colors (but only four at any one time) and could do so in a 320 pixel by 200 pixel (horizontal X vertical) format. CGA offered a limited color **palette**, but it was significant for the trend it would launch over the next ten years. CGA was the first of the so-called **RGB** (red/green/blue, for the colors of the electron guns in the tube) monitors, an acronym which Apple Computer still retains to describe its line of monitors for its Macintosh computers.

The demands of end users dictated that **high resolution** monitors were needed for more precise handling of visual data. The next development was the **EGA** (**extended graphics adapter**) monitor which offered a palette of 256 colors (depending on the model), with either 16 or 64 colors displayable simultaneously. EGA runs at 640 pixels by 350 pixels, effectively doubling the resolution (sharpness) of a CGA display. The next development was in **VGA** (**video graphics adapter**) monitors, which display 640 pixels by 480 pixels, and **super VGA** monitors, which display 800 pixels by 600 pixels. The next high standard is the so-called **8514/A graphics adapter**, which displays 1,024 pixels by 768 pixels from a palette of over one million colors. Present-day monitors can produce resolutions of as much as 1,280 by 1,024 pixels. Desktop publishing programs require a minimum of an EGA monitor for visual clarity, and a VGA or better resolution is preferred. The monitors at the very top of the line are typically used to run **computer aided design** (**CAD**) programs such as AutoCad, where extreme precision is required and on-screen measurements must be to exact scale. There are other video circuits such as **HGA** (**Hercules graphics adapter**) and **PGA** (**professional graphics adapter**) which are seen in many shops; however, because CGA, EGA, VGA and 8514/A are more or less the de factor standards, attention will focus on those models.

Libraries that are engaging in desktop publishing on a serious basis will need to realize that the software, because it is relatively complex, requires an extended (read "more expensive") PC or Macintosh setup and a knowledge of hardware slightly beyond the basics. For example, there is a significant gap between EGA and VGA/ 8514/A technology. EGA (and CGA) presents its displays via a **TTL** (**transistor/transistor logic**) circuitry; in other words, in a digital fashion where red is exactly red, green is exactly green, etc. VGA and 8514/A displays, on the other hand, use **analog** circuits; in the same manner as adjusting the level of the lights in your home using a rheostat (dial), analog displays allow for varying electrical levels to display light red, medium red, bright red, and so forth.

When PCs and Macintosh computers were first introduced, video graphics weren't an issue—monitors and displays were offered in only one or two configurations. Since the mid-1980s, the number of choices has increased considerably, and a consumer must shop with particular configurations in mind. The desired resolution, screen size, the choice of monochrome or color screens, the number of displayable colors, format, and intended software applications must all be taken into consideration. Along with configuring the PC itself, searching for the "right" video combination is much like shopping for a stereophonic sound system. You need to know what you want the CRT output to look like, and, as such, need to be armed with the appropriate information to make your choices work in harmony.

As important as selecting a video monitor is the choice of a **video card**. This is the circuit board that fits into an open buss slot in the PC or Mac and channels the video signals from the software onto the screen. Many desktop computers have the video card built into the motherboard. This is advantageous inasmuch as it makes the circuitry simpler and less expensive, but it makes upgrading the machine a bit more difficult. In most PCs and higher-end Macintoshes, video cards are separate devices and can be geared to a particular series of monitors. Typically, a video card will have its own on-board memory (**VRAM**, or **video RAM**), usually in increments of 256 kilobytes up to one megabyte or more. The purpose for this separate and larger amount of memory is for the computer to be able to display a larger palette of colors, with many more colors available simultaneously on the screen. Older PCs used a share of the computer's memory (*cf.* the memory map in chapter 6) to display images and colors, but, since screen displays typically use considerably more memory than programs or text, it became obvious that the video display should have its own RAM. As memory chip prices fell, the purchase of high-memory video cards became less demanding on the budget; hence, PCs of the 1990s are usually capable of displaying highly sophisticated graphics images.

Most of the Macintosh computers above the entry-level classics have sufficient video capabilities built in to drive a medium resolution RGB (color) monitor. Macintoshes with NuBuss slots allow the addition of more sophisticated video cards, in order that higher resolution and third-party monitors can be used for special applications. Most video cards for the IBM and compatible computers are built of the eight-bit or sixteen-bit varieties or for the Microchannel architecture, targeted for PC/XT or AT busses or for the IBM PS/2 busses respectively. The "wider" the card (one constructed for sixteen-bit slots as opposed to eight-bit slots), the faster it will run. In other words, "faster" determines the relative speed with which the screen can be redrawn from video memory. Also on the market are the so-called Windows enhancers, special video cards designed to work specifically with the Microsoft Windows interface platform, for greater input/output efficiency. Video cards can also be configured to work in a multisync mode, i.e., with a variety of monitors which have dissimilar electrical characteristics. Most video cards are also shipped with special device driver software written to enhance their performances with certain popular video-intensive programs. An example of the aforementioned is the add-on video driver which is supplied by various manufacturers to allow Ventura Publisher and Aldus PageMaker to access the capabilities of **full-page monitors**. The latter have a vertical rather than horizontal orientation and feature a greater number of scan lines arranged in such a manner that, as the name implies, the user of a desktop publishing program can view an entire page of text and graphics in actual size.

## DESKTOP PUBLISHING SOFTWARE

There have been a number of desktop publishing programs created in the past five to seven years to access the capabilities of the PC and Macintosh computers. Some are relatively primitive and feature their own self-contained repertoire of graphics, template formats, and typefaces. These programs usually do not interact with other popular software and will not be reviewed here. Two programs are outstanding,[1] and, because they are available for both the IBM PC and compatibles, as well as for the Macintosh, they will be detailed here as all-inclusive of a "wish list" of features desirable in a high-end desktop publishing program environment.

Ventura Publisher[2] first appeared as Xerox Ventura and was targeted initially at the IBM PC and clones. As of this writing, it is sold as version 2.0 for the Macintosh and as version 4.2 for the IBM and compatibles, the latter exclusively a Windows program. IBM Version 3.0 was available for both the DOS (in the so-called GEM Gold Edition) and OS/2 operating systems, as well as for Windows. In fact, Ventura's own literature proclaimed that, for a time, version 3.0 was more popular than the newly issued version 4.0. The newer version, however, took advantage of some advanced technology, including Pantone color separations and the accession of TrueType fonts (discussed later), and version 4.0 established its own following.

Aldus PageMaker[3] initially was issued for the Macintosh. While it is available also for the IBM and compatibles (it is currently version 6.0 on both Mac and IBM platforms), its roots in the Mac GUI are still very evident. PageMaker approaches desktop published documents from the point of view of a composer's storyboard, emphasizing the cut-and-paste methodology of page layouts. While both PageMaker and Ventura handle graphics and long documents with relative ease, PageMaker seems to have the edge with graphics, while Ventura is particularly suited for book-length documents. For example, PageMaker allows text to flow around irregularly shaped objects with but a few keystrokes; Ventura, on the other hand, requires a somewhat elaborate overlay of multiple, empty frames to sculpt the text flow as desired. However, both products are extremely sophisticated, and, in fact, have many more features than the average library will require. The dozens of tools that both PageMaker and Ventura provide allow publication quality, camera-ready copy for nearly any kind of brochure or report needed to carry out a library's goals and objectives for public relations and print communication.

Somewhat newer on the scene, but noteworthy, is FrameMaker.[4] This program migrated from a Sun workstation platform, and its page layout format somewhat resembles that of Ventura. FrameMaker is an attempt at cross-platform compatibility, and its strong point is its ability to handle long documents and multiples of long documents simultaneously. As the name implies, FrameMaker uses a collection of frames to handle text and graphics rather than allowing data to float freely throughout a document. The program runs under Windows and, as such, gives access to all the utilities provided by the Windows GUI. A significant feature of FrameMaker is its built-in drawing program which is more elaborate than either that of Ventura or PageMaker. With the latter two, a separate graphics editing package such as PC Paintbrush is required to create original artwork; with FrameMaker, the art can typically be created without leaving the DTP worksheet. The advantage of this all-in-one setup is that users need only learn one program as opposed to several, and tasks for creating published documents do not become separate or parceled.

## SPECIAL EFFECTS

Desktop publishing software has to be more fully featured than word processing software, otherwise, you probably wouldn't buy a DTP program just for the sake of owning another sophisticated editor. All the high-end DTP packages will allow some rather intricate manipulation of words and graphics, and it is these features that make desktop publishing software stand out.

The first PC- and Macintosh-based word processing software programs were line-oriented, as were CRT screens. That is, word processors, as described in chapter 3, were highly sophisticated manipulators of text. However, their manipulations were confined to the moving of characters, lines and paragraphs. Activities such as block move, block copy, cut and paste, and insert/delete words simply moved the chosen text around the document being edited. Word processors did not do anything to alter the appearance of text thus manipulated. Alternate typefaces, multiple sizes of text on the same page, ruling lines, background shading, and mixed graphics and characters on the same line were achievable only at a typesetter's shop. What this usually meant was that a person wishing to publish a document or book with special effects such as those just described would have to create two documents—one with text and the other with "pictures" or graphics of the special effects desired—and either hand-finish the meld of text and graphics or take the two sections to a professional artist or composer to complete the job.

The first convention of desktop publishing software that a new user notices as a radical departure from conventional hard copy printouts is the DTP program's ability to manipulate type **fonts**. Most desktop publishing programs ship with at least two fonts, variously called Times-Roman and Helvetica, to give a user a sample of one **serifed** and one **sans serifed** typeface to get started with creating publications. This is an example of a serifed font and **this is the same font in boldface** *and in italic.* This is an example of a sans serifed font, **again in bold** *and once more in italic.* Simply defined, serifed fonts are more fanciful and decorative and sans serifed fonts are plain, as the term translates, "without serifs." Another attribute of fonts which is supported nicely by desktop publishing is the feature of allowing either monospaced letters or proportionally spaced letters. Notice that, in the word "monospaced," each letter takes up an equal amount of space, whether it is a wide "m" or a narrow "l." This is desirable, for example, in financial statements and on spreadsheet printouts where columns of text and numbers must align precisely. On the other hand, the proportionally spaced letters give a pleasing, artistic effect desirable in formal documents. Desktop publishing programs provide **kerning tables** where the proper spacing of letters can be controlled mathematically. There are literally thousands of fonts available for desktop publishing, and the choicemaking is more an artistic than a technical issue; the selection of a typeface is more a matter of taste and the agreement between the designer and staff artist, if your library has one.

Desktop publishing programs and the accompanying laser or dot matrix printers originally required the use of **bitmapped fonts**. This technology created documents on a printer using patterns of dots much in the same manner as in the printing of newspaper pictures. Unfortunately, bitmapped fonts require a considerable amount of storage space on a hard disk drive. It is necessary to have a **soft font**, a file describing the typeface's bitmappings on disk, requiring anywhere from ten kilobytes of space or more, for each size and style of every font to be used. The two example sentences in the previous paragraph would require six soft fonts, one each for regular, bold and italic impressions, for both the serifed and sans serifed examples, if bitmapped fonts were being used. There are programs available which create fonts "on the fly" and place them on disk only as long as they are needed for a specific document project. Such a program is Glyphix,[5] which uses a font generator as a renewable resource, allowing a user to erase very large fonts after each use, freeing valuable hard drive space from the clutter of multiple font files.

Several methods of font management have been devised. As previously mentioned, bitmapped font files can be purchased in ready-made sets, as soft font files, and they are also available as **font cartridges** for selected printers. Cartridges store bitmap information in ROM circuits inside a plastic enclosure which fits into an expansion slot in many printers. Such an accessory negates the necessity of storing font information outside the printer, and, since the fonts are burned into printer ROMs as program files, they require no storage space on a computer's hard disk drive. Another way of eliminating the need for soft fonts is to purchase a printer with PostScript capabilities. **PostScript** is a printer language that is usually contained in a circuit inside the printer which, in addition to describing graphics images to printer output devices, contains the information necessary to output 35 different font styles in a variety of shapes and sizes. Fonts thus created are termed **scalable**, from the attribute that the style of the typeface is stored as a geometric description of each individual letter rather than as bitmapped images. Since geometric figures are mathematical models, PostScript fonts can be made smaller or larger merely by programming the desktop publishing software to alter the size multipliers for any given typeface. For older printers, cartridges of scalable images similar in construction to bitmapped type cartridges are available to upgrade printer capabilities to PostScript; the cost is in the $200-$400 range, depending on the brand of printer to be upgraded.

Font technology for computer-based processes has evolved at a rapid rate. Introduced on the Macintosh, and later on the PC in the Windows environment, is the **TrueType** technology.[6] TrueType font technology does not replace the PostScript method of typeface rendition; rather, the two font description techniques merely allow the end user alternatives. Because the TrueType system works under Windows, programs that access the Windows graphics user interface should also have access to a complete, installed repertoire of TrueType faces. TrueType font files must reside on the hard disk drive, as must bitmapped fonts; however, because TrueType files are scalable, only a descriptor file need be installed. All sizes of type derived from a TrueType file are realized, in a manner similar to PostScript rendering, as simply multiples of the outlines placed in the TrueType descriptor file. This results in a considerable savings of disk space, and, because TrueType descriptor files can be used by Windows to create screen fonts as well as printer fonts, separate screen font files are not required by most applications programs. Collections of 250 to 500 TrueType faces are available from several vendors, and many TrueType faces are appearing in the public domain. And, with the use of a simple translator program, TrueType fonts originating on the Macintosh can be ported to IBM and compatible computers.

The newer desktop publishing software programs, as well as some of the high-end word processors, eliminate the need for separation of text and special effects by making available a considerable repertoire of graphics and typographic manipulators that nest right in the midst of standard text copy. Consider, for example, the simple task of publishing a mathematics test that contains anything other than the elementary "+," "-," "*" (for multiplication), and "/" (for "divide") operators. A teacher wanting to adhere closely to the format in an elementary school arithmetic book might prefer to use "÷" so that division is clearly intended. Even on a first-year algebra examination, a teacher might want to represent the "power" formula, as $4^3$ to represent "four times four times four." A teacher with only a typewriter as an input tool for creating a test paper would have to manually roll forward the platen to type the "3" as a superscripted character, and an instructor with only a low-end word processor would have to enter the superscripted "3" by hand. Most word processors, however, will allow the emplacement of an **attribute byte** before and after the "3," making the equation appear in a manner similar to 4^T3^T (as in WordStar; the keystroke sequence is "Ctrl-P," "T," "3," "Ctrl-P," "T"), where the ^Ts are a signal to the word processor to instruct the printer (if it is capable) to print the "3" slightly above the baseline. However, in advanced mathematics, it is desirable to print more complex equations and formulas, and what follows is not possible from a keyboard alone:

$$\int_0^\infty x^2 \tan\theta \, dx$$

This formula was created "on the fly" in WordPerfect, at the same time the text for this chapter was being typed. WordPerfect for Windows, in fact, has an extensive dialog box which allows the author of an equation to pick from a list of functions, operators, mathematical symbols, Greek letters, and line draw symbols to create any formula desired. The "equation palette" is, in fact, an editor within an editor. As do Ventura Publisher desktop publishing software and as do several other word processing programs, WordPerfect outputs the formula as a bitmapped graphic. That is, what is actually seen on the computer screen and what is output to the printer are not actual printed type but pictorial representations of it. Aldus PageMaker does not currently support an equation maker, but

Ventura Publisher can also handle complex equations similar to the one above. With Ventura, the creator of an equation needs only to select the insertion point with the I-bar editor and invoke the equation tool with the mouse pointer. The equation tool guides the author through the creation process in a manner similar to that of WordPerfect for Windows.

Other typographic variations are easily accomplished with desktop publishing software. **Drop caps** are another example. At the beginnings of chapters, for example, a fanciful way to begin initial paragraphs is with a large, multiline capital letter. The letter can be ornamental or plain and can appear in a manner similar to the following:

> This paragraph has a large "T" as a drop cap. It is printed in this manner to get the reader's attention by varying the type-style. Chapter beginnings often use this convention for visual attractiveness. The capital letter need not be the same typestyle as the body of the paragraph.

Table construction is another feature of desktop publishing software. Both PageMaker and Ventura allow the creation of tables for publication; PageMaker accomplishes the task via a separately run utility program, and Ventura allows the creation of tables, in-line with other text, during the running of the main program. The following table was created with Ventura's table tool facility:

The table in Figure 9.1 exhibits some features that are difficult, if not impossible, to create with a regular word processor. Ventura allows you

| A line of text in a gray-shaded box | A different typeface in this box | This text is rotated ninety degrees | This text is inverted |
|---|---|---|---|
| Another line of text | 20 | Darker shading | 40 |
| Still another line | 30 | 30 | 50 |
| No background shading | 100 | 200 | 300 |

**Figure 9.1** Table created with Ventura Publisher

to decide how thick the ruling lines separating boxes are to be and whether the lines are single- or double-barred (using single lines for box separators and double lines for the table frame). Additionally, text within the boxes can be formatted as any other text, with choices of alignments and fonts. If your printer is capable of such output, Ventura tables will allow 90º, 180º and 270º rotations of box text. There are many degrees of background shading possible; if the preceding illustration were in color, the shaded boxes would appear in red and yellow instead of shades of gray. Other combinations are possible, making the table tool a powerful presentation feature for your publications.

## AUTOMATIC REFERENCING AND ADVANCED EDITING TECHNIQUES

While desktop publishing software is generally regarded as a tool for creating varied appearances for finished documents, most high-end DTP programs have toolboxes that allow for sophisticated manipulation of the *contents* of a document to be published. Such techniques are valuable timesavers, particularly for managing long documents and book-length manuscripts. In fact, a combination of advanced referencing techniques from several software packages was used in the preparation of this book. Such functions are usually invoked from the master document tool or publication manager (the name will vary with the brand of software), and these techniques eliminate much of the pencil-and-paper bookkeeping and notetaking, with the inherent chance of error, associated with projects of booklength magnitude.

For readers in the "fortysomething" (and even "thirtysomething") age groups, there is a vivid memory of the many nights spent at our typewriters preparing term papers and theses with the meticulously aligned and bibliographically correct footnotes and endnotes. The precise amounts of space to be left at the end of each page for the various two-line, three-line, etc., notes had to be "eyeballed" with the intention of leaving a precise one inch of space at the end of the pages. The penalty for guesstimating margins incorrectly was the necessity of retyping entire pages. The services of a skilled typist or of a typesetter for publication grade documents were often necessary, and the process could be slow and tedious, if not expensive.

A desktop publishing program, and, in fact, most of the high-end word processing programs, take advantage of the basic function of a PC to keep track of the spacing and placements of footnotes and endnotes: a DTP program *computes* the space necessary for keeping the margins and spacings uniform throughout a document. Whenever a writer makes an addition or deletion in a document, Ventura and PageMaker and most of the other DTP programs recalculate the positions of notes on each page throughout the document and make appropriate adjustments before the final printout. In fact, these programs allow for treating footnotes and endnotes as separate entities, for which unique typefaces, type sizes, appearances and positionings can be independently attributed. The enumerations of endnotes and footnotes can be controlled as well, and footnotes can be numbered consecutively throughout the paper, or the numbers can restart anew with each chapter of the document. The process is rather like keeping a separate catalog of notes, which can be edited and merged with the base document as necessary.

Other referencing tasks can be automated. Through the process of **tagging** paragraphs and headings within the document, tables of contents can be automatically generated. Once the TOC function is invoked, the desktop publishing software examines the entire publication for lines with TOC tags, usually at chapter beginnings or at major section breaks, such tags having been defined by the author. The tagged lines are extracted from the body of the text and duplicated in a generated file variously called "TOC" or "Table," which then becomes part of the publication and is editable with a word processor. Some programs apply the same technique in creating tables of authority lists or simply "general lists," in which recapitulations of figures, captions, and graphics labels can be printed separately if desired as part of the final draft of a publication.

A very powerful tool within desktop publishing software is the ability of such programs to generate indexes and cross references. The process used to index this book was already described briefly in chapter 3. The index functions of DTP programs can search an entire document in minutes and prepare lists of terms, with appropriate page references, alphabetized and formatted with subheadings (e.g., using both "movies" and "movies, silent" next to one another) if desired. Some programs (WordPerfect for Windows, for example) allow the use of **concordance** files as an authority to search documents for indexable terms. Typically, desktop publishing programs will allow text to be imbedded with tags, as described above in the creation of tables of contents, for which index subprograms scan the targeted text and generate the table of contents from the collection of tags they locate. An index file is thus created which can also be edited and formatted in the usual manner of any word processor file.

Through a similar tagging process, "see" and "see also" cross references can be generated. The advantage in allowing a desktop publishing program to manage the cross references in a document is that the "see page xx" entries change to reflect the appropriate page references whenever text is inserted or deleted anywhere within the master document. In a manual referencing project, in the presence of many cross references, it is easy to miss one or more pagination changes if the text is changed frequently or significantly. Using the lookup power of the computer, the DTP software can manage these changes, leaving the author more time to concentrate on the contents of the document rather than on the mechanics.

## OTHER HARDWARE FOR DESKTOP PUBLISHING: ALTERNATIVE INPUT SOURCES

Desktop-published documents typically carry a varied mixture of text and graphics objects. Both types of files originate from many sources—text can be created with numerous word processors and can exhibit a considerable number of formats, most of which are proprietary to the particular word processor from which they were generated. In fact, unless a text file was saved in pure ASCII format, with no special characters other than the carriage returns (<CR>) and line feeds (<LF>) embedded among the alphanumeric characters, the resultant .WP (WordPerfect), .WS (WordStar), .DOC (Microsoft Word), and .WRI (Windows Write) files must be translated or **filtered** by a DTP program in order to be usable. In other words, any particular desktop publishing program must be capable of handling a variety of word-processed formats, and usually from several different sources within one desktop-published document, in order to be of value as a timesaver and effective computerized publications manager to the institution that would rely on its capabilities to create a variety of professional quality publications.

Graphics objects such as line drawings, charts, grey scale art, and **screen dumps** (mirror images of video display contents) are output in formats which are even less standard than text files. For PCs and Macintosh computers, the most common graphics file formats are those generated from programs such as PC Paintbrush, HP Paintbrush, GEM Draw, MacPaint, Windows Paintbrush, and Aldus Persuasion which allow users to draw freehand pictures. These programs output graphics objects with the extensions .PCX, .IMG, .GEM, .EPS, .BMP, and others. Most desktop publishing software will handle at least two or more of these "standard" file formats. In terms of output, a reader of a document output from a desktop publishing program through a good quality laser printer will see little difference in publication quality, provided that the creator has used the drawing program and DTP package to best capability. For output to a file targeted for typesetting by a professional printer, the .EPS **(encapsulated PostScript)** format is generally preferred and may, in many cases, exhibit a higher print quality than graphics output from one of the other formats in the preceding list.

For those persons who cannot draw or who need a very high quality of graphics output, there are computer peripherals which make the task of creating pictures and graphics more manageable. Digital **scanners** are available from a number of manufacturers, and such devices make the task of inputting graphics as easy as photocopying a printed page; in fact, the process of scanning is nearly identical to that of making a Xerox copy. Scanners are manufactured in several configurations, the **flatbed** and **hand scanners** being the most popular. A typical scanner is pictured in Figure 9.2.

Books of scannable clip art are widely available,[7] and some clip art is available on floppy disks in the more popular file formats such as .PCX,

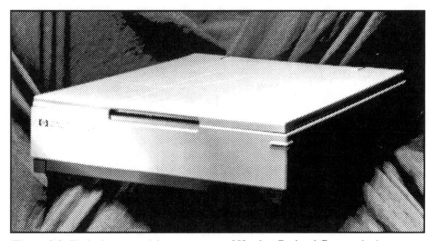

**Figure 9.2**  Flatbed scanner (photo courtesy of Hewlett-Packard Corporation)

.MSP, and .GEM.[8] Once scanned, clip art can be imported into drawing applications such as PC Paintbrush and HP Paintbrush for editing, enhancement, and colorizing. Many sources indicate that the drawings are royalty-free and may be included in an institution's published documents without additional permissions. On the next pages are some examples of book-based clip art available for use in desktop publications (see Figures 9.3, 9.4, and 9.5).

A number of peripheral devices have appeared on the market in the past few years which supplement scanners as graphics input devices. One popular device is the **frame grabber**, a circuit board which fits into an open buss slot in a computer and accepts television-based images for conversion into .TIF or .PCX graphics files. The process is similar to that used in boutiques in shopping malls where a person's photograph is converted into an ink screen for placement onto the front of a T-shirt. Where installed, a frame grabber is connected via a coaxial cable to a video camera (camcorder), a video cassette recorder (VCR),

**Figure 9.3** Clip art

or directly into a television antenna feed such as a commercial cable box. When the desired image is seen on the television screen, or, in some cases, directly on the computer screen, a combination of "hot keys" are pressed on the computer keyboard and the image is stored on the computer's hard disk drive. The image(s) can later be imported into a drawing program such as PC Paintbrush for editing and refinements.

A recent development that creates photographic .TIF and .PCX files is the **digital camera**. This device is approximately the size and format of a standard 35mm camera, except that, in place of film, the device is "loaded" with memory chips. The digital camera is used in the same manner as any still camera, with regards to the usual considerations of exposure and composition. Logitech, Dycam, and Apple Computer all manufacture models in the $600-$1,100 range (depending on configuration and accessories) which take from twenty-four to 100 pictures per session. Digital images are downloaded into a PC via the computer's serial or RS-232C I/O port and manipulated in a manner similar to those files obtained from any other graphics image source. Gray scale pictures are thus usable by any desktop publishing software capable of supporting .TIF, .PCX or .EPS formats. The camera's memories are erasable, and because their internal circuits are electrically erasable programmable read only devices (EEPROMs, *cf.* chapter 5), as is the case with any random access memory (RAM) devices, they can be reused indefinitely. Canon

**Figure 9.4** Clip art

manufactures a still video camera which employs a video floppy disk instead of internal RAM chips, but the end result is the same as with the Logitech and Dycam models. Canon's RC-250 system includes an optional Computer Imaging Kit, and the latter is capable of supporting color as well as grey scale pictures.

## FORMS DESIGN

One of the most cele-brated computer periph-

**Figure 9.5** Clip art

erals at the time of its introduction was the **impact printer**. The problem with using video displays exclusively in a computing environment is that the information such devices provide is only as permanent as the current screen. Printers leave a **hard copy** legacy; that is, they provide the user with a paper copy of the work that has been performed and the computations that have been made. **Dot matrix printers** provide an economical, personal consumer level output device which even the humblest of computing shops can afford.

On the downside, and to state the obvious, printers aren't typewriters. When the marriage of computers to printers was first consummated, the logical solution was to interface **teletype stations** (**TTYs**) with mainframe CPUs. TTYs had been used for some time prior to the 1940s for telegraph communications, and the meld of TTYs to computers was elegantly logical. Teletype machines, in fact, had an advantage over modern impact printers: they combined a keyboard and **platen** (a support roller upon which the keys strike the paper) and provided a complete input/output device for communicating with the CPU. In fact, the UNIX operating system still refers to the teletype ancestry in its commands GETTY and PUTTY for inputting from keyboard and outputting to a printer.

The appearance of personal computers was the impetus for creating cheaper printing solutions and for printers that were faster and less cumbersome than the TTY arrangements. In the early 1980s, manufacturers were experimenting with schemes to adapt existing electric typewriters to act as computer printers. Some of the inventions worked, but none really worked well. The crux of the problem was that there was no uniform **RS-232C standard**, the electrical protocol for interfacing serial communications devices (characteristic of printers in the late 1970s to early 1980s) to computer input/output ports. One manufacturer produced a device that fit on top of an IBM Selectric typewriter and pressed keys with a set of plungers forced downward onto the keycaps. All such devices were error-prone, and the methods of adapting typewriters as printers all but disappeared in the late 1980s.

What does all this have to do with forms design? One of the most powerful functions of a computer is its ability to read a database or file of information and transfer (i.e., paste) a share of that file's data into another software application. The procedure typically works as follows: a programmer designs a forms **template** to collect general information from various locations on the screen. During the data entry process, with the template displayed on the video monitor, an inputter types responses into various fields on the template. At the conclusion of the inputting, the data entry person keys a few codes, and the template program grabs (pastes) the remaining information from an appropriate database elsewhere in the program. A "Produce" or similar key is pressed on the keyboard, and the completed form is sent to the printer.

There is an example of the preceding activity which is familiar. A customer applies for a round-trip ticket at an airline counter. The airline clerk ascertains the passenger's destination, dates of travel desired, types of accommodations wanted, and other pertinent information. While the traveller waits, the clerk keys the passenger's responses into a forms template on the airline's video display screen. Other information is gathered from the database program in the computer, and a ticket, on a multiple-part form preprinted by the airline, is generated on a printer.

Another example relevant to libraries involves the OCLC workscreen. A cataloger wishes a set of catalog cards for a new book that the library has just received. He or she queries the OCLC bibliographic utility to which the library subscribes and brings up a forms template (workscreen) with information pre-entered in the form for that particular book. The cataloger makes any local changes to the form (e.g., alters the catalog number, deletes tracings, etc.) and presses "Produce" at the keyboard. In a few days, the library receives a printed set of catalog cards from OCLC. Unlike in years past, the cataloger does not have to run 3" x 5" cardstock through a typewriter and produce the cards manually. The time and money saved is obvious.

The outputting of standard forms such as airline tickets and catalog cards at a computer workstation is highly efficient, but there are many forms creation needs which are not so elaborate as to require nationwide computer hookups. Job applications, bills of lading, Postal Service declarations, courier shipping forms, and a host of other single-page or short, redundant papers can be best completed at a stand-alone computer terminal. The problem, until recent years, has been that the majority of forms were still best handled with a typewriter. To this day, an impact printer cannot easily be made to backspace, and it certainly cannot be placed in a correction mode with which to apply whiteout tape to a typographical error. Other solutions to the problems inherent with data entry into forms have been devised, and they are numerous.

A number of programs and devices have been created to expand the versatility of impact printers. The software program *The Typewriter*[9] allows entry of data from a PC keyboard and output to a dot matrix or daisy wheel printer and is useful for creating short memoranda or casually addressing a few envelopes. Characters are entered at the computer's keyboard one line at a time so that a typist can review what is to be printed before the "Return" or "Enter" key is pressed. There are other so-called "little" programs that allow completion of some standard forms (such as the U.S. government's lengthy SF-171 employment application), as well as some more elaborate programs which allow a user to custom design forms which can later also be completed and printed from the keyboard. One extension of dot matrix printer hardware technology that has made forms completion easier is the invention of a **sheet feeder**, also called a single sheet feeder. This device allows the use of nonperforated paper instead of **fanfold**, edge punched stock. Fanfold paper is sometimes difficult to load and often jams the **tractor mechanism** (sprocket feed) of impact printers. End users have often praised the single sheet feeder as a blessing and a miracle.

One of the less obvious problems with forms is the case where multiple copies must be produced. Such an instance requires an impact or dot matrix printer if carbon paper or **carbonless forms** (**NCR**, or **no carbon required forms**) are used. There is a trend to use desktop publishing techniques to produce multiples of the same form one after another, using a laser printer. This has become possible with the advent of high speed laser printers which can produce fifteen to seventeen pages per minute (PPM) or more. There are a variety of such printers currently on the market, and most are in the $3,000 to $7,500 price range (1995 dollars).

Desktop publishing has become the software of choice for in-house forms design in many offices. Using the table creation capabilities of programs such as Ventura and PageMaker (previously described), page layout techniques can be employed to create a variety of forms and templates. Such techniques have been around for many years, and they are just now being ported to PCs in small computing shops. These techniques round out the remaining discussion in this section.

All of us at one time or another have either praised or condemned any given form alternatively for its usefulness or unnecessary complexity. But forms are quite necessary in data gathering tasks. A poorly planned form, such as a lengthy or boring questionnaire, will be tossed in the wastebasket by the recipient. It is the job of a good systems analyst, in chorus with a competent layout designer, to create the most meaningful form for the job. To that end, there are four generally accepted principles of good forms design:

1. A form should collect specific kinds and definite amounts of data.
2. A form should make it easy for the user to enter the requested data, and with a minimal chance for error.
3. A form should exhibit a format from which data are easily absorbed and transferred (e.g., directly from the form to a ledger or data entry screen).
4. A form should be economical to produce and use, relative to its intended purpose.

There are five basic parts to any form:

1. **Title**. It should be self-explanatory and should imply the purpose of the form.
2. **Instructions**. These should be concise and to the point, or even absent (e.g., a blank, personal check needs no instructions).
3. **Heading**. This should include the control number and any internal references.
4. **Body**. The columns, blanks, checklist or grid to be completed by the respondent are part of this.
5. **Conclusion**. This contains a signature, disclaimer, and/or summary.

Forms are usually of one or two basic styles: open and boxed. An open style contains the title, instructions, heading, etc., in a narrative format. The information flows, as in a letter or instruction manual. The parts are distinct but not rigidly separated. With a boxed style, the sections are lined off as with a grid, and borders and dashes make each part distinct. Most forms are, in fact, a hybrid mixture of open and boxed styles, with some liberties taken for the sake of legibility and appearance.

**Cut forms** constitute about 90 percent of those produced. Cut forms consist of a single sheet, typically output on an offset printer or high-speed photocopier. This is the method of choice for forms that are to be completed by hand. **Specialty forms** are custom designed, usually to work on a specific machine. Such forms include those which ultimately will be bound into books, **continuous feed forms** (those repeated in a continuous strip), forms with detachable stubs, punched card forms, and credit card forms. Specialty forms can be single- or multiple-part and can use carbon paper or NCR techniques.

The cost of using a form far outweighs the cost of producing it. Therefore, the planning for an appropriate, efficient design is crucial. There are several considerations which will aid in ensuring the success of a form design:

1. Group all related information on the form.
2. Leave adequate space on the form to gather the information requested. If a form is to be completed on a typewriter, assume that the user will use the larger (pica) typeface. Allow for long names and oversized handwriting if a form is to be completed in pen or pencil.
3. Make your instructions clear and to the point. Tell the respondent exactly what you want to know.
4. Make field labels clear. If you want information to be placed in a certain box, place the label (e.g., "NAME," "ADDRESS") in or near that box. Don't digress from standard order (e.g., don't ask for the ZIP code before the name of the state). Allow for regional differences, e.g., dates in Europe are entered day/month/year, as 15/8/95 for August 15, 1995.
5. Use special techniques for improved readability but don't be too experimental. Don't clutter the form; use plenty of white space, and typeset the form with an appropriate typeface. And don't use more than three typefaces on any given page.

The appropriate use of color can greatly increase the efficiency of your forms. Many desktop publishing programs have incorporated the ability to use color in documents, and color separations can be displayed right on the computer's screen. Color printers have become available at consumer-level prices, and color printing in small computing shops is economically available. Certain color combinations have a greater "noticeablility" factor than others. LeCourier's legibility table[10] ranks these combinations as follows:

| Order of Legibility (Descending) | Color of Type | Color of Paper |
| --- | --- | --- |
| 1 | black | yellow |
| 2 | green | white |
| 3 | red | white |
| 4 | blue | white |
| 5 | white | blue |
| 6 | black | white |

| 7  | yellow | black  |
|----|--------|--------|
| 8  | white  | red    |
| 9  | white  | green  |
| 10 | white  | black  |
| 11 | red    | yellow |
| 12 | green  | red    |
| 13 | red    | green  |

Avoid the obvious clashes; any red with blue combination is usually unworkable, because the eye cannot process red and blue information simultaneously. Also, you should ascertain that your choice of paper is not so dark that information entered on it will be absorbed by the background. A similar caution should be taken for multiple part forms, to make sure that the color of the bottommost copy is not so dark as to absorb the carbon impression. Other typographic considerations can be made to enhance readability (left and right justifications, proportionally spaced typefaces, etc.), but care should be taken not to make the form appear too cluttered. As with any publication, good taste and common sense should prevail.

## OPTICAL CHARACTER RECOGNITION

**Optical character recognition**, or **OCR**, is the process of using a digital scanner to "read" a typewritten or typeset page of material and translate it into an ASCII or word processing file format. The subject has been placed here, at the end of the discussion on desktop publishing, because OCR employs many of the same peripheral tools as desktop publishing in the handling of file input and graphics processes. As a process, optical character recognition is somewhat of a luxury item that gives more versatility to a publications shop by allowing input of paper-only and archived documents into a machine readable format for republication and reproduction.

Optical character recognition begins with a scanned image. The poem in Figure 9.6 was created on a typewriter which, obviously, had seen many years of use. Consequently, the image, although created on an electric typewriter, appears less than perfect when viewed close up. This is typical of the quality of images that are often fed into OCR programs. While most OCR programs have fairly intelligent algorithms that provide a high degree of accuracy in "reading" such copy, the original documents must be relatively clean for the process to execute successfully and with a high degree of accuracy. In this example, there was also ink "bleed" on low-quality paper, and a fabric ribbon was used instead of a sharper, carbon film ribbon on the original. Moreover, the keyfaces in the machine were obviously worn to the point where most characters appear ill-formed and smeared.

To make it in a world
That takes so very much
I'm glad that I have your
Smile and your loving touch

With violence and despair
All around me everyday
Help me to escape the harm
That is sure to come my way

I need you to take my hand
And lead me to the light
So that I can live and learn
How to do everything right

With your help I will succeed
And make a difference too
By remembering to pass on
The things I got from you

**Figure 9.6** .PCX File for input to OCR software

Figure 9.7 shows the result of passing the .PCX file in the previous figure through an OCR program. Note that there are numerous characters that the OCR program could not recognize. The program either made a "best guess" or used a tilde ( "~" ) as a filler character. For this particular scan, the program also had a difficulty resolving the lowercase "i" and interpreted that vowel as requiring a leading colon. A user of an OCR software program must ascertain whether or not the error rate is too high with the particular batch of documents to be scanned before committing to a long term inputting project. With older or poor originals, it may well be more efficient to re-enter copy from scratch.

Some libraries use light pens or light wands to input data for automated circulation systems. For those systems that support it, data on book card and borrowers' card labels can be created with a typewriter using **OCR-A** or **OCR-B** typefaces. Data elements for these typefaces are available for various brands of electric typewriters, and, using a high-quality carbon ribbon, input labels can be created with a high degree of accuracy and readability. Such a machine-readable label for input to a light-pen-based terminal might appear as follows, in OCR-A as

# MITCHELLGONEWITHWIND

in a library which is using simply the last name of the author and the book title as input to the automated system.

While scanners are the typical input devices for OCR activities, **pen technology** has gained some acceptance as a spinoff from OCR algorithmic processes. The devices used in pen technology should not be confused with light pen hardware, in which the pen is used solely for inputting bar codes or typed characters or bar codes as in an automated

```
To make :it in a world
That takes so very milch
I'm glad tbat I have your Smile
and your Loving touch

With vialence and despair
ALL around me everyday
Help me to escape the harm
That is s~?re to come my way

I need you to take my hand
And Lead me to the Light
So that I can L:ive and Learn
How to do everyth:ing right

With your he Lp  I w:ill succe ed
And make a difference too
By remembering to pass on
The things I got from you
```

**Figure 9.7** Result of .PCX File in an OCR program

circulation system. The process surrounding pen technology is one in which a **digitizer pad**, or **tablet**, is used as an input device connected to the computer's serial port. The pad can display a template, much like a data input screen for a database program, into whose fields a person with an appropriately connected pen can enter information (usually in block, capital letters). Using OCR algorithms, the database program's "engine" can recognize these handwritten patterns and enter them as ASCII or text data into the database proper. There has been some experimentation with recognition of script handwriting, although (at the time of this writing), the processes have not been perfected.

Pen and tablet input has been used for a number of practical applications, including the taking of physical inventories and the recording of data in field situations, using portable or laptop computers as pen support until the recorded data can be further refined in an office environment. Couriers such as United Parcel Service have been using digitizing tablets to collect signatures of consignees, thereby having a computer-based record of delivery acceptance signatures on file in standard graphics formats. Library applications would, of course, follow typical business practices, and the need for pen technology would be dictated by circumstances. But on a widespread basis, OCR input by pen does not (yet) have a wide following.

## NOTES

1.  Harrel, William. "High-End Desktop Publishing Software." *Windows Magazine*, October 1992, pp. 174.
2.  Ventura Publisher, published by Corel Corporation, 1600 Carling Avenue, Ottawa, ON K1Z 8R7. $249.00.
3.  PageMaker, published by Aldus Corporation, 411 First Avenue South, Seattle, WA 98104-2871. $895.00.
4.  FrameMaker, published by Frame Technology Corporation, 1010 Rincon Circle, San Jose, CA 95131. $795.00.
5.  Glyphix, published by Swifte International, Ltd., P.O. Box 219, Rockland, DE 19732. $99.95.
6.  Mendelson, Edward. "TRUETYPE: The Second Font Revolution for the Desktop." *PC Magazine*, April 28, 1992, p. 144.

7. Thematic collections of clip art are available in book form from Dover Publications, 31 East 2nd Street, Mineola, NY 11501, at about $3.95 per copy. Many art supply stores also carry a number of Dover titles.

8. Disk-based clip art can be purchased from shareware vendors; see Bibliography, chapter 2, "Catalogs" section for list.

9. *The Typewriter*, published by Power Up!, P.O. Box 7600, San Mateo, CA 94403-7600. $39.95.

10. Gore, Marvin and John Stubbe. *Elements of Systems Analysis for Business Data Processing*, 1975. P. 75.

# Chapter 10

# Specialty Software

This is a "cleanup" chapter, that is, a discussion of programs of significance to information science but ones that cannot fit into any of the categories of previous chapters. They are included here because they round out the concepts of applications programs and provide a number of useful examples of information- and instruction-based activities germane both to librarianship and formal classroom instruction.

## APPLICATIONS PROGRAMS FOR STATISTICAL ANALYSES

In the first half of this text, software was lumped into major categories: word processors, spreadsheets, database programs, operating systems, graphics user interfaces, and developmental languages. There are other programs that are to be found in libraries and educational institutions and which are widely used in instruction and strategic planning.

There are a number of statistical programs which provide for highly sophisticated handling of mathematical data for research and instruction. Some of the popular titles include: SPSS, or Statistical Program for the Social Sciences, Minitab, Epistat, and Systat. Most of these are available in mainframe, PC, and Macintosh versions. Their functional capabilities are similar, and it is a matter of individual preference which is to be used.

SPSS[1] has been around for quite some time, and the earliest versions required the user to input data for analysis on punched cards. The current mainframe version works in a batchlike mode in which the user types data onto "cards" (lines of text in a separate file) to submit to the main program. The PC version is available in both unabridged and abbreviated versions, the latter being shipped with a textbook and diskettes for student use. The only difference in the two PC versions, other than price, is that the student version can handle a limited (although generous) number of variables in the various analyses.

Minitab[2] operates in a more conversational mode, and, as such, is said to be interactive in the same manner as program language interpreters (see the discussion on BASIC interpreters in chapter 8). In the mainframe version, for example, a user can submit data for analyses in one of two ways, either by typing numbers at the command prompt one by one and signaling Minitab when the input is complete, or by submitting data in a text file to any particular process (regression, averaging of means, etc.) in a manner similar to that of SPSS. In such interactive modes, the posting of results is immediate, and screen reports can also be directed to a printer or to a disk file for later study. Minitab is available for the IBM PC and compatibles and for Macintosh computers, as well as for the DEC VAX and for the VMS, VM, CMS, and MUSIC operating systems.

SYSTAT[3] is a full-featured statistical program that runs under DOS, Windows, UNIX, or on the Macintosh. It must be licensed on an annual basis (there is no provision for purchase of a permanent usage license), and SYSTAT requires that you keep a log of the locations of individual users on the license arrangement within your organization. Aside from this atypically tight control of its user sites, SYSTAT provides a powerful, easy-to-learn product that handles a wide variety of analyses and number-crunching, databased activities.

## APPLICATIONS PROGRAMS FOR OTHER LIBRARY-BASED FUNCTIONS

It is obvious, then, that there are many programs that appear from atypical sources that are quite useful in the library sector. There are a number of programs in the public domain that satisfy libraries' requirements to generate their own **bar code labels** (sometimes called **z-bars** or **zebra labels**). In chapters 13 and 14 there are some detailed discussions of planning and implementing automated circulation and cataloging systems. While bar code labels can be purchased from professional printing houses, in boxes of preprinted sets, there are times when libraries might find it more economical to print their own labels in-house. Several programs make this possible, and bar code labels can be generated with a minimum of equipment.

UNIKEY Systems has released for shareware distribution the Bar Code printing programs USC39H91, USC39M91, USC39L91, USUPAM91 and USI25H91.[4] The program group is written for IBM PC compatible systems, and each routine is menu-driven. Several bar code formats are supported, including universal product code, code 39 (alphanumeric and mostly used for inventory and tracking), and 2 of 5 (numeric and requires very little space left to right). The routines work on nine-pin dot-matrix printers with Epson or IBM graphics capabilities. There is a menu choice for 1-inch-high labels and variable vertical spacing for others. Bar code labels generated on dot matrix printers can usually be read efficiently by laser scanners, but libraries intending to use homemade bar codes should check their scanners' user manuals before making an investment in additional printers and software.

Zbar[5] is a barcode printing shareware program which will print the barcode, two comment lines above it, and the code in human readable characters below it. It is menu driven and features a windowed interface which runs under DOS and OS/2, in either real or protected mode. The interface makes use of the up and down arrow keys for menu scrolling and the "Enter" key to select your choice. Zbar supports both interactive and command line input modes. This allows you to create input files from other programs (such as inventory control) and feed them right into Zbar without the need for entering all the data again. It currently supports the following barcode symbologies: UPC-A, UPC-E, EAN/JAN-13, EAN-JAN-8, code 39, extended 39, interleaved 2 of 5, code 128, CODABAR, Zip+4 Postnet, MSI Plessey, code 93, extended 93 and UCC-128. Because of the new U.S. Postal Service regulations adopted in 1993 involving user emplacement of Postnet codes on presorted first-class mail, libraries can realize considerable postage savings from this feature alone. Several printers can also be used, including emulation for 9- and 24-pin Epson, 9- and 24-pin IBM Proprinter, 24-pin Toshiba, Okidata Microline, HP LaserJet and DeskJet, as well as PostScript printers. Zbar also allows you to print several times across a page, as would be the case for adhesive labels, price tags, and shelf IDs.

As a matter of example, the bar codes with which we are probably most familiar are the so-called **universal product code** (**UPC**) labels used by grocery stores. The laser scanners used in the supermarkets are fed into a control program not unlike those used in automated circulation systems for libraries, and the scanning/reading mechanics are nearly identical. What do these UPC labels mean, and how do the systems translate them at the checkout line? The following summary, in brief, outlines "how to crack the universal product code" (*cf.* Figure 10.1):

- A—the two thin "guard bars" don't mean anything; they frame the real message. They are repeated in the middle of the label and at the other end of the bar pattern.
- B—a wide space, a bar, a narrow space, and a thin bar encode "0" at the left of the symbol. "0" means that the label is for regular groceries; "3" would indicate drugs.

**BIG SECRETS**
**How to Crack the Universal Product Code**

**A B    C       D   E**

**A** Two thin "guard bars" don't mean anything; they frame the real message. Repeated in middle and at other end of bar pattern.

**B** Wide space, bar, narrow space, thin bar encode the 0 at left of symbol. 0 means it's regular groceries. 3 is for drugs.

**C** Ten spaces and ten bars encode the 12345 at bottom, which identifies the manufacturer. 21000 would be Kraft, etc.

**D** Encodes the 67890, which identifies the product, including size of package. Price in not encoded.

**E** A secret "check digit" (here 5) to catch any error or tampering. If someone widens a bar with a felt-tip pen, the check digit helps the scanner detect it.

**Figure 10.1.** Universal Product Code label

- C—ten spaces and ten bars encode the "12345" at the bottom, which identifies the manufacturer. "21000" would be Kraft, etc.
- D—encodes the "678 90," which identifies the product, including the size of the package. The price is not encoded.
- E—a secret check digit (here, the number "5") to catch any error or tampering. If someone widens a bar with a felt-tipped pen, the check digit helps the scanner detect it.

It should be noted that the UPC label does not include the price of the item. In this manner, price changes can be made in the control program, without the necessity of affixing a second bar code label to the package. This has caused consternation with grocery store customers who sometimes contend that the scanned price is not the same as that on the shelf label; in fact, the accusation is that the overcharges are excessive, possibly in the millions of dollars per year.[6] Libraries should be aware of this potential for negative public relations; not that book prices are ever changed (if, indeed, the library sells its collection anyway), but variables such as loan periods and overdue fees, if triggered by bar codes, can represent the bases for arguments. It is probably best to advise patrons, with signage, if necessary, to check their borrowers' transactions before leaving the circulation desk.

## GUIDE TO SELECTING AND EVALUATING SOFTWARE FOR LIBRARIES

Because the bulk of the discussion in the first half of this book has involved the use and application of computer software, it seems fitting to conclude with a section on the examination and purchase of programs for in-house use. Software runs the gamut of very cheap to very expensive, but regardless of price, the time and effort required to install and run any particular program represent a considerable investment of hardware and human resources. This section will provide (again) some criteria for intelligent consumerism and give some insight into the procurement of this now common, nonprint medium.

Obviously, you'll want to purchase the most recent version of any program you choose. This can be a problem when purchasing software from department stores, electronics specialty stores, or smaller mail-order houses. Often the inventory of those establishments has been allowed to grow out-of-date, and you may find that the package you take away is one or two versions behind the most recent publication. You can protect yourself by noting revision numbers in the literature, or by calling the software company prior to purchase to ascertain date and number of the latest release.

Software is typically released in version numbers of integer digits. The initial release is commonly version 1, and major updates are incremental whole numbers as version 2, version 3, etc. **Incremental updates** of software are usually listed as decimal numbers, as version 2.1, version 3.01, and so on. These versions are **maintenance updates**, sometimes called **patch releases**, issued to incorporate corrections or fixes of minor flaws, or bugs, in the most recent program version. When you buy, particularly through mail order, make certain that the solicitation or advertisement is specific about the version that is to be sold. Then be specific on your purchase order exactly which release you expect to receive.

Sometimes it is advantageous to purchase software that is one or two versions behind the next current release, but you should exercise caution in doing so. Many software houses will allow you a free update, with proof of purchase, if you can demonstrate that a superseded version was purchased by you within a certain timeframe. The window for the free update is usually 60 to 120 days, and you sometimes must pay for shipping and handling. If you are a savvy bargain hunter and pick up an older (and cheaper) copy of a software program at a computer flea market, you might be able to upgrade to the latest version for a nominal fee and for considerably less than the price of a brand-new package. You can also attempt to exercise this option if you inadvertently buy an old version of a program from a store which has an "all sales final" policy; caveat emptor. In any case, if you are upgrading, you should ascertain that newer versions of a program maintain **downward** (i.e., **backward**) **compatibility** with older releases. It is highly inefficient to upgrade to a newer version of a program only to discover that files created with the older release must be converted manually to conform with the filing conventions of the newer program. The process is time-consuming and can entail many dollars for staff to reconstruct hours of previous work.

It is common nowadays for retail computer software stores to handle upgrades in-house. Because some of the upgrade kits are specially configured, you must have the previous version of the program in your possession. Such upgrades examine the contents of your hard disk drive and alter some older files, while installing new ones. Moreover, stores that handle upgrade packages usually require proof that you own a license to a previous version. This proof can be in the form of the printed software license from the original package, or, many times, the title page from the user's manual or the master diskette. Title pages and diskettes must usually be surrendered, for the store must also provide proof to the manufacturer that it sold a legitimate update. Also in current practice is for one vendor to accept an upgrade offer from a competitor's product. One spreadsheet vendor may accept the title page from another product's user manual and allow a similarly priced upgrade as from its own customers. It is a variation on the idea that "we honor competitors' coupons," and you need to do some shopping to determine whether this approach works for you. Don't forget, if you switch products, you may face considerable amount of work time converting your old data and document files to conform to the structures required in the new program.

Barden[7] outlined a number of tips that are timeless in their value for the intelligent purchase of computer support programs. They are presented in the following sections.

### Software May Not Follow the Machine

In the mid 1980s, this was more of a problem than now. However, computer manufacturers have come together in their adherence to standards so if a software package states "IBM or 100-percent compatibles," the program will run all right on any of the clones in the IBM PC family. For older machines, the manufacturers were charged with the task of compatibility, requiring the customers to have faith that the programs they wanted were, or would be, available for a particular brand of hardware. Regrettably, a number of companies went bankrupt, leaving their users with collections of attractive hardware but few programs on which to run them.

If your computer or operating system is an issue that might be considered one of the more "exotic" varieties, scan the literature to ascertain whether programs for your environment are in the mainstream. dBase IV, for example, is available for a number of platforms other than DOS— UNIX, and OS/2 versions are also available. The Oracle database package is also available in PC, Macintosh, minicomputer, and mainframe versions. Check with the vendor *before* you buy. And run like the wind if you even hear the slightest hint of "real soon now" when new software is being developed!

## Buy as Few Software Packages as Possible

This is commonsense advice; the fewer programs you must learn, the more proficient you will become on the ones you have ultimately chosen. Some vendors make available an integrated package that combines a word processor, spreadsheet, and database manager into one program. Examples of this type of software are Framework, Symphony, Microsoft Works, and Microsoft Excel. The advantage is that when you switch between functions (from word processing to database manipulation), the keystrokes and macro commands of one module are identical to the conventions of the others.

It is less of a problem nowadays to use several programs from different vendors in your computing environment. Most major software packages, and many from the so-called **third-party** vendors, allow the exchange of data files between each other's programs. This ability to convert file formats is called **importing** and is a highly useful feature when several processings must take place on the same data file. For example, a database of names and addresses created with dBase IV can be used with Ventura Publisher to output a typeset telephone directory. But the advice to keep the physical number of programs to a minimum is still valid. Simply check the software you are considering to ascertain exactly which vendors' programs are compatible. It is far too time-consuming to have to create the same data files twice or to be required to modify a large database manually to make it usable across programs and platforms.

## Beware of Free Software

This caveat should be added to the material in chapter 2. "Free" doesn't necessarily mean "bad," it simply means "be cautious." The one element that shareware and public domain software cannot place against the major brands is development time. Keep in mind that commercial software houses have teams of programmers who can devote hundreds and even thousands of hours to developing and refining individual programs. Many of the programs available on the commercial market are ones first developed by independent programmers. These programmers sell the rights to their ideas and concepts to software houses that can invest large sums of money for marketing and program support. However, after all the lavished praise on low-cost software presented in chapter 2, this does not now mean that public domain software is to be dismissed. "Caution" is the watchword; if you discover a program that seems to fulfill your needs at low cost, and after a reasonable trial of its functions it doesn't seem to exhibit any quirks, stick with it and congratulate yourself for identifying a bargain.

## Use the Documentation as a Guide

It is a shame to pay hundreds of dollars for a computer program only to discover after opening it that the printed instructions leave much to be desired. If this has happened to you, you should have insisted in the store that you be permitted to review the documentation as a condition of purchase. Shrinkwrap laws do not typically apply to program manuals, so even if you decide to refuse the software after taking it out of the store, as long as you have not discarded any materials you should be allowed a return privilege.

As a rule of thumb, the more comprehensive the written documentation is, the better the program runs. This is a very sweeping statement, and librarians and educators have a decided advantage of evaluation: they can judge a software product also by the quality of its accompanying technical manual. Further, book selectors have an additional tool: the various book reviews. Computer software, particularly PC and Macintosh programs, has spawned an industry which no longer can be termed "cottage": the publication of third-party documentation. Books are available as supplemental reading for most major, and many minor, software packages. Care must be taken to find out if the text under consideration is more than just a rehash of the program manual. Also, there is much redundancy between publishers. You should judge a third-party text as you would any other print medium, particularly to discover whether the book has a unique perspective or additional information to offer about the software.

## Buy Programs Written in Assembly Language

This is easier said than done; do so *if* you can determine the language of the original source code, that is. This advice was much more important in the past than today. The bulk (approximately 75 percent) of microcomputer-based applications programs are written in the C programming language (see chapter 8). C handles PC resources in a manner similar to that of assembly language; in other words, C and assembler **optimize** the executable code. This attribute is desirable to obtain speed and computing efficiency from a program. No one wants to wait ten or twenty minutes for the printout of a single page of text, and good, "tight" code makes the machine "run faster." Your best bet before purchasing any applications package is to read the results of the **benchmark tests** (comparisons of performances of similar programs) in the product reviews. If the review reports the language of program source code origin, so much the better. Benchmarks will allow you to compare like products to one another for speed of execution. And if a review states that a program was written in C language or assembler, you can lend greater confidence to the test results.

## Avoid Software That Cannot Be Backed Up

In chapter 2, the matter of copyright as it applies to computer software was discussed at length. However, history has proven that morality and ethics cannot be legislated. It has been estimated that for every legal, legitimate copy of a computer program in use, there is at least one illegal, pirated copy running elsewhere. Illegal copies of any program deny authors and vendors revenue to which they are entitled. Because of rampant duplication and general ignorance of copyright restrictions by end users (with a bit of paranoia thrown in) in the early 1980s, producers of software decided to take matters into their own hands. Thus, the concept of disk-based **copy protection** was born.

As with many restrictive schemes, the honest consumers were the ones hurt most by copy protection methodologies. Copyright allows an end user to make duplicates of properly licensed programs as archival disks, to protect against damage to the original, master copies. As mentioned in chapter 2, this is a legal act as long as the end user does not run two or more copies of a single-license program simultaneously. Copy protection schemes prevent any archiving, and typically, a user who has damaged a master diskette so protected must appeal to the company for a replacement, and sometimes must purchase an entirely new package. Obviously, a customer who has many documents based on a particular word processor or spreadsheet cannot afford the downtime waiting for the restored program to arrive. In a worst case scenario, a software company can go out of business and leave a substantial user base in the lurch when replacement copies of master programs cannot be obtained ever again.

Software manufacturers employ a variety of techniques to ensure payment of license fees. A common practice once was to furnish a **key disk** with a program package. This required an end user to insert a special floppy diskette into the computer (even if the program was to be run from the hard disk drive) to activate the executable files. Another disk-based method was to allow installation of a program from a floppy disk to the hard drive, but requiring the program to be "uninstalled" back to the same floppy disk if the program needed to be moved to a different computer. This technique disallowed the running of sometimes necessary housecleaning programs on the computer. A method used primarily on mainframe computers was the encoding of a "drop dead date" in the software. The CPU compared its internal clock to a date in the program; if the software had not been updated (usually by payment of the renewal fee to purchase a regeneration number), the program ceased to function. There is a not too humorous story of a computer used to monitor environmental controls for a large office building; its software consisted of a module with one of the so-called "drop dead" codes imbedded. A license renewal and fee payment date of January 1 was missed and the program shut itself down. So did the furnace in the building, much to the chagrin of the maintenance and MIS staffs. Needless to say, a new vendor of environmental control software was immediately sought.

Variations on copy protection schemes abound. Typically, a manufacturer places a hidden file or "secret" routine on a disk that is unviewable by the end user and thereby uncopyable. Other techniques are more drastic: one manufacturer devised a method of drilling a small hole (sometimes known as a **worm**) in the floppy disk with a laser beam that could not be reproduced magnetically on the computer and therefore could not yield to copy commands. There are also some hardware-based techniques that require the end user to attach an encoded plug to the serial (printer and communications) port to make the program run. There are also documentation-based techniques that require a user to enter one of many "secret" codes in the sign-on screen before the program will run. There are hundreds of random codes issued for such programs, and the paper on which they are printed is a deep purple and cannot be photocopied. Complaints abound that these schemes are aggravating, and consumer attitudes have all but eradicated the once widespread practice of copy protection for computer software.

Human nature being what it is, not long after copy protection schemes arrived on the market, a cottage industry of programs that break such protections flourished. For several years, it was rather like watching a game of leapfrog; as soon as a more sophisticated copy protection methodology was invented, a commensurately sophisticated copy protection removal program appeared shortly thereafter. At length, the software houses decided that the protection wasn't worth the hassle, and copy protection schemes have all but disappeared from new software on the market. However, some copy protection still lingers, and the advice here is to shun programs that continue to insist that it be applied. Be mindful that freedom to copy implies certain ethical obligations, and it is best to follow the dictates of software copyright as closely as the law governing print media.

## Buy Software from Responsive Companies

Reliable software vendors are like reliable publishers and book jobbers—you'll come to recognize the ones you can trust by reading reviews and perusing the literature. And, as with other media, you'll develop a list of your favorites. But don't let this discourage you from trying the "little" publishers from time to time. Many of the well-known, expensive programs began as products of lesser known software houses. It is common for major publishers to purchase the ideas and programs of independent vendors and develop such programs on an elaborate scale. The Microsoft C language compiler, for example, originated from a product written by

Lattice, Inc. Many useful products are never advertised (see the discussion of shareware in chapter 2) or appear only in the classified sections of computer periodicals. When considering a major, expensive program, ask the publisher for a demonstration disk and do some comparison shopping before making a final purchase decision.

## See the Software Demonstrated

Barden makes a subtle point which can prevent considerable frustration and regret: "The initial cost of the package is negligible compared to the time and data that you'll be investing in it if you use it frequently." In other words, the real cost of software is the amount of time and effort spent using it after the initial purchase. Once again: it is not unrealistic to ask for a demonstration of a software package before it is sold. If you are uncomfortable with the program in the store, there is little chance that you will "grow into it" once you get it installed on your own PC. Be mindful of shrinkwrap and licensing laws; you might not be able to return a program for a refund if the seal is broken on the diskette package. Thus, better safe than sorry; take a "test drive" before you issue a purchase order or sign the check—you'll save yourself a considerable amount of grief.

To summarize, there are a number of considerations that should be taken into account before selecting a particular software package. Keeping in mind that the initial cost of software represents only a fraction of your investment, be certain that you can respond affirmatively to the majority of the following criteria before paying your money:

- Does the software use the operating system that is standard for your computer, or will you have to buy an additional operating system just to run one program?
- Does the program run as an executable file, or do you have to use a runtime module (sometimes a separate purchase) in conjunction with it?
- Does the program require a graphical user interface such as Windows or Mac System 7 in order to run?
- How much disk storage space is required for the program *and* for the resulting data files and work files?
- How much random access memory (RAM) does the program require? Does your system require extended or expanded memory to run the program? More to the point, is the program a "memory hog"?
- Can you define the input and output formats of the program, or are they fixed? Will the program import and export file formats to and from other programs of the same functional category?
- Will the software support your brand of printer?

- How much are new versions or revisions? Is the charge for an upgrade nominal, or are you required to purchase a completely new version? Do you receive new manuals with an upgrade, or are you furnished only supplement sheets or **release notes**?
- Does the vendor notify you of new releases automatically, or do you have to pay for a support service in order to get such news?
- Is the program unconditionally guaranteed to be free of bugs and defects? What must you do to obtain a replacement?
- Does the vendor use a copy protection scheme, limiting you to the number of archival or backup copies you can make? Is a separate piece of documentation or key disk required to run the program?
- Is the program user-friendly? Is it self-prompting or menu-driven?
- Is the documentation complete, well written, and in a readable format?
- Are there seminars or videotapes available for user training?
- Is there a body of literature available from reputable publishers to supplement the vendor's documentation?
- Do third-party authors write utility programs to supplement the base package?
- Is there technical support available by telephone, mail, or electronic bulletin board? Is there a fee for such support?
- Is the program customizable to work with nonstandard input/output devices? For example, could a particular word processor be configured to work with a printer not included on the basic installation list?
- Are there any reviews available on the program?
- Can you identify other libraries or individuals using the program that can comment on its functionality?
- Are there local user groups for the software, or is there a list of users available for comment on their experiences with using the program?
- How much does it cost?

## APPLICATION: SOFTWARE TO INSTRUCT MATHEMATICS

Computers make natural learning tools for mathematics. After all, the term "computer" implies that something is going to be calculated. By extension, then, the machine can be set up to instruct its native "language." All that is needed are some programs to access the **arithmetic/logic unit (ALU)** and to provide tutorials and feedback on the particular branch of mathematics that must be learned.

It should be immediately obvious that computer instruction in mathematics has one drawback: it cannot delve much into the realm of theoretical mathematics. However, the bulk of applied mathematics is fair game. Here, the computer can return a discrete answer, display a graph, plot coordinate points, work an equation, plug numbers into statistics formulas, and resolve complicated matrices. As soon as a child can navigate a keyboard, mathematics exercises are available to him/her for interactive study. It doesn't matter whether the problem is addition or subtraction or advanced calculus; the computer becomes the tool for the introduction and review of concepts.

For the sake of brevity, this section will illustrate study aids and tutorial programs that emphasize more advanced mathematical concepts. The reason is that there are far more "little" software programs for teaching basic concepts of arithmetic and counting than utility programs on the "high" end. Indeed, concept- and curricular-based software gained momentum with the many programs published for the Apple II computer, and a number are in the public domain. Resource catalogs will also show that a number of good elementary mathematics programs can be had for as little as two dollars per title.

This section emphasizes programs which are first available as shareware. However, there are some good programs in the commercial sector as well. For example, Power Up! publishes a two-volume set of tutorial disks called AlgebraPlus[8] which takes the user from beginning concepts through logarithms and quadratic equations. Published for IBM and compatible computers, the arrangement of material is in a format suitable for study preparation for the SAT and ACT examinations. The publishers of Cliffs Notes also makes available a number of Studyware programs that include physics and mathematics tutorials. There is one for statistics and another for calculus.[9] The questions are multiple choice, and the drills can be taken either in tutorial (feedback) or quiz format. The programs are intended to be supplements to text material, not as teaching tools in themselves. Regrettably, Cliffs has chosen to invoke a document-based copy protect scheme to inhibit unauthorized duplication.

Most higher mathematics classes are requiring students to purchase a hand calculator with a considerable range of functions built in. While it might not be possible to carry the following program to class on any machine but a portable or laptop computer, MATHX[10] serves as a PC-based version of a very sophisticated programmable scientific calculator. MATHX (MATH EXTRA) and its companion MATHXR (MATH EXTRA RESIDENT, a memory resident version of the MATHX program), can handle variables, labels, and equations. Written in assembly language for greater speed, the program also provides a repertoire of trigonometric and hyperbolic functions and can also handle hexadecimal numbers. Its popup menu format makes it very useful as a learning companion for others shareware mathematics programs described below.

Two programs are available to take a student through precalculus mathematics. LIMITS[11] allows a user to create and edit systems (equations) of limits for $f(x)$, and then calculate them whether $f(x)$ is a limit from above or below or is two-sided, or if x approaches $+\infty$ or $-\infty$. There is a Projects section that provides the user with a learning tool when not using the program to solve individually entered problems. LINEAR ALGEBRA[12] is a companion program and takes a student through matrix operations and vector operations, with an editor for creating systems of both. The program solves linear equations and determinant sets, computes the sums and differences of matrices, and performs scalar multiplication. There is both a Homework (exercises) section and a Projects section, and there are built-in mathematics tables. Both LIMITS and LINEAR ALGEBRA provide extensive online help by pressing the F1 key, and the programs are driven by pulldown menus. Permission to copy is given of both programs, and libraries might want to consider these titles for a circulating software collection.

For those who would be satisfied with a simpler, more user-friendly equation solver, Calculus and Differential Equations V 9[13] provides a line-oriented approach to higher mathematics aids. Its various components self-document the operations of the software: CALCULUS.COM is used to solve functions of x; DE.COM, of course, calculates differential equations; ODE.EXE and EULER3D.EXE work on systems of linear points; and STRING.EXE draws and animates various functions based on values and points specified on the workscreen. The program was written in Microsoft C version 5.0 for greater accuracy and speed. A similar program, Diff: Differential Equations,[14] can differentiate almost any analytical function, show the complete step-by-step breakdown of the differentiation process, and plot a graph of the function and its derivative on screen or a dot matrix printer. Diff can be used as a teaching aid for showing how to differentiate complicated functions or for engineers and scientists who need to find nontrivial derivatives. Diff is very easy to use and incorporates online help with over 130 screens of information for those who want to delve deeper into its facilities. The graphics utility lets you see with as few as two keystrokes what the function and its derivative look like over any range of values, and the program takes advantage of colors on RGB monitors.

Advanced mathematics courses are usually prerequisites for courses in the sciences, from intermediate levels and up. This is especially true for physics and electronics courses, and high-level study aides are difficult to locate. Through an interactive programming technique, the Electronic Circuit Designer[15] takes much of the tedium out of designing the more common electronic circuits. There are sixty-two programs that comprise the Electronic Circuit Designer and help the design engineer or technician play "what if?" with circuit drawings. A technician can quickly substitute component values, change parameters and design specifications, and immediately see the effects. Electronic Circuit Designer will free the technician to concentrate on the circuit design instead of studying reference tables and books of equations and entering numbers into a calculator. A monitor capable of supporting graphics images is required, and monitors with resolutions through VGA are supported. The DC Circuit Analysis[16] program is intended as an educational tool for introducing the user to the concepts of direct current (DC) circuits in general, and digital computer circuits in particular. Circuits can be created and evaluated on the computer screen. The documentation can function as a tutorial to learn about semiconductors, microprocessor logic, and digital computer circuits. Numerous sample circuits are used throughout the documentation and can be displayed and evaluated using this program. The program will support mouse and graphics resolutions as high as VGA.

## NOTES

Where either "PBS" or "TSL" is noted following addresses of program vendors, shareware versions of the programs listed below can be obtained from Public Brand Software or The Software Labs respectively; PBS and TSL catalogs are annotated in the Bibliography.

1. SPSS, published by SPSS, Inc., 444 N. Michigan Avenue, Chicago, IL 60611, (312) 329-3500. Price varies according to program configuration, accessory components included, and machine upon which the program is to be run.
2. Minitab, available from Minitab, Inc., 3081 Enterprise Drive, State College, PA 16801-3008, (814) 238-4383. Price varies according to version desired and number of licenses ordered.
3. SYSTAT, available from SYSTAT, Inc., 1800 Sherman Avenue, Evanston, IL 60201-3793, (708) 864-5670. Price varies according to version desired and number of licenses ordered.
4. UNIKEY Systems, 20210 Laceyland, Katy, TX 77449. Price of program varies with licensing arrangements (PBS disk #20.0).
5. Zbar, published by Al Borges, 263 Ashsale Ave., Syracuse, NY 13206. $35.00 (TSL disk #9060).
6. Bartholomew, Doug. "The Price Is Wrong." *Information Week*, September 14, 1992, pp. 27-30.
7. Barden, William, Jr. "What Do You Do After You Plug It In?: How to Buy Software." *Popular Computing*, January, 1983, pp. 54-57.
8. AlgebraPlus, published by Power Up! Direct, P.O. Box 7600, San Mateo, CA 94403-7600. $39.95 per volume.
9. Studyware for Calculus, published by [Cliffs] Studyware Corporation, P.O. Box 80728, Lincoln, NE 68501. $39.95.
10. MATHX and MATHXR, published by Denker Software, 204 4th Ave. S., P.O. Box 115, Isanti, MN. 55040. MATHX, $30.00; MATHXR, $20.00; printed manual, $10.00 (PBS disk #38.0).

11. LIMITS and LINEAR ALGEBRA, published by David Lovelock, Department of Mathematics, University of Arizona, Tucson, AZ 85721. No fees (TSL disks #2344 and #2338).

12. Ibid.

13. Calculus and Differential Equations V9, published by Byoung Keum, Department of Mathematics, University of Illinois, Urbana, IL 61801. No fee. (Shareware version available from Shareware to Go, P.O. Box 574575, Orlando, FL).

14. Diff: Differential Equations, published by David I. Hoyer, 31 Rossian Place, Cherrybrook NSW Australia 2126. US$38.00, AUS$50.00 (TSL disk #2326).

15. Electronic Circuit Designer, Published by Diatom Software, P.O. Box 262, Northfield, Ohio 44067. $25.00 (TSL disk #2333).

16. DC Circuit Analysis, published by Arthur Tanzella, 4613 Clubvue Drive, Pittsburgh, PA 15236-4803. $15.00 (TSL disk #7533).

# Chapter 11

# CD-ROMs and
# CD-ROM Networks

The term **ROM** has appeared several places in previous sections of the text. In chapter 1, ROM was defined as hardware—a microchip into which was burned a computer program. In chapter 8, ROM took on a different connotation, that of the engine of BASIC programming in an IBM PC. In this chapter, ROM will be considered as a different entity, that of a storage medium with incredible capacity at low cost.

Because of the popularity and virtually overnight success of the medium, the average person will equate "CD-ROM" with "compact disc," a music source. This perception is not unjustified, since CDs replaced 33-1/3" RPM vinyl phonograph records as the standard home music medium. CDs reproduce music with higher fidelity than vinyl recordings which must be played with a diamond needle, because CDs can be used again and again without wear and tear or detriment to the physical medium; the thousandth playing of a CD is as true to the original performance as the first. Moreover, compact disc players can be programmed to play music in a predetermined sequence, and the discs take up less space on a bookshelf.

However, the keyword for librarians as applies to this compact disc medium is "information." Music is information, as are text and graphics. This **CD-ROM**, in an information sense, stands for <u>c</u>ompact <u>d</u>isc-<u>r</u>ead <u>o</u>nly <u>m</u>emory. A CD-ROM, then, is nothing more than an optically readable medium capable of storing ones and zeros—binary digits—in patterns that can be read by the appropriate equipment and translated into ASCII text, graphics images, animated pictures, binary files, sound, or any combination of all of these. CD-ROMs are sometimes referred to as **optical**

*171*

**discs**, and the two terms are more or less interchangeable. The medium was first introduced in the mid-1980s, and, after a brief decline in popularity for a year or so, has made a comeback whereby it is now increasingly popular as a delivery medium for large databases and subscriptions which generate mass quantities of text. Many government agencies and the Superintendent of Documents issue publications on CD-ROMs, in lieu of microfiche. There are also many commercial vendors who issue their subscription series on CD-ROM. The list is growing, and the medium has found a permanent niche in the personal computing environment.

Technically, CD-ROMs function the same as magnetic disks, by manipulating binary data.[1] The differences are in the physical setups: a CD-ROM is impressed with lands and pits to represent the ones and zeroes of the binary system. When a CD-ROM is being "written," a laser beam is focused on a plastic substrate (base material) on the CD-ROM proper. With bursts of laser light in synchronization with the "on" and "off" states of the information to be recorded, the beam burns a hole resulting in a pit in the plastic or leaves it alone, making a land. The read process does just the reverse, with the laser beam sensing the presence of substrate material (the land) or the absence of it (the pit) to determine states of "one" or "zero" respectively. The advantage of using laser-based techniques is the density of information allowed by such technology—a data track of some three-and-one-half miles can be recorded onto a standard 4.8" (actually 120 mm) disc. This is a spiral (not concentric) track which begins at the center hub of the disc, instead of from the outside as with

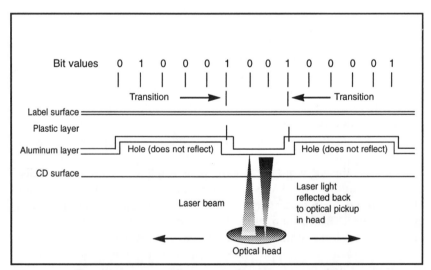

**Figure 11.1** Compact disc read/write process (diagram courtesy of Procom Technology, Inc)

a phonograph record. All of this results in a very high compression of information, and, with current technology, a very accurate and precise retrieval mechanism.

This is where the technology stands at the time of this writing. For the present, CD-ROM is a **WORM** (**write once, read many**) device. The write process is destructive, that is, once the pits are burned into the CD-ROM substrate, they cannot be erased. There currently exists an optically erasable/rewritable technology, and it is just beginning to break its way into the commercial and consumer market. There are several variations of this optically rendered medium, one called a **floptical** (for floppy/optical) disk, and the price range is dropping to where the technology is affordable outside of industrial and laboratory environments. When CD-ROM drives were first introduced, some analysts predicted the death knell for hard disk drives and other high-density, magnetic-based storage media. The "demise has been greatly exaggerated," however, and the prediction is now that rewritable CD-ROM devices will be commonplace around the mid 1990s, although they will share the marketplace with most of the traditional storage media.

## CD-ROMS AS REFERENCE SOURCES

CD-ROMs as optically readable media are naturals for holding huge quantities of data. A typical CD-ROM can hold upwards of 660 megabytes of information.[2] It is thus possible to place entire sets of books on one CD-ROM, and perhaps have enough room left over to include some graphics images and pictures.

The first mass-market CD-ROM was Grolier's *The Electronic Encyclopedia*,[3] introduced in January 1986. Other titles quickly followed, and the McGraw-Hill *Science and Technical Reference Set, The Original Oxford English Dictionary*, and H. W. Wilson's *Reader's Guide to Periodical Literature* were among the originally available titles. Prices of CD-ROMs which appeared on the market for the first few years ranged from $300 to $1,100 per title. CD-ROM players were targeted at the consumer market as well and could be purchased for under $1,000 as add-ons for personal computers.

CD-ROM technology evolved along with PC technology, and the number of available titles increased geometrically. As disc capacities increased, problems for personal computers began to surface. The PCs of the mid-1980s reached the upper bounds of memory capacity with the architecturally-imposed 640,000 bytes of RAM—able to contain hardly a fraction of the contents of a CD-ROM disc in the computer's memory at any given time. Further, the limitations of the first few versions of MS-DOS thwarted PCs from accessing CD-ROM drives with any efficiency—early versions of

DOS couldn't read a single hard disk drive of a capacity greater than 32 megabytes. Engineers at the time had not conceived of a drive necessary to hold any more than 32 million bytes of material; programs and databases (at least, on personal computers) just weren't that large yet!

A solution was devised to overcome the limitation, and it is one that is still widely used for its simplicity. The Microsoft Corporation furnished a device driver called the **Microsoft Extensions** which adequately allows DOS to access disk partitions far larger even than the 640 megabytes presented by CD-ROM discs. The Extensions attach themselves as a .SYS (system) file at bootup time and act as a memory resident utility program to intercept DOS requests for large sectors of information. Installation is simply a matter of including a line in the CONFIG.SYS (system configuration file) for DOS to access, similar to the following:

DEVICE=DRIVER.SYS /B:300 /M:P /T:1 /U:1 /D:device_name

To translate, this is where DRIVER.SYS is a device named by the CD-ROM drive's manufacturer to correspond to the hardware furnished by that manufacturer, e.g., HSONY.SYS or SONYCDU.SYS for a Sony CD-ROM drive. /B:300 sets the base memory address for input/output activities. /M:P allows a choice of interrupt driven or polled device setups (here polled has been chosen). /T:1 is the DMA (dynamic memory allocation) channel 1, 2, or 3, and /U:1 advises DOS of the number of CD-ROM drives attached. /D:device_name tells DOS the name of the device driver specified in the MSCDEX.EXE file (the program that actually loads the CD-ROM access program into memory when the CD-ROM drive is invoked at the command promt).

Actually, the majority of the settings just given need not concern the end user. Whenever a CD-ROM drive is installed, the only switch that needs to be programmed is the interrupt level (3, 4, or 5). Most drive manufacturers furnish an installation program with their own versions of the Microsoft Extensions, and this utility takes care of determining the proper CONFIG.SYS settings and writing them to the CONFIG.SYS file. If the drive has not been installed by the dealer when the computer was purchased, the user needs only to answer a few questions, and the drive is attached to the system, ready to query CD-ROM discs.

CD-ROM hardware is available in a wide variety of configurations. CD-ROM drives are usually in the class of **SCSI** (pronounced "scuzzi"), or **small computer systems interface** devices. The technology is now affordable at the consumer level, such that a single drive, internal CD-ROM player is available for a few hundred dollars. Units with external drives add a hundred dollars or so to the price, because of the addition of case hardware and an additional power supply. There are multi-unit CD-ROM setups, configured typically in a **tower** (upright case) format, or, for larger setups, in **rack mounts**. Many of the larger configurations are just multiples of single-unit systems, typically governed by one or more **server units** (see discussion on local area networks in chapter 15). A variation on the multi-unit system is that of a **jukebox** setup, where there is a carousel type CD-ROM changer inside a single CD player unit. While the jukebox has the advantage of economy, unlike the units with separate, discrete player drives, only one of usually six or more CD-ROMs can be accessed at any given time. Setups with individual (single platter) drives can be programmed in such a way as to access one or more CD-ROM-based databases simultaneously, in a multisharing environment.

It is easiest to explain data-oriented CD-ROMs in terms of musical compact discs. Because the foundation of CD-ROMs is a digital technology, data, whether music, graphics, or text, are encoded in approximately the same manner on any given disc ("compact dis_c_" is the actual trademark). In fact, all three forms of data can exist simultaneously on one disc. If you examine most CD-ROM drives installed in (or on) a personal computer, you will notice a small jack marked "audio" or "voice" or something similar. There are several programs which will allow you to play music on the drive while you are attending to other computing tasks. One such program is SoundWorks,[4] which allows you to output music to a set of personal stereo headphones or to small, low wattage speakers. This is also a good example of multitasking (see chapter 6), allowing a program to run "in the background" while you are attending to something else on the screen. Procom Technology also ships with its CD-ROM drives a utility called PLAYCD.EXE which plays audio CDs while the computer is attending to other tasks. If you are the kind of person who must have a "bit of noise" while attempting to concentrate, these programs are for you!

## APPLICATION: CD-BASED PROGRAMS ESPECIALLY USEFUL IN LIBRARIES

This chapter does not purport to act as a selection tool for a CD-ROM collection. Persons desiring to evaluate titles are pointed to the standard review media; *Library Journal* publishes a regular column called "CD-ROM Review" which presents annotated reviews of new titles, and there are several periodicals and catalogs (see Bibliography) which provide similar assistance. However, there are some representative titles which are noteworthy for their reference value in libraries. Rather than place them in the Bibliography (which is reserved for print media), they are described below and discussed in the context of applicability to library management, as representatives of the various classes of CD-ROM topics available.

One bit of advice when considering CD-ROM-based titles surrounds the issue of copyright. As mentioned above, CD-ROM setups are possible over a local area network, a factor which dilutes the issue of high cost that many CD-ROM titles exhibit. It is highly cost-efficient to place CD-ROMs in jukebox setups or arrangements of stacked CD-ROM drives, particularly where the discs can be accessed from multiple workstations along a network. However, the silver lining has a cloud: copyright protection. CD-ROM-based works enjoy the same authors' rights as do other software programs and hard copy titles. It is prudent to check with the publisher as to whether a particular CD vendor will allow multiple location accesses to a title or requires that one CD-ROM must be purchased for every workstation that will access it. There is no set pattern; some publishers are quite strict about accesses, others state that accesses over local area networks are allowable with purchase of but a single copy, and many are vague in their policies or state a "don't care" attitude. Many will demand that a CD-ROM be returned before an update is mailed, and others retain ownership of the disc, demanding that the medium be returned when its lease to the library expires. Again, it is best to check usage policies before committing budget dollars or inadvertently erring against copyright restrictions. Further, you should consult the publisher and not the jobber in order to ascertain policies straight from the source.

One other consideration that should be addressed is the requirement of the CD-ROM itself for a compatible hardware as well as software environment. Many CD-ROMs exhibit a dual functionality; that is, they will run on either a PC-based CD-ROM drive as well as on an AppleCD player. Most systems will specify that CD-ROMs to be used must conform to the **International Standards Organization (ISO) 9660** or **High Sierra** standards—sets of protocols that dictate how data and files must appear on the CD-ROM proper for compatibility with programs such as the aforementioned Microsoft Extensions. CD-ROMs and their associated software usually dictate that a relatively recent version of the operating system be in place on the target computer. In the case of PCs, it is usually a requirement that DOS version 3.1 or higher be available, with Microsoft Extensions version 2.0 or later running concurrently. Macintosh computers typically must present System 6.0.5 or later. You should also check the computer hardware requirements in the CD-ROM publisher's literature to find out if your machine has an appropriate memory capacity. Many CD-ROM programs require the bulk of the 640 kilobytes of available lower memory in a PC, and you might even be forced to install a memory management program such as QEMM or EMM386.EXE to free up additional RAM. Also, many CD-ROM database programs require that a **loader program** be installed on the hard disk drive, and some of the larger of these setup and menuing utilities can use two or three megabytes of disk space. The CD-ROM titles furnished by the Superintendent of Documents use such loaders, and there is usually a different one for each GPO title.

A couple of notable titles have already been mentioned. There are hundreds of titles available by subscription and as trade publications; catalogs for these are listed in the Bibliography. Those that have been especially helpful in constructing this textbook are as follows: where the discussions of public domain software were concerned (chapters 2 and 10), the *PC-SIG Library*[5] was invaluable. This compendium of some 4,500 public domain programs for the IBM and compatible computers is presented with an interface of on-screen descriptions (blurbs) of the programs, from which you can download the samples to your own hard disk, or, in some cases, run the sample programs directly from the interface screen. The interface rivals the print publication of PC-SIG, its *Encyclopedia of Shareware*,[6] in content and organization. If it were attached to a CD-ROM network, this disc would serve as a valuable resource to patrons browsing through a selection of programs to seek one for their particular needs (see chapter 12 on public access computers). A similar CD-ROM is *Phethean's Public Domain Library*,[7] which has many unique shareware titles but lacks the user interface and hard copy backup of the PC-SIG disc.

Library reference departments are finding that more and more shelf space can be cleared when general encyclopedias and reference books can be made accessible on CD-ROM. The Software Toolworks' *Multimedia Encyclopedia*[8] and *Reference Library*[9] are often available for free in hardware bundles with CD-ROM drives. The contents of these two discs are quite useful for quick reference of even relatively complex inquiries. The *Multimedia Encyclopedia* is actually the 21-volume Grolier *Academic American* edition, and includes 3,000 pictures in VGA resolution, 250 maps, 50 video clips, and 30 minutes of sound bites. While the multimedia presentations require special equipment such as a sound card (e.g., Sound Blaster or Ad Lib card), the pictures are nonetheless displayable on a standard PC workstation with a VGA monitor. The *Reference Library* contains *Webster's Dictionary of Quotable Quotations*, *Webster's New World Dictionary*, *Webster's New World Thesaurus*, *Webster's Guide to Concise Writing*, *The New York Public Library Desk Reference*, the Prentice Hall *Dictionary of Twentieth Century History*, *J.K. Lasser's Legal and Corporation Forms for the Smaller Business*, and *The National Directory of Address and Telephone Numbers*. Because all the various reference works are linked by a common menu-driven interface, searches can easily be shifted from one book to another, and cut-and-paste of text from any of the on-disc material can easily be transferred into a word processor. Probably the greatest advantage, though, is to a reference librarian on a busy public desk; a search on a topic can be made through any of the volumes in a matter of seconds. The *Microsoft Bookshelf*[10] is another alternative to a ready reference shelf, and this CD-ROM includes the *American Heritage Dictionary*, the *Houghton Mifflin*

*Spelling Verifier and Corrector*, *Roget's II: Electronic Thesaurus*, *The 1987 Newspaper Enterprise Association World Almanac and Book of Facts*, *Bartlett's Familiar Quotations*, *The Chicago Manual of Style*, *The U.S. Zip Code Directory*, the *Houghton Mifflin Usage Alert* (usage of commonly misused words), and the directory of *Business Information Sources*.

Chapter 8 discussed the use of languages in building and developing software programs. Language compilers and interpreters at one time could be shipped on just one or even two diskettes. But languages have evolved in complexity, and nowadays it is typical for PC-based compilers to ship on ten or twelve or more high-density diskettes. For its C/C++ compiler, Microsoft Corporation gives the end user the option of receiving its product (beginning with version 7.0) on diskettes or on a single CD-ROM. The latter has a decided advantage: compiler libraries take up a considerable amount of space on a hard disk, and most serious programmers will frequently swap between setups to accommodate different target machines or clients. The fact that the various setup options and libraries can reside on a CD-ROM allows voluminous free space on a programmer's hard drive that ordinarily must be kept in reserve to hold all the permutations which may be required for any new computing environment. Programmers typically require a considerable amount of support (print) documentation to which to refer for syntax rules, coding conventions, and sample programs for the programs they develop. Microsoft Corporation, because it publishes several different language compilers and utilities for developers, has also placed a set of all the manuals for all its compilers (C, Pascal, FORTRAN, assembly language, etc.) on a CD-ROM called the *Microsoft Programmer's Library*.[11] As with the text-based reference books mentioned in the previous paragraph, all the manuals are searchable as a unit, and the inquirer can request that material on a programming topic be sent to a printer. It is not required to purchase a copy of any of Microsoft's software compilers to buy the *Programmer's Library*, and libraries with heavy technical collections would do well to include this CD-ROM title to perform searches for patrons.

A number of indexes are now being published on CD-ROM. A noteworthy issue is the *Computer Library*,[12] which provides indexes and abstracts for a year's worth of magazine articles on computer science from about 120 different periodicals. Its monthly issues cover over 55,000 articles, making it an ideal candidate for appearing, as it does, on CD-ROM. *The Reader's Guide to Periodical Literature*[13] is also now available on CD-ROM, and it includes the WilSearch query mode for applying complex search parameters (see chapter 17). Benchmark tests on the CD-ROM *Reader's Guide* showed an average of twenty seconds required to deliver query results. And a number of other high-powered reference tools that were once available only in hard copy have appeared on CD-ROM. The

McGraw-Hill *CD-ROM Science and Technical Reference Set*[14] should be familiar to students of scientific bibliography, and its capability of allowing a researcher to look up a word up in the dictionary and immediately continue in the encyclopedia's main text makes it a highly efficient cross-reference tool. *The Oxford English Dictionary (Second Edition) on Compact Disc* has also been "computerized," and this Windows-based *OED* on CD-ROM includes algorithms for searching for words in groups (e.g., all those ending in "-ism,", "-ology," or "-phile") and for locating words even if the search stratagem contains a misspelling.[15]

Finally, there are some specialty programs that would not have been possible, or would have been very expensive to provide, without the availability of the CD-ROM medium. *Clip Art 3-D*[16] is a collection of 2,500 objects, including state and national maps, flowers and trees, automobiles and trucks, and a host of other line art pictures importable into desktop publications and word-processed documents. The objects can be shaded, rotated, expanded, sized, combined, and altered with the draw package, then saved as graphics files in standard (including .PCX) file formats. There are both Macintosh and IBM format discs, the latter running under Microsoft Windows. *Monarch Notes* and *Cliffs Notes* have variously appeared in CD-ROM format, as have collections of the *Great Books* and other assorted unabridged classics under collective titles such as *Library of the Future*. Finally, DeLorme Mapping publishes a CD-ROM-based atlas which lists, by name, nearly every street in all fifty states. Called *Street Atlas USA*,[17] the disc allows searches by town name, area code, Zip code, and by specific street name. Even named rural routes are identified, and both federal and state designations are given for numbered routes. The on-screen maps can be zoomed into or out of, and they can be sent to a file for incorporation into a published document. Figure 11.2 gives an example of a customized map using *Street Atlas USA*.

There is a current trend, a sort of "second wave," in CD-ROM publications toward multimedia presentations. This trend, which first appeared in the early 1990s, involves the combination of text, graphics, animation, and sound onto one screen. An example might be a lookup of Dr. Martin Luther King's "I Have a Dream" speech. Superimposed upon a portrait of Dr. King might be a thirty-second film clip of the delivery of the speech, with the actual speech itself playing through the computer's speaker or through a media board such as the Sound Blaster or Ad Lib card. The applications for this type of reference tool in a media center or classroom situation are many and varied. It is a chance for multisensory reinforcement of what might ordinarily be a text-based reading assignment. Those students who "learn with their eyes" can now use the computer to compete scholastically with those whose learning experiences have been mainly verbal.

There are more than 3,000 commercially available CD-ROM titles in print, and the list is doubling each year.[18] Many of the new publications are following the multimedia trend, and subject offerings are varied. The Microsoft Bookshelf is now issued in a multimedia edition, as is the Software Toolworks' *Multimedia Encyclopedia* (previously mentioned). *Battle Chess*[19] teaches the game with a thirty-minute animated tutorial, and pieces move about on a three-dimensional chessboard. The *Amanda*

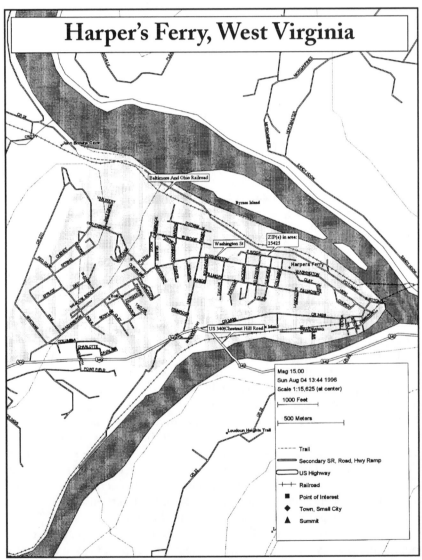

**Figure 11.2**  Street Atlas USA's rendition of the Harper's Ferry, West Virginia, area

*Stories*[20] provides ten interactive stories by Amanda Goodenough, including "Indigo the Cat" and "Your Faithful Camel," for children ages three and up. *Stingers*[21] includes ninety-eight clips of music in multiple computer formats as well as in audio CD-ROM format, and the *Digisound Sound Solution Disc*[22] contains over 1,000 sound effect and music tracks, including 200 licensed music tracks on **Musical Instrument Digital Interface (MIDI)**. The list is growing, as are the possibilities for integrating the technology into library science. The prices of multimedia CD-ROMs are coming down to "affordable," where a core collection of titles will be possible to integrate with sound recordings and films for enhancement of any media center's offerings.

## DOCUMENT IMAGING

**Document imaging** is the process of scanning records, reports, typewritten pages, pictures, graphics—any information that is reproducible on a flat, printed page—and storing it on a computer disk as a bitmapped or vectorized descriptor file. As a newer area of information retrieval systems, document imaging is particularly helpful in circumstances where high volumes of data, not necessarily in text form, need to be stored and indexed. Specific applications for this technology in libraries and educational institutions, which are targets for document imaging solutions, include the following:

1. **Transcripts and student records**. While most schools are computerized for the purpose of recording and issuing grades, transcripts issued prior to the time of an automation conversion may still be in paper form. Document imaging reduces the need for bulk and may render the retention of source documents unnecessary.

2. **Scientific literature**. The handling of loosely disseminated literature concerned with distributing information to the appropriate receivers is a critical time problem. Distribution of such material on CD-ROMs speeds the search time and eliminates the possibility of separation of unpublished materials.

3. **Project communication**. Large projects, such as new library building construction, require a considerable amount of inter- and intraproject communications, often between cities if the architects and construction managers are distantly separated. Particularly for technical information, blueprints and specifications, each member of the advisory, decision-making and planning teams needs access to the same body of voluminous information.

**4. Special files**. Drawings, flow sheets, completed studies, graphics, and support documents need to reside elsewhere than in damp basements. Often dictated by statute, they cannot be discarded for a number of years; document imaging techniques ensure that stored papers don't have to be intrusive.

**5. Special reference collections**. The handling of relatively short-life, but out-of-print books, books too rare or fragile to be circulated freely, extraordinarily long government documents not provided on microfiche, and artwork needs special protection. The originals can be stored in special environmental conditions after they are scanned (once) onto CD-ROMs for reference and investigation.

**6. Museum collections**. It is surprising how many samples and specimens are not on public display. Document imaging can provide visions (still or animated) of the contents of drawers and display cases not generally on view; moreover, such collections on CD-ROM can travel outside the museum, while, in most cases, the original artifacts cannot.

## NOTES

1. Ogg, Harold C. "CD-ROM Setups on a Zenith Data Systems Computer." *REMark*, December 1990, pp. 39-43.
2. Quain, John R. "CD-ROM Drives: Mass Appeal." *PC Magazine*, December 22, 1992, pp. 293-343.
3. O'Brien, Bill. "Archives in Miniature." *PC Magazine*, January 31, 1989, pp. 185-224.
4. Soundworks, published by The Software Toolworks, Inc., 60 Leveroni Court, Novato, CA 94949. $39.95.
5. *PC-SIG Library, 13th Edition*, published by PC-SIG, Inc., 1030-D East Duane Avenue, Sunnyvale, CA 94086. $39.95.
6. *The PC-SIG Encyclopedia of Shareware*. Sunnyvale, CA: PC-SIG, Inc., fourth edition, 1991. Paper, 690 pp., $19.95.
7. *Phethean's Public Domain Library #1 for IBM and Compatibles*. La Habra, CA: Peter J. Phethean, Ltd., $39.95.
8. Software Toolworks *Multimedia Encyclopedia*, published by The Software Toolworks, Inc., 60 Leveroni Court, Novato, CA 94949. $33.32 (when bundled with CD-ROM hardware).
9. Software Toolworks *Reference Library*, published by The Software Toolworks, Inc., 60 Leveroni Court, Novato, CA 94949. $33.32 (when bundled with CD-ROM hardware).
10 *Microsoft Bookshelf*, published by Microsoft Corporation, 16011 NE 36th Way, Redmond, WA 98073-9717. $295.00.
11. *Microsoft Programmer's Library: CD-ROM Database of PC Programming References*, published by Microsoft Corporation, 16011 NE 36th Way, Redmond, WA 98073-9717. $295.00.
12. *Computer Library*, published monthly by Ziff Communications Company, One Park Avenue, New York, NY 10016. $790.00 per year.
13. *Reader's Guide to Periodical Literature*, published by H.W. Wilson, Bronx, NY 10452. $1,095 for a yearly subscription.

14. *CD-ROM Science and Technical Reference Set*, published by McGraw-Hill Book Co., 1221 Avenue of the Americas, New York, NY 10020. $325.00.

15. Rabinovitz, Rubin. "An Etymologist's Dream: The OED on CD-ROM." *PC Magazine*, October 27, 1992, p. 49. The CD-ROM version of the *Oxford English Dictionary* is published by the Oxford University Press, 200 Madison Avenue, New York, NY 10016. $895.00.

16. *Clip Art 3-D*, published by NEC Home Electronics, Inc., 1255 Michael Drive, Wood Dale, IL 60191-1094. $399.00.

17. *Street Atlas USA*, published by DeLorme Mapping, Lower Main Street, P.O. Box 298, Freeport, ME 04032. $169.95.

18. Hicks, Adam A. "CD-ROMs for Your Multimedia PC." *PC Magazine*, December 22, 1992, pp. 358-368.

19. Battle Chess Enhanced CD-ROM, published by Interplay Productions, Inc., 3710 S. Susan, #100, Santa Ana, CA 92704. $79.95.

20. *Amanda Stories*, published by The Voyager Company, 1351 Pacific Coast Highway, Santa Monica, CA 90401. $59.95.

21. *Stingers*, published by The Music Bank, P.O. Box 3150, Saratoga, NY 15070. $99.00.

22. *Digisound Sound Solution Disc*, published by Presentation Graphics Group, 270 N. Cannon Drive, #103, Beverly Hills, CA 90210. $249.00.

# Chapter 12

# Public Access Computers

In chapter 2, computers were introduced as tools, machines that can make poeple's lives easier by performing useful work. The idea that computers could make library tasks easier, and perhaps more enjoyable, was given as a motivation for exploring in depth this idea of automation. Chapter 10 further explored the possibility of using computers in library settings to handle vast quantities of information using CD-ROM technology to make searching and storage more manageable.

The assumption of this chapter, which concerns "public access" as an "environment" of computer science, is that public domain software and CD-ROM databases will be purchased and collected for browsing by library patrons and perhaps used in shared settings. This study will examine the sometimes controversial issues of providing computers to patrons and the collection and dissemination of libraries of software programs.

## PUBLIC ACCESS WORKSTATIONS

Public access computers are really a phenomenon of the 1980s. Until the advent of the IBM PC and the Apple II computers, workstation terminals for patron use were out of the question for one simple reason— expense. In the decades prior to 1980, terminals for uses other than data publication were the bailiwick of researchers and students in colleges and universities who could pay the high laboratory fees to support their studies. Computer time was "sold," and CPU access was billed in fractions of seconds that the processor was dedicated to any given task. Casual use, then, was out of the question.

In order to discuss public access computers in light of a library issue, this text offers a somewhat focused definition. "Public access computer" refers to any workstation, usually a PC, that is not (or *may* not be) dedicated to an administrative function of the library and is available either free of charge or for a small fee for use by patrons. Uses will vary, and uses include the study of computer techniques and programming, the running of applications programs, the accession of databases, and the playing of games.

Many librarians consider an investment in public access computers a gamble. After all, budget money for workstations for patron use typically takes a low priority, right after all other computer equipment, especially for staff work areas, has been purchased. Because of ever-changing advances in computer technology, and particularly in PC technology, it is also a frustrating experience for a librarian to have to explain to a budget-conscious board of trustees why a hefty expenditure was made on equipment that soon became obsolete. Library boards have keenly acute memories of such purchases as delivery vans with rotary engines, quadraphonic stereo systems, and wet process photocopy machines. For big-ticket items such as workstations, librarians need to be armed with serious purchase justifications to obtain such things, and it helps to have done a lot of homework prior to financial planning meetings.

When called upon to construct a list of reasons for purchasing and installing computers for public access, most librarians must explain why they want to do it at all. Indeed, with "home" computers so ubiquitous and sold even in drugstores and shopping malls, why should public libraries or educational institutions not connected to timeshare hookups consider a service that may already be covered in other business sectors? This question is usually followed closely by: why should the library provide public access computers when it doesn't yet have all the terminals it needs for its own processes? The natural rejoinder becomes: will the technology be universally acceptable? Unbiased market figures are difficult to obtain, since many of these data are accurate for sales but not for applications. Perhaps the best technique to use is inductive reasoning: who would have access to a terminal for shared personal use? Students of elementary school up through college age are becoming computer-literate through hookups in classrooms. The media tries to convince people that within the next few years the microcomputer will become a typical household appliance, second only to the television. Thus, it becomes difficult to justify tax dollar purchases of such items in light of the presumption that a microcomputer is so common that inclusion of one or more in the library is merely a subsidization of what the general public should be able to afford on its own.

But the latter argument is akin to the old favorite, "Shouldn't people purchase all their own books?" The argument is obvious: just as there is a public mandate for literature and information, so there is also one for technology. This thesis can extend to a survival issue—the element of the citizenry that possesses computer literacy will have a decided advantage over the sector that does not. Here is precisely where the public and community college libraries step into the picture. There will always be people who do not have access to counseling services, business offices, books, and computer hardware environments. These potential users of PCs must turn to their old reliable standbys, the libraries. The remainder of this section will be devoted to constructing a convincing list of legitimate, potential uses for public access computers in order that a library administrator who is proposing so great an expenditure will have ammunition to show that the purchase is not merely a reaction to current fad.

There are going to be three cost outlays to the library that decides to provide computers for public access: the cost of the hardware, the cost of the software, and a salary for the person who will oversee and maintain both programs and computers. The choice of hardware will usually be an IBM PC or compatibles, a Macintosh, or an Apple II. The latter is still widely used in elementary and secondary schools, and students and teachers may bring disks to the library for out-of-class study. One collection of Apple II software still popular is *Public Domain Software on File*.[1] A library would typically not use machines larger than PCs, because high-end equipment such as minicomputers, UNIX boxes, Sun workstations, etc., are not considered part of the consumer or retail market. The library should decide how many locations are to be equipped, should purchase machines from one central source (adhering to bid laws), and should include a maintenance contract in the purchase. Shareware and public domain programs (see chapter 2) are good sources of inexpensive software, and a library can build a significant collection of shareware titles without spending a lot of money. The one ongoing cost is for a librarian to maintain the various hardware setups. It should be decided that, if public access computers are to be offered, the upkeep on such machines should not be casual. If maintenance of a public access environment is not taken seriously, there will be patron complaints because of broken equipment, lost programs, and even dirty workstations. It is better to decide that there will be a permanent budget entry for computer support than to have a potentially valuable service create negative public relations.

Several groups of applications are typically offered in public access environments.[2] They are as follows:

- games
- educational and tutorial programs

- user-contributed software
- text editors and word processors
- accounting, personal finance, budget and spreadsheet programs
- informational databases (library fact files and bibliographies)
- message boards (local or dialup)
- programming language tutorials
- program language interpreters, such as BASIC

There will be some controversy over the first item in the list. It is up to the individual library to decide whether to provide entertainment media. Some libraries separate games into two categories, arcade (video) and educational, purchasing only one or the other from selection criteria. For all software, user manuals must be provided, and they should not circulate. Usually, if a program manual is lost in circulation, it can be replaced only with the purchase of a complete, new set of software disks; this policy is followed by most software vendors to discourage piracy (illegal copying) of programs to be distributed with a photocopied manual. There are third-party manuals in trade format for all of the major software programs, and these should be the only ones not assigned to the reference collection.

The same rules that apply to the purchase of public domain software and shareware for internal library use also apply to the selection of programs for public access and circulating collections. Regarding the matter of circulating software, the individual library must decide whether it will circulate returnable media, or whether it will insist that patrons copy the programs they desire onto their own floppy disks. The latter has money-making possibilities if the library wishes to run a concession to sell blank floppy disks at a premium charge. Bear in mind also that floppy diskettes, if they are to be circulated and returned, must be given the same physical considerations as other magnetic-based media such as videotapes. In other words, theft detection strips and sensitizers, as well as metal detectors, can have a detrimental effect on computer software disks. Thus, whether the disks are to be used in the library (reference only) or out of house is a question that the library must decide before committing the cash outlay to public access programs.

Equipment security will be a problem, and the library will have to spend dollars above the cost of the basic equipment to ensure that computers do not disappear from public work areas. This is another point that might have to be "sold" to the policymaking body that approves the purchase. Probably the most secure protective device is a metal "cage" that completely surrounds the CPU (and possibly the video display) and can be opened only with a key. Nearly as effective, and somewhat more economical, are metal lockdown plates which affix to the bottom of computer equipment with 400 pounds-per-square-inch (PSI) adhesive.

Depending on the brand, the latter cost between $50 and $100 apiece, depending on size. Cable-and-lock sets, widely advertised and available at low cost ($10-$20 each) will usually slow down a potential thief, but such devices' effectiveness against a strong crowbar is limited. As with any planning, each individual library will have to decide what areas of the building are most vulnerable. The old adage that "locks thwart only honest people" should be remembered by those administrators who proclaim that their buildings are perfectly secure from thieves.

Security problems can affect programs and software as well. The most common vulnerability to public access computers is the computer virus. A **virus** is a piece of executable code which, as the name suggests, is transmitted from machine to machine via floppy disks or from files uploaded from a public (electronic) bulletin board. This code, typically written to cause harm (or at least, nuisance value) to computers, attaches itself to the computer's system files (e.g., COMMAND.COM in DOS) and lurks until a certain condition is met. Viruses range from **time bombs**, which usually react when a certain date is read from the system clock/calendar, to **worms**, which move around the system, attaching themselves to whatever strikes their creators' fancies. The results vary, from wisecrack messages appearing at inopportune moments on the computer's screen to lockups of input/output processes (e.g., with the accompanying message, "Your CPU has been STONED!") to outright destruction of the computer's **file allocation table (FAT)**. The FAT is an operating system construct that is essential for proper functioning of the hard disk drive; a virus attack to this area of the disk effectively wipes the drive clean. The best protection against viruses on public access terminals is to install a virus intercept program such as the Norton Antivirus[3] or Virucide[4] or any of several dozen other protective programs. These programs can be set to automatically subject new disks to a scrutinization process so that errant viruses cannot be brought in by patrons. Such programs are in the $40.00 to $60.00 range and should be updated periodically to ascertain that newer viruses are not missed by older software.

Another problem for software security is the matter of outright theft of confidential material. Some libraries allow dial access of public access computers in addition to dial access of the automated card catalog, and the two systems may be integrated. It is not uncommon for public access processes to share the same physical disk drives as the business office or other nonpublic facilities. While most patrons will honestly investigate the public bulletin board for legitimate activities, there are those who would test the system, to ascertain just "how far inside" they can pilfer. Such individuals are (rather derogatorily) known as **hackers**, so named for the "hacking around" that they do over the telephone lines. There is perhaps a shred of truth in the assertion that hackers and the authors of virus code are of the same breed. The results of such activities range from minor irritations to pure terrorism. However, this should not cause libraries to hesitate at providing public access services; there are protections available. The most obvious protection is to have the public access files on physically separate machines from internal files and documents. If this is not possible, there are **encryption programs** which, when applied to files, make any attempts to print them output as garbage. There are also **cloaking programs** such as Lattice's SecretDisk[5] which render entire hard disk drives invisible until a user with a password "unlocks" the drive. **Password protection** is available with a number of utility programs and in computer operating systems hosting user accounts (e.g., UNIX and NetWare). These types of programs are safe enough and can also be used in offices where computers with sensitive files are left unguarded after hours.

One selling point for public access computers is the possibility that the computers could generate some revenue. Coin boxes can easily be adapted to computer CPUs to sell computer time, much in the same manner as libraries have traditionally vended time on electric typewriters. The installation of a coin box also introduces an added element of security risk, because coin boxes, especially in unsupervised areas, are invitations to theft. A possible compromise is to seek a vendor who would lease coin boxes *and* computer equipment as a concessionary arrangement, thereby sharing the risk and relieving the library from making a large cash outlay at the same time. Time cards, similar to copy cards for photocopy machines, could also be considered if the library anticipates a heavy demand for time on public access machines. In sum, all the elements— need, cost, payback, security, and operation—will have to be brought to the governing body before a public access arrangement can be established and maintained.

## ACADEMIC COMPUTER DEPARTMENTS

Depending on the locality, a library might be responsible for facilities that support curricula and instruction. This is particularly true of school and university libraries, and it places the librarian in the role of technician. Obviously, information science comes heavily into play in academic computer departments, and the job description of the librarian in charge often seems to include the catch phrase, "responsible for anything that plugs into the wall."

In a real sense, computer laboratories fall under the heading of "public access facilities," although the implication here is that lab resources are open only to a limited, authorized clientele. But the librarian will have similar responsibilities for administering laboratory equipment and programs as for managing public workstations. The librarian must be an intelligent consumer of computer equipment and be able to negotiate with vendors for quantity purchases of processors, video terminals, printers, and appropriate peripheral devices. Additionally, the librarian must be able to work with teachers and faculty to ascertain that software titles and version releases properly support what is being taught in the classroom. To do this, a librarian must be a materials selector with a grasp of the technical requirements of the programs to be included in the laboratory repertoire. It may also be a requirement of the facility that a collection of supplemental literature (e.g., journals and third-party manuals) be maintained separately in the laboratory proper.

In a manner of speaking, an academic computing facility is a specific kind of special library. There are materials to purchase, budgets to administer, cataloging and classification chores to attend to, check in/check out activities to manage, and personnel matters with which to keep abreast. Additionally, a librarian in charge of such a facility must tend a database of software licenses to be sure that copyright licensing is strictly followed. Some teaching activities may be required, if the librarian is expected to present bibliographic instruction of the various program offerings on the computers' disk drives. And, there may be the necessity for seminars to introduce newcomers to the proper methodologies of accessing their user accounts or of using the various operating systems installed in the facility. It may be necessary for the librarian to create and distribute handouts explaining steps for using the facilities and programs—an excellent application for desktop publishing programs. Finally, the librarian may be required to speak at conferences and publish papers about public access and academic computing facilities, especially if the librarian's position carries a tenure-track faculty status. Anyone who has read this textbook completely from the beginning will readily see that all aspects of hardware and software technology covered in the first half of the book are germane to administering such a facility—making the position of librarian in charge of public access stations a highly skilled and involved job assignment.

## NOTES

1. Public Domain Research Staff. *Public Domain Software on File Collection - IBM.* Facts on File, 1989 (includes 32 pp. *Program Description,* 16 pp. *User's Guide,* and 16 pp. *Librarian's Guide,* 12 diskette basic set with Satellite disk supplement). Also available as *Public Domain Software on File Collection - Apple* (for Apple IIe computers). Either basic set, $195.00; IBM supplement, $50.00, Apple supplement, $40.00.
2. Ogg, Harold C. "Public Access Computers in Libraries: A Justification for Existence." *Indiana Libraries 3:* Winter 1983, pp. 114-121.
3. The Norton Antivirus and The Norton Antivirus for Windows, published by Symantec Corporation, 10201 Torre Avenue, Cupertino, CA 95014-2132. $129.00.

4. Virucide, published by Parsons Technology, Inc., One Parsons Drive, P.O. Box 100, Hiawatha, IA 52233-0100. $31.99.
5. SecretDisk, published by Lattice, Inc., 3010 Woodcreek Drive, Suite A, Downers Grove, IL 60515 (mailing address P.O. Box 3072, Glen Ellyn, IL 60138). $129.00.

# Chapter 13

# Automated Circulation Systems and Public Access Catalogs

Chapter 5 has already discussed database programs. The following sections will move beyond the principles of database programming and outline the more extensive, computerized circulation and cataloging systems. As a motivation for espousing the highly technical, and sometimes expensive automated systems, the text will briefly examine the traditional circulation control methods as well as place them in their proper, historical perspective.

**Hand charging** was, obviously, the first system of circulation control. Sometimes called the **Newark System**, in its simplest form, hand charging requires only that there be an identifier card in the book (usually in a paper pocket) on which is typed the author, title, and call number of the book. It is necessary, then, that a borrower sign the card (sometimes including his/her address) and exchange it for a date due slip or rubber stamped date to indicate the latest time the book may be returned without penalty. This system, still widely used in many school libraries and in rural areas, requires only a file of book cards that must be accessed whenever a book is returned or at the occasion that a book must be considered delinquent.

Hand charging is advantageous in that it is inexpensive to maintain, and a separate patron file is not required. However, it is workable only with relatively small collections and in instances where there is not a large number of patrons. Moreover, the borrower population must be more or less local and known to the staff, and the system must assume that there are few out-of-district or reciprocal borrowers. Magnitude of use is therefore sacrificed for the sake of simplicity.

Other noncomputerized systems have been developed over the years. The **Gaylord System**, vended by Gaylord Brothers, employs a stiff cardboard borrower's card about the size of a standard credit card, with a metal tab affixed that contains a unique borrower number. A title/author/call number book card is also used with this system. When a book is charged, the borrower's card is inserted in the machine along with as many book cards, one at a time, as the patron wishes. The book card is imprinted with the number from the metal tab, along with a date due.

The Gaylord System's advantage is that a large number of books can be charged in a short period of time, since no writing or signing is a part of the chargeout transaction. However, book cards still must be filed as with a hand charging system, and a separate, numeric cross reference file of patron numbers must also be maintained. Nonetheless, it is still an inexpensive system; the majority of the costs are for supplies of tabbed borrower's cards, book cards, date due cards, and rental of the imprinting equipment. It is useful in libraries where there is a high turnover in books and materials circulated.

The McBee Corporation has sold a system generically known as the **McBee Keysort**. It is a variation on hand charging and machine charging systems, offering a supplemental facility whereby files of date due and book cards can be quickly filed and retrieved. The system works on the principle of punched holes along the edges of cardstock through which a metal rod can pass. Depending on how the cards are coded, the hole-or-notch system allows cards to stay on the rod if an edge hole is intact, or fall to the table if the hole has been cut away on the outside. Cards can be separated into two categories, then four, then eight, and so on until desired categories have been partitioned. The cost of such a system is low, and it is advantageous where large volume card files must be maintained. The drawback of the McBee system is in cases where the notched cards are lost from the book pockets, then the transactions must be completed by hand.

The **Recordak System** uses a 16 mm microfilm camera to take a picture of every single circulation transaction. Being a photographic activity, every check in/check out is memorialized on film. This system is also advantageous in situations where a considerable amount of materials are turned over in circulation because transactions are accurate and speedy. This is also a particularly handy system for proving to a skeptical (or larcenous) patron that he or she did, in fact, check out a particular book—a picture doesn't lie! However, the Recordak System is paper intensive, and a library must maintain a (sometimes voluminous) file of serialized date due and transaction cards. And, there is the matter of the microfilm itself—one or more microfilm readers must be maintained in the library for retrieval of overdue book information, and film processing bureaus often impose a time lag between acceptance of film for development and return of the processed run.

## PUBLIC ACCESS CATALOGS

Traditionally, when you arrived at the library in the years B.A. (before automation), if you wanted to look up a certain book or subject, you headed straight for the card catalog. "Card catalog" had a singular meaning: a cabinet full of trays of alphabetized 3" x 5" cards, upon which references to every book in the library were inscribed. The card catalog is (was) an institution; there are accounts of library schools teaching a handwriting technique called "the library hand," in order that the cards be properly inscribed with no spaces or punctuation out of place. In some circles, the catalog card symbolized a religion.

The card catalog serves a useful function, and there is no denying its importance or the fact that it and its format are still the basis for proper bibliographic assignment to the materials in the collection. However, the 3" x 5" card catalog is not without its drawbacks. First of all, it is labor intensive and expensive to maintain. In larger libraries, duplicate catalogs were needed for high traffic areas, and additional catalogs meant a duplication of efforts to produce cards and to file the results. There is also the cost of typing cards and the cost of cardstock, although service bureaus such as OCLC, WLN and Bro-Dart will furnish preprinted cards for a price. Paper card catalogs always were vulnerable to fire and mildew, and, in recent years, to vandals seeking a few thrills.

Photographic technology has made a significant inroad into the way card catalogs are handled. With the advent of finer-grained films, it became possible to take microfilm pictures of complete catalogs, sacrificing no detail or bibliographic element on the cards. Roll film was typically used, and **microfiche** and **ultrafiche** were often employed in lieu of 16 mm or 35 mm transparency film. At first, such records were used as a basis for disaster recovery—if a card catalog was destroyed, its contents could be duplicated from film records. It became obvious that such films could be offered at public access stations for patrons to perform catalog searches. Such microfilm was sold by service bureaus under many labels, including ComCat, and it provided a searcher with a quick and compact way to search the holdings of a library. And, since film can easily be duplicated, multiple catalogs were simply a function of duplicating the original film.

Microfilm catalogs were a leap forward for automated catalog technology, but they, too, had drawbacks. Since film is a linear medium, if a patron wanted to search for "Smith" in the catalog and the film was positioned in the reader in the "A's" or "B's" from the last person's search, the new searcher would have to spool through a (sometimes lengthy) piece of film to arrive at "S." Later releases of microfilm incorporated timing marks on the edges of the film so that a selected frame could be stopped at a predetermined point, but the film still required a finite time to spool from one end to another. Microfiche and microcards posed a similar problem as paper card catalogs; that is, loose cards could easily be misfiled. Card catalogs in 3" x 5" format could, theoretically, have been as up-to-date as the most recent card typed or received, provided that filers placed cards in the appropriate drawers immediately upon receipt. Photographic media, however, have a three-to six-month time lag because cards and machine readable tapes have to be converted to film. Conceivably, a microfilm catalog could have been many months out-of-date before its update supplement was received. Many a "new acquisitions notebook" has graced the counters of readers' services desks to supplement patron demand for knowledge of new titles received and not yet cataloged!

Nowadays, when librarians refer to public access catalogs, they mean automated, computerized terminals and typically use the acronym **PAC**. Indeed, in many libraries such terminals have taken the place of traditional 3" x 5" card catalogs. Some libraries now proclaim that they are "fully automated" and have relegated the card catalog and all its file drawers (or microfilm readers) to the darkest recesses of the basement. Other libraries have viewed the transitions as traumatic experiences and maintain computer terminals in the same area as the 3" x 5" drawers, although the latter may no longer be updated. The public access points may be simply **dumb terminals** (terminals with no processing power, and wired directly into a computer port), or they may be personal computers running special software interfaces so that the PC can double as a catalog inquiry terminal. There may be keyboards and/or **touch screens**. The latter are of the "point-and-shoot" variety, that is, you are given several choices on the screen, and you touch your finger to the item you wish to view. Whatever the format, the PAC is usually the tip of the iceberg and indicates a farther reaching, more elaborate circulation and cataloging environment behind the scenes.

Computerized public access catalogs have some obvious advantages over previously existing manual formats. One significant advantage is that of instantaneous update of titles in the database. Typically, a library that uses an automated circulation and cataloging system will also use the services of a **bibliographic utility,** such as OCLC or WLN online, or a CD-ROM based service, such as Bibliofile. Vendors of automated circulation systems provide one or more interfaces that link the computer providing the cataloging information to the local library's main book database. When a book or other piece of material is received, it is entered as a holding into the bibliographic database, and the library's computer database is simultaneously updated with the new bibliographic information. It is quite possible that a newly cataloged book is available for a patron search before it leaves the technical processing department.

There are other advantages to computerized catalogs. Very little paper is needed to maintain records, since the database is usually on magnetic disk in the main computer. Whenever additional access points are needed, it is a matter of running cable and plugging another terminal into an available port on the computer; there is no additional filing or alphabetizing needed for one or a hundred additional screens. Searches are rapid and efficient—you can locate a screenful of items on your topic in seconds using a computer terminal, compared to hopping from drawer to drawer with the traditional catalog setup. For global searches, you usually have a choice of **keyword searches** or **Boolean searches** (see chapter 17) in addition to title and author inquiries. In some locales, it is also possible to search a library's catalog from your home, via dial access (see chapter 16). And it is almost always possible to obtain full bibliographic entries for the items you have located, an advantage when constructing footnotes or reading lists for term papers or research documents you may be writing.

Computerized catalogs are not without their disadvantages, however. The most prohibitive factor is the cost, not only in the startup capital, but also in the replacement cost five to seven years (typically) in the future. Maintenance is another cost factor, and service contracts can run several hundred dollars per year per terminal and can include a general charge for the CPU and associated peripherals such as printers as well. Another rule of thumb: an automated circulation/cataloging system will almost *never* eliminate staff positions. In fact, the library which is newly automating should create in the budget the position of systems administrator, and for large, multibuilding computerized systems, two or more such *full-time* positions should be anticipated. Also for multilocation setups, there will be local telephone charges for exclusive use and **dedicated lines** to connect buildings. And finally, there is the one drawback that *never* happened with traditional 3" x 5" catalogs—you're only up and running as long as the electricity is on and the CPU is healthy!

There are numerous considerations which surround the planning and installation of public access catalogs along with a more expansive automated circulation and cataloging system. Vendors and procedures for automating a library will be discussed in the following sections.

## VENDORS AND SYSTEM ATTRIBUTES

Numerous brands and publishers of turnkey automated circulation systems have appeared over the years. Alys II, DataPhase, GEAC, LCS,

OCLC, CLSI, WLN, Notis, Dynix and many others have variously appeared on the library scene. Many are still viable, and many others have long disappeared. Still others have combined forces: in early 1993 Geac and CLSI consummated a merger; in the previous year, Ameritech acquired Dynix and Notis.

It is uncommon for all but the largest libraries to write their own automated circulation/cataloging systems using in-house programmers. Such a project is prohibitively expensive and highly impractical in light of the many vendors that offer **turnkey**, or ready-made systems. Turnkey vendors have been around since the 1970s, each company surviving (or not) with varying degrees of success. While this chapter will not focus on any one vendor's system but will describe automated circulation systems generically, a partial list of vendors who were the pioneers in the field is provided below for name recognition. Frequent readers of library literature should find these companies familiar. Included is the computer language in which the vendor authors and compiles the various system components and subprogram routines.

- CLSI—uses DEC assembly language and C language; newer modules are UNIX-based
- Classic—writes in FORTRAN (company now out of business)
- Gaylord—uses Pascal and some assembly language
- Geac—runs assembly language burned into firmware, under the UNIX operating system
- Ringgold—writes programs in COBOL
- Ulysis—uses compiled BASIC

It is interesting to note the variety of languages the original vendors used in creating their systems. The survivors were the ones who programmed in C and assembler, most likely because those two languages are less machine dependent than others. Additionally, the UNIX operating system, being an extension of the C language, has been a pivot point for the development of some of the newer, more successful turnkey systems.[1] The majority of vendors in business in the 1990s still focus on these two platforms, and C and assembler will probably be the languages of choice in information systems development for some time to come.

## PLANNING AND INSTALLING AUTOMATED CATALOGING AND CIRCULATION SYSTEMS

The planning for automating a library, once the financial decision is made to proceed with such a project, can take months. The process is further complicated for libraries that are converting from manual systems rather than upgrading existing computerized environments. Nonetheless, the process is methodical and can be accomplished with a minimum of anguish if a well-established plan is formulated beforehand. Methods of systems analysis (chapter 14) should be an integral part of all planning, and communication, both with budgetary powers and the persons who will be using the system, is imperative at all steps in the process. Success or failure, both in procuring and implementing the system, depend on perseverance until the switch is thrown on "conversion day."

Naturally, every library setting is unique. However, there is a skeletal process which can be followed, with modifications as needed, to establish the work plan and see the automation through to conclusion.

## Step 1: Determine What Is Needed

This may seem like a trivial part of the planning, but the glitz of computers many times has inspired an automation project merely for the prestige of owning machinery. Answer the question honestly: Does the library really need to computerize? More than a few persons must be enthused about such a project, because there will be a great deal of work involved before the process is concluded. If there are many questions or doubts about the value of an automated circulation/cataloging system, it might be money well-spent to bring in an outside consultant who can impartially study the library's current and future needs.

The process must also involve decision makers at all levels. Several groups of people are going to have to be consulted about this thing called "automation." The library needs to actively involve the following people:

1. **The library board or governing body**. The idea for automating a library may have come from within the board or from the administrative staff. Large expenditures nearly always have a formal origin, usually from a policymaking individual or individuals. And, as such, these leaders are going to have their own concepts of what "automation" means. It is the library director's task to educate the policymakers and provide as much accurate and concise information as possible about a computerization project, in language appropriate for the group who will vote to proceed or not proceed.
2. **The public**. Because the minutes of most public bodies are subject to scrutiny, or, in the case of colleges and universities, to a review by senates and committees, the library must prepare for a sales job which may encounter varying amounts of resistance. Many times, taxpayers cannot fathom an expenditure of a minimum of a quarter of a million dollars for "wires and tubes." Once a need is determined, the library staff and board must be prepared to speak enthusiastically about the project to all challengers.
3. **The staff**. Because computerization is an involved and sometimes lengthy project which will change working conditions forever, the

staff must be made to feel that their involvement in the design and planning for the new system is wanted and needed. It is well taken at this point to identify those staff members who have some background in computers and automation for input to the project, and, if necessary, allow them freedom to discuss, caucus, and even make some policy regarding the impending months of work ahead.

## Step 2: Study the Physical Layout and Environment

Realize from the onset that a considerable amount of wiring will be needed. To make bidders' and contractors' jobs easier, you should have, or have drawn, a current set of blueprints for the entire library (and branches, if the system is to span buildings). With floor diagrams, sketch locations where public and staff terminals are desired. Allow also for future expansion; inevitably, you will want to add terminals during the life of the system. Set aside a separate room—not the corner of a room or the basement—for the central processing unit, line printers, staff workspace, and storage for backup tapes and printouts. It is a good idea to obtain an opinion of an electrical contractor of the suitability of your building for an automated system; the need for specially air conditioned rooms, drilling through concrete, the shielding of cables, and partitioning of space can add considerable cost to the base price of the system.

## Step 3: Plan the Financing

This step should be taken early in the project. If you cannot pay for the system and provide for continuing maintenance, support and equipment replacement, all the subsequent planning is useless. Ideally, the library will have been placing funds aside into a capital layback fund in anticipation of a cash purchase, but this case is exceptional. If such a reserve fund is not available, the next most desirable scenario is to have approved a line item in the annual budget for an outright purchase of the desired system. Otherwise, one of several other avenues must gain approval: in a college or university, a special appropriation must be sought from the governing board. In a public school or public library, it is possible that a bond issue for capital improvement must be levied. The latter can take a considerable amount of advance planning. In some states, a bond issue is approved through a petitionary process, subject to taxpayer remonstrance. In other states, bond issues are placed on a ballot and are subject to a referendum. And in others, bond issues are approved or disapproved by elected representative bodies outside the library. Whatever the case, the library should be prepared for the bond issue to fail the first time, and possibly a number of subsequent times. Upon failure of an issue, there is often a statutory cooling-off period of several months to a year, during which time the matter of a bond issue cannot be resubmitted.

Before making its request to the appropriate financial powers, the library should have prepared a comprehensive financial statement covering all possible elements of the automation project. The plans should include a long range contingency fund for replacement of the entire system in five, but no more than seven, years. The statement should also include funds for the hiring of additional personnel who will administer the system. If the library has been on a completely manual system, monies to perform a **retrospective conversion** (see step 6 below) of the card catalog into machine readable format must be included. While the best financial planning cannot predict the unforeseen, the financial statement of the project should be as complete as possible; taxpayers and governing boards do not like "surprises" of added costs after they have approved the original plan especially if they were caused by careless accounting. Be prepared to defend the financial proposal in a manner similar to defending a graduate thesis; be calm and professional when asked questions about the project or challenged on account of its feasibility.

## Step 4: Generate the Request for Proposal

The **request for proposal,** or **RFP**, will become the primary working (if not legal) document of the entire automation project. It can also become the single most costly piece of paperwork of the entire venture. Ideally, if the library has staff expertise and human resources time to construct its own RFP, a considerable amount of funds will be saved from the budget. If a bond issue is to finance the project, it may or may not be possible to fold the cost of having a consultant prepare the RFP document into the bond proceeds. Sometimes the RFP is a sunk cost; that is, if the project does not proceed to conclusion, the money invested in a proposal is lost. You should make the RFP specific enough to cover all the major points of what you expect in the proposed automated system, but not so specific as to discourage potential bidders on the basis of standards being too high or parameters being too complicated.

One way of saving money on the drafting of the request for proposal is to identify a library similar to yours that has purchased an automated system akin to the one you are seeking and to copy its proposal. In tax supported agencies, an RFP is usually considered a public document subject to inspection by the general population and reproducible for the cost of photocopying. You should respect any wishes or restrictions of the library that provides you with its proposal and adhere to any copyrights relevant to the document. Within reason, you can consider the document a **boilerplate**, a template model of what you are seeking for your own library, and replace numbers and names with those of your own institution.

When constructing your RFP, you should engage in site visits. In doing so, you will undoubtedly notice features not in the vendors' literature and, sometimes, features not desirable in a particular system. Other libraries will be more frank and candid about the pros and cons and problems of their system, and by talking to recent customers, you will be spared the vendors' biases. State and national library associations' exhibitor areas (such as those of the American Library Association and Canadian Library Association) can act as springboards for provision of literature and specifications, and at these meetings you sometimes make initial, important contacts with the vendors with whom you will be dealing for the next several months or years.

Once you have your completed Request for Proposal (and hopefully your funding), you will probably have to "sell" the plan to your governing board. A committee of the whole is a good way to cause the board members to feel that they "own" the document, and this bit of diplomacy can go a long way in getting the plan approved at a formal board meeting. Immediately thereafter, your RFP becomes a plan of action. You must check local and state or provincial bid laws to ascertain the proper procedure for advertising for your system and soliciting bids. It is a good idea, and money well spent, to hire counsel who is well versed in governmental matters and can oversee your issuance of bonds and acceptance of bids. There will be other legal papers to consider (most specifically, the purchase contract), and the library will have other, technical matters to attend without having to worry about running a legal gauntlet.

### Step 5: Prepare the Staff

The coming of automation to the library will be a joy for some, and a trauma or catharsis for others. The staff should have been involved from the beginning (see step 1). It is quite necessary to obtain a psychological acceptance of the "new computer"; technophobia is often a common dysfunction among library staff, if not an outright fear that their jobs are threatened. It must be realized that some persons simply do not like computers! Nevertheless, you need a high level of cooperation to make the project work successfully. As soon as a system is chosen, arrangements for scheduling pre- and post-installation training should be established. Near the beginning of the actual physical installation, job descriptions for appropriate personnel should be drawn, and individuals should be interviewed and hired or promoted for the various jobs of computer operator and system manager. Technical services and circulation department personnel such as catalogers and data inputters already on staff should be an integral part of the training, for their skills and knowledge will provide a vital support function in the conversions and adaptations required of the new system.

## Step 6: Perform a Retrospective Conversion

It is rare the library that has 100 percent of its holdings in machine readable format prior to the commencement of an automation project. A retrospective conversion project is going to be necessary to load paper-based records into a bibliographic utility and/or into the library's new computer's central storage database. This is a large project that cannot be performed casually. Moreover, conversions require a considerable amount of human resources and are a costly part of any automation scheme. Prior to the issuance of a budget document for the project, a time study needs to be performed to include the number of titles to be converted, the resources available to perform the conversion, and the number of person hours required to complete the project. Typically, retrospective conversion projects are performed as piecework, by staff moonlighting and working after hours. If this framework is to be used by your library, you should check on rates of payment as dictated by state, provincial, and federal laws regarding overtime and minimum wages. It is often desirable to hire outside workers qualified to perform online inputting, although the dictates of library labor unions, if not the feelings and opinions of the staff, must be considered regarding out-of-house and temporary employees.

## Step 7: Prepare the Site

Immediately after bids have been accepted for the new computer system, plans will have to be prepared for installation of equipment. The electrical plans should be prepared immediately, and most installation jobs are of sufficient magnitude that the contract work will constitute a separate bid situation. In any case, unless your library has a staff of electricians, trained electrical workers must be employed to run the cables and ascertain the power requirements and proper emplacement of hardware and surge protectors. Regardless, specialists in computer installation and network cabling will have to be engaged at some point in the project because of the sensitive nature of high-tech equipment. Once the locations are prepared and the computer room is constructed, equipment can be received. A vendor's representative should be on hand for the unpacking and for the supervision of the connections of the various components.

## Step 8: Turn the Key

There is still work to be performed even after the switch is turned in a so-called turnkey system. Before the automated system can be used, **parameters** (system attributes) must be established. These parameters include matters such as loan periods, rates of overdue fees, timing for generation of automatically printed notices, and the like. Additionally, a library representative must be present when the vendor's representative performs a systems acceptance demonstration, a session at a selected terminal or terminals to prove that the entire system will perform as the request for proposal, and vendor's specifications, claim it should.

Beyond these eight steps, the library staff will be performing behind the scene tasks as well. Borrowers' cards will have to be reissued or affixed with special machine readable labels. Books will also have to be affixed with machine readable labels, usually bar codes or z-bar labels. The latter project should have been started as soon as the go-ahead on the specific system was received. This is an excellent project for volunteer help, and many a library has generated valuable goodwill among its volunteer workers by making them feel that they have contributed to such an extensive project. Some specific programs for generating bar code labels are mentioned in chapter 10, if the library cares to print its own rather than purchasing them from a commercial preprinting source. If the library's theft detection system has been replaced at the time of automating, the occasion of the emplacement of bar codes and labels is a good time to affix simultaneously the detection strips for the theft sensors. This is also an excellent time to weed unneeded and wornout books from the collection, before costly bar codes and sensor strips are applied.

Every library is different, and each will perform the eight steps with variations and modifications; consider the preceding steps a "launching pad" to get through a lengthy process. It is said that the planning for the next automation process begins before the conclusion of the current one; a methodical approach such as the one above should help to make the process more livable. Formal, detailed planning techniques will be discussed in the next chapter.

There are many possible variations for cooperative arrangements of automated circulation and cataloging systems. Setups can be local, as clusters of libraries pooling their computer resources, or state- and province-wide, underwritten by regional library authorities. The possibilities for wide area resource sharing will be discussed further in chapter 15.

## NOTE

1. Brandt, D. Scott. *UNIX & Libraries.* 200 pp.

# Chapter 14

# Library Systems Analysis

Systems are all around. From the time people get into their automobiles (a mechanical system) in the morning until they turn off the television evening news (a communications system), they are inundated with systems. Libraries and businesses are flanked with dozens of systems. All of these systems must and do operate in harmony to allow people to accomplish work, get from place to place, and recreate. For this integrated harmony to function, there must be procedures for planning, implementing, and improving all the systems that are encountered.

A **system** is defined many ways. It is "an assembly of components united by some form of regulated interaction to form an organized whole"; "a collection of operations and procedures, persons, and machines, by which business activity is carried on"; "any purposeful organization of resources or elements"; "a collection of operations and procedures united to accomplish a specific objective"; "a devised and designed regular or special method or plan or methodology or procedure"; "the organization of hardware, software, and people for cooperative operation to complete a set of tasks for desired purposes"; and so on.[1] Any specific definition from the above list depends on the environment to be used (e.g., computerized or manual) and the work to be accomplished. The determination of tools and resources to be used depends on a systematic planning scheme. Such a scheme is called a systems analysis.

A **systems analysis**, then, is the process by which a given task or project is accomplished in the most efficient and economical manner, utilizing the personal skills and hardware available, in an optimum fashion through time and motion studies, qualitative and quantitative observations and logical investigations. A systems analysis can include any or all of computers, flowcharts, forms, narrative and numerical reports, and performance studies.

## PARALLELS BETWEEN BUSINESSES AND LIBRARIES

Systems analysis is used extensively in businesses and in corporations. In recent years, libraries and educational institutions have used system methods and techniques with modifications to accompany processes indigenous to academic and bibliographic settings.

There are many parallels between businesses and libraries. Like a library, a business is an information system. Businesses and business executives will pay for information. In the corporate arena, good information equals profits. A credo among many executives is that "I make money by possessing information that you don't have." Another paralled is that businesses rely on extensive documentation (e.g., books) outlining their processes, procedures, marketing, and trade strategies. They also invest heavily in systems, both computerized and manual, for the storage and retrieval of information. Lastly, libraries and businesses share key tools in the management and planning for services and administration of their respective organizations. The following tools are common to both organizations:

- computers and computing machinery
- organizational charts, to denote who's responsible to whom
- procedures manuals, e.g., in libraries, lending policies manuals; in business, sales manuals
- policies and staff (personnel) manuals
- forms control manuals, e.g., in libraries, compendia of forms for book ordering and processing; in business, notebooks of various applications for the services and products to be sold or models for advertisements and styles for correspondence

Businesses and libraries must both be concerned with general issues such as accounting, taxes, and financial reporting, and appropriate systems must be established to satisfy the boards of directors or auditors who might examine the records. Libraries must satisfy the one or more statutory bodies that control their funding, and businesses must pay heed to the demands of their stockholders. In any case, all systems and procedures dictate a logical path that must be followed. These paths are many times quite formal; for example, in financial accounting for an organization, the reports must follow generally accepted accounting principles (GAAP). The various paths followed often evolve into universal procedures called **standards** and must be interrelated into the system. It is the job of the systems analyst to correlate these standards and properly integrate them into the mainstream of an organization's activities.

## LIFE CYCLE

Systems do not spontaneously generate. Innovative businesses and progressive libraries attack problems with a four-pronged approach, called the **Life Cycle**, in order to implement a new or revised system or procedure (e.g., a method of circulating books). The phases of the Life Cycle are detailed as follows:

1. The **study phase** is the setup of a problem investigation. The study phase includes
   a. The **initial investigation** asks whether a problem actually exists and what do you want to do about it.
   b. The **problem identification** asks how many elements are contained in the problem and what are its parameters.
   c. The **information service request** is a formal plea for help from the systems staff. "Staff" can consist of the consultants, architects, analysts, committee members, or task force charged with conducting systems problem investigations. There may be a systems coordinator or ombudsperson assigned to the project who, although he or she might have no real authority over others, must be able to circulate among departments and obtain cooperation and information from others whose input into the systems analysis is vital to its success.
   d. The **initial investigation**, or fact finding/gathering mission, may involve visual observations, sampling studies, literature searches, or statistical compilations performed in such an investigation. It is comparable to the first half of a thesis (i.e., the proposal and summary of the research relevant to the topic), which contains charts, graphs and uninterpreted raw data.
   e. The **system performance definition** will establish the following for the data collected:
      What data are to be entered into the system?
      How are the data to be acted upon?
      What desired results are expected of data studied?
      What data processing tools are to be employed?
      What are the expected levels of reliability of any results?
      What constraints are to be placed on the data?
   f. The **feasibility analysis** is a published opinion of whether the proposed system will work.

2. **The design phase** is the actual creation of the work components necessary to implement the systems analysis. This phase includes the following activities:
   a. allocation of functions to various personnel and machines
   b. configuration of manual tasks
   c. procurement of equipment and designation of uses for each piece
   d. writing of computer programs, including flowcharting, coding and debugging of source code
   e. establishment of the format of databases, file structures, appearance of forms and printouts (see chapter 9 for forms design)
   f. testing and retesting of the design components
3. The **development phase** is a continuation of the design phase but is involved with the actual implementation of components and procedures established by the design team. Activities include the following:
   a. user orientation and review
   b. preparation of reference manuals and bibliographies
   c. recruitment of personnel and presentation of training workshops and seminars for use of the new system
   d. presentation of the changeover plan, if the new system replaces an existing one
   e. review of user acceptance and/or criticism
4. The **implementation phase** is sometimes an overlap from the development phase, inasmuch as it proceeds from the evaluations generated from part 3.e. above. Many times the implementation phase circles back to a new study phase, if it can be determined that the system does not function as desired, or if user acceptance is negative. The implementation phase includes:
   a. a retest of methods and procedures
   b. the final installation of hardware and software
   c. a conversion team to implement final changeover to the new system
   d. a final review and evaluation

Some organizations include a fifth component to the Life Cycle, called the **operation phase**. This phase is not as much a series of steps or activities as a signal that the cycle has been broken and that the study phase will not be repeated. There may be new Life Cycles in the future, but the operation phase generally indicates that the new systems project has come to a (hopefully successful) conclusion.

# COMPUTER PROGRAMMING AS A SUBSYSTEM OF SYSTEMS ANALYSIS

It should be emphasized that the creation of a system does not automatically mean that a *computerized* system is implied. In systems analyses, many times a computer is never included as a part of the overall solution. It is just that, as a matter of course in strategic planning in recent years, it is taken for granted that some kind of high-level computing hardware will be involved. "Use a computer" tends to be the universal panacea of the 1990s.

To include a computer and its attendant programs as a part of our systems planning is nonetheless taken for granted. With all the programming tools, peripheral devices, and accessories available, this is not an illogical course of action. As such, this chapter considers the major phases of systems analysis and focuses on computer programming as a major component of one or more of these phases, although not itself one of the main phases of the Life Cycle of the planning process. Finally there is a discussion of systems planning and information systems management, as an entry-level example of how work and planning fit into the overall methodology of scientific management of library systems.

Three specific elements comprise the foundation for creating and maintaining computer programs:

1. **Personnel**. The staff members who create the logic setups and author the code perform their tasks in a specific hierarchy. It should be noted that jobs and persons do overlap and that no job is performed exclusively or without input from above or below. Typically, the personnel are grouped as follows:

    a. **Users** originate a programming request from job specifications. Such job specs can be from library- or company-approved forms, from ledger sheets, from printed reports and studies, or from bibliographies. Almost any form or report that is relevant to the programming task can be considered a **source document**.

    b. **Systems analysts** study a job as an entity requiring various utility programs and subprograms that can be addressed with computer code. Such persons can (and do) cross departmental lines, study and design work flow, and place every task in a logical order. Systems analysts have numerous tools at their disposal, including various charts and charting techniques. The latter will be discussed in detail at the end of this section.

    c. **Programmers** use various computer languages and **subroutine libraries** (see chapter 8) to author code to submit to a computer for execution. And within the **programmer** hierarchy, there is typically a rank level of persons with progressive responsibilities. A junior programmer is a person who writes code from rigid specifications handed down from a **senior programmer**, a person who decides the components and program flow of the various language routines. Some organizations may also employ a patch programmer, a person who writes fixes and update routines (**patches**) to existing, previously implemented programs.

d. **Computer operators** submit the various programs and run them on the appropriate equipment. There may also be a **lead operator** in larger computer shops; this person is responsible for the scheduling of program jobs and may be authorized to make minor changes in programs or runtime decisions in order to generate alternate or special reports as needed.

e. **Technicians**, or **technical support specialists**, maintain and repair the hardware which run the programs. Larger organizations may further divide their technical staffs into specialty areas, such as mainframe support, personal computer support, and the like. Alternatively, some computer shops purchase service contracts on their equipment, for which a certain amount of maintenance is prepaid at a fixed price for time and materials. Such a arrangement is called **outsourcing** and is particularly advantageous for libraries where budgets do not allow funding for unexpected breakdowns in the middle of a fiscal year.

2. **Software**. This is the set of programs that comprises the computing environment. In a larger sense, the software includes the operating system, compilers, interpreters, platforms, interfaces, languages and syntaxes, that make up the tools of programming. These tools are building blocks that, when used in proper arrangement, allow a computer to perform work from stored programs that were first described as a concept back in chapter 1.

3. **Hardware**. These are all the machines which work in harmony with program code to accomplish the end results of jobs for which the software was originally written. Included are all the peripheral devices which perform specialty tasks, such as **dumb terminals** for fast, noncomputing data entry, and **smart terminals**, which perform some preliminary computing work before the central processing unit even begins to execute the program. Depending on the system to be installed, the hardware can include specialty devices such as **bar code readers** and **laser**

**wands** (in the case of an automated circulation sytem) or any other mechanical devices germane to the task. The choice of hardware is an integral part of the systems analysis, and its functionality in terms of the software and personnel included in the program-authoring process cannot be overlooked if the system is to work at all.

Before continuing with the discussion of systems analysis, it is time to deal with one of the most fundamental tools of systems analysis and programming construction—the flowchart.

## FLOWCHARTING

One of the oldest tools available to systems planners is the flowchart. A **flowchart**, as the name implies, is a method of graphically illustrating the flow, or progress, of a task or problem. As is true with most tools used to define a problem or illustrate work flow, a flowchart does not necessarily imply that a computer is the object of the illustration. However, computer programmers often use flowcharts to study the logic patterns and results of program statements before writing the actual language code. Flowcharts have a variety of other planning applications, as the illustrations in this section will show.

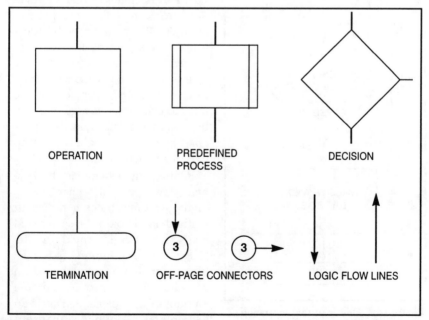

**Figure 14.1** Standard flowchart symbols

While there is no formal standard for the symbols used in flowchart layouts, there is general agreement of the function of the symbols used. Typically, the set is as described here.

The **operation** symbol denotes an action or single event in the course of the work flow. If an operation consists of several steps, or can be considered a subroutine or predefined task, the rectangle includes two vertical bars and is called a **process**. The **decision** diamond handles "what if?" or alternative choices, and directs the work flow to **branches** or **loops** in the flowchart. Using these three basic shapes, most work projects and computer programs can be represented in their entirety. A planner usually has at his/her disposal a stencil, or **flowchart template**, for drawing the symbols neatly on a preprinted flowchart grid.

Several other symbols are available to refine a flowchart. **Termination** ovals indicate the beginning and end of work flow; **connector** circles denote connections from one column or page to another. **Flow lines** with directional arrows act as the wires to connect everything together, and instructions or choice **flags** can be inscribed along or on top of the lines to clarify the flow of information. Language used in the flowchart symbols can be either narrative or mathematical.

Almost any activity can be broken down into flowchart steps. Figure 14.2 illustrates a flowchart method for cooking a soft-boiled egg. The path indicated by the "have three minutes passed?" block launches a choice based on a predetermined quantity, i.e., the amount of time elapsed. This is an example of a loop or **program**

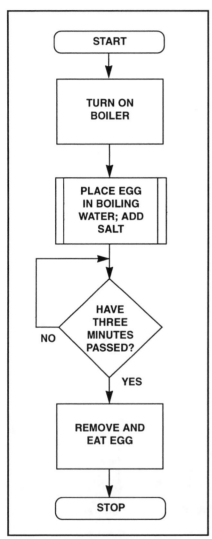

**Figure 14.2** Flowchart for preparation of a three-minute egg.

**loop**, an event that will continue to occur until a specific condition is met. In the example above, the condition to be met is "time passed = three minutes." For this reason, the decision symbol is sometimes called a **condition block**, one which tests the work flow to ascertain whether the actions can be allowed to continue and in what directions. Clusters of diamonds can be drawn to test for multiple conditions, or **cases**, and flowcharts can become quite complicated in such instances.

It is also possible, through logic error, to construct a work or program flow whose condition can never be met, i.e., one which can never evaluate to "true." In this instance, the construct is called an **infinite loop** which, in most cases, must be corrected for the program or system to function properly. In computer programs, the conditions for test can be "greater than or equal to?", "less than or equal to?", and "not equal to?", among others. Such conditional tests are also applied in database searching, a topic which will be covered in more detail in chapter 17.

Other types of charts and techniques play a role in systems analysis. Several of these will be considered in the following section.

## MANAGEMENT INFORMATION SYSTEMS

The term management information system connotes different meanings to different organizations. It is not to be considered merely a business concept; an information system can be a marketing type, or scientific and technical, medical, educational, legal, and, of course, library. In fact, in terms of library application, the "information" component of "management information system" embodies the very essence of what libraries purport to do: collect and handle facts and knowledge. It is fitting, then, to examine how the scientific management of information in other professions applies to library situations. Considering how this management fits into the greater concept of systems analysis is the focus of this chapter.

A **management information system**, or **MIS**, is any integrated system for the planning, managing, and evaluation of programs, which collects, merges, and stores information in a common database. Further, the MIS will display two specific characteristics: at least one level of vertical integration and feedback and control.[2] A management information system can include communications technology and computers. Note, however, that MIS is *not* required to include any mechanical or electrical devices or tools at any level. A management information system can be created exclusively with pencil and paper. A library example of the latter is a manual book charging system: lots of cards, file boxes and rubber stamps—but not necessarily a computer!

A management information system is comprised of three major subsystems:

1. The **operating subsystem** includes the data and files used in everyday business operations.
2. The **reporting subsystem** includes all the studies and reports that may (or may not) be derived from the operating subsystem.
3. The **decision-making subsystem** involves the mathematical models, charts, programs and instruments of evaluation for implementing and refining the MIS. Decision making within MIS involves two elements, namely (a) the inclusion of objectives, the measurement of performances against those objectives, and any corrective action necessary; and (b) the availability of appropriate information on which to base decisions. Decision making provides feedback, a necessary process for control over the systems analysis process.

As the flowchart acted as a standard tool for computer programmers, there are standard tools available to systems analysts for supporting the decision-making subsystem. For developing data processing systems and studying the processes of information handling, the following are included:

1. **Simulations** can be computer or noncomputer based hypothetical models that answer "what if?" conditions in a systems study. A recently issued computer game program which exemplifies simulation programs is *Sim City*.[3] Some college curricula include it in applied computer science courses for its simplicity, ease of learning, and graphic illustrations of this category of computerized planning tools. In this game, you become a city manager/city planner who begins with an uninhabited, mythical terrain and develops it into (ultimately) a metropolis. You, the planner, are in control of budgets, space allocations, resource management, and disaster recovery. Related programs include *Sim Earth*, a more ecologically-oriented version of the simulation, and *A-Train*, another "citified" version of *Sim City*, but oriented around railroad building and stock acquisitions.
2. **Linear programming** is a type of decision tool that is a mathematical model which manipulates combinations of resources to show optimum results of various uses of one commodity against the others. For example, a linear model of bookmobile routes might show the best schedules and routes for optimum patron coverage, best materials circulations, and most efficient gasoline mileages.

3. **Program review and evaluation technique (PERT) charts, Gantt charts,** and **critical path method charts** are tools that assist in the planning of time against available resources, illustrating diagrammatically the options for work flow based on due dates and deadlines. The general overview of such charts resembles maps of railroad marshalling yards, and the ordering and organization of tasks are not unlike the classification and connection of railroad cars for the best delivery of goods.

4. **Organization charts** should already be included in the staff handbook, subject to modifications as circumstances arise. Organization charts are also useful in the planning for scientific management of making decisions. There are two basic types of organization charts, **superior-subordinate linkage** and **vertical-horizontal linkage**. Both types of charts illustrate authority from the top downward. However, the vertical-horizontal linkage type adds dashed lines between levels to demonstrate formal relationships between peers. Superior-subordinate is more authoritarian, but it keys on the "link pin" elements; there is no doubt who reports to whom. Vertical-horizontal linkage charts imply staff rather than line relationships and are usually indicative of participative management.

5. **Database management systems (DBMS)** are techniques for modifying, structuring, and accessing combinations of data elements to meet undefined, future needs.

6. **Life Cycle management** is a scientific method for the definition, study, design, development, and operation of an effective business or library system. This decision-making tool is a standard methodology and has already been detailed above in the discussion of systems analysis.

## INFORMATION LEVELS IN LIBRARIES AND BUSINESSES

In light of the availability of all these tools to aid the decision-making process, it is necessary to consider also the information that emanates as a result of having employed such tools. In any information system, the level of information used or generated depends on the rank of the person requesting or creating the information. Restating the concept of "information levels" in a more concise form, the hierarchy answers the question: "Who needs to know what, and why?" The four information system levels are described on the following pages.

## Strategic

Strategic is usually top management. In a medium-sized organization, this constitutes the library board; in a university, this is the board of regents or board of governors. These persons set philosophies of the institutions, sometimes answering directly to voters or, in businesses, to stockholders. This group needs information upon which to base decisions on major, sometimes costly issues. The information provided to strategic managers will have been read, summarized, and condensed by researchers one or perhaps two levels below them. Leadership regarding programs and institutional policies is launched from this level. The information generated from the strategic level has an impact throughout the organization, and in many instances, an impact on other organizations and agencies as well.

## Tactical

Tactical is middle management. Characterized as "administrative," this group of workers has extensive decision-making power but uses it in synchronization with the philosophies established by the strategic managers. Their decisions are made from the repertoire of choices (implied or written) dictated by the organization's philosophies. These persons would construct organizational manuals containing job descriptions, work rules, staff policies, and procedures and forms for the accomplishment of tasks. Typical of this level is a library director or dean of a college unit containing the learning resource center or information-providing division of the organization.

## Supervisory

Supervisory is lower management and includes the department or division heads of the library. By "management" implying a professional level of competence, these persons organize and run specific units within the organization, adhering strictly to the rules and regulations dictated by tactical personnel. Supervisory staff assign work responsibilities, assign work schedules, maintain public contact as liaisons with patrons and clients by officially representing the organization, and act as first-contact personnel managers. Their decision-making power is limited to the parameters and guidelines established by tactical management.

## Functional

The last level is comprised of the operational workers. The lowest level of the pyramid, these are the "rank and file" workers of the organization. Included here are clerks, secretaries, and shelvers, some or all of whom may be members of an organized labor union. Note—and this is stated emphatically—the intent in describing this group is not to equate clerks with janitors or any category with another; it is merely to show that, as the pyramid widens at the base to accommodate a broadening level of workers, it includes those persons who, at any place within the functional level, have no discretionary power or authority to make rules or decisions. In fact, the persons in this level may actually be the most productive, in terms of measurable results, of any of the four groups. Although each of the other three levels of management set goals and objectives, it is the functional personnel that ultimately provide the labor to achieve the results. It is an example of the "trickledown" process in its purest form: a library cannot provide information or circulate a book unless someone has returned the volume to its proper location in the shelves!

## A FUNCTIONAL BUSINESS SYSTEM FOR LIBRARIES

It should now be evident that both libraries and businesses constitute "systems of systems." Both consist of combinations of personnel, materials, facilities, and equipment to accomplish specific objectives and to achieve specific goals.

In planning, the terms "goal," "objective," and "task" are often used interchangeably and usually incorrectly. A **goal** is a very broadly stated purpose. There may be goals directed toward earning profits, educating students, or circulating books. A goal is the most abstract of the three concepts and is not always stated in specific terms. An **objective** consists of the concrete and specific accomplishments necessary to the achievement of goals. If the goal is made to "circulate more books," the objectives of that goal might be stated in terms of public relations campaigns, intelligent book selection techniques, and the encouragement of readership through summer reading programs for children. Objectives are further broken down into **tasks**, or specific jobs necessary to realize those objectives and ultimately the organization's goal or goals.

Businesses can be broken down into two broad categories: production enterprises and service enterprises. Libraries usually comprise only the latter, although (arguably) a library's production "commodity" can be defined as information. Because of the multiplicity of objectives and subobjectives that must be achieved within an enterprise, businesses and libraries can be divided into major elements called **systems**. A **generalized system environment** may include the following elements and divisions:

| Businesses | Libraries |
|---|---|
| Purchasing from vendors | Purchasing and acquisitions |
| Processing raw materials | Processing books and A/V items |
| Inventory | Inventory |
| Production (manufacturing) | Reference and readers' advisory |

| | |
|---|---|
| Sales and marketing | Public relations and programming |
| Distribution (supply customers with goods) | Circulation |
| Mailing of billing statements | Mailing of overdue book notices |
| Collections (accounts receivable) | Collections (fines and fees) |
| Paying vendors | Paying vendors |

As the list demonstrates, there are many parallels between the business environment and the library world.

## APPLICATION: BUDGET PLANNING FOR ESTABLISHMENT OF NEW LIBRARY SERVICE

The following example has its roots in a library school exercise that has been repeatedly assigned, with variations, for more than twenty years. The purpose is to demonstrate systems analysis as it pertains to setting up a department, constructing a new building, or just reorganizing some existing procedures. Whatever the magnitude of the project, the steps are the same, and the planning sequences and considerations hold true for any size budget. It is not intended to report an actual event in any particular library, but to serve as a hypothetical example of what can happen (with permutations) in many management instances.

For the purpose of this application, the reader would benefit from a review of chapter 4 and of spreadsheet principles in general. The exercise is presented as a setup for a hypothetical library and is not based on a case study of any institution in particular.

### An Exercise in Budget Planning

On September 1st of this year, you began a new assignment as department head, Acquisitions Division, in a medium-sized library. You were hired from the outside, but the director felt that, with your supervisory background, you would assimilate the procedures and practices of the organization very quickly.

Because of the nature of the organization, most of the titles the various divisions select are nonfiction. To save dollars, the library does purchase paperback copies of the more expensive books, when available in that format. Because of heavy use, paper book covers soon disintegrate and the Acquisitions Division must also assume responsibility for prebinding (the Technical Services Division assumes the cost of binding titles already in the collection). Altogether, a gross total of some $250,000 is spent by the divisions on books in any fiscal year, which is coincidental with the January 1 to December 31 calendar.

The greatest drawback of the organization is that there is not a comprehensive procedures manual. Worse, your predecessor left in such a hurry that she did not have an opportunity to teach you the procedures for creating a proposed budget or justifying expenditures for the incoming fiscal year. In effect you have a blank slate and must make a good impression without any real guidelines. Fortunately, you have draft copies of previous years' budget workups, and they contain some information you can use.

Every division or department (the terms here are synonymous) has an independent appropriation; when it is all spent, there's no more money available (literally) until January 1. The Acquisitions Division must include for its budget, in common with all other divisions, the following items:

1. Staff salaries (including your own)
2. Benefits:
   a. FICA, employer contribution @ 7.15 percent of gross pay
   b. State retirement, employer contribution @ 4 percent of gross pay, but for full-time employees only
   c. Health insurance at a flat $125 per month for each full-time employee
3. Supplies—paper, 3" x 5" cards, pens, pencils, etc.
4. New equipment
5. Service contracts
6. Books and continuations (e.g., Books in Print) that are used only in the Acquisitions Division
7. Computer software
8. Prebinding costs

In figuring the budget, the following parameters are to be used:

1. The gross budget for the Acquisitions Division in 1996 (here, the current fiscal year) is $100,000. There is just enough money to finish the year, with no carryover.
2. For staff salaries, you do not have to figure the cost of vacations or holiday time. Departments are very cooperative about "pinch hitting" for absent colleagues, so you do not have to worry about pay for substitutes.
3. The only staff permanently assigned to the Acquisitions Division are you and one other full-time, professional librarian. The rest of the staff is classified under civil service and may be reassigned to other departments on January 1. You are at liberty to request a person to fill any declared position (within reasonable definitions) which your budget will afford. Once declared, all positions are valid for one calendar year; in fact, in computations for this example, you may assume that all civil service and clerical

employees will be on the payroll for the full twelve months. You may declare any combination of positions you wish, but each employee is to be guaranteed at least ten hours of work per week. You must pay a minimum wage of $4.75 per hour. No position descriptions or base rates of compensation will change during the calendar year.

4. The library has a policy that only one-half of the monthly insurance premium is paid for part-time personnel. Further, those workers to be eligible for this benefit must work at least a half schedule, i.e., 18 to 34 hours per week (full time is 35 hours/week). You may assume that, if there is a union agreement, the rate of premium compensation is the same for both union and nonunion personnel. Note: for full-time, nonunion employees working 36 to 40 hours per week, straight time is paid; time over 40 hours is compensated at 1.5 times the hourly rate *unless the employees are considered supervisory.* All union employees are compensated at 1.5 times their hourly rate for time over 35 hours.

5. You do not have to worry about utilities or janitorial services because these are paid out of the library's general fund. The library also takes care of major repairs and painting and decorating.

6. You do not have to purchase major furniture items such as desks and shelves, but tabletop equipment is your responsibility. You have two IBM-PCs and a host of other equipment, but it is obvious that you will need to replace an electric typewriter as soon as possible. It would be welcome to have an additional printer upon which to output booklists and some correspondence.

7. The Acquisitions Division maintains service contracts on all its typewriters, computers, duplicating machines, copiers, and the like. Some of the equipment currently in use is old and/or used heavily, and service calls can average $50 a visit. There are twelve pieces of equipment in the department, and the service contracts in 1996 have all cost $100 apiece. The repair companies have all complained that they lose money on these contracts, and it is a certainty that the cost of these contracts will each increase by $25 per year. There is a judgment to be made within the year: should you drop these contracts to save dollars, and, if so, what will be your contingency for breakdowns?

8. You do not have to worry about any OCLC hardware or similar cataloging equipment; this line item is absorbed by the Cataloging Division. That division also maintains the budget for

hardwire connections of terminals and production charges for catalog cards.

9. The Acquisitions Division does not pay directly for books ordered by other departments, i.e., Acquisitions does not purchase books for other departments from its own funds; Acquisitions does, however, maintain the invoices and record debits against departmental book budgets when funds are encumbered. (Note: it is not the intent of this example to design an encumbrance system for book purchases.) Nor does the Acquisitions Division write the actual payments (checks) to vendors for goods received; this is done by the Business Office.

Note also that the previous section introduces the actual "research" work for the project. In other words, you need to determine a method to figure the time unit per book necessary for processing. Using the tools and procedures in chapter 14, you should be able to derive a formula which is reliable for the duration of the calendar year, subject to modification(s) if extraordinary circumstances warrant.

10. Five percent of all the titles ordered are requested prebound. The cost for this service is $4.00 per title.

This is a typical "ringer" that creeps into every well-planned formula and budget. The trick here is to ascertain the number of books that will require prebinding, based on how many books will be processed during the year. Remember, the total *value* of books handled will be $250,000, a figure which can be used to determine the number of books that will pass through Acquisitions in that period of time. Assume that the average cost of a book has been determined to be $25.00. Therefore, 250,000 ÷ 25 = 10,000 books. But only five per cent of these items will need prebinding; therefore, 10,000 x .05 = 500 books. At $4.00 per book, the year's prebinding charges will be 500 x 4 = $2,000.

11. One suggestion left by your predecessor was that you judge personnel needs by the number of books ordered. You have it on "good estimation" that the total library book budget will be no more than the $250,000 originally stated. Your intuition and colleagues, fearing the worst, however, tell you that a budget cut could bring that figure down as low as $175,000.

A good way to construct this part of the cost equation is to estimate the average cost of a book (the *Bowker Annual*[4] is helpful for researching such figures), based on the types of books purchased in your library, divide that figure into the total book budget or your best estimate of it, and judge, through time and motion study, how many persons would be needed to process that many books in a year. For simplicity, assume that your institutional discount will average 20 percent for the year.

For presentation to the budgetary powers, the format left by your predecessor seems to have worked well, so at least for the first year, you decide not to "reinvent the wheel." The outline to be maintained will contain the following information:

1. In three columns, enter the current year's allocations (total budget), your needs for the incoming year, and a projection for the year after next. As a final note, you should make your estimates a bit on the high side. For all calculations, your best information tells you that the library's revenues will increase by two per cent per year. However, the cost of living figures will increase by four per cent per year. Suggestion: for staff salaries, consider norms only in your immediate area of the country.
2. Show staff salaries and benefits on separate lines for each individual position.
3. The expenditure for the Acquisition Division's books, since there probably won't be many, may be a lump-sum item.
4. Each piece of equipment desired is to be a separate line item entry if it costs more than $500; everything else (such as pencil sharpeners and the like) may be lumped.
5. Supplies need only be broken into three or four categories, i.e., "paper," "copy machine," "secretarial," etc.
6. Quarterly totals are not necessary; grand totals are required for complete years.

The complete spreadsheet should not exceed two or three pages. Either a vertical or horizontal format is acceptable.

In addition to your formatted spreadsheet (see Figure 14.3) you should submit a support letter footnoting the various expenditures, justifying each one. You should state a two or three sentence reason for the purchase of extraordinary items such as telefacsimile machines. For the purpose of this exercise, there would be no single set of arithmetically correct figures. There are two global rules: make your estimates reasonable, and explain any line item which is not immediately obvious. You may fabricate any conditions or assumptions not specifically mentioned in the rules, as long as the fabrications are realistic.

A brief analysis of the spreadsheet in Figure 14.3 shows that this is neither a right nor a wrong way to solve the budget problem in the preceding outline. It does, however, point out some issues that arise in any library financial planning cycle. Here, the department head assumed that

|   | A | B | C | D | E | F |
|---|---|---|---|---|---|---|
| 1 |   |   |   |   |   |   |
| 2 |   |   | Acquisitions Division |   |   |   |
| 3 |   |   | Annual Budget |   |   |   |
| 4 |   |   |   |   |   |   |
| 5 |   |   | 1996 | 1997 | 1998 |   |
| 6 |   |   | Current Year | Incoming | Following Year |   |
| 7 |   |   |   |   |   |   |
| 8 |   | Salaries |   |   |   |   |
| 9 |   | Dept. Head | $35,000 | $36,400 | $37,856 |   |
| 10 |   | FICA | $2,503 | $2,603 | $2,707 |   |
| 11 |   | Retirement | $1,400 | $1,456 | $1,514 |   |
| 12 |   | Insurance | $1,140 | $1,380 | $1,620 |   |
| 13 |   | Librarian | $25,000 | $26,000 | $27,040 |   |
| 14 |   | FICA | $1,788 | $1,859 | $1,933 |   |
| 15 |   | Retirement | $1,000 | $1,040 | $1,082 |   |
| 16 |   | Insurance | $1,140 | $1,380 | $1,620 |   |
| 17 |   | FT Clerk | $16,500 | $17,160 | $17,846 |   |
| 18 |   | FICA | $1,180 | $1,227 | $1,276 |   |
| 19 |   | Retirement | $660 | $686 | $714 |   |
| 20 |   | Insurance | $1,140 | $1,380 | $1,620 |   |
| 21 |   |   |   |   |   |   |
| 22 |   | Supplies |   |   |   |   |
| 23 |   | Paper | $1,000 | $1,000 | $500 |   |
| 24 |   | Copy machine | $2,000 | $2,000 | $1,500 |   |
| 25 |   | Secretarial | $950 | $629 | $612 |   |
| 26 |   |   |   |   |   |   |
| 27 |   | Equipment |   |   |   |   |
| 28 |   | Typewriter | $500 | $0 | $0 |   |
| 29 |   | Laser printer | $1,100 | $0 | $0 |   |
| 30 |   |   |   |   |   |   |
| 31 |   | Service Contracts | $1,500 | $1,800 | $2,100 |   |
| 32 |   |   |   |   |   |   |
| 33 |   | Books | $1,000 | $1,000 | $500 |   |
| 34 |   |   |   |   |   |   |
| 35 |   | Software | $1,500 | $1,000 | $0 |   |
| 36 |   |   |   |   |   |   |
| 37 |   | Prebinding | $2,000 | $2,000 | $2,000 |   |
| 38 |   |   |   |   |   |   |
| 39 |   | Totals | $100,000 | $102,000 | $104,040 |   |
| 40 |   | Baseline | $100,000 | $102,000 | $104,040 |   |
| 41 |   |   |   |   |   |   |
| 42 |   |   |   |   |   |   |

**Figure 14.3** Acquisitions Department budget plan.

she would require an additional, full-time clerk for the two projected years. She has applied a multiplier of 1.04 to salaries, which, from cell formulas in columns D and E, has increased the expenditures for personnel much faster than that for all other items. A baseline (the last line on the sheet) has been created to show the anticipated 2 percent increases in available revenues in the next two years. Obviously, revenues are not keeping in line with salary expectations, and most non-personnel items have had to be cut.

Contributing factors to the costs of personnel are insurance and employer's Social Security (FICA) taxes. Here, it is assumed that health insurance premiums will increase $20.00 per year for each of the next two years, perhaps a conservative estimate. FICA, of course, increases proportionally with gross salary amounts. The department head has taken advantage of some surplus money in the current year's budget to obtain a typewriter and laser printer rather than delaying these purchases until the incoming year, effectively taking the worry of buying new equipment out of a future budget. While it is not anticipated that new equipment will be purchased in the next two years, a zero allocation is dangerous inasmuch as it does not allow for unanticipated wearouts of existing hardware. Regrettably, the equipment line is often one of the first to be cut when the bottom line must be balanced. An alternative might be to cancel some of the service contracts and take a chance on pay-as-you-go maintenance.

It could be concluded that, if the service level of the Acquisitions Division in this example is to be continued, an influx of revenue or redistribution of cash resources to the department must be found. The department head would have to prepare justifications that the amount of personnel to provide the service is warranted, if arguments for additional funds are to be taken seriously by a budget committee. It should be remembered that other departments will be making similar pleas, and, as is almost always the case, the budget "pie" can be split only so many ways.

## NOTES

1. Sippl, Charles J. and Charles P. Sippl. *Computer Dictionary and Handbook.* Indianapolis: Howard W. Sams & Co., second edition, 1978, p. 435.
2. Gore, Marvin and John Stubbe. *Elements of Systems Analysis for Business Data Processing.* Dubuque, IA: William C. Brown Company, 1975, p. 49.
3. Sim City, published by Maxis, Two Theater Square, Suite 230, Orinda, CA 94563-3346. DOS version, $49.95; Windows version, $49.95; Macintosh version, $49.95.
4. *Bowker Annual Library & Book Trade Almanac 1992.* 37th edition. R. R. Bowker, 1992, 800 pp.

# Chapter 15

# Local Area Networks and
# Peer-to-Peer Networks

"Networking" has a number of meanings depending on context. People "network" with persons in a quest to identify and land a job. There is a network of telephone companies that bind voice communications devices nation- and worldwide. A circle of friends or business acquaintances could be considered as a network. A network, then, connotes a group of objects or persons somehow bound together in order that the function of the group be stronger when it functions as a unit. But, for any piece of equipment or individual in the network, it is important that the specific function or personality thereof not be lost.

"Local area network," which will be used interchangeably with the acronym **LAN**, has a different meaning when given a computer context. Very simply stated, a **local area network** is a collection of interconnected computers or PCs which share common resources and are interfaced to one another for the purpose of exchanging information. If you consult six other reference books, you will doubtlessly find a half dozen other definitions. Perhaps it is clearer to define a LAN by describing briefly how one is constructed and perhaps more importantly, why. Imagine an office or library with a dozen or so PCs and Macintosh computers. The organization can afford only one laser-quality printer, but at least five users with their own PCs have a demonstrated need for a printer's services. Further, the administrative secretary's computer holds some budgetary files which several department heads need to access, but changes and alterations to the budgets must be done in such a way that the modifications are updated to a common file and not to those files dispersed to individuals' workstations. These two circumstances point to the basic reasons for networking:

**resource sharing** and **file sharing**. Described graphically, a solution to accomplish printer sharing might be illustrated as in Figure 15.1.

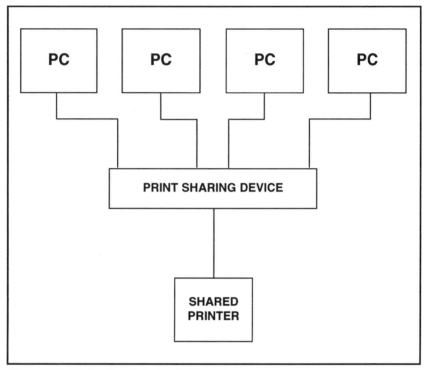

**Figure 15.1** Printer shared electronically by four computers

The motivation for interconnecting PCs is not new. With the advent of desktop computers as common tools in the late 1970s, and after the introduction of the CP/M operating system (chapter 6), it became obvious that a kind of **distributed processing** would have to take place. That is, once out of a mainframe environment, no PC was sufficiently large (or so it seemed in 1970) to run all the jobs and hold all the files in one office. Somehow, computing tasks were going to have to be distributed and performed locally, at specified workstations. Such a need created the necessity of gathering PCs and Macintosh computers into zones of interest, or **interest clusters**. It was not only a necessary arrangement for grouping work flow and consolidating related tasks, it was also needed to establish an efficient arrangement electrically for the computers to function as a system.

The ideas of "local" and "area" are relevant. "Local" can denote a single office, a single building, or a department or group of departments. It

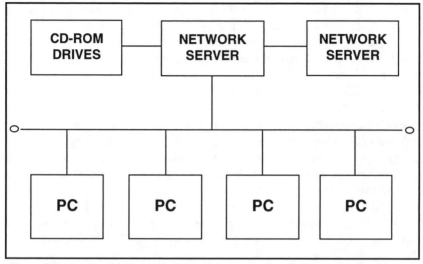

**Figure 15.2** Local Area Network, in daisy chain arrangement

is the same for "area," which can have an abstract meaning as an area of administrators, an area of catalogers, or an area of accountants. Using a well-conceived plan and analysis (see chapter 14) involving potential users, systems programmers, and electrical installers, the definition of "local area" can be set diagrammatically. It is a matter of identifying users' needs, the physical capabilities and limitations of the building in which a network is to be installed, the available budget, the relative sophistication of users, and the availability of talent and staff to administer the network. For the remainder of this section, to keep the discussion uniform, it will center on a local area network as a one-building setup, in a medium-sized public library, and connected in such a way that business, technical processes, and public access functions are integrated. The automated circulation system, if the library has one, will be treated as a separate entity because such a dichotomous setup is a more or less typical one found in modern libraries.

All local area networks begin with a consideration of the topology necessary to support a particular environment. The **topology** of a LAN means nearly the same thing as it does in mathematics; for computers, it is the manner by which the various components are connected and the rules which must be observed for the arrangement to work. For PCs, the network topology can be that of a **daisy chain**, with computers connected elephantine-style with each one connected to the next, and so forth, radiating away from a central **server** computer, also known as a **file server**. The daisy chain is a typical connection pattern for IBM and compatible PC networks as well as for Macintosh AppleTalk software. Keep in mind, however, that while inclusion of a file server is the rule for networks, a network *can* function without a server. The arrangement can also be that of a **star LAN** topology, in which each machine is connected to all others. It can also be a **token ring** setup, in which the machines are connected in a circle or circles; in such an arrangement, an electronic "token" is passed from computer to computer in a kind of **device polling** setup to ascertain which workstation has information to place on the LAN or to select which machine various bits of information are to be targeted.

Connections on the network will be of one of several types, which usually also are supported as network boards bearing the same name. A popular connection setup is **Ethernet**, designated as thick Ethernet, thin Ethernet or **fiber optic**, each depending on the type of connecting cable used. Fiber optic, also known as the **fiber distribution data interface** (**FDDI**), is an emerging technology with the potential for high-speed data transmission coupled with relatively low cost. Another popular type is

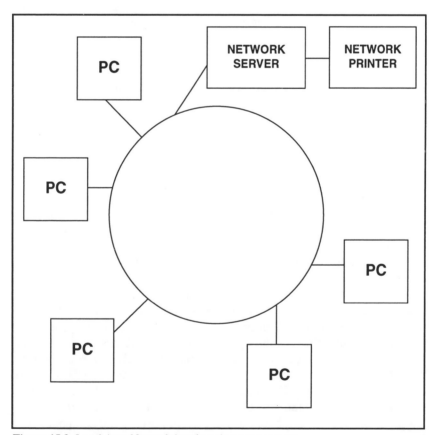

**Figure 15.3** Local Area Network in token ring arrangement

**ArcNet**, which can support either **twisted pair wiring** similar to ordinary telephone cable or coaxial cable (also called "coax") similar to the cable used to bring cable television signals (CATV) into the home. Several networks might be interconnected using **dedicated** (usually telephone) **lines**, and, to conserve the physical number of lines needed, signals can be combined on one wire using a **multiplexer** (**MUX**) device. Electrical signals will be monitored and gathered into manageable groups with **concentrator** hardware, and the signals will be distributed to their proper destinations by microprocessor-based **routers**. The photograph in Figure 15.4 illustrates a collection of rack-mounted concentrator and router hardware with cable connections to distant clusters of networked PCs and Macintosh computers.

A network management software must also be selected, and for larger LANs, products such as NetWare, 3Com, Microsoft LAN Manager, OS/2 LAN Server, Banyan Vines, or LANtastic might be employed. Microprocessor-based devices other than PCs might also have to be interconnected.   For instance, if several LANs were to be connected in a **wide area network** (**WAN**) arrangement as with a multibuilding campus, bridges and routers would be selected for electrical and signal support. **Bridges** close the gaps between two or more servers so that communications over a larger area are possible, and routers "police the traffic" in order that electrical signals (**packets**) take the most efficient (in terms of **throughput** speed) and appropriate pathways from one point on the LAN to another. For setups which involve workstations separated from each other by great distances, it may be necessary to install signal **repeaters** at various

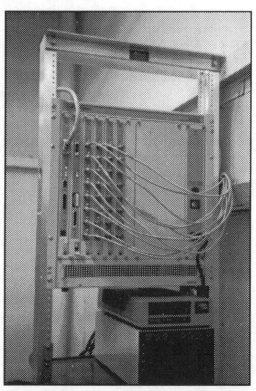

**Figure 15.4** LAN hardware, Ethernet cables are routed to various locations.

intervals to amplify the electrical information sent down the lines. All the hardware might be supported with one or more **uninterruptable power supplies** (**UPS**) to ensure that data are not lost en route if there are momentary (or longer) lapses in electrical services.

Although some smaller LANs function without one, a typical network will have one or more servers which permit administration of network software and hardware. A server performs several functions: It stores the executable (binary) files necessary for the LAN to function as a system, holds the common applications programs available to all workstations on the network, handles information necessary for keeping track of user accounts and allowable usage of the various services and programs on the LAN, and supports the peripheral devices such as printers and plotters available for sharing. As an accountant, the server will have been set up by a LAN supervisor to determine **privilege levels** of users and to determine whether a user may sign on with a password or can use the system only as a guest. Where one or more printers act as shared devices, a server will determine in what order (priority) each print job is to be executed by establishing a **print queue**, or holding area, for the **spooler** (print job execution program) to output hard copy printouts in proper turn. A server may also have a degree of control over access to records in various databases and may invoke **file locking** procedures in order that important records cannot be corrupted by **collisions** (i.e., two users attempting to alter the same record simultaneously) or unauthorized enquiries.

## NETWORK SOFTWARE

As listed in the previous section, several vendors author and publish network management software for PCs and Macintosh computers. These programs vary in degree of sophistication and, in fact, can be classified as operating systems. A number of nonmainframe operating systems such as SCO UNIX (chapter 6) are shipped as multiuser versions so that standard network boards (e.g., Ethernet cards) will interface with the software to form true local area networks.

IBM-compatible PCs and Apple Macintosh machines can easily be connected for file and resource sharing using off-the-shelf programs. On the PC side, the most popular vendor for network management (LAN) software is Novell, which supplies the NetWare line of programs. The Novell Corporation has extended its popularity by supporting a division which works closely with schools and educational institutions and grants software to those institutions who would use it and acknowledge Novell as a benefactor. At the time of this printing, NetWare is shipped as version 4.1 and is available in 5, 10, 25, 50 100, and 250 user versions with increasing prices according to the respective larger numbered user version.

NetWare version 3.12, the predecessor to versions 4.0 and 4.1, is still sold and supported by Novell. Because Novell redesigned some functions in version 4.0 and because there are yet many active 3.12 sites, version 3.12 remains "in print." In fact, version 3.12 is only slightly less costly than 4.1 (street price). Much of version 4.1's popularity is that its administrative functions can be handled pictorially, from a graphics user interface run under Windows version 3.1. However, as with any enhanced product, NetWare 4.1 takes time to learn. Many NetWare administrators are thus staying with version 3.12 until support is no longer available.

NetWare has variously appeared as Advanced NetWare and NetWare SFT (system fault tolerance). There is also a NetWare Lite for users who do not require the full range of features offered in standard NetWare. NetWare Lite is supplied in a building block arrangement in order that users on an existing network are able to purchase additional nodes as needed, in an add-on fashion, to grow at the same speed as the computing environment that requires LAN services. Standard NetWare must have a computer built with at least an Intel 80386 processor; it will not run on a machine which uses the 80286 (or older) chip. Further, a network environment must have a **dedicated server** to run the Novell software; a **nondedicated server** (one that can alternately be used for tasks other than NetWare) is not supported with NetWare versions later than 3.0. NetWare supports many popular network standards, including Ethernet and ArcNet. Novell also uses a proprietary packet transfer called **IPX (information packet exchange)**, which is supported by many other network software programs.

Because it has become a de facto standard for LAN software, Novell also deals with certification of network hardware manufactured by third-party vendors (**VARs**, or **value-added resellers**). The company also manufactures a small line of network interface boards and connection hardware, and it conducts certification classes for network installers and administrators. Among network professionals, Novell's CNE (Certified NetWare Engineer) certificate is the coveted credential. Study guides for the several phases of the CNE examination are good additions to any library's technical collection. Novell also deals in publications and user literature for its own software and network products. A recent publication, the *Network Support Encyclopedia*,[1] has placed on CD-ROM a compendium of all NetWare documentation, users' manuals, application notes, patches and fixes, troubleshooting bulletins, and corporate information articles. Like the *Microsoft Programmer's Library* (chapter 11), it is a keyword and Boolean searchable medium and eliminates the need for several feet of bookshelves full of loose manuals and release notes essential for efficient administration of NetWare-based local area networks.

Users of the MS-DOS operating system will have little trouble adapting to NetWare. In fact, many of the same commands such as DIR (directory listing) and file handling conventions such as the eight-and-three (name plus filetype extension) rule are exactly the same in NetWare as in DOS. NetWare is an extension to DOS of commands necessary for the operation of a multiuser system, with a lengthy repertoire of reserved words and operators for taking command of both the server and workstation environment. The following typify commands from the several groups of NetWare utilities and subprograms, and their uses are easily inferred from context:

**Console** (network administrator) **commands**:

- BROADCAST message—sends announcement to all stations logged onto the server
- MOUNT [PACK]—adds additional disk drives to the system
- PRINTER nn START—add a numbered (nn) printer to the system
- DISK [volume name]—displays information about the specified volume (i.e., hard disk)

**Command line** (workstation) **commands**:

- LOGIN—log in to a file server
- SETPASS—create or change a user's password
- RIGHTS [path]—view your privilege levels in a particular directory (path)
- CHKVOL—similar to DOS CHKDSK command, view a summary of how much of that space is currently being used
- USERLIST—view a list of all the users currently logged onto a file server
- PURGE—permanently delete erased files
- SEND message [TO] [USER]—send a broadcast or message to a particular user or group of users
- LARCHIVE [path]—archive or save network files to local floppy disks or hard disks

**Menu utilities**:

- FILER—create, rename, or delete directories and subdirectories
- COLORPAL—add or change color palettes (video screen appearances)
- SYSCON—list users on a particular server
- SESSION—send messages or broadcasts to groups of users

The number of commands and command variations in NetWare is actually in the hundreds. It should be obvious that in NetWare, as with DOS, there are usually two or three different ways of performing the same task or command. Further, not all commands are available to all users on the system. NetWare allows for user accounts, as do other operating systems such as UNIX and MUSIC, and there are assignable **privilege levels** based on users' "needs to know" and allowable activities within the system. NetWare classifies users into three groups: **administrator**, to designate the person(s) who is responsible for the physical setup and overall maintenance of the LAN; **supervisor**, who plays a subordinate role and typically assigns accounts, performs software troubleshooting, and maintains applications software programs on the server; and, of course, **user**, who accesses the various devices and services attached to the network and to the one or more servers containing the programs and utilities available to everybody with entry-level privileges. Users may have official or account-holder status, or they may have unofficial, minimal-level access and be classified as **guests**.

The most commonly used Macintosh network manager software is the Apple-produced AppleTalk system. AppleTalk uses the familiar icon-based desktop environment that is supplied with every Macintosh computer, attaching itself to the computer's system files and extending the Mac's capabilities to interconnect with other Apple Macintosh boxes. The Macintosh is advantageous in its physical construction because it is the simplest of all the so-called microcomputer devices to connect in a LAN configuration. Because the AppleTalk system invokes the serial communications ports inherent in every Macintosh computer, there are no additional network cards or circuits to purchase in order to set up a LAN environment. The person designated as LAN manager merely attaches the necessary interconnect cables and associated interface boxes from computer to computer, sets up the software to reflect the kinds and numbers of the various equipment on the network, and the job is done.

Macintosh computers can be interfaced into larger local area networks which also contain IBM-compatible computers by inserting appropriate network boards (such as Ethernet cards) into the Macintoshes' busses. NetWare, incidentally, contains a Macintosh component for interfacing Apple products to the IBM side. However, for Apple-only LAN setups, cables, and software are all that are required. AppleTalk is quite flexible, and LANs with central file servers, or no servers at all, can be created in fairly elaborate configurations. The only drawback is that, because AppleTalk uses the serial ports (which would ordinarily be used for modem or printer hookups), the LAN has a slow throughput relative to some of the higher speed, IBM networks. This is a minor inconvenience, however, and the tradeoff for simplicity more than compensates for the slight lethargy of the Macintosh system.

AppleTalk LANs provide many of the same services as NetWare. Where cost is a major consideration, AppleTalk can be configured economically with twisted pair (e.g., telephone) cables, using Farralon and PhoneNet products as hardware support. Several AppleTalk networks can be connected or bridged, and printers on several networks can be shared from outside the "home" network to which they are connected. Files can also be shared from network to network, and in more elaborate setups, programs can be executed over network lines, making it necessary to load only one copy of an executable file on a server rather than individual copies on each user's workstation. Many such schemes are possible to conserve computer memory and storage resources, and configurations are limited only by rules of network topology and the creators' imaginations.

A spinoff of full-blown local area networks are the so-called **peer-to-peer LANs**, sometimes known as "cheapLANs" and "boss/secretary" setups.[2] These have become quite popular in recent years and are especially useful in small offices and libraries where there is not sufficient budget for hiring a network administrator and where expenditures for exclusive, dedicated network equipment are not possible.

Peer-to-peer LANs typically support two to four computers. While there is ordinarily not a separate server PC in such arrangements, one of the workstations in the setup is usually classified as the "main" computer because of its size or the rank of its owner. This "main" computer contains sharable files and may be the PC to which the common printer is connected. The physical setup of peer-to-peer LANs varies, but it is usually nothing more than a hard-wired setup from one computer's serial (RS-232) port to another, in a daisy chain fashion similar to that of AppleTalk described above. Some of the more elaborate peer-to-peer LANs (such as MainLAN Easy) require that a circuit board be installed in the PC, the accompanying loss of a buss slot resulting in faster communication (i.e., throughput) times and additional features in the software. Board-based peer-to-peer LANs are usually upwardly compatible with network arrangements such as NetWare, a feature built into the smaller system so that the office that can afford to upgrade does not lose its investment in the more compact, starter system.

## ACADEMIC AND RESEARCH COMPUTER NETWORKS

Local area networks grow and give way to **wide area networks** (**WANs**). At some point, growing organizations find that their LANs proliferate from one building to many. In companies and multicampus universities, multiple LANs may be separated by miles and even by states. This separation evolves into a wide area network situation, and it becomes necessary for the various LANs to be able to communicate with one another.

It is not difficult to make similar LANs "talk" to each other. Electronically, the server of each respective LAN setup must bridge to an external communications device. A physical bridge can be as simple as a communications card (i.e., circuit board) that plugs into an available slot inside the computer. The bridge is connected to remote servers via a dedicated line, which is typically a private, data-grade telephone line leased to the organization by the telephone company. In the case of multiple server locations there may be a router device to direct network traffic, but the principle is the same as in the case of just two LANs connected together.

What is involved if two or more organizations wish to share their LANs and computer resources? It would be ideal if every LAN-using organization were to install NetWare or 3Com or Banyan Vines as network software. But this is almost never the case. The problem arises, then, how to cause dissimilar LANs to communicate transparently with one another and operate fast enough and simple enough to make interLAN sharing useful and desirable for those who would benefit from it.

Such a condition is achieved through the establishment of communications standards called **protocols** and the installation and use of software programs that incorporate these standards. For data communications, the earliest protocols were somewhat less than reliable and errors in sending and receiving data were rampant. Basically, two computers would establish a **handshake** situation of transmission speed, composition (length) of a data byte, and type of **parity** (a device for fault checking in transmissions), if error checking were present at all. This fundamental protocol was all right if simple text or ASCII files were being shared, since misspelled words could usually be inferred from context. With higher transmission speeds and more sophisticated files being shared, however, newer, more reliable protocols were needed.

For modem-to-modem communications, several protocols have been developed, and many are still in use. Some of these are Xmodem, Ymodem, and Kermit. Kermit is in the public domain and is under continuous development and refinement by Columbia University. Some packages which include Kermit infer that Kermit is the name of a program when actually it is the basis of the communications software. Most telecommunications programs include Kermit as a file transfer protocol along with Xmodem and others, although Kermit can be run as a standalone utility in the releases issued by Columbia.

More specific to network communications are the protocols Telnet, FTP, and TCP/IP. FTP, or **file transfer protocol**, sometimes offered as a package under the name FTP,[3] and TCP/IP, or **transmission control protocol/Internet protocol**, are used to support internal, local area network communications within a single organization's network as well as for access to the Internet (described in the next section). Users receive individual addresses such as 192.175.66.43, octets recognized by the Internet but which may translate to such slogans as "jrsmith@ academic.edu" for J.R. Smith at Academic College, an *edu*cational institution. This addressing scheme forms the basis for wide-area-network and Internetwork communications, making such connections workable and searchable.

TCP/IP is becoming the protocol of choice in a multivendor, disparate operating system environment.[4] It includes SMTP (simple mail transfer protocol), SNMP (simple network management protocol), ICMP (Internet control message protocol), NFS (network file server) and PING (packet Internet grouper). With all these protocols and addressing schemes as ammunition, we are "armed and ready" to begin the quest of branching out beyond our respective institutional walls. There are a number of national and international computer networks of value to libraries and to educational organizations. All that is needed for access is a knowledge of these networks' existences and a connection to a host computer providing a gateway into the systems. The information pool and potentials for sharing ideas await those who would log on and explore.

## BITNET AND INTERNET

This section will not attempt to focus in depth on the subject of the Internet. When the idea for this textbook was conceived not so very long ago, the notion of a universally accessible, global network of unseemingly endless sources of information was just beginning to gain momentum. As all librarians can attest, there are hundreds of books available with copyright dates no older than 1994 and 1995 on every aspect of the Internet. And, it is almost impossible to pick up a bibliography or enter a bookstore without immediately being presented with a handful of titles on the Internet. Because there is so much literature available on the subject, this section will only briefly introduce the concept of a global network, to provide a sense of continuity with the idea of local area and wide area networks introduced earlier in this chapter.

BITNET (**B**ecause **I**t's **T**ime **Net**work) was formed in 1981 from a cluster of computers centered at the City University of New York. Its membership exceeds 500 worldwide, and the network adds about 100 new members per year. It is chartered "for the purpose of facilitating noncommercial exchange of information consistent with the academic purposes of its members."[5] An Executive Committee elected from its membership governs BITNET.

The Internet is not a "thing" or separate network; rather, it is a collection of computer networks worldwide. These networks are separately administered and are of many sizes and types. Some of the individual networks might have more than 10,000 separate computers or workstations. The collective total of users on the Internet is in the millions. In the United States, the National Science Foundation Network, called NSFNet, administers the backbone of the Internet. NSFNet is a high speed network that connects appropriate key regions across the country. The High-Performance Computing Act of 1991, which was signed into law on December 9, 1991, will likely cause NSFNet to become NREN, the National Research and Education Network.

Connections of the various networks that comprise the Internet are of varying types from coaxial cable to fiber-optic cable to microwave setups. Typically, groups of organizations with similar interests form groups within regions to form regional networks. These networks, in turn, connect into the Internet through a collective **gateway** and access the various networks as one consortium to another. The method is similar to the way libraries access the OCLC bibliographic database, not via direct connection to OCLC headquarters but through state and regional cooperatives that "broker" the utility through library services authorities.

Access is made to the Internet using the transmission control protocol/Internet protocol (previously described). Other compatible protocols may work as well, but TCP/IP establishes how users of the Internet can successfully accomplish electronic messaging, online connections, and the transfer of files. The e-mail (electronic mail) facility is a feature of Internet, and it allows communications worldwide between academic colleagues to share new developments, research, and papers in various fields. There are also forums and conferences available which expand the versatility of the basic e-mail, and an e-journal facility, for the exchange of complete periodicals and individual articles, is evolving. Graphics-based "home pages" running under the World Wide Web are very popular.

Once connected, the user is presented with a host of powerful search tools. Because the majority of the Internet's host sites are based on the UNIX operating system (see chapter 6), a searcher with a working knowledge of UNIX will have a decided advantage. However, third-party software houses are writing a number of user-friendly interfaces (or "front-ends") based on Windows and other GUIs, and navigating the Internet is not the cryptic experience it once was. Now familiar utilities such as USENET forums, the Wide Area Information Servers (WAIS), the World Wide Web (WWW), and the Gopher resources make communicating between New York or Chicago and Johannesburg or Melborne as easy as dialing a local telephone call. Some of the more popular Internet browser utility programs include NetScape, Mosaic, and NetCruiser.

The Internet allows for remote login, a facility whereby a computer user can establish a connection to a remote computer and manipulate the remote machine as though it were directly connected to the user's workstation. To accomplish this, a user invokes a facility of TCP/IP called **telnet**. Telnet is particularly adept at accessing bibliographic databases and library catalogs where such online services exist. FTP, the file transfer protocol mentioned above, allows the sharing of full-text documents, and the Archie service indexes files from over 900 sites available for download, even for users who do not have accounts on the host system.[6]

There is much discussion in the mid-1990s centering on the so-called "information superhighway." It is beyond the scope of this text to elaborate on the specifics of Internet techniques and services; as previously stated there are many good manuals and reference materials available for that purpose. In fact, the Internet's overnight rise in popularity has caused an instant explosion in the number and proliferation of titles available to explain the online system. There is considerable redundancy in the literature, and you can get along quite well with one or two directories and a simple comprehensive reference; use your book selection skills to decide which meet your library's needs.

## NOTES

1. *Network Support Encyclopedia, Professional Volume*, published by Novell, Inc., 122 East 1700 South, Provo, UT 84606. Irregular, $1,395 per year.
2. Ogg, Harold C. "CheapLANs: Resource Sharing on a Budget." *Library Software Review*, May-June, 1991, pp. 179-185.
3. PC/TCP Network Software for DOS, published by FTP Software, Inc., 26 Princess Street, Wakefield, MA 01880-3004. Price varies according to number of copies on site license.
4. Force, Stephen. "What is TCP/IP?" *Technical Support*, November 1992, pp. 32-38.
5. BITNET and the BITNIC: The BITNET Network Information Center at EDUCOM. Informational brochure published by EDUCOM, P.O. Box 364, Princeton, NJ 08540.
6. Tennant, Roy. *Internet Basics*. Unpublished paper, 11/1/92.

# Chapter 16

# Dial Access Facilities

No one library can afford to purchase every new book published. Further, no library can expand its materials collection to engulf the span of recorded knowledge—even for just that of the twentieth century. Nonetheless, demands for comprehensiveness in research, whether it is for a short essay or an exhaustive thesis project, insist that this expanse of writing be made available.

Sometimes the difference between a good research paper and an outstanding one is only the degree of perseverance and legwork backing it. Yet due to busy schedules, researchers often do not have the time to drive the miles, write the letters, make the telephone calls, etc., necessary to identify all the relevant materials for their projects. The more successful researcher will arm himself/herself with an evolving, state-of-the-art technique for completing a bibliography for a work- or school-related report—the technique of dial access.

This chapter is an introduction to the process of dialup communication for library card catalog databases. While the focus of this chapter is on dialup to library catalogs, it should be noted that library vendors, too, have taken advantage of dialup procedures to sell their wares. Notably, Baker and Taylor, Ingram and Blackwell North America have hardware set up to accept book orders via computerized telephone hookups, and EBSCO and Faxon can consummate periodical orders in a similar fashion. Access to materials found through dialup can take a variety of forms— personal visits, direct loans, interlibrary loans, or the borrowing of materials through one or more reciprocal arrangements. The emphasis here, however, is on techniques for eliminating much of the legwork by using electronic communications lines.

## A GUIDE TO PC DIALUP ACCESS: WHAT YOU'LL NEED

This chapter does not purport to teach the intricacies of data communications. Rather, it will list the basics and some resources for further information. Fortunately, dial access is a relatively simple activity once a connection to a remote computer is made. Most of the online systems described below will "walk you through" a search to some extent. This section will tell you what you need to know to go shopping, and what to look for in the documentation to get properly connected.

Of course, you'll need a PC with the capability of accepting the installation of a **modem** device. This is the circuit, which may be placed inside (internal) or outside (external) the machine, with which you hook the PC to your telephone line. The physical appearance of a modem makes little difference; just be certain to let your dealer know the make and model of PC to which you intend to connect it. Modems are available for both IBM and compatible computers and for Macintoshes. External modems for the IBM usually plug into the **COM: port** (serial communications port), and those for the Macintosh also plug into a designated communications port, which is also sometimes used for printer connections.

Modems are usually manufactured to the so-called **Hayes compatibility standard** (protocol). The Hayes corporation is also a manufacturer of modems and modem software. What this suggests is that other brands of modems should be able to run software whose programming was targeted for the Hayes instruction set (as most are). Be certain that Hayes compatibility is specified on the shipping box or in the documentation. Modems are usually sold according to speed, measured as the **baud** (transmission) **rate**. The available baud rates are usually 2400/9600/14,400/28,800, and modems become progressively more expensive as the top speed increases. A suggestion: since most online systems vary between supported speeds, purchase a 14,400-baud modem as an economical compromise. Check the modem's documentation to be sure that the baud rate is "software selectable" (switchable between several speeds). Even for the systems that will handle 14,000-baud transmissions, 9600 baud is sufficiently fast for home dialup accesses. A quality, 14,400-baud internal modem costs (as of the date of this publication) less than $100.00.

Although not delicate instruments, modems must contend with precise signals. Any given modem should be capable of handling a **parity check**, a verification of data integrity which uses one bit of each byte of incoming data to ascertain that the transmission's **carrier signal** did not become garbled since its time of origin. Causes for errors in transmission, or **glitches**, include static electricity, "dirty" telephone lines, lightning striking the telephone equipment, atmospheric disturbances of satellite hookups, and a host of other natural phenomena. In environments where extremely precise transmissions must be employed, other integrity verification techniques such as **cyclic redundancy checks**, mathematical formula imposition schemes, are used. Where line voltages are subject to frequent dropouts and fluctuations, a variety of signal protection devices such as **power conditioners** and **surge protectors** are used. But most of the telephone and electrical services in the United States, Canada, and Western Europe are relatively stable, and users should be able to use the protections built into the modems and their accompanying communications software programs with little danger of data loss with dial accesses.

A growing phenomenon is for modems to be packaged as circuit boards capable of sending telefacsimile transmissions. These so-called **fax modems** are typically capable of taking documents produced by popular word processors such as WordPerfect or Microsoft Word and sending them to standard telefacsimile (fax) machines. For offices whose PC environments have an attached digital scanner, many fax boards allow the transmission of scanned graphics images in .PCX and .TIF graphics formats. And, for setups that also include a laser or inkjet printer, it is possible to set up the system to print out received faxes on plain paper.

A number of modems are packaged with basic communications software which are included at no additional cost. Sometimes these programs are older versions of software currently available on the market (at additional cost), but many times the included products will work quite well for library dialup access activities. Be certain to read the documentation thoroughly in order to install the software properly. Some of the typical brands of communications software are: Zstem,[1] PROCOMM,[2] BitCom,[3] FtTerm,[4] SideKick,[5] and SmartCom.[6] Many of these packages are inexpensive (under $100) and some are among the programs packaged with modems as a bonus. All have similar features, but they may appear differently on your PC's screen. You may want to request a demonstration of one or two of the packages at the dealer's location to determine which format best suits you.

One of the important accessory components of communications software is the set of **emulator files**. Your PC, as shipped, probably uses an **ASCII keyboard** or an **ANSI** (American National Standards Institute) **keyboard**, both keyboards being versions of standard, text-oriented alphanumeric layouts. These keyboards are capable of various keystroke combinations, such as the **control** (Ctrl) **sequences** (e.g., Ctrl-C or ^C for program abort, and others) used for software and program flow control. Note, however, that some of the systems described below specify keyboards other than either of the two aforementioned. This is because the dialup software on remote computers does not (or cannot) anticipate what kind of keyboard each and every dialup user will present to the system. Because this is so, each system usually must insist on one particular keyboard protocol from all incoming users. The communications software you purchase will have documentation on how to install the emulator components when necessary. The emulator files will, in turn, trap codes such as control sequences and interpret them properly to the system with which you are attempting to communicate. Some of the more popular keyboard emulations are: VT52, VT100, VT102, IBM 3101, Wyse, Televideo, and Wang. Check the software's documentation before you purchase a communications program to ascertain that the software includes a sufficient number of these emulator files and terminal capabilities.

## SPILL FILES AND CAPTURE FILES

Unless otherwise stated, none of the dialup databases in this chapter require you to establish a user account or pay a fee for services. However, when using dial access to a remote computer, you do incur charges on your household telephone bill, the same as charges for making a voice call of the same time length and distance. While most of the dialup computers specified in this chapter allow you to browse at will, casual and inattentive use of a dialup database can become expensive. If it is necessary for you to examine detailed bibliographic data in an online catalog, it might be more economical to record the general information to a disk file and read the details later, after you have logged off the database. Your communications software should have a provision for what is variously called a **capture file**, **spill file**, **log file**, or some similarly named utility. The idea of this feature is to create a file on your computer's disk that is an exact duplicate of everything that has been shown on your PC's screen from the time you made a connection until you hang up; in other words, a mirror image of your dialup session. The strategy is for you to go into the database, enter your enquiries quickly (with some preplanning) and exit immediately when you're done, keeping connect time to a minimum. Once offline, you can examine or edit the spill file with your favorite word processor. Another important advantage with this spill file method is that you can "capture" full bibliographic information for the references you identify, an essential step for creating a final reading list for your term paper or thesis.

## HOW TO SEARCH FOR THE MATERIALS YOU WANT

Once you've logged on, searching an electronic library catalog database is not much different from searching the familiar 3" x 5" card catalog.

Generally, you need to know the author, title, or subject of the book(s) you seek; some systems will allow you to search on the book's call number, if you have it. In general, you need not be concerned with matters of punctuation or capitalization when entering search words or names. Because rules of these aspects of grammar sometimes vary with the persons or organizations using them in their publications, opinions regarding propriety cataloging conventions and syntaxes can differ. Database programmers have taken this into consideration, and search algorithms usually ignore special characters such as hyphens and accent marks, and they usually translate anything you type into upper case before processing.

While this can be an advantage when searching, it is helpful if you copy (through screen capture, if possible) the *exact* information returned on the computer screen. That way, when you enter the information in your report's footnotes, it will be in a correct research style. Library catalogers make great efforts to enter information about a book into a catalog/database in precise detail, maintaining what is known as **bibliographic integrity** for each entry. This ensures that your citations will be accurate, and you should use this fact to your advantage when it comes time to write your report's final draft.

To elaborate further on search algorithms, programmers usually maintain a list of **stopwords** for the database. These are words (typically "a," "and," "the," and sometimes "or," "of," or "not") which are in such common usage that they are of no value for a search to identify a certain book. If you type them, as in the title, *The Day of the Jackal,* you could have saved yourself typing time by entering "Day Jackal" since the two "the's" and the "of" would be ignored as stopwords. Different systems strip (parse) different words; for example, one system strips "history" and "national" as stopwords, along with many others. If you use a particular online database on a regular basis, it would be advantageous to learn that database's stopword list as an abbreviation to the amount of necessary keystrokes. While some databases will allow you to search only with names or words in the title, others will allow keyword subject searches. Some will allow Boolean, or logical searches; these can be timesavers and powerful aids in limiting searches only to those topics which are relevant to your research. The more sophisticated databases will allow at least the use of Boolean operators AND, NOT, and OR, and some will allow nesting of search terms with parentheses. Those persons who have performed online database searches in systems such as ERIC, DIALOG, and others, will already be familiar with the Boolean search stratagem. There is a further explanation of Boolean searching in chapter 17. For now, as a matter of example, the following line of pseudocode assumes that "ti=" is the instruction for a title search:

ti= (children OR video) AND education >> 1980

This formula defines any book whose title has the keyword "education" along with either the keyword "children" or the keyword "video" and was published after 1980.

Most online library catalogs are clustered, i.e., shared by more than one library. Dialup access points cannot determine where you are calling from, nor which library's collection you wish to search. The LCS (Library Computer System in Illinois) system, for example, defaults to the University of Illinois library and assumes that you wish to search that University's collection. **Scoping codes**, two-letter abbreviations of the various schools in Illinois, are available to focus a search on a particular library or group of libraries. You should take a few moments to familiarize yourself with the scoping codes developed for the particular system in your area. If a searcher wished to confine a title enquiry to one school, an online search might take the following format,

F T gone with the wind $NI

to search for *Gone With the Wind* in the catalog database at Northern Illinois University.

Finally, many dialup systems require you to log off formally, releasing the dialup port you've been using for others to use. Dialup facilities are not inexpensive, and libraries typically buy only what they think they can afford to accommodate an average number of users. It is a courtesy for you to provide the logoff command at the end of your session; otherwise, a busy port may be rendered unavailable to others for a period of time, or, worse, until a systems operator manually resets it. Be considerate also with the amount of time you stay connected to the remote system. Persons who monopolize dialup facilities or do not plan their searches intelligently are denying others their right to access the information. And, persons who leave their PCs connected but idle are doing little other than lining the pockets of the telephone company's stockholders!

## RECIPROCAL BORROWING ARRANGEMENTS AND INTERLIBRARY LOAN

Once you have identified the books and materials you need, the next logical step is to obtain them. Depending on the time and transportation available to you, there are several options to connect you with the reading matter for your project.

### Apply in Person

It may be necessary for you to go to several libraries to obtain all the materials you want. Most libraries will not charge a fee for use of their facilities. As long as you do not need to check out books, all libraries will generally afford you the same privileges and reference services as for local patrons or registered students. There are almost always photocopy machines available for you to copy materials that you are not permitted to take from the library.

Many libraries in North America belong to consortia that afford some kind of reciprocal borrowing arrangements with other libraries. This means that a library card (or student I.D. card) in your possession may be honored for the purpose of borrowing books from a library away from your home or school of registration. Such arrangements are usually accomplished within clusters of libraries engaged in cooperative setups. In many states and provinces, public libraries are typically members of systems, while colleges and universities form their own cooperatives, usually indifferent to geography. But while most public as well as private colleges allow open access to their facilities, some of the nonaffiliated institutions and corporate libraries do not. Since the latter are not always tax-supported bodies, they have the right in many cases to deny you access to their book collections. But usually these schools and corporations will, nonetheless, allow you the use of their facilities for a bona fide scholastic purpose. Admission to most of these facilities can sometimes be obtained through your own college or university library in some form of written pass program. You should apply in person to your home library, typically to the main reference desk, to obtain whatever written documentation might be required for special access to a nonaffiliated library. The librarian must sometimes ascertain that the information you seek is not available at the local level. He/she may then request to see your student I.D. card to complete the written pass. You may also be required to state the purpose of your intended visit to the other library, along with the date and approximate time of your expected visit. Instructions for use are usually printed on the pass itself; part of it will be surrendered by you to the library at which you will perform your research. Generally, you will not be permitted to borrow books and materials from the library you visit.

## Direct Loan

If your search has scoped to a school or library with which your local institution has reciprocal borrowing privileges and you have identified a book you need, you can often have that book sent directly to the circulation desk of the library with which you are affiliated. You can use direct loan in two ways: when you read the computer record from the screen, note the catalog number. Take that number, the book title, the owning school's scoping code, and your student I.D. card to the library circulation desk. Your request will be processed, and the books will be ordered for you. You may order several books at a time, and usually they need not be from the same remote library.

If you are accessing a library catalog through dialup facilities, you can often initiate a request for materials yourself, directly from your PC screen. Libraries with such a facility usually provide pamphlets of written instructions for completing this process. What triggers or validates your request is your borrower's ID number, typically your Social Security number or some other unique code issued by your home library, activated from your student identification card or library card at the library circulation desk. As with in-person requests, books are shipped to your library's circulation desk for pickup. It is courteous to notify circulation personnel of your action so that they can be expecting your order, one for which they (depending on the system) might not have received an advice of transmission. When requesting books from a dialup facility, you should pay particular attention to records that read "REF" (or something similar) before the call number—such books may be designated "reference only" and therefore not available for use except in the owning library. If the computer records read "CHGD," "SNAGGED," "RECALL," "HOLD," or a variety of other similar flags, the books so marked are currently unavailable for you to borrow, and you should not attempt to enter a request for one or more of them.

Direct loan is probably the quickest way for you to obtain materials short of going to other libraries yourself. Depending on the time of the year, the waiting period is typically between three and seven working days.

## Interlibrary Loan (ILL)

If your search results in no items located within your local system, you may want to branch out. Dialup access is usually not available for patrons through bibliographic utilities such as OCLC; you must make application with the librarian for such materials. However, for interstate searches, you may be able to search distant libraries' catalogs through the Internet (see chapter 15); check with your network administrator to see if a list of participating (i.e., networked) libraries is available.

You should be prepared to provide as much information about the book you want as possible. You will also be asked for your student I.D or borrower's card. Be advised that some lending libraries charge a fee for ILL, and you may be expected to pay the charge. There is often a line on the ILL form upon which you are allowed to place a dollar limit on charges you will allow. If the lending library's charge exceeds your specified amount, the materials will not be sent. Bear in mind that this option should be used only if time is not at a premium. Interlibrary loan deliveries can take from two to six weeks, and this should be taken into account if you are depending upon such materials to complete a research project within a deadline.

# APPLICATION: CATALOG DIAL ACCESS TO SPECIFIC SYSTEMS

In chapter 13, a number of automated circulation and cataloging systems were discussed. Most of these have dialup facilities; however, for the sake of variety, examples of several other systems' dialup components will be illustrated in the section below. Each of these examples is from a college or university library setting.

**INNOPAC** is a relative newcomer to the online system arena and is growing in popularity. While it does not offer some of the detailed search strategies of other systems, it is outstanding in its user friendliness and ability to prompt the user for the next logical step. With INNOPAC it is usually not necessary to press the "Enter" key after typing single keystrokes, i.e., as with responses to input prompts. You still must hit the "Enter" key after typing authors, titles, etc., to complete the entry information. Other than this idiosyncracy, INNOPAC is more or less foolproof and can help you identify the materials you want with a minimum of difficulty.

INNOPAC supports the following searches:

* **Author**. Search by last name, first name, middle initial, as "Jones, Mary B." Pseudonyms should be searched by the popular name such as "Twain, Mark" for Samuel L. Clemens. If the author is a corporation or organization, search by that organization's name, such as "Standard and Poor's Corporation."

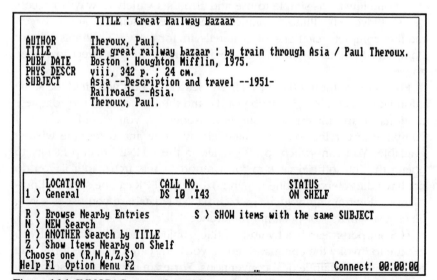

**Figure 16.1** INNOPAC screen from title search

- **Title**. Enter words in the title in the exact order they appear. You may eliminate some words if the title is very long. You may omit "a," "and," and "the."
- **Subject**. Use the Library of Congress subject headings. If you are uncertain of the correct words or formats, consult an official copy of the *Library of Congress Subject Headings*.
- **Words in Title**. Use this option if you do not know the first word of the title, if you are unsure of the order of the words, or if you do not remember all the words in the title.
- **Special Features**. Boolean searching is somewhat limited; however, you may use the Boolean operators AND, OR, and NOT. Nesting (i.e., the use of search stratagems featuring parentheses) is difficult for INNOPAC to interpret properly. If what you actually want is a keyword search, use the Words in Title option for best results. Capitalization (or the lack of it) will not affect the results of your searches.

INNOPAC does not have an automatic disconnect on hangup. When you leave the system, be sure to return to the main menu screen and type "D" (disconnect) to free the port for others.

LCS (Library Computer System) with FBR (Full Bibliographic Record) is the familiar name of the online database shell of ILLINET Online in Illinois. In 1992, ILLINET replaced its line-oriented interface with a more user-friendly, full-screen utility for catalog inquiries. Available once only on PC terminals running GW-BASIC and directly connected to ILLINET telephone lines, it is simple to use and affords a variety of ways to access items at over 800 Illinois libraries. LCS is the system of choice if you require complete citations of materials in forty ILCSO (Illinois Library Computer Systems Organization) libraries and items for direct loan (see above).

FBR is the authority file for ILLINET. Searching FBR will yield the same information as on 3" x 5" catalog cards, and the file contains the complete citations of any materials in question. Generally, you would use LCS if you were just trying to locate materials by name and determine what is available. You can switch to FBR while in the ILLINET dialup facility to obtain the full, official citation for a report or research paper if you do not have the referenced title in hand. However, FBR can be searched pursuant to determining holdings; which ILLINET database you use is sometimes just a matter of personal preference.

LCS supports searches by author, title, subject, and call number. If you choose to invoke the command mode, you can search in a free form style by following certain lexical conventions. For example, you can search in command mode, where "F A" is the operator for "find author" as

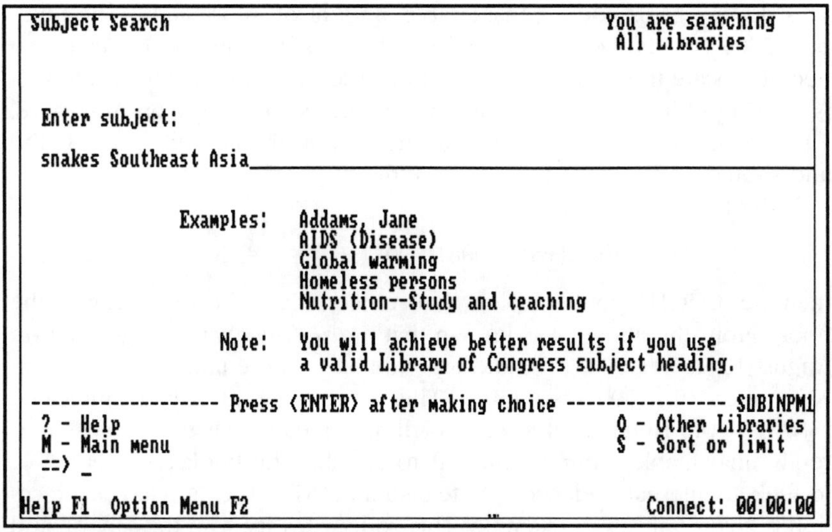

```
┌─────────────────────────────────────────────────────────────────────┐
│ Subject Search                                      You are searching │
│                                                     All Libraries     │
│                                                                       │
│                                                                       │
│   Enter subject:                                                      │
│   snakes Southeast Asia_____│
│                                                                       │
│                                                                       │
│             Examples:   Addams, Jane                                  │
│                         AIDS (Disease)                                │
│                         Global warming                                │
│                         Homeless persons                              │
│                         Nutrition--Study and teaching                 │
│                                                                       │
│                 Note:   You will achieve better results if you use    │
│                         a valid Library of Congress subject heading.   │
│   ------------------ Press <ENTER> after making choice ---------- SUBINPM1│
│   ? - Help                                      O - Other Libraries   │
│   M - Main menu                                 S - Sort or limit     │
│   ==> _                                                               │
│                                                                       │
│ Help F1  Option Menu F2                              Connect: 00:00:00│
└─────────────────────────────────────────────────────────────────────┘
```

**Figure 16.2** ILLINET screen for subject search

   F A Terkel, Studs $ALL

to find all books by author Studs Terkel in all ('ALL') libraries in the database; as "F T" for "find title" as

   F T Great Railway Bazaar $UI

to find the book, *Great Railway Bazaar* at the University of Illinois; as "F S" for "find subject" as

   F S economic geography $LCS

to locate books on the subject of economic geography in all LCS (Illinois college) libraries; and as "F A .and. F T" in Boolean style to combine search stratagems as

   F A Mitchell, Margaret .and. F T Gone Wind $NU

to find Margaret Mitchell's *Gone with the Wind* at Northern Illinois University. Note that "with" and "the" are not entered in the search because they are stopwords and would be ignored. Note also that the use of periods as delimiters around the Boolean operator ".and." distinguishes it as part of the stratagem and not a stopword.

   The result of an ILLINET search might yield the following record:

E806.T45   TERKEL, LOUIS.  HARD TIMES  $NEW YORK  69-20195
81918 1970 1 ADDED:800828
01 001 16-3W STX

This display gives you a considerable amount of information. The number "E806.T45" is the library's call number (catalog number), which you need to locate the book on the shelf or order from the dialup window. It is a 1970 publication, and the library purchased one copy on August 28, 1980 (800828). Copy 1 ("001") is on the shelf in the library's stacks (STX) and should be available for you to retrieve.

If the third line had read:

01 001 16-3W STX CHGD 900810/901130

then the "CHGD" would indicate that someone had already borrowed the book. From the above, it is known that *Hard Times* was charged out on August 10, 1990 ("900810"), and was due back in the library on or before November 30, 1990 ("901130"). This line might also have indicated "SNAGD" or "HOLD," either of which also means that the book is currently unavailable. Your recourse is to ask that the book be reserved or to seek an alternate selection. Note also that "STX" (i.e., stacks) as a location is given only as an example. This code will vary with the school, and you should check with individual libraries to determine the exact meanings of the codes.

Northwestern University's NUCat OPAC (online public access catalog) has evolved as the basis of user access to its proprietary NOTIS integrated information system. Terminals hooked up through LUIS, the Library User Information System, including the dialup interface, can query the collections of the University and users can accomplish relatively complex

```
Subject Search: SNAKES SOUTHEAST ASIA              You are searching
No. of Items: 2

  1. TITLE:  Fascinating snakes of Southeast Asia : an introduction /
Enter subject:                                                       1989
     AUTHOR:  Lim, Francis Leong Keng.
sn
  2. TITLE:  Venomous snakes of southeast Asia and some physiological and
             biochemical aspects of their venoms /                  1975
     AUTHOR:  Lin, M. Wai




+-
          Use E - Expand search to look for additional items.
------------------ Press <ENTER> after making choice ------------- SUBDMBBM
? - Help                                          O - Other libraries
M - Main menu D - Detailed record  T - Try new subject  S - Sort or limit
==> _ No.: _ E - Expand search  L - Location/Call no.

Help F1  Option Menu F2                ..             Connect: 00:00:00
```

**Figure 16.3** Result of ILLINET subject search.

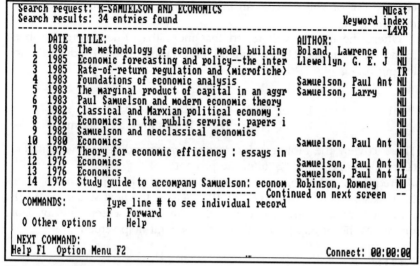

```
Search request: K=SAMUELSON AND ECONOMICS                          NUcat
Search results: 34 entries found                            Keyword index
-----------------------------------------------------------------------L4XR
        DATE  TITLE:                                    AUTHOR:
     1  1989  The methodology of economic model building  Boland, Lawrence A  NU
     2  1985  Economic forecasting and policy--the inter   Llewellyn, G. E. J  NU
     3  1985  Rate-of-return regulation and (microfiche)                       TR
     4  1983  Foundations of economic analysis            Samuelson, Paul Ant  NU
     5  1983  The marginal product of capital in an aggr   Samuelson, Larry    NU
     6  1983  Paul Samuelson and modern economic theory                        NU
     7  1982  Classical and Marxian political economy :                        NU
     8  1982  Economics in the public service : papers i                       NU
     9  1982  Samuelson and neoclassical economics                             NU
    10  1980  Economics                                   Samuelson, Paul Ant  NU
    11  1979  Theory for economic efficiency : essays in                       NU
    12  1976  Economics                                   Samuelson, Paul Ant  NU
    13  1976  Economics                                   Samuelson, Paul Ant  LL
    14  1976  Study guide to accompany Samuelson: econom   Robinson, Romney    NU
------------------------------------------------- Continued on next screen --
   COMMANDS:        Type line # to see individual record
                    F   Forward
   0 Other options  H   Help

   NEXT COMMAND:
Help F1   Option Menu F2                                  Connect: 00:00:00
```

**Figure 16.4** Northwestern University's online public access catalog

searches by following instructions on the computer screen. An example of NWU's LUIS is in Figure 16.4.

## PUBLIC ACCESS CATALOG

The University of Chicago uses a proprietary online catalog system which is very user-friendly. With a minimum of input, a dialup user can obtain very detailed information about the holdings of the U of C libraries. From the preliminary signon screens, online help is available to guide the searcher through even the most detailed inquiry.

As with other systems, you can search the University of Chicago's online catalog by author, title, and subject/keyword. However, the system is intuitive, which means that the online catalog can infer what you want from a single search line. For example, after you have logged onto the system, the prompt "Enter Search:" will appear and you can begin to enter search terms. For example,

Enter Search: Terkel, Studs
Enter Search: Terkel, Hard
Enter Search: Hard Times

would all access a reference to Studs Terkel's *Hard Times*. Regardless of the terms used, you should separate each word with a comma. If one record is found, the screen entry will display full bibliographic information along with the call number and the book's location. If "Circulation Status:" appears, the display will indicate whether the book has been charged out or will provide an instruction to type "C" for further information.

Often, the inquiry will report that more than one record has been found. For example, "Enter Search: Terkel, Hard" could produce the following listing:

| List# | Uses | |
|---|---|---|
| 1 | 3 | Terkel, Studs, 19xx-./Hard times |
| 2 | 1 | Terkel, Studs, 19xx-./Hard times, a criticism |

Thus, to view the bibliographic record corresponding to line number 2 (List# 2), simply enter "2" after the prompt.

Frequently, a bibliographic record will occupy multiple screens. If this is the case, enter "N" (or F8 on an IBM PC) for the next screen or "P" (F7 on a PC) for the previous screen. Extensive help screens are available online. At the prompt, press F1 for the general help screen

## NOTES

1. Zstem, published by Zenith Data Systems Corporation, St. Joseph, MI 49085. $99.95.
2. PROCOMM PLUS, published by Datastorm Technologies, Inc., P.O. Box 1471, Columbia, MO 65205. $129.00.
3. BitCom, published by BIT Software, Inc., 830 Hillview Court, Suite 160, Milpitas, CA 95035. $39.00.
4. FtTerm, published by International Business Machines, Inc. (IBM) as part #75X3286. $145.00.
5. SideKick, published by Lattice, Inc., 3010 Woodcreek Drive, Suite A, Downers Grove, IL 60515 (mailing address P.O. Box 3072, Glen Ellyn, IL 60138), Inc. $89.95.
6. SmartCom for Windows, published by Hayes Microcomputer Products, P.O. Box 105203, Atlanta, GA 30348. $49.00.

# Chapter 17

# Boolean Logic, Structured Query Language, and Data Searches

In order for any database to be of use, there must be a standard method or methods for retrieving the information it contains. It doesn't matter whether the database consists of a few dozen records or many thousands, whether it is floppy disk-based or residing on the inner sanctum drives of a mainframe computer complex, there must be a logical, straightforward way to make use of the data that persons have diligently input.

Data searching is both an art and a science. As an activity, there are rules and formulas, both general and proprietary, that surround the process of data retrieval for any given database. As a skill, each searcher will devise his/her own tricks and techniques for getting a database to yield its contents quickly and with accuracy and relevancy. Without structures and algorithms for extracting information from databases, all the collection, sorting, manipulating, and indexing performed in setting up the database amount to little more than rote exercises.

In the simplest form, data searching is performed with **keywords**. **KWIC (keyword in context)** systems evolved from this arena, and, for simple data searching, the technique remains valid. For the sake of simplicity for patrons who might not be computer-literate, online catalog searches using only keywords in the subject title are a simplistic but effective way of locating materials on the shelves. For more elaborate searches, keywords provide the foundation for nouns and modifiers in search stratagems.

One search stratagem that has its roots in applied mathematics is **Boolean logic**. Also called **Boolean algebra**, it is a system devised by the English mathematician George Boole. In a mathematical sense, it is a system of logic formulas represented by **gate diagrams**; in fact, microprocessor circuits are usually first represented by gates and connections before they are processed as transistors and capacitors inside an integrated circuit chip. A simple microprocessor circuit might appear as in Figure 17.1.

A logic diagram is a representation of some binary signal, consisting of ones and zeros (as described in chapter 1), that must pass through transistors and wires from point A to point B, to carry information from one side of a circuit to another. All modern computers are made up of many thousands of such circuits, and all microcircuits, no matter how complex, have their origins as Boolean diagrams on the drawing board. It is the bringing together of the many circuits that make the computer operate as a system entity.

Boolean algebra, then, is a simplified mathematical system used to deal with binary or two-value functions. Boolean sentences allow us to express various logic functions and, when used in information searches, allow both simple and complex lookups to be expressed in a convenient, mathematical format. And, since Boolean searching *is* an algebra, a very complex search equation may be reduced to simpler terms. Boolean logic uses a number of **operators** to construct logic and search equations. The most common are "**AND**," "**OR**," "**NOT**," and "**NOR**." In simplest terms, using ones and zeroes to illustrate the use of these operators, single- and two-term Boolean AND statements resemble the following:

1 AND 1 = 1 (true)
1 AND 0 = 0 (false)
0 AND 1 = 0 (false)
0 AND 0 = 0 (false)

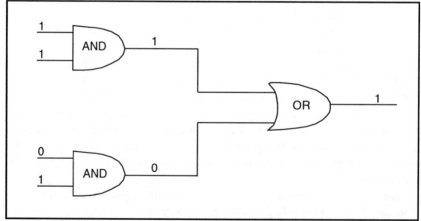

**Figure 17.1** Boolean logic diagram of (1 AND 1) OR (0 AND 1) = 1

In other words, when "AND" is the operator, the number 1 must be the value of both elements in the left side of the equation before the statement returns "true," i.e., "1." If any other combination of ones and zeroes is stated where one or both of the variables is not a 1, the statement returns "false." Likewise, if there is a complex statement of three or more elements, all the elements must be ones before the statement = "1" i.e., "true." Thus, 1 AND 1 AND 1 AND 1 = 1 (true) but

1 AND 1 AND 0 AND 1 = 0 (false).

Before reviewing Boolean operators other than AND, consider a somewhat restricted example of a data inquiry. Suppose you were searching a database for an article with the title, "Use of Video Recorders in Public Libraries." This article could have been coded with the keywords "video," "recorders," "public," "libraries," "television," or any number of other nouns and adjectives. In a very small database, it might be possible to retrieve the article using only two of the possible keywords. Suppose the searcher typed

video AND libraries

at the keyboard. Assuming that the original inputter of the article had indexed the article with the keywords that were just listed, there would be a **hit** on the search, and the article's title, along with any accompanying information, would be printed at the console.

In terms of Boolean operators, use of only the AND operator severely limits search capabilities, so OR and the other operators must be brought into the picture. Once again using ones and zeroes to illustrate the concept in the abstract, a two-element search using OR would resemble the following:

|   |    |   |   |   |         |   | A | B | C |
|---|----|---|---|---|---------|---|---|---|---|
| 1 | OR | 1 | = | 1 | (true)  |   | 1 | 1 | 1 |
| 1 | OR | 0 | = | 1 | (true)  | = | 1 | 0 | 1 |
| 0 | OR | 1 | = | 1 | (true)  |   | 0 | 1 | 1 |
| 0 | OR | 0 | = | 0 | (false) |   | 0 | 0 | 0 |

With the OR operator, only one element of the statement need be a 1 for the statement to equate "true" (i.e., = 1). The column on the right—the A, B, and C block—is a graphic illustration of all the possible combinations of elements of this two element Boolean equation called a **truth table**. It follows that, if elements are added to the equation, the principle of "at least one element needed for truth" holds no matter how many elements are in the statement; that is, 1 OR 0 OR 0 OR 0 OR 0 = 1 (true), regardless of how many zeroes are appended. There need be only one "1" for the equation to render truth!

To return to the data search example: the original AND statement could be changed to read

video AND (libraries OR academic)

"Academic" does not appear in the title "Use of Video Recorders in Public Libraries," but that doesn't matter—all that was asked for was for an article that had at least "video" in the title, but it could have either "libraries" or "academic" (or both, for that matter) to satisfy the remainder of the search statement. In this small database, "Use of Video Recorders in Public Libraries" would have been retrieved, but if there had been an article with the title "Use of Video Recorders in Academic Institutions," that title would have been returned also.

Electrically, this is how a search works inside the computer: recall in chapter 1 the discussion of how a byte of data is made of bits, or logical ones and zeroes, held inside an integrated circuit. Suppose each keyword in a database is assigned a numeric code, which is translated into a binary number and limited (in this example) to one byte in length. A list of such "legal" keywords, called a **thesaurus**, can be created and establish it as the foundation of the database. The thesaurus' lookup table might look something like this:

| | | |
|---|---|---|
| academic | 1010 | 1000 |
| librar# | 1010 | 1001 |
| public | 1010 | 1010 |
| recorder# | 1010 | 1011 |
| television | 1010 | 1100 |
| video | 1010 | 1101 |

The bit pattern is unique for each keyword. Suppose a searcher enters "public" at the keyboard in an effort to retrieve article references with that word in the title. The keyword "public" is translated into the appropriate bit pattern, 1010 1010, and passed on to the computer. The database program makes a **bitwise comparison** to ascertain that "public" is a legal keyword in the thesaurus. If so, then "public" is passed on to another part of the database program to compare its bit pattern with those of keywords in each of the articles stored. For each article that contains a byte keyword value of 1010 1010, a hit will be registered and reported back to the searcher in a few moments on the computer screen or teletype writer. Naturally, in large databases more than one keyword at a time is entered, and the keywords will have multiple bit pattern assignments. However, this simple example will serve to illustrate the underlying theory behind computerized database searching.

A Boolean search can use any combination of operators and any line length of search formulas limited only by the capacity of the database program assigned to interpret it. To recapitulate, the following are the major elements of Boolean database searching:

1. **AND**—the process of **conjunction**. Graphically, a search might be stated:

video ∩ librar# ∩ television ∩ public

( "∩" is the Boolean symbol for "AND".) All four keyword terms must be present for the search formula to yield an article from the database. If any one keyword is missing, the other three will be rejected. The effect of AND is that its use decreases response (the number of hits) and narrows **specificity** (i.e., increases detail of the search).

2. **OR**—the process of **disjunction**. This type of search is stated as

video ∪ librar# ∪ television ∪ public

( "∪" is the Boolean symbol for "OR".) In this search, any one or more of the keywords will yield an article. Obviously, this search is far too general to be of benefit when searching a large database. Practically, the OR operator is used in combination with other operators, usually AND, to give a bit of generality to the search. The effect of OR is that it increases response and broadens specificity.

3. **NAND**—the process of **exclusive alternation**. An example is

video NAND librar# NAND television NAND public

Here, any combination of the four terms *except all* will produce a hit and find an article title. The effect of NAND is that it decreases response and narrows specificity but with less effect than AND.

4. **NOR**—the process of **contradiction**. A NOR search might be stated

(neither) video NOR librar#

such a search displaying all article titles that are void of either or both keywords. This is the "everything but" operator; in other words, for every title qualifying as a "hit," all the search terms influenced by NOR must be absent from the article's keyword association. The search will reject any article that contains at least one of the terms in the search formula. The effect of NOR is that it increases response and broadens specificity, but with less effect than OR.

5. **NOT**—the process of **negation**. An example of the use of NOT is

NOT (video ∩ libraries)

NOT is typically used with parentheses, and these have the same meaning as in ordinary algebra. This particular search occurs in two phases: first, the computer evaluates the AND statement "video ∩ libraries" and then negates it. In other words, the database program will search for all articles with both the keywords "video" and "libraries" and reject what it finds in favor of everything else. Like OR, NOT is typically used in combination with other Boolean operators and never alone. NOT is sometimes written as a bar across the top of the statement instead of using parentheses. Its effect is to narrow the detail of the search.

**6.** = —**equality**; the "all or nothing" operator. An example of the use of "=" is

= (video + librar# + television + public)

The "+" sign is another way of stating "AND". The "=" operator is not frequently used in database search algorithms. Its effect is to find articles if all four terms are present (as with AND) and also if *none* of the terms are present. Its effect is to decrease response and narrow specificity, but with less effect than AND.

**7.** > **and** < —**scoping operators**. These signs are typically used with dates and ranges of numbers, as

(video ∩ librar# ∩ television) > 1980

Assigning the "greater than" (i.e., ">" operator) to mean "dates after," the search would be limited to articles published only after 1980. A particular database could assign other numeric values to mean "before" and "after." For example, if articles were assigned reading levels, "≤" or "<=" might mean "reading levels of eighth grade or less" if stated as "(video ∪ librar#) ≤ 8". The effect is that response decreases drastically with minor effect on specificity.

**8. # (and others, such as $ and @ and \*)—universal characters.** Nearly every example above has contained the keyword "librar#". When universal characters are appended to keywords, it is a process similar to the use of wildcards in the DOS operating system (see chapter 6). In this instance, the search formula is conveying that "all variations of keywords beginning with 'librar' are permissible." In other words, "library," "libraries," and "librarianship" would all be acceptable in the list of articles found. The effect is to increase response and decrease specificity.

Bear in mind that, in the preceding examples, no particular search language was being illustrated. Although the Boolean statements above will closely resemble the search stratagems of many databases currently in use, the examples are made of an artificial search language for the sake of illustrating principles. To reinforce the concepts of Boolean and

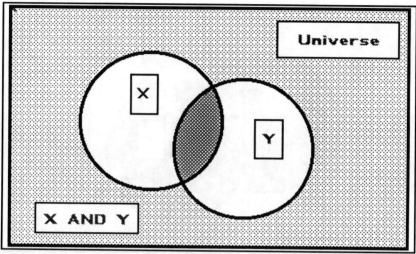

**Figure 17.2** Conjunction (AND) diagram

word searching one last time, Figures 17.2 through 17.6 illustrate database constructs graphically.

A number of colleges are including a course in finite mathematics in the first year curricula for social sciences and business. To be sure, many of the concepts of Boolean algebra and practical logic are included in such a course. Further, these topics relate directly to library science and to the concepts introduced in this chapter. Specifically, we turn to the idea of a Venn diagram to illustrate database searches from a mathematical point of view.

A **Venn diagram** is a graphic way of illustrating sets of data and showing the methods in which those data can be accessed. The Venn rectangle in its entirety constitutes the **universe**, as indicated inside the boxes in Figures 17.2 through 17.6. The universe contains exactly what you would logically expect, i.e., all the data elements (samples, titles, subjects, etc.) that are possible to include in any related group of items. And this universe contains a **population** of all valid items, represented by circles. The result of keyword or Boolean searches is represented by the intersection of these circles. Thus, with a Venn diagram as a drawing tool, we can talk about searches without resorting to the use of made-up phrases. Keep in mind that a population can represent any number of data from a few dozen items to a few billion. It all depends on the nature of the data being discussed.

Repeating the Boolean terms at the head of this section, Venn diagrams for the various operators appear as follows:

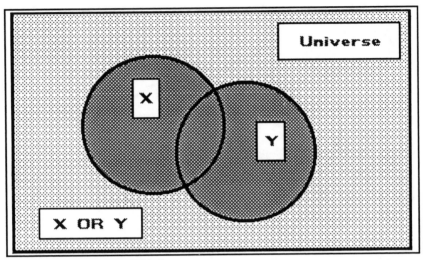

**Figure 17.3** Disjunction (OR) diagram

**Conjunction AND
(Truth Table)**

**Explanation**

X • Y
0 • 0 = 0
1 • 0 = 0
1 • 1 = 1

only both x and y; document
must contain both (or all)
terms to be considered a
"hit."

Note that there are two ways to illustrate Boolean equations; at the head
of this section, the "set logic" method of using "∩ s", "∪ s" and words
was illustrated; the truth tables above use mathematical notation.

**Disjunction or
(Truth Table)**

**Explanation**

X + Y
0 + 0 = 0
0 + 1 = 1
1 + 0 = 1
1 + 1 = 1

either x or y or both must be
present; the left side must
contain at least one (true)
term.

**Exclusive Alternation NAND
(Truth Table)**

**Explanation**

X + Y
0 + 1 = 1
1 + 0 = 1
0 + 0 = 0
1 + 1 = 0

either x or y but not both;
anything but all or nothing.

**Contradiction NOR
(Truth Table)**

**Explanation**

X • Y

not x, not y, not (x and y);

0 • 0 = 1

inclusion of any (true) term

1 • 0 = 0

voids a search. Everything is

0 • 1 = 0

"outside the circles."

1 • 1 = 0

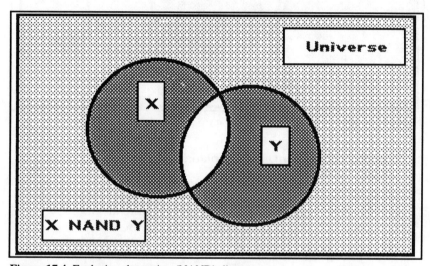

**Figure 17.4** Exclusive alternation (NAND) diagram

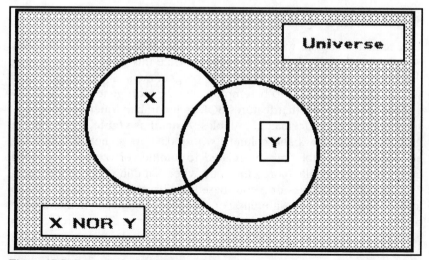

**Figure 17.5** Contradiction (NOR) diagram

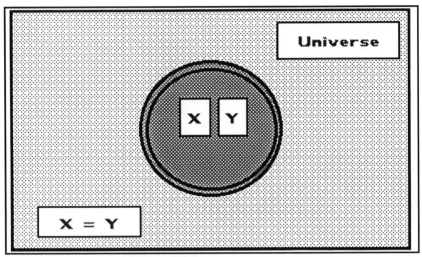

**Figure 17.6** Equality (Equivalence) diagram

| **Equality (Equivalent)** **(Truth Table)** | **Explanation** |
|---|---|
| X + Y | x and y; not x and not y; |
| 1 + 1 = 1 | not (x and y); all terms or |
| 0 + 0 = 1 | none must be present. |
| 1 + 1 = 1 | |
| 0 + 1 = 0 | |
| 1 + 0 = 0 | |

## STRUCTURED QUERY LANGUAGE

A search stratagem which has gained rapid popularity in recent years is **structured query language**, or **SQL**. While this method of searching databases is still performed chiefly by programmers, SQL nonetheless is sufficiently user-friendly to be employed as a report generating facility.

Database software that features SQL as its primary query facility considers its data to be formatted in tables. A **database table** is just that—a grid, or table, of rows and columns whose data are somehow interrelated. Further, one table can be related to another or others. Sequential query language works more efficiently when handling data in this manner; it's not that flat files or record-based databases are in a less desirable format than tables, only different. For end-user programs, whether a table or random access database is being used is irrelevant. The search criteria are basically the same, as are many of the commands. SQL is merely an attempt at standardization of language and at getting the job done in a more timely manner.

The following is a short subroutine in SQL which is more or less self-documenting. It resembles very closely the dBase code with which it was written to execute and is not unlike the pseudocode used for planning search strategies in other language environments. The CURSOR (line 2) is "like a file containing the rows of a result table created by an SQL SELECT statement."[1]

```
* SQL source code to compute bonuses for salespersons
* 'Sales' is the file containing salesperson data
* and 'Salestab' is the resultant work table.
* A commission will be awarded to those salespersons
* whose sales for the period is at least $25,000 gross
* on the specific item 'thingamajigs'.
STORE 0 TO Sales_ID
DECLARE Salestab CURSOR FOR
SELECT sperson_id_no
FROM Sales
WHERE item_desc = 'thingamajigs'
AND item_price * no_units >= 25000;
OPEN Salestab;
        DO WHILE .T.
                FETCH Salestab INTO Sales_ID;
                IF SQLCODE = 100
                EXIT
                ENDIF
                UPDATE Salesperson
                SET commission = commission + 1000.00
                WHERE Sperson_id_no = Sales_ID;
        ENDDO
CLOSE Salestab;
```

The preceding[2] illustrates exactly the philosophy behind so-called high level languages, i.e., that the code itself tells, even to a novice programmer, the purpose of the program or subroutine. SQL uses common English verbs and modifiers to accomplish its task. The choice of variables and field names is left to the creativity of the individual programmer, and such user-defined nouns should keep with the spirit of simplicity of the program language. Note also the use of the Boolean operator "AND" to specify that a salesperson must meet both of two conditions to receive a commission, namely, that "thingamajigs" must be the item sold to qualify for the bonus, *and* that a minimum of $25,000 worth of these items must be sold. If either one of these conditions is not met, there is no commission awarded. ".T.'"("true") is another Boolean operator, in this case, included to fetch data from the salestab(le) as long as there are still items in the table. As soon as the DO loop returns ".F." ("false"), the subroutine ends, and this portion of the query program terminates.

## DATABASES AND COMMERCIAL SOURCES OF ONLINE INFORMATION: OCLC AND WLN

Bibliographic databases encompass a considerable amount of detailed material. It is therefore the purpose of this final section to introduce such entities only as information utilities, for the sake of awareness. Extensive discussions of OCLC and WLN are more appropriate for texts and courses on cataloging and classification. Thus, the following will discuss such databases as they apply to the theme of computer science that has been the foundation of previous sections of this book.

OCLC, the Online Computer Library Center, Inc.,[3] has its roots as a cataloging and classification utility, although it has progressed far beyond the original scope. The organization began in 1967 as the Ohio College Library Center for the purpose of developing a cooperative, computerized regional library network. OCLC quickly evolved the Online Union Catalog, its bibliographic database, which currently holds about 25 million records. For years, OCLC was best known for its system of providing sets of 3" x 5" catalog cards from such terminals as its popular M300. OCLC's facilities have progressed far beyond a singular cataloging purpose, and the organization is now international. Many types of libraries, as well as governmental organizations, use the OCLC bibliographic database for reference services, resource sharing and interlibrary loans, telecommunications and hardware support, and retrospective conversion assistance (chapter 13), as well as for traditional cataloging services and support.

OCLC services are not vended outright; a library must apply for a membership, and services are then handled through various regional networks and agencies (e.g., AMIGOS for libraries in the Southwestern United States, Utlas for Canada, etc.). Services are then offered through various OCLC subsystems—for example, PRISM for online cataloging and creation/retrieval of **MARC (machine readable catalog) records**, EPIC for subject and keyword searches of the Online Union Catalog, RETROCON and MICROCON for conversion of local library records not originally in electronic format into records usable by various automated circulation/cataloging systems, and FirstSearch for queries of databases such as PsycINFO and Periodical Abstracts, which are not a regular part of the OCLC Union Catalog. Many of OCLC's services are delivered in CD-ROM format, and others, such as the interlibrary loan subsystem, are available via dialup.

WLN, the Western Library Network,[4] is a smaller bibliographic utility than OCLC, showing more than six million records in its database as of 1990. Until recently, WLN was primarily a regional entity which restricted most of its activities to 350 libraries in the Pacific Northwest region of the United States. WLN began in 1967 when the Washington State Library assumed responsibility for developing a statewide library network. In 1972, ten libraries in the state of Washington implemented resource sharing by participating in a batch pilot system to produce the *WLN Resource Directory* union book catalog. In 1975, an online system was designed and programmed by Boeing Computer Services under a $4.5 million contract in conjunction with the Washington State Library.

## INFORMATION SERVICES AND DIALUP FACILITIES

There are dozens of searchable databases that will, for a price, allow very detailed and sophisticated inquiries to be made online. These are available to all libraries and are, indeed, used for scholarly research by major universities and Fortune 500 companies alike.

The one service that perhaps needs little introduction to librarians is the DIALOG information service. DIALOG uses many of the Boolean search techniques and algorithms described above and in itself has evolved a rather sophisticated query language. DIALOG currently advertises availability of over 350 databases,[5] accessible along several pathways. Information can be obtained online through DIALOG's DIALMAIL, an electronic mail and conferencing service; through its KNOWLEDGE INDEX, a service of selected databases for "home professionals, students and other end users;" via DIALOG Menus, a menu-driven access to over 250 DIALOG files; through DIALOG's Business Connection, another menu-driven service targeting databases of interest to managers and financial planners; and via the gateway service to such facilities as the OAG (*Official Airline Guide*) Electronic Edition Travel Service, DIALOG QUOTES AND TRADING and DIALOG/MONEY CENTER. A communications software package called DIALOGLINK is available for IBM and IBM-compatible computers to aid in the login processes and to keep track of account usages and search costs.

Off-line, many of DIALOG's databases are available in CD-ROM format. DIALOG OnDisc has the advantage of a fixed annual subscription rate and allows for unlimited searching which can be used in conjunction with the online facility. DIALMAIL is available as an electronic mail and conferencing facility, and it also serves as a handy inbox for overnight delivery of recent searches on the DIALOG system. KNOWLEDGE INDEX is an evening and weekend service targeting the individual user who prefers to work at home. There are over ninety-five databases available through this facility, and it is a very economical way to use DIALOG because accesses are made at nonpeak hours. Because of the wide variation in materials and telecommunications times within DIALOG, it is impossible to generalize on costs. A potential user would benefit by contacting DIALOG directly to inquire about charges, which are a combination of the length of connect times, the particular database(s) queried, the time of day a search is made, the length and breadth of printouts requested, and the communications vehicle by which a search or searches are performed. The cost also depends on whether a searcher requests a **full-text** (unabridged) **copy** of search results or an abridged version, containing only bibliographic data and summary information. Dialog Information Services, Inc. makes an effort to help the searcher use the databases to best advantage, and the DIALINDEX and OneSearch facilities allow users to query multiple files simultaneously. The intricacies of DIALOG searching cannot be fully described in a few paragraphs; indeed, many library schools focus an entire course on electronic database searching. The interested student would profit well from investigating such coursework.

Other database services are widely used by research libraries. LEXIS, known as LEXIS 2000, is a service which supports legal research and offers full-text citations of information on litigation, potential clients, government and business activities, technology and general news. The scope of LEXIS' and of related services coverages includes patents and trademarks in the LEXPAT library; articles in more than 730 law reviews and legal journals in its Legal Resource Index; banking and brokerage analyses in the Exchange Service; medical trends and currents in the Medis Service; and information on more than 4,200 publicly traded companies in the NAARS (National Automated Accounting Research System) service.[6] News Plus includes periodical and newspaper journal articles and features up-to-date securities quotes from the NASDAQ, all North American stock exchanges, the Dow Jones averages, Standard & Poor's indices, and from brokers of bonds, mutual funds, and money market funds. Many of the databases in LEXIS are international in scope of subject content, and the arrangement of data is in "libraries," or file drawers, to make searches more logical.

LEXIS is designed to work with IBM-compatible computers and with its own specially designed LEXIS 2000 keyboard. Like OCLC, LEXIS has a number of database functions which are best invoked with single keystrokes from special function keys. If a subscriber's computing environment features multiple workstations, LEXIS software can be configured to operate with a local area network. LEXIS is accessed through a variety of communications avenues, many of which are common to other online database services: LEXIS' own MEADNET lines are available for standard modem connections, as are SprintNet (formerly Telenet), TYMNET, AlaskaNet and Datapac, so that regular long distance telephone lines are, in effect, bypassed. There is still a charge for telecommunications, however, which is built into the connect charges for the database. The LEXIS user guides are shipped to subscribers on floppy diskettes, and the signon/login scripts are customized by each user along with system and search parameters. The LEXIS software appears in menu format for each user, and **macros** (predefined search strategies and online processes) are supported in the PC programs.

A companion service to LEXIS is NEXIS; in fact, the two utilities are sometimes collectively cited as LEXIS-NEXIS since they are both services of Mead Data Central, Inc. Search strategies and operation of the two services are similar and both use the same PC interface for accessing the various databases.[7] NEXIS' focus is on news items and current information on business and political topics, although it goes into considerable detail on many other topics as well. NEXIS includes a NEXIS library of over 140 business, financial and general interest publications which include some wire services. As adjunct services from Mead, there is an INFOBK (Information Bank) library of full-text articles from major publications such as the *New York Times* and *Wall Street Journal*; a GOVDOC library of U.S. government documents, which includes the *Code of Federal Regulations* and *The Federal Register*; the EB (*Encyclopedia Britannica*) library; and an APOLIT (Associated Press Political Service) library of information on political candidates and elections.[8] The NEXIS library itself contains numerous other libraries, namely, the Entertainment Library, the Market Library, the Company Library, the Assets Library, the Environment Library, the Legislative Library, the Executive Library, the Campaign Library, the Europe Library, and the World Library.

Another company that makes available online databases in a variety of subjects is **CCH**, Incorporated. The company, formerly known as Commerce Clearing House, has transformed many of its traditional loose-leaf services into electronic and CD-ROM formats. Using the CCH Online or Online for Windows software, either of which is furnished with the purchase of an online or CD-ROM subscription, a user can search more than forty databases of CCH information. The topics are updated at least monthly and include both Federal and state tax codes (all fifty states, the District of Columbia, and Puerto Rico), Health Law (with Medicare), Securities Law, Human Resources, and Pension and Welfare Benefits. There is also a tool (CD-ROM format only) which provides tax forms for Federal reporting, as well as forms for tax reporting in all fifty states. The latter is updated two or three times a month during the tax season. The online service is obtainable over a dedicated (800 number) telephone line at speeds up to 28,000 baud, using either DOS or Windows 3.1 interface. A version of the Online software that runs under newer Windows software was planned for release in June 1996. A handy feature of the Online package is the ability for the user to "point and shoot" at desired topics. All that is necessary is for the user to highlight, with the mouse cursor, the desired keyword(s) or citations shown on the screen, and the cross-references to a studied topic will be listed. If a user subscribes to multiple databases, this cross-reference capability spans whatever titles and topics are recognized as valid by the Online software.

Numerous other commercial database services exist. Dow Jones News/Retrieval contains a number of newspaper and business publications with full-text retrieval capabilities in as little as two weeks after date of publication. Westlaw for Law Students is a powerful educational tool which uses a proprietary WALT (West's Automatic Law Terminal) to teach contemporary legal research. There are dozens of others: BRS Information Technologies, Dun & Bradstreet Business Credit Services, Investext, The Human Resources Information Network, and DataTimes all supplement and automate the reference process for libraries that require an in-depth, exhaustive coverage of research topics. The modern reference librarian needs to enhance his/her search skills to include online querying as an everyday tool and as an element on one's personal résumé to ensure marketability when job interviews become necessary.

There are several general use, consumer-oriented information services available. America Online,[9] CompuServe Information Service,[10] Delphi,[11] GEnie,[12] and Prodigy Interactive Personal Service[13] are among the most popular, and the services of these five online utilities are generally within affordable reach of the average member of the computing public. There are common denominators of features to be found among all the aforementioned, and typical of the utility programs offered are electronic mail, financial services (stock quotes, online checking, portfolio management, etc.), weather forecasts, clipping services, online encyclopedias, games and entertainment, travel services, home shopping, and college coursework instruction and tutorial. Connection charges vary, and it is typical for a user to incur costs beyond the basic monthly charges for extraordinary services such as sales of securities, document delivery, and categorical purchases. An example of the latter is CompuServe's "bookstore" setup, whereby a subscriber can place an order for any title listed in *Books in Print*, the confirmed order delivered to the subscriber's home in a matter of days via United Parcel Service. All that is required is for the subscriber to enter a valid Visa, MasterCard, or American Express card number onscreen—and CompuServe takes care of the rest! While many of the online information services just mentioned might not have in-depth reference value to libraries, it is important that such services be recognized for the body of third-party literature that has been generated on their use. As part of a comprehensive materials collection reflecting our computerized society, libraries will no doubt want to purchase several titles detailing the use and benefits of online information services for their patrons.[14]

## NOTES

1. Hursch, Jack L. and Carolyn J. Hursch. *dBASE IV SQL User's Guide*, p. 171.
2. ibid., p. 178.
3. OCLC Online Computer Library Center, Inc., 6565 Frantz Road, Dublin, OH 43017-3395. Inquiries (800) 848-5878 [(800) 848-8286 in Ohio].
4. WLN Inc. (Western Library Network), 4224 6th Avenue SW/3, Lacey, WA 98503. (206) 459-6527.
5. *Searching DIALOG: The Complete Guide*, August, 1991, p. 9-11.
6. *Learning LEXIS: A Handbook for Modern Legal Research*. Mead Data Central, Inc., 1986, 36 pp.
7. *NEXIS Quick Start: A Guide to Searching Nexis and Related Services*. Mead Data Central, Inc., 1992, 20 pp.
8. *Learning NEXIS: The Basics*. Mead Data Central, Inc., 1987, 12 pp.
9. America Online Inc., 8619 Westwood Center Drive, #200, Vienna, VA 22182-2285. (800) 827-6364; (703) 448-8700.
10. CompuServe Information Service, P.O. Box 20212, Columbus, OH 43220. (800) 848-8199; (614) 457-0802.
11. Delphi, c/o General Videotex Corp., 1030 Massachusetts Avenue, Cambridge, MA 02138. (800) 695-4005; (617) 491-3342.
12. GEnie Service, 401 N. Washington Street, Rockville, MD 20850. (800) 638-9636; (301) 251-6415.
13. Prodigy Interactive Personal Service, 445 Hamilton Avenue, White Plains, NY 10601. (800) 776-3449; (914) 993-8000.
14. Steinberg, Don. "On-Line Services: Making Meaningful Connections." *PC Magazine*, February 23, 1993, pp. 303-320.

# Appendix A

# BASIC—A Library Application Example

In the mid-1980s, before utility programs were available ubiquitously for a few dollars per disk, much of the applications code for small programs was being created in-house. "Home-brewed" software typically provided only one or two functions and consisted of only a few hundred lines of code. But such programs served useful purposes such as check writing, budget planning, forms generation, and scheduling. And, more likely than not, the code was written in BASIC.

One such program is the Personal Résumé Generator. It was written in conjunction with a Library Services and Construction Act grant to enhance the availability of materials to assist jobseekers. The original program was written for an 8088 microprocessor-based Osborne I microcomputer placed in a public access area of the library. The idea was for a patron seeking assistance in résumé writing to use the program as a self-guided document generator. The program works quite well, but even the final version has too many trap doors for errors to creep in. After about two months of various frustrations, the librarians decided that the program was best handled by a staff member working the keyboard while interviewing the patron desiring a résumé. It was a noble effort, but it proved that even the best-intended programs sometimes require a bit of familiarity and practice by users to be of any benefit.

As a teaching tool for BASIC, the résumé generator is a good example of string manipulations and interactive keyboard I/O techniques. It has been tested on several versions of BASIC and should run with little, if any, modification under GW-BASIC and Quick Basic. The source listing in its entirety is as follows:

271

```
1'
2'
3'    * * * * * * * * * * * * * * * * * * * * * * * * * * *
4'    *                                                   *
5'    *      PERSONAL RESUME GENERATOR                    *
6'    *                                                   *
7'    * * * * * * * * * * * * * * * * * * * * * * * * * * *
8'
9'
10 REM RESUME GENERATOR 'RESUME.BAS'
15 DIM L$(15), S$(20)
20 PRINT CHR$(27); "E" :REM CLEAR THE SCREEN
30 PRINT:PRINT TAB(20); "RESUME WRITER" :PRINT:PRINT
40 PRINT "THIS PROGRAM CREATES A PERSONAL JOB RESUME
   FROM "
50 PRINT "YOUR TYPED INFORMATION. YOU MAY MAKE COPIES
   OF "
60 PRINT "THE RESULT AND REPRODUCE IT AT WILL. " :PRINT
70 PRINT "USE THE COMPUTER'S KEYBOARD AS YOU WOULD A "
80 PRINT "REGULAR TYPEWRITER. YOU WILL RECEIVE A PROMPT
   ( ? OR — "
90 PRINT "OR : ) WHERE INFORMATION IS REQUIRED." :PRINT
100 PRINT "HIT 'RETURN' WHEN A LINE OR ENTRY IS FINISHED."
110 PRINT "TO BACKSPACE, HOLD DOWN 'CTRL' AND PRESS 'H'. "
120 PRINT "DO NOT BE OVERLY CONCERNED ABOUT MISTAKES.
    THE "
130 PRINT "PROGRAM IS DIVIDED INTO SECTIONS SO THAT
    EVERY "
140 PRINT "FEW LINES YOU CAN MAKE CORRECTIONS BEFORE "
150 PRINT "PROCEEDING." :PRINT
160 LINE INPUT "ARE YOU READY (TYPE 'Y' AND HIT 'RETURN')? "
    ;R$
170 IF LEFT$(R$,1) <> "Y" AND LEFT$(R$,1) <> "y" THEN PRINT "
    INVALID ENTRY; TRY AGAIN." :GOTO 160
180 '
190 '
200 PRINT CHR$(27); "E" :REM CLEAR SCREEN
210 PRINT:PRINT "THIS SECTION PREPARES THE PAGE HEADINGS. "
220 PRINT "(NOTE: YOU MAY ENTER DATA IN BOTH lower and "
230 PRINT "UPPER CASE LETTERS; USE 'shift' or
    'alpha lock' or 'Caps Lock'. "
240 PRINT:PRINT "ENTER YOUR NAME EXACTLY AS YOU WANT IT
    TO APPEAR."
```

```
250 LINE INPUT " —";PERSON$
260 PRINT "ENTER YOUR HOUSE NUMBER AND STREET ADDRESS. "
270 LINE INPUT " —" ;ADDRESS$
280 IF LEN(ADDRESS$) >25 THEN PRINT "CAN YOU SHORTEN
    THAT TO LESS THAN 26 LETTERS?" :GOTO 260
290 PRINT "AND YOUR CITY, STATE AND ZIP CODE. "
300 LINE INPUT " —" ;CITYSTATE$
310 IF LEN(CITYSTATE$) >25 THEN PRINT "CAN YOU SHORTEN
    THAT TO LESS THAN 26 LETTERS?" :GOTO 290
320 PRINT "ENTER YOUR HOME PHONE NUMBER WITH AREA
    CODE. "
330 LINE INPUT "E.G., (219) 555-1212. —"; HOMEPHONE$
340 PRINT "YOUR BUSINESS PHONE, IF YOU HAVE ONE, SAME
    WAY. "
350 LINE INPUT "(HIT 'RETURN' IF YOU HAVE NONE) —"; BUS-
    PHONE$
360 PRINT CHR$(27); "E" :REM CLEAR SCREEN
370 PRINT:PRINT "THIS IS THE WAY YOUR HEADER WILL
    APPEAR:"
380 PRINT:PRINT STRING$(80, "_")
390 FOR X = 1 TO 5: PRINT: NEXT X: REM SPACE DOWN 5 LINES
400 PRINT TAB(33); "PERSONAL RESUME OF" :PRINT
410 PRINT TAB(INT(42 - (LEN(PERSON$)/2))); PERSON$ :PRINT
420 IF LEN(BUSPHONE$) <7 GOTO 460
430 PRINT ADDRESS$; TAB(50); "Home Phone: "; HOMEPHONE$
440 PRINT CITYSTATE$; TAB(50); "Business: "; BUSPHONE$
450 GOTO 480
460 PRINT ADDRESS; TAB(50); "Home Telephone:"
470 PRINT CITYSTATE$; TAB(50); HOMEPHONE$
480 PRINT: PRINT: PRINT "DO YOU WANT TO LEAVE THE
    HEADERS THE "
490 PRINT "WAY THEY ARE <1> OR DO YOU WISH TO START
    OVER"
500 PRINT "AND MAKE CORRECTIONS <2>?"
510 LINE INPUT "ENTER '1' OR '2' AND 'RETURN' TO CHOOSE— R$"
520 IF LEFT$(R$,1) = "2" GOTO 180
530 IF LEFT$(R$,1) <> "1" THEN PRINT CHR$(27); "E": PRINT:
    PRINT: PRINT "PLEASE ENTER ONLY '1' OR '2'.
    TRY AGAIN." :GOTO 480
540 '
550 '
560 LPRINT TAB(33); "PERSONAL RESUME OF" :LPRINT
570 LPRINT TAB(INT(42 - (LEN(PERSON$)/2))); PERSON$ :LPRINT
```

```
580 IF LEN(BUSPHONE$) <7 GOTO 620
590 LPRINT ADDRESS$; TAB(50); "Home Phone: "; HOMEPHONE$
600 LPRINT CITYSTATE$; TAB(50); "Business: "; BUSPHONE$
610 LPRINT:LPRINT:GOTO 670
620 LPRINT TAB(20); ADDRESS$; TAB(50); "Home Telephone:"
630 LPRINT TAB(20); CITYSTATE$; TAB(50); HOMEPHONE$
640 LPRINT:LPRINT
650 '
660 '
670 PRINT CHR$(27); "E" :REM CLEAR SCREEN AGAIN
680 PRINT:PRINT "IN THIS SECTION YOU WILL TELL SOMETHING
    ABOUT "
690 PRINT "THE KIND OF WORK YOU ARE LOOKING FOR AND
    WHAT KINDS"
700 PRINT "YOU HAVE DONE.":PRINT
710 PRINT "IN ONE OR TWO LINES, STATE YOUR 'JOB OBJECTIVE'
720 PRINT "SUCH AS 'Entry level sales representative for "
730 PRINT "a tool and die manufacturing, firm'. DO NOT "
740 PRINT "SPLIT WORDS AT THE END OF A LINE. WHEN YOU "
750 PRINT "HAVE TYPED AS MUCH AS YOU WISH. TYPE 'ZZZZ' "
760 PRINT "AFTER THE '-'. NOW TYPE YOUR 'JOB OBJECTIVE'. "
770 X=0
780 X=X+1
790 LINE INPUT " —"; L$(X)
800 IF L$(1)= "ZZZZ" OR L$(1) = "zzzz" THEN PRINT :PRINT
    "YOU MUST ENTER AT LEAST ONE LINE. TRY AGAIN."
    GOTO 790
810 IF LEN(L$(X))> 50 THEN PRINT
    "SHORTEN THAT LINE TO 50 SPACES OR LESS AND RE-ENTER.":
    GOTO 790
820 IF L$(X)<>"ZZZZ" AND L$(X)<>"zzzz" GOTO 780
830 PRINT CHR$(27); "E"
840 PRINT:PRINT
    "HERE IS HOW THE PREVIOUS INFORMATION WILL APPEAR: "
850 PRINT :PRINT :PRINT "  OCCUPATIONAL"; TAB(20); L$(1)
860 IF L$(2)="ZZZZ" OR L$(2)="zzzz" THEN
    PRINT "  OBJECTIVE": GOTO 920
870 PRINT "  OBJECTIVE"; TAB(20); L$(2)
880 X=2
890 X=X+1
900 IF L$(X)="ZZZZ" OR L$(X)="zzzz" GOTO 920 ELSE
    PRINT TAB(20); L$(X)
910 GOTO 890
```

```
920 PRINT:PRINT:PRINT:PRINT
930 PRINT "DO YOU WISH TO CONTINUE WITH THE PROGRAM
    <1> "
940 PRINT "OR DO YOU WANT TO REDO THE ABOVE <2>? "
950 LINE INPUT "ENTER '1' OR '2' AND 'RETURN'— ";R$
960 IF R$="2" GOTO 670
970 IF R$<>"1" THEN PRINT
    "ENTER ONLY '1' OR '2'. TRY AGAIN.": GOTO 930
980 '
990 '
1000 LPRINT "  OCCUPATIONAL"; TAB(20); L$(1)
1010 IF L$(2) = "ZZZZ" OR L$(2) = "zzzz" THEN LPRINT
    "  OBJECTIVE": GOTO 1050
1020 LPRINT "  OBJECTIVE"; TAB(20); L$(2)
1030 X=2
1040 X=X+1
1050 '
1060 IF L$(X) = "ZZZZ" OR L$(X) = "zzzz" GOTO 1080 ELSE
    LPRINT TAB(20); L$(X)
1070 GOTO 1040
1080 LPRINT:LPRINT
1090 '
1100 PRINT CHR$(27); "E": REM CLS
1110 FLAG=0
1120 PRINT:PRINT
    "YOU WILL NOW LIST YOUR WORK EXPERIENCES. ": PRINT
1130 PRINT
    "IF YOU HAVE NO EXPERIENCE, TYPE '1' ELSE TYPE '2' "
1140 LINE INPUT "AND HIT 'RETURN'— "; R$
1150 IF R$ = "1" THEN GOTO 1850
1160 PRINT:PRINT
    "WHAT IS THE NAME OF THE COMPANY OR ORGANIZATION "
1170 LINE INPUT "FOR WHICH YOU MOST RECENTLY WORKED? ";
    C$
1180 LINE INPUT "CITY, STATE IN WHICH LOCATED? "; L$
1190 PRINT:PRINT
    "IF YOU ARE CURRENTLY EMPLOYED, TYPE 'present' IN "
1200 PRINT "SMALL LETTERS; ELSE TYPE THE LAST YEAR WORKED
    "
1210 LINE INPUT "(AS '1992') AND 'RETURN'— "; LY$
1220 PRINT:PRINT "FIRST YEAR YOU WORKED FOR THE ABOVE "
1230 LINE INPUT "ORGANIZATION? "; FY$
```

```
1240 PRINT:PRINT "WHAT WAS YOUR JOB TITLE (OR AS CLOSE
     AN "
1250 LINE INPUT "APPROXIMATION AS YOU KNOW)? "; JT$
1260 PRINT CHR$(27); "E": REM CLS
1270 PRINT:PRINT "YOU WILL NOW TELL A LITTLE ABOUT YOUR
     WORK "
1280 PRINT "AND RESPONSIBILITIES. THIS WILL TAKE UP ABOUT "
1290 PRINT "TWO TO FOUR LINES ON YOUR RESUME. THE FIRST "
1300 PRINT "LINE WILL BE SHORT (YOU'LL SEE WHY ON THE "
1310 PRINT "PRINTOUT), SO YOU MIGHT WANT TO WRITE
     DOWN "
1320 PRINT "YOUR RESPONSES BEFORE TYPING INTO THE COM-
     PUTER. "
1330 PRINT "AGAIN, TYPE 'ZZZZ' WHEN YOU WISH TO STOP
     ENTRY. "
1340 X=0
1350 PRINT:PRINT "FIRST LINE;"55-LEN(JT$); "LETTERS OR LESS. "
1360 X=X+1
1370 LINE INPUT "— "; L$(X)
1380 IF LEN(L$(X)) >(55-LEN(JT$)) THEN PRINT:PRINT
     "ENTRY TOO LONG; TRY AGAIN. ": GOTO 1370
1390 PRINT "NEXT LINE; 55 LETTERS OR LESS. "
1400 X=X+1
1410 LINE INPUT " — "; L$(X)
1420 IF LEN (L$(X)) >55 THEN PRINT:PRINT
     "CAN YOU SHORTEN THAT A BIT? TRY AGAIN. ":
     GOTO 1410
1430 IF L$(X) <> "ZZZZ" AND L$(X) <> "zzzz" THEN GOTO 1390
1440 X=X+1: PRINT CHR$(27); "E": REM BACK UP 'X' AND CLS
1450 PRINT:PRINT
     "HERE IS THE 'EXPERIENCE' ENTRY YOU JUST TYPED: "
     PRINT:PRINT:PRINT
1460 PRINT:PRINT:PRINT TAB(47-(LEN(C$)/2)); C$
1470 PRINT TAB (47-(LEN(L$)/2)); L$: PRINT:PRINT
1480 IF L$(1) = "ZZZZ" OR L$(1) = "zzzz" THEN L$(1)= " "
1490 IF L$(1) = "ZZZZ" OR L$(1) = "zzzz" THEN L$(2)= " "
1500 PRINT TAB(6); FY$; " to"; TAB(20); JT$; ". "; L$(1)
1510 PRINT TAB(6); LY$; TAB(20); L$(2)
1520 IF X<3 THEN GOTO 1550
1530 FOR Y=3 TO X: PRINT TAB(20); L$(Y): NEXT Y
1540 PRINT:PRINT
1550 PRINT:PRINT
     "DO YOU WISH TO CONTINUE WITH THE PROGRAM <1> "
```

```
1560 PRINT "OR DO YOU WANT TO REDO THE ABOVE <2>? "
1570 LINE INPUT "ENTER '1' OR '2' AND 'RETURN' — "; R$
1580 IF FLAG=0 AND R$="2" THEN PRINT CHR$(27); "E":
     GOTO 1160
1590 IF FLAG=1 AND R$="2" THEN PRINT CHR$(27); "E":
     GOTO 1800
1600 IF R$<>"1" THEN PRINT
     "ENTER ONLY '1' OR '2'. TRY AGAIN.": GOTO 1550
1610 '
1620 '
1630 IF FLAG=0 THEN LPRINT " EXPERIENCE";
     TAB(42-(LEN(C$)/2)); C$ ELSE
     LPRINT TAB(42-(LEN(C$)/2)); C$
1640 IF FLAG=0 THEN LPRINT " RECORD";
     TAB(42-(LEN(L$)/2)); L$: LPRINT ELSE
     LPRINT TAB(42-(LEN(L$)/2)); L$: LPRINT
1650 LPRINT TAB(6); FY$; " to"; TAB(20); JT$; ". ";L$(1)
1660 LPRINT TAB(6); LY$; TAB(20); L$(2)
1670 IF X<3 THEN LPRINT:LPRINT: GOTO 1720
1680 FOR Y=3 TO X: LPRINT TAB(20); L$(Y): NEXT Y
1690 LPRINT:LPRINT
1700 '
1710 '
1720 PRINT CHR$(27); "E": REM CLS
1730 PRINT:PRINT "YOU MAY LIST AS MANY JOBS AS YOU WISH. "
1740 PRINT "IS THERE ANOTHER PRIOR TO THE ONE YOU LISTED
     "
1750 PRINT "ABOVE? IF SO, ENTER 'Y' FOR 'YES', ELSE ENTER "
1760 LINE INPUT "'N' FOR 'NO' AND HIT 'RETURN'—"; R$
1770 IF LEFT$(R$,1)="N" OR LEFT$(R$,1)="n" THEN GOTO 1840
1780 IF LEFT$(R$,1)<>"Y" AND LEFT$(R$,1)<>"y" THEN PRINT
     "INVALID ENTRY; TRY AGAIN.": GOTO 1730
1790 FLAG=1; PRINT CHR$(27);"E": PRINT:PRINT:PRINT
1800 LINE INPUT "NAME OF THIS COMPANY FOR WHICH YOU
     WORKED?"; C$
1810 LINE INPUT "CITY, STATE IN WHICH LOCATED? ";L$
1820 LINE INPUT "LAST YEAR WORKED FOR THIS COMPANY? "; LY$
1830 GOTO 1220
1840 '
1850 '
1860 PRINT CHR$(27);"E": REM CLS
1870 PRINT:PRINT "YOU WILL NOW LIST YOUR EDUCATIONAL
     QUALI-"
```

```
1880 PRINT "FICATIONS. START WITH THE MOST RECENT
     SCHOOL "
1890 PRINT "OR COLLEGE YOU ATTENDED AND WORK BACK-
     WARD. ":
     PRINT
1900 FLAG=0
1910 PRINT "NAME OF SCHOOL (AS 'Mytown Vocational "
1920 PRINT "Technical School, Mytown, IN')"
1930 LINE INPUT " —"; S$(1)
1940 IF LEN(S$(1))>55 THEN PRINT:PRINT
     "CAN YOU SHORTEN THAT A LITTLE? PLEASE RE-ENTER. ":
     PRINT: GOTO 1910
1950 PRINT:PRINT "GIVE THE NAME OF THE DIPLOMA OR
     DEGREE "
1960 PRINT "YOU EARNED WITH THE YEAR THAT YOU EARNED
     IT "
1970 PRINT " (AS 'Diploma: Secretarial Studies, 1988'). "
1980 PRINT "NOTE: IF YOU DID NOT GRADUATE, ENTER THE "
1990 PRINT "YEARS OF ATTENDANCE AS 'Attended 1976-78'. "
2000 LINE INPUT " —"; S$(2)
2010 IF FLAG=1 GOTO 2060
2020 PRINT CHR$(27);"E": PRINT:PRINT
     "HERE IS YOUR FIRST 'EDUCATIONAL EXPERIENCE: ":
     PRINT:PRINT
2030 PRINT "  EDUCATION"; TAB(20); S$(1)
2040 PRINT TAB(20); S$(2): PRINT
2050 GOTO 2080
2060 PRINT CHR$(27);"E": PRINT:PRINT
     "HERE IS THE NEXT 'EDUCATION' ENTRY:": PRINT:PRINT
2070 PRINT TAB(20); S$(1); PRINT TAB(20); S$(2): PRINT
2080 PRINT "DO YOU WANT TO PRINT OUT THIS ENTRY <1> "
2090 PRINT "OR DO YOU WISH TO DO IT OVER <2>? "
2100 LINE INPUT "ENTER '1' OR '2' AND 'RETURN—'"; R$
2110 IF R$="2" THEN PRINT:PRINT
     "RETYPE YOUR CORRECTED ENTRY. ": PRINT:GOTO 1910
2120 IF R$<>"1" THEN PRINT:PRINT
     "PLEASE ENTER ONLY '1' OR '2'; TRY AGAIN.": PRINT:
     GOTO 2080
2130 IF FLAG=0 THEN LPRINT "  EDUCATION"; TAB(20); S$(1):
     LPRINT TAB(20); S$(2): LPRINT
2140 IF FLAG=1 THEN LPRINT TAB(20); S$(1): LPRINT TAB(20);
     S$(2): LPRINT
2150 PRINT:LINE INPUT "ANY MORE SCHOOLS <Y OR N>? ";R$
```

```
2160 IF LEFT$(R$,1)="Y" OR LEFT$(R$,1)="y" THEN
     PRINT CHR$(27);"E": FLAG=1: PRINT:PRINT: GOTO 1910
2170 IF LEFT$(R$,1)<>"N" AND LEFT$(R$,1)<>"n"" THEN PRINT:
     PRINT "PLEASE ANSWER ONLY 'Y' (YES) OR 'N' (NO);
     TRY AGAIN. ": PRINT: GOTO 2150
2180 '
2190 '
2200 '
2210 '
2220 PRINT CHR$(27); "E": PRINT:PRINT
2230 F$(2)="0"
2240 PRINT "FOR THE LAST ELEMENT, YOU WILL GIVE SOME "
2250 PRINT "REFERENCES, IF YOU WISH. IF YOU PREFER "
2260 PRINT "NOT TO DO THIS, ENTER <1> TO PRINT 'References "
2270 LINE INPUT "furnished on request', ELSE ENTER <2>—"; R$
2280 IF R$="1" THEN LPRINT:LPRINT "  REFERENCES";
     TAB(20); "References furnished on request.":
     FOR X=1 TO 20: LPRINT: NEXT X: GOTO 2760
2290 IF R$<>"2" THEN PRINT:PRINT
     "PLEASE ENTER ONLY '1' OR '2'; TRY AGAIN. ":PRINT:
     GOTO 2240
2300 PRINT:PRINT
     "THIS PROGRAM WILL ASK FOR ONLY TWO REFERENCES. "
2310 PRINT
     "IF YOU WISH TO ADD MORE, USE THE SAME FORMAT AND "
2320 PRINT "TYPE THEM ON THE BOTTOM OF THE PAGE. ":PRINT
2330 LINT INPUT "NAME OF THE REFERENCE (PERSON)? ";F$(1)
2340 IF LEN(F$(1))> 25 THEN PRINT:PRINT
     "CAN YOU SHORTEN THAT A LITTLE? TRY AGAIN. ":PRINT:
     GOTO 2330
2350 PRINT:PRINT
     "THAT PERSON'S ADDRESS (GIVE City, State ONLY). "
2360 PRINT
     IF YOU HAVE THE PHONE NUMBER, ELSE GIVE ONLY "
2370 LINE INPUT "THE NUMBER AND STREET FOR THIS LINE—";
     N$(1)
2380 IF LEN(N$(1))>25 THEN PRINT:PRINT
     "CAN YOU SHORTEN THAT A LITTLE? TRY AGAIN.":PRINT:
     GOTO 2350
2390 LINE INPUT
     "City, State OR TELEPHONE (AS (219) 555-1212)—";
     P$(1)
2400 IF LEN(P$(1))> 25 THEN PRINT:PRINT
```

```
     "CAN YOU SHORTEN THAT A LITTLE? TRY AGAIN. ":PRINT:
     GOTO 2390
2410 PRINT:LINE INPUT
     "DO YOU HAVE ANOTHER REFERENCE <Y> OR <N>? ";R$
2420 IF LEFT$(R$,1)="N" OR LEFT$(R$,1)="n" THEN GOTO 2510
2430 IF LEFT$(R$,1)="Y" AND LEFT$(R$,1)<>"y" THEN PRINT
     "PLEASE ENTER ONLY 'Y' OR 'N'; TRY AGAIN. ":PRINT:
     GOTO 2410
2440 LINE INPUT "NAME OF OTHER REFERENCE? "; F$(2)
2450 IF LEN(F$(2))>30 THEN PRINT:PRINT
     "CAN YOU SHORTEN THAT A LITTLE? TRY AGAIN. ":
     PRINT: GOTO 2440
2460 LINE INPUT "City, State or Street Address? ";N$(2)
2470 IF LEN(N$(2))>30 THEN PRINT:PRINT
     "CAN YOU SHORTEN THAT A LITTLE? TRY AGAIN. ":
     PRINT: GOTO 2460
2480 LINE INPUT "AND City, State of Telephone—"; P$(2)
2490 IF LEN(P$(2))>30 THEN PRINT:PRINT
     "CAN YOU SHORTEN THAT A LITTLE? TRY AGAIN. ":
     PRINT: GOTO 2480
2500 GOTO 2550
2510 PRINT CHR$(27);"E": PRINT:PRINT
     "HERE IS YOUR 'REFERENCES' SECTION:": PRINT:PRINT
2520 PRINT " REFERENCES"; TAB(20); F$(1): PRINT TAB(20);
     N$(1): PRINT TAB(20); P$(1): GOTO 2600
2530 '
2540 '
2550 PRINT CHR$(27);"E"; PRINT:PRINT
     "HERE IS YOUR REFERENCES SECTION:": PRINT:PRINT
2560 PRINT " REFERENCES"; TAB(20); F$(1); TAB(50); F$(2)
2570 PRINT TAB(20); N$(1); TAB(50); N$(2)
2580 PRINT TAB(20); P$(1); TAB(50); P$(2)
2590 '
2600 PRINT:PRINT:PRINT
     "DO YOU WISH TO PRINT OUT THIS SECTION <1> "
2610 LINE INPUT "OR REDO IT FROM THE START <2>? "; R$
2620 IF R$="2" THEN GOTO 2220
2630 IF R$<>"1" THEN PRINT
     "PLEASE ENTER ONLY '1' OR '2'; TRY AGAIN. ":PRINT:
     GOTO 2600
2640 '
2650 '
2660 IF F$(2)<>"0" GOTO 2700
```

```
2670 LPRINT:LPRINT "  REFERENCES"; TAB(20); F$(1)
2680 LPRINT TAB(20); N$(1): LPRINT TAB(20); P$(1): GOTO 2760
2690 FOR X=1 TO 15:LPRINT:NEXT X
2700 LPRINT:LPRINT "  REFERENCES"; TAB(20); F$(1);
       TAB(50); F$(2)
2710 LPRINT TAB(20); N$(1); TAB(50); N$(2)
2720 LPRINT TAB(20); P$(1); TAB(50); P$(2)
2730 FOR X=1 TO 15:LPRINT:NEXT X
2740 '
2750 '
2760 PRINT CHR$(27);"E": REM CLEAR SCREEN
2770 PRINT:PRINT:PRINT
       "YOUR RESUME MAY BE LONGER THAN A STANDARD "
2780 PRINT
       "ELEVEN INCH PAGE. THE SPACING IN THIS PROGRAM IS "
2790 PRINT
       "DESIGNED TO ALLOW YOU TO CUT AND TRIM THE FIN-
       ISHED "
2800 PRINT "DOCUMENT BEFORE PHOTOCOPYING."
2810 PRINT:PRINT:PRINT
       "THE PROGRAM AND SERVICE CREATED HEREIN WERE "
       2820 PRINT "MADE POSSIBLE THROUGH A LIBRARY SER-
     VICES AND "
2830 PRINT
       "CONSTRUCTION GRANT ADMINISTERED BY THE STATE "
2840 PRINT "LIBRARY OF INDIANA."
2850 END
```

Those persons familiar with BASIC programming will immediately note room for improvement. There are redundant strings, for example, and the repetitions of "CAN YOU SHORTEN THAT A LITTLE." could be better coded using a table or **array** of strings so that there would be only one incident of any given string in the code. Also, the repeated PRINT statements could, in some dialects of BASIC, be replaced with the "?" character. Programming aficionados will also shudder at the repeated use of GOTO statements, verboten in many computer language classes for their potentially disastrous results. Inclusion of these improvements and other nuances could result in a "tighter" code, and in a program which would probably run faster.

# Appendix B

# Certificate Program in Computer Literacy for Librarians

The following is a four-course curriculum in computer science for librarians who may not have completed such work as a part of their masters' degrees. It was originally planned as a four-semester, post-master's sequence to fill gaps in training on a pragmatic level, particularly for graduates of NCATE and school librarianship programs where the courses of study may have veered away from technical matters. However, such a curriculum could be placed in the mainstream of any master's program, somewhat as a "major" in the field. The emphasis is on the study of personal computers (PCs) and Macintoshes (but not on minis or mainframes) that are typically to be found in all types of libraries.

As continuing education for graduate credit, the first three courses of the sequence could result in the award of a Certificate of Computer Studies in Library Science (or similar). Upon successful completion of the fourth course in the sequence, a student might be awarded a certificate "... with Computer Hardware Endorsement." It would, of course, be at the discretion of faculty committees and senates which kind of credit to offer or whether merely to award continuing education units (CEUs) at the termination of some rather intense workshops and seminars. An alternative for those who seek some kind of automation credential are referred to certifying agencies such as the Institute for Certification of Computer Professions which issues the Certificate in Data Processing (CDP).

Each of the topics listed each comprise about one to two weeks of class time. All four courses are intended to be hands-on practicums, with about one third (first course) to one-half (last course) of the instruction presented in laboratory settings. The amount of lab time increases with progression through the four-course sequence. The first two courses would typically be completed in group settings. The final two courses are more individualized, and laboratory sessions therein are meant to be conducted as seminars.

This program is not possible without some budgetary ramifications. The first course can be completed in a more generalized setting such as an academic computer facility, and software and utility programs can be run on workstations available to students of other disciplines. MS-DOS (PC-DOS) and GW-BASIC are now somewhat universal, usually shipped as a bundle with PC workstations and would not generate an added cost to the program. The PC-Type, PC-Calc, and PC-File programs are available at low cost or as shareware, and their impacts, too, on the budget are minimal. It is about midway into the second course that things get costly. To teach the fundamentals of database searching, a library science program should ideally have an institutional subscription to DIALOG and to one or more of the other commercial academic database services, as well as to consumer-based utilities such as CompuServe or Prodigy. Additionally, some searches would be performed on CD-ROM-based databases such as ERIC and Compact DisClosure; ideally, these resources would already be available in the library proper, to be shared by students with a library's reference department. Students should also have access to more than just the basics of the available automated cataloging and circulation system, and they should have privilege levels above those of regular students, although not as high as library staff, to be able to explore the intricacies of online systems. The sophistication of the latter will largely be an advantage of geography; i.e., students in the more populous states and provinces will have more extensive systems to play with!

The last course in the sequence is the one for which the cash outlay would be the most prominent. Students pursuing the computer hardware course will need a number of machines, and relatively new ones, to take apart, troubleshoot, reassemble, and reconfigure at the workbench. Additionally, some test equipment and digital logic hardware is desirable for thoroughness of training, and the latter should *not* be hand-me-downs from the college of engineering. Good purchasing agents will be cognizant of quantity discounts and institutional pricing, and a sharp-eyed grants coordinator will keep abreast of the opportunities for corporate donations of relatively new equipment for tax purposes.

There is some spillover from one course to the next, and the beginnings of the second, third, and fourth courses assume that approximately the first two weeks of class will consist of a review of material already covered; the sequence is quite comprehensive. Program directors might want to establish a set of competency examinations requisite for passing from the lower courses into the upper ones.

The material is open to changes and modifications as individual circumstances dictate. For example, more time could be spent on desktop publishing in the first course (with the obvious increase in expenditures for DTP software and hardware). "Commercial" programs might be substituted for the more generic titles—Lotus 1-2-3 or Microsoft Excel for PC-Calc, WordPerfect, or Microsoft Word for PC-Type, etc., here, also with the understanding that individual copies (perhaps one for every two students) can run in the hundreds of dollars. Finally, the coursework need not be limited to the classroom or laboratories because the material on local area networks, automated circulation systems, and PCs as audio/visual media, for example, lends itself to some highly imaginative field trips. The order of presentation of the various topics may be altered, within reason, without detriment to the progression of the learning cycle.

The curriculum, with no particular reason for selecting the numbering system presented, is as follows:

## Library Science 501: Introduction to the Use of Computers in Libraries

**Concepts and topics covered:**
1. Basic terminology
2. Identification of the parts of a personal computer
3. Operating systems; MS-DOS and System 7
4. Word processing and document creation
5. Spreadsheets
6. Library budget planning on a computer
7. User interfaces; Windows and the Macintosh GUI
8. Flowcharting
9. Library systems analysis
10. Desktop publishing
11. Practical applications of PCs in libraries

**Programs studied (written exercises assigned):**
1. MS-DOS or PC-DOS
2. Macintosh System 7
3. PC-Type or commercial word processor
4. PC-Calc or commercial spreadsheet program
5. Aldus PageMaker or Ventura Publisher (optional)

**Term project:**
A departmental budget plan using a computer (cf. chapters 4 or 14).

## Library Science 502: Library Information Retrieval Systems

**Concepts and topics covered:**
1. Review of operating systems
2. Boolean searching
3. Database construction

4. Automated circulation systems
5. Online catalogs (in-house and dialup)
6. Principles of data communications
7. Modems and communications hardware
8. Electronic bulletin boards
9. Commercial (consumer-oriented) databases
10. CD-ROM technology
11. Subscription databases (online and disc-based)
12. Local area networks
13. File transfer programs (e.g., Carbon Copy, PC Anywhere)
14. Electronic mail (e-mail); PROFS
15. Telefacsimile (FAX) machines and FAX modems
16. Voice digitizers and answering machines

**Programs studied (written exercises assigned)**:
1. MS-DOS (review)
2. PC-File
3. dBase III +/dBASE IV or R:BASE

**Term projects**:
1. The Electronic Rolodex (database creation, cf. chapter 5)
2. A literature search of a commercial database (e.g., DIALOG) or CD-ROM database

## Library Science 503: Library Computer Applications and Bibliography of Information Sciences

**Concepts and topics covered**:
1. Review of the body of literature relevant to computers in libraries
2. Software and hardware review media
3. The basic reference tools for computer science
4. Major publishers of computer science literature, with emphasis on consumer-oriented publishers
5. Subject areas of information science and strategies for cataloging and classification of technical materials
6. Specific subject areas of applications programs:
   A. Education
   B. Graphics
   C. Document delivery (CAD, desktop publishing, etc.)
   D. Languages (BASIC, COBOL, etc.)

**Programs studied (written exercises assigned)**:
1. GW-BASIC interpreter (be able to write a simple program applicable to libraries (cf. chapter 8)
2. File transfer program such as SmartCom, CrossTalk, Kermit

**Term projects**:
1. A critical review of one area of applications software programs

(i.e., a review of word processors, spreadsheets, and the like), using appropriate media to make a report to a committee, to (a) establish a selection policy for library software and (b) recommend specific purchases.

2. Creation of a subject bibliography using an online catalog over a telephone line, employing appropriate communications/file capture software.

## Library Science 504: Library Computer Hardware Maintenance

**Concepts and topics covered**:

1. The personal computer as an audio/visual medium
2. Experiments and demonstrations with PC and Macintosh hardware
3. Principles and interfacing of peripheral hardware
4. Survey of installable boards (cards) and internal circuits
5. PC repairs and maintenance; troubleshooting
6. Maintenance of a parts and subassemblies inventory
7. PC architecture
8. Digital electronics fundamentals; circuit logic
9. Evaluation and purchase of equipment
10. System planning and construction
11. Floor layouts, blueprints, and automation needs assessments; working effectively with contractors
12. Writing requests for proposals (RFPs) and electrical specifications
13. Writing grants for automation funding; technical writing

**Programs studied (written exercises assigned)**:

1. The UNIX operating system; and
2. The C and C++ programming languages, both for their close relationships with the hardware systems on which they run

**Term projects**:

1. A proposal for the purchase and installation of workstations in the business office, i.e., a needs analysis, review of software literature, and narrative of the recommended configuration
2. Construction of an RFP for automating the circulation and cataloging functions of a small (one building) library; project will include schematic drawings
3. Construction, from subassemblies provided, of a working PC which supports at least one peripheral device (e.g., a printer or a modem); parts provided *may* require some troubleshooting or determination that they must be submitted for repairs.

# Annotated Bibliography

The titles in this annotated list are recommended purchases for circulating, reference, and support collections. Catalogs are listed as comprehensive sources and agents of hard-to-find items, as well as for those programs and accessories that have proven to be unusually good bargains. Periodicals are given where contents of such journals have proven to have reference value or sometimes go as unnoticed resources worth a consideration. Most of the tools listed below were used to assist in the preparation of this textbook. Although the list is not comprehensive and should not be considered a substitute for standard, unabridged reading lists, it is hoped that the reader will find the list of value as a starter for building a subject collection on computers and automation. In any case, it is the author's wish that readers might find a gem or two among the items listed.

## CHAPTER 1

Conlan, Roberta, series editor. *Understanding Computers*. Alexandria, VA: Time-Life Books. $14.99 per title.

The value in these works is the generosity and clarity of the illustrations and the straightforward presentation of highly technical issues in laypersons' terms. These are recommended first purchases for libraries of high school level and above, and there is much amplification of the material found in the introductory chapter of this text. Series titles include

*The Chipmakers*. 128 pp., 1990.
*Communications*. 128 pp., 1990.
*Computer Basics*. 128 pp., 1989.

*Computer Languages.* 128 pp., 1990.
*Computer Security.* 128 pp., 1990.
*The Computerized Society.* 128 pp., 1990.
*The Human Body.* 128 pp., 1989.
*Illustrated Chronology and Index.* 128 pp., 1989.
*Memory and Storage.* 128 pp., 1990.
*Revolution in Science.* 128 pp., 1990.
*Software.* 128 pp., 1990.
*Speed & Power.* 128 pp., 1990.

Mueller, Scott and Alan C. Elliott. *Que's Guide to Data Recovery.* Carmel, IN: Que Corporation, 1991. Paper, 498 pp., $29.95.

In addition to a being manual on recovering lost files, the *Guide* is a comprehensive reference on disaster recovery. Detailed and technical information is given on hard disk drives, floppy disk drives, virus detection and eradication, DOS internals, and disk format and structure. Tips for computer maintenance and techniques for preventing file loss are included.

Simonson, Michael and Thompson, Ann. *Educational Computing Foundations.* New York: Macmillan, 1990. Paper, 428 pp., $35.00.

Textbook format presents an overview/introduction to information science from a school administrator's point of view. In addition to some non-technical but theoretical background, it outlines features of word processors, spreadsheets, and database programs. Additionally it presents material on the Logo and BASIC computing languages and uses of computers in the classroom. Emphasis is on Apple II machines and microcomputers.

Williams, William F. *Principles of Automated Information Retrieval.* Elmhurst, IL: The Business Press, 1965. 439 pp.

One of the earliest textbooks on the fundamentals of indexing, abstracting, coding, and storing data. It serves better now as a retrospective view of bygone storage and retrieval techniques. The theories are still valid, however, and the book is a solid voyage into the mathematics of information theory. It also contains an extensive glossary.

## Catalog

*Heath: Catalog of Educational Systems, Computer-Aided Instruction Series, Home Electronics, and Home Automation Gear.* Free. Heath Company, P.O. Box 8589, Benton Harbor, MI 49022-8589. Orders (800) 253-0570.

Heath Company, a.k.a. Heathkit Electronics, once sold an extensive line of consumer-grade and professional-level electronics equipment in kit form. The company's main product line now consists of continuing education courses, and all are of high caliber. Most courses feature experimental trainers with electronics parts, and the high quality of the tutorials and their associated laboratory components make them ideal for self-study of computer and electronics principles, as well as computer programming. Beginner to advanced studies are available, and many courses offer optional instruction by videotape. C.E.U.s (continuing education units) are awarded with certificates of completion if a student submits the optional final examinations.

## Periodicals

*BYTE: The Small Systems Journal.* Monthly, twice in October, $3.50 per issue/$22.00 per year. BYTE Subscriptions, P.O. Box 7643, Teaneck, NJ 07666-9866.

A first purchase for general collections, *BYTE* offers a variety of hardware and software reviews in every issue. This is a layperson's technical magazine which features both IBM and compatible computers and Macintoshes. *BYTE*'s philosophy is not to compare products but to present features and test results, allowing a program to stand on its own merits.

*InfoWorld.* Weekly, $2.95 per copy/$100.00 per year. InfoWorld, P.O. Box 5994, Pasadena, CA 91107.

A newspaper which claims to be a magazine, *InfoWorld* is comprehensive and highly respected. Because it covers new releases of software and hardware, the issues tend not to be thematic although products are reviewed very systematically and statistically. While not intended as seals of approval, high *InfoWorld* ratings and "good numbers" tend to appear in subsequent advertisements of products tested.

*PC Magazine.* Biweekly except in July and August, $2.95 per copy/$39.97 per year. PC Magazine, P.O. Box 54003, Boulder, CO 80322.

*The* definitive journal for IBM and compatible computers. Reviews are thorough and comprehensive, and "Editor's Choice" of a product under review is tantamount to a "best in show" anywhere. The articles are scholarly, and the periodical has reference value. Sophisticated, it will be read by technicians and managers alike. It is also available in CD-ROM format, issued quarterly at $49.95 per year. Each CD-ROM contains a year of back issues and is keyword searchable.

*T.H.E. Journal (Technological Horizons in Education).* Monthly except July, $3.50 per copy/$29.00 per year. T.H.E. Journal, 150 El Camino Real, Suite 112, Tustin, CA 92680-3670.

It exhibits a classroom slant, and not always about computers. But *T.H.E. Journal* is useful for insights into the various ways that information is disseminated. It contains news, new product blurbs, and reviews of software applicable to the learning process.

## CHAPTER 2

Callahan, Mike and Nick Anis. *Dr. File Finder's Guide to Shareware.* Berkeley, CA: Osborne McGraw-Hill, 1990. Paper, 1019 pp., $39.95 (includes two 5 1/4" diskettes in IBM format, which contain several of the programs described in the text).

In this encyclopedic and exhaustive presentation, the authors go far beyond the basics, and include material on the use of commercial online system libraries, participation in shareware user groups, invocation of bulletin board telecommunications, and mastery of file transfer protocols. Hundreds of programs are described in major categories from applications programs to systems utilities. Appendices include names and addresses of members of the Association of Shareware Professionals, telephone numbers of hundreds of online bulletin board systems, and several dozen pages of mail-in offers for shareware programs, including twelve disks full of programs described in the *Guide* but not provided on the "free" disks included with the book.

Gralla, Preston. *PC Computing Guide to Shareware.* Emeryville, CA: Ziff-Davis Press, 1992. Paper, 413 pp., $34.95 (includes two 5 1/4" diskettes in IBM format, which contain several of the programs described in the text).

This source presents the usual overview of the range of currently available shareware, along with descriptions of programs that commonly appear in vendors' shareware collections. It details the concept and spirit of shareware, and tells "how to put a shareware toolkit together." Included is a comprehensive chapter on viruses and how to avoid them. Of particular value are the appendices on shareware sources and dialup bulletin boards, both of which include locations and telephone numbers.

Ottensmann, John R. *IBM PC Shareware: PC-File, PC-Write, PC-Talk and ExpressCalc.* Blue Ridge Summit, PA: Tab Books, 1987. Paper, 246 pp., $15.95.

After an introduction to DOS-based shareware, it gives about equal treatment to each of the four programs. Here are featured (in order) a database program, a word processor, a communications program, and a spreadsheet. One wonders why the PC-Calc program, the third member of the so-called Buttonware trio, was not included, but the coverages and explanations are good, with a final section detailing how to share files among the four programs featured in the book.

Remer, Daniel. *Legal Care for Your Software: A Step-by-Step Guide for Computer Software Writers.* Berkeley, CA: Nolo Press, 1982. Paper, 247 pp., $19.95.

A writer's manual for computer programs, it explains in detail the law of copyright, patents, and trade secrets as it applies to program code with advice on programming by contract and on negotiating work-for-hire agreements, as well as material on protections and remedies for aspiring software authors.

Sawusch, Mark R. *The Best of Shareware: IBM PC Utilities.* Blue Ridge Summit, PA: Windcrest Books, 1990. Paper, 219 pp., $29.95 (includes a 5 1/4" diskette containing eighty-three of the programs annotated in the text).

This text contains a generous, well-represented sample of currently popular utility programs either in the public domain or available at low cost. Subjects include file and directory management utilities, keyboard and screen manipulation programs, clocks and calendars, operating system enhancements, and batch file utilities. Sources for obtaining the executable program code and accompanying documentation are included, as are descriptions and features of the various software programs.

## Catalogs

*The Connection: Programmer's Connection Buyer's Guide.* Quarterly, free. Circulation Department, 7249 Whipple Avenue NW, North Canton, OH 44720-7143. Orders (800) 336-1166. Product information available by telefacsimile.

Each issue contains well over a hundred pages of annotated products. The guide contains many items not elsewhere advertised, as well as numerous unusual and exotic utility programs. A resource for developers, this catalog should be on the shelves of technical libraries. It is meant for PCs (running DOS, XENIX, UNIX, OS/2), Macintoshes, Sun Microsystems, and VAX computers, and it lists no mainframe products, but has occasional short feature articles, which are more newsy than technical. Most products in the catalog are sold at a discount.

*Diskette Gazette: Computer Accessories and Macintosh Software.* Irregular, free. International Datawares, Inc., 2278 Trade Zone Blvd., San Jose, CA 95131-1801. Orders (800) 222-6032.

In tabloid format, illustrated and annotated, it includes hardware and commercially available programs, the latter in both diskette and CD-ROM format. Articles that accompany several of the programs have reference value, and there is a Library Catalog in an annual edition. Public domain programs start at about $5.50 per disk.

*EDUCORP Software Encyclopedia: Affordable Software, Hardware, CD-ROM Products, and Accessories for Macintosh Computers.* Annual edition, $4.95; update supplements, $2.95. EDUCORP Computer Services, 7434 Trade Street, San Diego, CA 92121-2410. Orders (800) 843-9497.

This is an exhaustive list of products, annotated and illustrated. Shareware titles predominate, but commercial software and some hardware products are included. Indexed, the annual compendium has over 375 pages of entries.

*800-SOFTWARE.* Quarterly, free. 800-SOFTWARE, Inc., 1003 Canal Blvd., Richmond, CA 94804. Orders (800) 888-4880.

This company handles software, hardware and network products, and its catalog's descriptive entries are exhaustive. *800-SOFTWARE* provides a great deal of information on hundreds of discounted IBM-PC and Macintosh products. Once on its mailing list, you can also receive the monthly and bimonthly newsletters: *NewsLine,* a publication featuring announcements and particulars of new and upgraded programs; *TechFlash,* a broadcast letter of "bugs and tips" regarding software currently on the market; *TechLine,* an information manual for various groups of products; the *Upgrade Report,* a monthly summary of newly released software versions with instructions for ordering them; *It's Academic,* a newsletter of software program information of particular interest to libraries and educational institutions; and *MacLine,* a version of *NewsLine* for Macintosh users. The company is particularly helpful in obtaining upgrades for your existing software packages. Newsletters arrive prepunched for a three-ring binder; place these bulletins in your reference room.

*The Programmer's Shop Buyer's Guide.* Quarterly, free. The Programmer's Shop, 90 Industrial Park Road, Hingham, MA 02043. Orders (800) 421-8006.

This guide features compilers, utility programs, code libraries, and tools for "power" programmers. The annotated catalog has reference value; your library will want to keep the current issue for information on high-level developmental software. It is heavier on advertisements than most, but the ads, too, contain valuable information not generally publicized with programs for DOS, UNIX, OS/2, Windows, and networks but no Macintosh software. It also sells specialty interface and connectivity hardware, although no complete systems.

*$ave-On $oftware.* Free. $ave On $oftware, P.O. Box 2837, Wilkes Barre, PA 18703. Orders (800) 962-6107.

An annotated listing of 1,600 shareware titles for IBM and compatibles, it has no ratings, but blurbs show registration fees (if any) required by program authors. Disks are about $3.00 each, depending on format and quantity ordered with some CD-ROM listings. The complete collection is available on CD-ROM, and the company also maintains a subscription bulletin board for customers who prefer to download specific titles.

*Shareware Catalog and Reference Guide.* Quarterly, $2.00/copy. Public
Brand Software, P.O. Box 51315, Indianapolis, IN 46251. Orders (800)
426-3475.

More than 2,000 programs are reviewed in each issue, and the list is
continually updated. Public Brand uses a five-level rating system, whereby a "trophy" rating indicates "best disk anywhere for the task." A significant part of the annotations concentrates on the programs' attributes;
each entry gives information regarding technical support, licensing, availability of supplemental documentation, updates, and registration fees or
royalties expected by the author(s). Each disk in the catalog costs $5.00,
and both 5 1/4" and 3 1/2" formats are available. There are a number of
programs in Public Brand's repertoire of particular interest to librarians
and educators. Those ordering disks will also receive a copy of the pamphlet *Beginner's Resource Guide,* which explains how to use shareware
disks to best advantage.

*The Software Labs.* Monthly, free. The Software Labs, 100 Corporate
Pointe, Suite 195, Culver City, CA 90231. Orders (800) 569-7900.

It offers several thousand shareware programs in its annotated and illustrated catalog and there is some redundancy with Public Brand Software
(above), but many unique titles also. The only drawbacks of the catalog
are that there is no rating system for the various programs, and there is no
indication of royalties to be paid to shareware authors upon acceptance
and use of the programs provided. Disk prices begin at $3.69 each, with a
$1.00 premium for 3 1/2" format; there is a downwardly sliding price scale
which increases in percentage with the quantity of disks ordered.

### Periodical

*Shareware Magazine.* Bimonthly and occasional special issues, $2.95 per
copy. PC-SIG, 1030D East Duane Avenue, Sunnyvale, CA 94086.

Emphasis is on details of PC-SIG's public domain and shareware collection. It includes reviews of new software titles and updates and supplements the group's *Encyclopedia of Shareware* between editions. It
ceased publication in July 1994, but back issues should be collected for
their reference value.

## CHAPTER 3

Harvey, Greg and Kay Yarborough Nelson. *Encyclopedia WordPerfect
5.1.* San Francisco: SYBEX, 1990. Paper, 1100 pp., $29.95.

This is a text for the DOS (IBM) version of the popular word processor and it is exhaustive, and particularly helpful for aspects of on-screen
text editing that sometimes "just don't come out right"—columns, tables,
alternate styles, fonts, and equations. Valuable also is the discussion of

macros, utility programs (including the speller and thesaurus), and supplemental WordPerfect software. It is not updated for version 6.0, but the information is still useful for its detailed treatment of specific WordPerfect features.

McComb, Gordon. *WordPerfect 5.1 Macros and Templates.* Toronto: Bantam Books, 1990. Paper, 677 pp., $39.95 (includes two 5 1/4" disks of macros and style sheets described in the text).

This takes over where the WordPerfect manual leaves off; it illustrates macro programming by creation of alternate keyboard layouts, macro recording, file merging, and creation of menu systems. Practical examples include memoranda, boilerplate letters, legal forms, publication documents, invoices, mailing labels, and resumes. Over 400 of the book's examples are included on the floppy diskettes.

Shuman, James E. *Application Software for the IBM PC.* Santa Cruz, CA: Mitchell Publishing, Inc., 1988. Second edition. Paper, 318 pp., $29.95 (bundled with seven 5 1/4" diskettes which include shareware versions of PC-Type, PC-Calc, and PC-File and example files).

A tutorial on the Buttonware trilogy of PC-Type, PC-Calc and PC-File software, its chapters are arranged so that the programs can be used as an integrated package, and many practical examples, with instructions for creating them, are included. An excellent teaching tool, it is an inexpensive way to set up a working office computing environment.

Simpson, Alan. *Mastering WordPerfect 6 for Windows.* San Francisco: SYBEX, Inc., 1994. Paper, 1190 pp., $27.95.

Encyclopedic, it emphasizes the special features of the Windows version, along with hints for customizing the editor program, running macros, and performing desktop publishing and typesetting. The amount of detail is almost overwhelming. Containing nearly 200 pages of tutorials, it has a section on Windows basics; a DOS version of the text is also available.

## Periodicals

*WordPerfect for Windows.* Monthly, $3.00 per copy, $24.00 per year. WPWin Magazine, 270 West Center Street, Orem, UT 84057-4637. (801) 228-9626.

Published by the vendor of WordPerfect for Windows word processing software, it emphasizes the special considerations and features provided by the Microsoft Windows interface, with tips and tricks for getting the most out of the Windows GUI. The *Disk of the Month*, a diskette with macros, templates, and user code featured in the magazine, is available for $7.95 per copy or $69.95 per year.

*WordPerfect: The Magazine.* Monthly, $3.00 per copy/$24.00 per year. WP Magazine, 270 West Center Street, Orem, UT 84057-4637. (801) 228-9626.

Another publication of the WordPerfect vendor, it is an insider's view of the word processor, with tips on macro construction, page layouts, typographical considerations, and special effects. It tends to be a user forum; good for insights on new releases and interrelating WordPerfect's other utility programs with the flagship product. The *Disk of the Month* (see *WordPerfect for Windows,* above) is also available for standard WordPerfect featured in this periodical.

## CHAPTER 4

Person, Ron. *Using Excel Version 5 for Windows.* Carmel, IN: Que Corporation, 1993. Paper, 1276 pp., $29.95.

Another encyclopedia, with emphasis on spreadsheet design, chart-building, macro execution, and importation of "foreign" spreadsheets, such as those of Lotus 1-2-3, it features material on data consolidation when working with multiple sheets, linking with database programs, and integrating with other Windows applications.

Shuman, James E. *Application Software for the IBM PC* (see chapter 3 entry above for full bibliographic citation).

This text includes how-to material on PC-Calc spreadsheet.

## CHAPTER 5

Beiser, Karl. *Essential Guide to dBASE III-plus in Libraries.* Westport, CT: Meckler, 1986. Paper, $35.00.

Beiser, Karl. *Essential Guide to dBASE IV in Libraries.* Westport, CT: Meckler, 1991. Paper, 400 pp., $40.00. (IBM format 3 1/2" or 5 1/4" diskettes with program listings, $80.00.)

The author uses dBASE code to illustrate various library procedures applicable to database management. Full source code is given for those who wish to customize the various programs. Taken collectively, the assortment of programs constitutes an extensive, sophisticated automation scheme for a small- to medium-sized library supported by PC workstations.

Finkel, LeRoy and Jerald R. Brown. *Data File Programming in BASIC: A Self-Teaching Guide.* New York: Wiley, 1981. Paper, 338 pp., $9.95.

This tutorial presents a detailed explanation of the principles of random and sequential database file programming. Included are material for creating error checking routines and utilities for altering and updating existing files. As titled, the book assumes reader knowledge of the BASIC programming language (see chapter 8 of this text) and an elementary familiarity with file structure terminology.

Shuman, James E. *Application Software for the IBM PC* (see chapter 3 entry above for full bibliographic citation).
This text includes material on PC-File database management program.

## CHAPTER 6

Ashley, Ruth, and Judi N. Fernandez. *Job Control Language: A Self-Teaching Guide.* New York, Wiley, 1978. Paper, 157 pp., $5.95.
While it cannot detail the JCL for every mainframe operating system, the *Guide* offers a general overview of the principles of IBM-command language for system control. There is a generous number of sample "cards" along with illustrations of JCL coding sheets; it is a useful handbook for training beginning computer operators.

Fernandez, Judy N. and Ruth Ashley. *Using CP/M: A Self-Teaching Guide.* New York, Wiley, 1980. Paper, 243 pp., $8.95.
Presented are fundamentals of the CP/M operating system in tutorial format. It is very detailed and covers CP/M utility programs STAT, ED, and PIP.

Fernandez, Judy N. and Ruth Ashley. *CP/M for the IBM: Using CP/M-86.* New York: Wiley, 1983. Paper, 262 pp., $14.95.
An extension of Fernandez and Ashley's first book on CP/M, this edition is for the 16-bit (PC) version of the operating system.

O'Reilly, Tim, Series Editor. *UNIX in a Nutshell System V Edition.* Sebastopol, CA: O'Reilly & Associates, Inc. Paper (spiral bound), $19.95.
The text is a comprehensive handbook of all UNIX commands with a summary of editor commands, NROFF and TROFF text formatting utilities, macro packages, and Bourne shell and C shell syntaxes.

Rann, Lavona S. *Using the Macintosh with System 7.* Carmel, IN: Que Corporation, 1992. Paper, 440 pp., $24.95.
Both a tutorial and a reference, it provides a smooth transition for Mac users who have upgraded from System 6.x. A considerable amount of material is presented on installation, troubleshooting, and customization with focus on new features, including the expanded Desktop, sound capabilities, interapplication communications, file sharing, and data exchange with Apple II and MS-DOS computers.

Waite, Mitchell, Stephen Prata, and Donald Martin (a.k.a. The Waite Group). *UNIX System V Primer.* Indianapolis: Howard W. Sams & Co., 1987. Revised edition. Paper, 442 pp., $22.95.

One of a number of books on operating systems on this publisher's reading list, *UNIX System V Primer* is exemplary for its clear presentation to aspiring learners of UNIX, its commands and its utility programs. This title is a foundation on which to build a UNIX collection and could be considered first purchase by faculty who need a text for efficient teaching of beginning UNIX.

Wolverton, Van. *Running MS-DOS*: Version 6.2. Redmond, WA: Microsoft Press, 1994. Paper, 616 pp., $24.95.

A definitive reference on DOS, it is written in a straightforward, layperson's language. A new edition is issued with each major release of DOS, and each revision includes a summary of the features and compatibilities of all DOS versions prior to, and including the current one. Wolverton includes much information on PC technology in general (at press time, version 6.22) and presents DOS in guidebook format with an unabridged reference of DOS commands.

## Catalog

*UNIX Central: Products for SUN, SCO, INT, HP, IBM, AT&T 386 and a dozen other UNIX systems.* Quarterly, free. UNIX Central, 474 Potrero Avenue, Sunnyvale, CA 94086-9406. Orders (800) 532-1771.

Some hardware, but mostly software, are presented and it is very useful and informative if you're running a Sun Microsystems workstation. Presenting a good collection of applications packages, along with a number of utility and developmental programs including X Windows systems and C++, it also offers software for interconnectivity with Novell NetWare and Macintosh AU/X—a must for university and technical collections.

## Periodical

*Unix Review: The Magazine for Systems and Solutions Developers.* Monthly, $3.95 per copy/$55.00 per year. Miller Freeman, Inc., 600 Harrison Street, San Francisco, CA 94107.

Supports all versions of UNIX from PC- to mainframe-based systems. Articles focus not only on operating system software, but also on hardware specifically designed for running in conjunction with UNIX. Articles are scholarly and technical; product reviews are thorough and exhaustive, although a rating system is not included in comparison summaries. The marriage between UNIX and the C language is apparent; this journal will be of great interest to power programmers.

## CHAPTER 7

Johnson, Eric F. and Kevin Reichard. *X Windows Applications Programming*. Portland, OR: MIS: Press, 1989. Paper, 562 pp., $29.95

(program listings are available on 5 1/4" diskettes from the publisher for an additional $29.95).

The text covers the basics from drawing, manipulating text, managing windows, and processing events and continues through the building of a complete X Windows application. Advanced techniques of multiple window handling and programming popup windows and dialog boxes are also considered. You need an X Windows system processor to run the programs, but the text is an excellent summary of what the X graphics user interface is all about.

LeBlond, Geoffrey T. *Windows 3.1 Power Tools.* Second edition. New York: Bantam Books, 1992. Paper, 664 pp., $49.95 (includes a 3 1/2" high density diskette).

This looks at Windows from a programmer's point of view. The material focuses on fine tuning the .PIF (program information) files as well as the WIN.INI and SYSTEM.INI system files, and details how to share data between applications, how to run non-Windows programs from within Windows, and how to run Windows over a network. It is recommended as a reference work in libraries where there is a significant technical book collection.

Person, Ron and Karen Rose. *Using Microsoft Windows 3.* Indianapolis: Que Corporation, 1990. Paper, 662 pp., $22.95.

An advanced guide to using Windows, although not a programming manual, it shows efficient management of the Windows interface, control of the MS-DOS executive, the use of macros, and how to run non-Windows applications effectively from within Windows. It contains valuable information for shops where there are many DOS-based programs running side-by-side with Windows applications.

Petzold, Charles. *Programming Windows.* Redmond, WA: Microsoft Press, 1990. Paper, 944 pp., $29.95.

A technical reference manual for Windows version 3, this is an advanced handbook for persons who want to obtain more than just the basic services from the Windows GUI. It includes management of computer resources, the Dynamic Data Exchange, the Multiple Document Interface, and use of the Dynamic Link Library. Examples are given in the C programming language. It should be a first purchase for technical collections.

## Periodicals

*WINDOWS Magazine.* Monthly, $2.95 per copy/$29.94 per year. WINDOWS Magazine, P.O. Box 58649, Boulder, CO 80322-8649. (516) 562-5000.

Bold, glossy, and comprehensive, it addresses the rapidly growing library of products, both from the Windows publisher (Microsoft Corporation) and from third-party vendors. It is lavishly illustrated, as it should be, with features and product reviews (critical, but with no numerical ratings), "first impressions" of new Windows utility programs, analyses for "power users" of Windows, and a "how to" section.

*Windows User.* Monthly, £2.50 per copy/£30.00 per year (U.K.), £44.40 (North America). Windows User, Oakfield House, Perrymount Road, Haywards Heath, West Sussex, England RH16 3DH. (0444) 441212.

Scholarly, the issues have exhaustive directories of sources for products and hardware mentioned in the articles' contexts. There is material of interest to Windows developers and end users alike, although the essays do not get overly technical. Big, glossy, and colorful, with clear and precise illustrations, its past issues will have archival value.

## CHAPTER 8

Hendrix, James E. *A Small C Compiler.* Redwood City, CA: M & T Books, 1990. Second edition. Paper, 628 pp., $29.95 (includes a 5 1/4" IBM format diskette with source code of programs described in the text).

The public domain contains several compilers which are subsets of the ANSI C language; few are documented. Schools will want this book to supplement curricula on compiler design and for experimenters who wish to learn C at the system level without dissecting one of the high-end compilers or wading through unnecessary technical material.

Stern, Nancy, Alden Sager and Robert A. Stern. *RPG II and RPG III Programming.* Second edition. New York: John Wiley & Sons, 1991. Paper, 666 pp., $44.95.

It is an exhaustive documentation for all versions (mainframe, mini- and microcomputer) of the report program generator language. Well-illustrated with sample code on standard RPG forms. Because of the relatively thin amount of available RPG literature compared to that of other languages, this book is needed for its reference value.

Stevens, Al. *teach yourself . . . C++.* Portland, OR: MIS: Press, 1990. Paper, 272 pp., $29.95 (includes a 5 1/4" IBM format diskette of source code examples).

One of the few tutorials of the superset of the C language, and one which covers a half dozen C++ compilers, this text assumes a basic knowledge of the C language, and covers C++ extensions, structures, classes, overloaded operators, and advanced input/output streams. The explanations are informal and the examples are pragmatic, with the learning presented in manageable chunks which build on material of previous chapters.

## CHAPTER 9

Crane, Mark W. and Joseph R. Pierce. *Laserjet Companion*. Louisville: The Cobb Group, Inc., 1988. Paper, 707 pp., $24.95.

The Hewlett-Packard line of laser printers has set the standard for publications-quality printers for desktop publishing. The *Companion* tells owners how to take best advantage of their expensive printers and how to care and maintain them for longest service life. Considerable information is lent to the use of fonts and font cartridges as well as to the printing of graphics. It is particularly useful if yours is a non-Postscript printer.

Danuloff, Craig and Deke McClelland. *The PageMaker Companion: PC version 4.0 Edition*. Homewood, IL: Business One Irwin, 1992. Paper, 600 pp., $24.95.

Beginning with a summary of features new to version 4.0, *The PageMaker Companion* zips through the basics and gets quickly into projects of interest to librarians. Generously illustrated, the text covers publication of a simple newsletter, a flyer of relative complexity, a catalog with advertisements and price lists, and longer documents. PageMaker's close tie-in with the Windows interface is strongly acknowledged.

Holzgang, David A. *Understanding PostScript Programming*. San Francisco: SYBEX, Inc., 1988. Second edition. Paper, 472 pp., $24.95.

Emphasis is on the Adobe PostScript language, and many code examples supplement the text. It has reference value for presentation of language fundamentals and definitions of PostScript verbs and operators and has a technical approach that assumes a bit of artistic ability on the part of the reader. Material is included on font manipulation, and there is a lengthy discussion of the structure of encapsulated PostScript files.

Kleper, Michael L. *The Illustrated Handbook of Desktop Publishing and Typesetting*. Blue Ridge Summit, PA: Tab Professional and Reference Books, 1987. Paper, 770 pp., $29.95.

This text is one for the reference shelf. Its value is in the wealth of illustrations and examples of relatively complex documents. It covers a number of DTP and auxiliary utility programs and word processors, both for IBM and compatibles and Macintosh, and includes some basic (and necessary) personal computer theory and terminology with an exhaustive bibliography and source list.

Lubow, Martha and Jesse Berst. *Style Sheets for Business Documents.* Thousand Oaks, CA: New Riders Publishing, 1988. Paper, $39.95 (includes two 5 1/4" diskettes).

Lubow, Martha and Polly Pattison. *Style Sheets for Newsletters.* Thousand Oaks, CA: New Riders Publishing, 1988. Paper, $39.95 (includes two 5 1/4" diskettes).

Canfield, Byron and Chad Canty. *Style Sheets for Technical Documents.* Thousand Oaks, CA: New Riders Publishing, 1988. Paper, $39.95 (includes two 5 1/4" diskettes).

Ventura Publisher ships with about twenty style sheets (templates) for various types of document design, and version 4 ships with an additional collection known as the Design Gallery. This trilogy generously supplements the basic Ventura collection and, with the various accompanying .STY files provided on floppy disks, makes using the style sheets quite easy. While the templates are for Ventura versions 1 and 2, they are easily upgradeable to versions 3 and 4. There are many ideas and illustrations; each book contains suggestions and directions for manipulating the settings to obtain customized documents.

Miller, Michael. *Ventura Publisher Techniques and Applications.* Carmel, IN: Que Corporation, 1989. Paper, 378 pp., $24.95.

This is a "tips and tricks" book rather than just a makeover of the Ventura documentation and features newsletters, directories, business documents and book-length documents. Written for version 2, its suggestions are universal for more current releases. Of particular assistance is the pickup of the Professional Extension, a version 2 add-on that extends the ability to create tables and formulas. There is a generous amount of illustrations and examples.

Smith, Ross. *Learning PostScript: A Visual Approach.* Berkeley, CA: Peachpit Press, 1990. Paper, $22.95. A companion diskette which contains code for sample programs and batch files shown in the book is available from the publisher for $20.00.

A more organized tutorial than that of Holzgang (above), *Learning PostScript* teaches the language using brief code segments to create building blocks of simple to complex graphics. Text concludes with projects to create a calendar and various document cover pages.

Will-Harris, Daniel. *WordPerfect Desktop Publishing in Style.* Berkeley, CA: Peachpit Press, 1990. Second edition. Paper, 645 pp., $23.95.

The WordPerfect word processor has matured sufficiently that it can be used to produce a range of reasonably sophisticated publication quality documents. Will-Harris covers both versions 5.0 and 5.1 of WordPerfect in a chatty, conversational style of text full of practical examples. Given particular emphasis are fonts, graphics, boxed pictures and the use of utility software for creating original drawings. If you cannot afford one of the high-end desktop publishing programs, this guide will allow you to take full advantage of the publication capabilities of your WordPerfect to accomplish nearly the same ends.

## Catalog

*Personal Computing Tools for Engineers, Scientists, and Technical Professionals.* Quarterly, free. Personal Computing Tools, 550 Division Street, Campbell, CA 95008. (800) 767-6728.

The company offers a line of hard-to-find computer accessories, including digitizer boards, video frame grabbers, cameras and printer enhancers. Many higher-priced peripherals are to be found here, but there are also many necessities included that are of interest to power users of desktop publishing paraphernalia.

## Periodicals

*Aldus Magazine.* Bimonthly, $4.00 per copy/$20.00 per year. Aldus Corporation, 411 First Avenue South, Seattle, WA 98104-2871. (206) 628-2321.

The PageMaker publisher's house organ, the journal itself is a model of techniques and styles you can use with desktop publishing. Included are hints and tricks and much information specific to using PageMaker to best advantage. A bit heavy on advertisements, its references to third-party products, as well as to summaries of Aldus' own PageMaker add-on utilities, make it valuable for sources of further information.

*Business Publishing.* Monthly, $6.00 per copy/$24.00 per year. Hitchcock Publishing Company, 191 S. Gary Avenue, Carol Stream, IL 60188.

This text looks at desktop publishing from a composition and typesetter's viewpoint and is of value for the connection it makes between in-house publishing and its relationship to professional typesetting projects. Articles feature fonts and type, printer technology, paper quality, and considerations which must be made if documents will be output both by computer (laser) printers and high-resolution (printshop) hardware. It is a good periodical for browsing collections.

## CHAPTER 10

Carey, Joan. *MINITAB Mini-Manual: A Beginner's Guide to MINITAB Statistical Software.* State College, PA: Minitab, Inc., 1992. Paper, $6.95.

Full of examples and well-illustrated, this introductory handbook covers all platforms for which Minitab is available. The book assumes that the reader has a knowledge of elementary statistics and of the particular

PC on which Minitab is to be run. It provides a "quickstart" format to get the new user up and running.

Norusis, Marija N. *SPSS/PC+ Studentware Plus.* Chicago: SPSS Inc., 1991. Paper, 483 pp., $49.95 (includes ten 5 1/4" IBM format diskettes with student version of SPSS and example files).

A tutorial for the abridged version of the Statistical Program for the Social Sciences, it is an economical alternative to the mainframe or full-featured PC versions of the software, which can cost $500 or more per copy. Probably best used as a textbook, it has reference value for technical collections.

### Periodical

*Library Software Review.* Bimonthly, $125.00 per year. Meckler Corporation, 11 Ferry Lane West, Westport, CT 06880.

Programs featured in *Library Software Review* undergo lengthy narrative descriptions. Special features, macro operations, relevant code segments, and sample outputs are all considered. The reviews tend to reveal features about a program which are not covered in other periodicals, and writeups of software with parallels between the library and business worlds are often demonstrated. Bibliographies are included with reviews.

## CHAPTER 11

Hendley, Tony. *CD-ROM & Optical Publishing Systems.* Westport, CT: Meckler Publishing Corporation, in association with Cimtech and the British National Bibliography Research Fund, 1987. Paper, 150 pp., $39.50.

Similar to Myers' *Publishing with CD-ROM* (below), it presents a technical overview of CD-ROM as a publishing medium and the workstation configurations necessary for access to CD-ROM data. It discusses the marketplace of CD-ROM-related products and includes a modest source list of vendors specializing in the arena of compact disc data bases.

Holz, Frederick. *CD-ROMs: Breakthrough in Information Storage.* Blue Ridge Summit, PA: Tab Books, 1988. 215 pp., $22.95.

This is a very detailed essay covering the technology and theory of CD-ROM electronics and construction. Written on an engineering level, the discussions contain many numeric specifications and descriptions of the mechanics of the players (drives) as well as the media. There is an exhaustive section on standards, as well as appendices of suppliers and manufacturers. The value to librarians is the annotated bibliography of databases currently on CD-ROM and collection of essays on the future and applications of the technology.

Lambert, Steve and Ropiequet, Suzanne, editors. *CD ROM: The New Papyrus*. Redmond, WA: Microsoft Press, 1986. Paper, 619 pp., $21.95.

A collection of essays explains the (then) new CD-ROM technology, predicting its potential, and issuing a call for standards. Included are passages illustrating the possibilities for library applications, authoring, archive management, and research support. Extensive footnoting and appendix of supplemental resources.

Myers, Patti. *Publishing with CD-ROM*. Westport, CT: Meckler Publishing Corporation, in association with The National Composition Association, 1987. Paper, 98 pp., $22.95.

The audience of this guide is "providers of publishing services," and it includes information on both literary and technical considerations for using disc media. There is a good overview on the mechanics of CD-ROMs, and the principles are outlined in lay terms. The book is rich in terminology and includes bibliographic sources and a list of companies involved of CD-ROM publishing services.

Ropiequet, Suzanne, editor, with Linberger, John and Zoellick, Bill. *CD ROM: Optical Publishing*. Redmond, WA: Microsoft Press, 1987. Paper, 358 pp., $22.95.

Volume two of *CD ROM: The New Papyrus*, it is also in essay format, and a bit more technical than the original publication. It focuses on information delivery, text retrieval and database indexing, and the creation of information systems on disk, including the cataloging utility BiblioFile, and has reference value for its description of the High Sierra standard and provision of an extensive glossary.

## Catalogs

Several dealers make available single and bundled CD-ROMs containing useful information for library reference departments. These are not the vendors that sell CD-ROMs on a subscription basis, and the material is not highly technical. But for ready reference and as supplements to basic collections, the offerings in the following catalogs can save search time and shelf space.

[Catalog of] CD ROM, Inc., 1667 Cole Boulevard, Suite 400, Golden, CO 80401. Quarterly, free. Orders (800) 821-5245.

The catalog is grouped by subject areas, and titles are annotated; it sells titles for both IBM PC and compatibles and Macintosh computers. It also deals in CD-ROM hardware with a considerable variety of brands offered.

[Catalog of] DAK Industries Inc., 8200 Remmet Ave., Canoga Park, CA 91304. Quarterly, free. Orders (800) 325-0800.

This catalog sells in bundles, usually with purchase of hardware. Many titles are offered as superseded annual editions, but prices are at bargain levels.

*EDUCORP Software Encyclopedia: Affordable Software, Hardware, CD-ROM Products, and Accessories for Macintosh Computers* (see chapter 2 entry above for full bibliographic citation).

[Catalog of] Mr. CD ROM, P.O. Box 1087, Winter Garden, FL 34777. Quarterly, free. Orders (800) 444-MRCD.

This catalog is annotated with several hundred titles and includes some hardware.

[Catalog of] Tiger Software, 800 Douglas Entrance, Executive Tower, 7th Floor, Coral Gables, Fl 33134. Quarterly, free. Orders (888-4437.

It contains color illustrations with annotations and is similar to DAK (above) in that CD-ROMs are sold with hardware, but there are CD-ROM-only bundles sold as well. It also has discount pricing.

[Catalog of] Ztek Co., P.O. Box 1055, Louisville, KY 40201-1055. $5.00 per issue. Orders (800) 247-1603.

Selling "interactive videodiscs & CD-ROM for education," the catalog is annotated and indexed. and deals with IBM PC and Macintosh formats.

## Periodicals

*CD-ROM Librarian.* Published eleven times per year, $82.00 per year. Meckler Corporation, Eleven Ferry Lane West, Westport, CT 06880.

This journal began life as *Optical Information Systems Update/Library and Information Center Applications,* titles which still accurately describe the format and contents of the latest incarnation. While the emphasis is on compact discs, laser discs and other optical media are considered as well. It contains reviews and technical articles, including discussions of standards. Bibliographies at the ends of articles make *CD-ROM Librarian* a powerful selection tool.

*CD-ROM Professional.* Published six times a year, $86.00 per year. Pemberton Press, Inc., 462 Danbury Road, Wilton, CT 06897-2126.

A more technical treatment of CD-ROMs, with feature articles, product reviews, and special treatment of CD-ROM publishing, its essays are detailed, and reviews and tests are thorough and exhaustive, although no rating scales are included. It presents screen dumps and code segments where applicable. Both hardware and software are included.

*CD-ROM Review.* Published monthly, $34.97 per year. IDG Communications, Eighty Elm Street, Peterborough, NH 03458.

The magazine contains technical articles and CD-ROM title reviews, the latter of which emphasize academic/educational rather than consumer-oriented databases. Discussions of hardware are included, and selection guides and writeups of CD-ROM specifications help wade through the (sometimes confusing) mire of this establishing standard.

*CD-ROM Shopper's Guide.* Published quarterly, $12.95 per year. DDRI, Inc., 510 N. Washington Street, Suite 401, Falls Church, VA 22046-3537.

The content consists of addresses and sources for some very obscure and hard-to-find CD-ROM hardware and software products.

*Imaging: The Imaging Industry Magazine.* Monthly, $2.95 per copy/$17.95 per year. Imaging Magazine, 12 West 21 Street, New York, NY 10160-0371.

Emphasis is on CD-ROM data storage and optically rewritable disk drives. Many product reviews (more for hardware than software) are included, although they are presented without ratings. Nonetheless, the reviews by themselves add much value to the journal because optical storage technology is a relatively new phenomenon. Has reference value for discussions on creation of CD-ROM data bases and optical disk publishing.

*Imaging World.* Monthly, $5.00 per copy/$48.00 per year. IW Publishing, Inc., 49 Bayview St., Camden, ME 04843. (207) 236-8524.

A glossy tabloid, containing signed news articles of developments in this relatively new technology, it has a commercial rather than technical slant, although the new product descriptions are quite detailed.

## CHAPTER 14

Dougherty, Richard M. and Heinritz, Fred J. *Scientific Management of Library Operations.* Second edition. New York: Scarecrow Press, 1982. 286 pp. $20.00.

Almost ancient history (first published in 1966), the book contains timeless information on the study, planning, charting, recording, and evaluating of library business procedures. Written well before even the embryonic stages of library automation; nonetheless, it offers principles and methods of performing a systems analysis on many library procedures.

## CHAPTER 15

Hahn, Harley and Rick Stout. *The Internet Yellow Pages.* Berkeley, CA: Osborne McGraw-Hill, 1994. Paper, 447 pp., $27.95.

There are several Internet reference books with a telephone directory-like format, and this one is typical. As with most network directories, the information is slightly out-of-date even on the day of release. However, the *Internet Yellow Pages* is a good springboard for browsers and to demonstrate the various kinds of data available on the Net. This volume is particularly useful for locating Usenet groups and anonymous FTP sites. It has directory entries only and very little "how-to" information is included.

Kehoe, Brendan P. *Zen & the Art of the Internet: a Beginner's Guide.* New York: Prentice Hall, 1993. Paper, 112 pp. $22.00.

A nontechnical approach to the Internet, it answers the questions "what is there on the system for me?" and "how do I sign on with a minimum of hassle?" Kehoe explains FTP and Telnet, the two basic software utilities for accessing Internet, along with pointers for using the various subcomponents to best academic advantage.

Krol, Ed. *The Whole Internet User's Guide and Catalog.* Second edition. Sebastopol, CA: O'Reilly & Associates, 1994. Paper, 543 pp., $24.95.

Written with new users in mind, *Whole Internet* includes background material, a description of the "inner workings" of Internet, and a summary of functions and services available. The author professes that he has featured the "reference librarians" of Internet, focusing on recently developed services such as Archie, an archive of free software; Gopher, a general tool for accessing Internet resources; WAIS, a tool for searching large libraries and collections, based on keywords; and WWW, the World Wide Web, for organizing all the Internet's resources in terms of a hypertext model. It has a generous list of resources, an annotated bibliography, and glossary of Internet related terminology.

LaQuey, Tracy L., editor. *The User's Directory of Computer Networks.* New York: Prentice Hall, 1990. Paper, 630 pp., $35.00.

Exhaustive encyclopedic directory compiled by the Computation Center of the University of Texas at Austin, it outlines BITNET, the Internet, NSFNET, JANET, and several other regional academic networks, and invaluable for locating electronic mail addresses. The names directory is somewhat dated, but the institutions list is complete and accurate. There is a great deal of information on affiliated organizations and principles of connectivity.

Sheldon, Tom. *Novell NetWare: The Complete Reference.* Second edition. Berkeley, CA: Osborne/McGraw-Hill, 1992. Paper, 912 pp., $39.95.

Encyclopedic, it covers several versions of NetWare. Material is for both installers of NetWare-based network hardware and administrators and users of the program itself. Particularly useful as a supplemental volume for software management in places where the Novell documentation can be somewhat confusing to first-time installers, it includes details about account and file management, with emphasis on security and server maintenance.

## Catalog

*Black Box Catalog: The Source for Connectivity.* Black Box Corporation, P.O. Box 12800, Pittsburgh, PA 15241-0800. Quarterly, $5.00 per copy.

Comprehensive source for all types of PC-based local area networks, the catalog has items that represent everything from wire and cable to complete systems to supported LANs, including ArcNet, EtherNet, token ring, and others. The catalog is well-illustrated and has some reference shelf value.

## Periodical

*Internet World: The Magazine for Internet Users.* Monthly, $4.95 per copy/$29.00 per year. Internet World, P.O. Box 713, Mt. Morris, IL 61054-9965.

This magazine features scholarly articles, from beginner how-to instruction to advanced uses of the Net. The book reviews are comprehensive, and each issue offers lists of new Internet services with online addresses. It has reference value for publicizing upcoming Internet events and describing services too new to appear in other trade (i.e., book) literature.

## CHAPTER 16

Campbell, Joe. *C Programmer's Guide to Serial Communications.* Indianapolis: Howard Sams, 1987. Paper, 672 pp., $29.95.

This one-of-a-kind book is comprehensive. Particular emphasis is given to the Hayes protocol and RS-232 standard. This is a first purchase if you have a significant collection on system level computer programming.

Schuyler, Michael, ed.. *Dial In, 1992: Annual Guide to Online Public Access Catalogs.* Westport, CT: Meckler, 1992. Paper, 250 pp., $55.00.

Begun in 1991, this compendium of U.S. and Canadian libraries with dial access to their online computerized catalogs includes access parameters, hours of operation, communications protocols and system vendor affiliates for many academic and public libraries. Introductory material on data communications, modem usage, and online catalogs in general is included. Cross indexes by states/provinces, libraries, Zip/postal codes and automation system vendors are also featured.

Smith, Bud E. *On-Line With BitCom.* New York: Bantam Books, 1989. Paper, 333 pp., $39.95 (includes a 5 1/4" IBM format diskette with BitCom and fifty script files).

BitCom is a popular and inexpensive full-featured modem control and communications program, and this book provides a thorough description of the software and its capabilities. Protocols are included, as are instructions for accessing on-line (commercial) services. It is very complete in its description of BitCom's script (command) language, for which examples are given on the included disk.

## CHAPTER 17

Hursch, Jack L. and Carolyn J. Hursch. *dBASE IV SQL User's Guide.* Torrance, CA: Tate Publishing, 1989. Paper, 280 pp., $24.95.

This is a comprehensive manual for sequential control language as it integrates with the dBase IV database software. Many examples of applications code are given with a practical slant. It is a useful tutorial for those who already have a working knowledge of the dBase language to learn the more universal SQL techniques.

*Searching DIALOG: The Complete Guide.* Palo Alto, CA: Dialog Information Services, Inc., 1991. Notebook, $30.00.

A textbook, as well as user guide, for the search strategies, methodologies, commands and contact names/addresses of Dialog, it is a definitive reference which would be present in any library using or offering DIALOG services.

### Periodical

*Online: The Magazine of Online Information Systems.* Published six times per year, $89.00 per year. Online, Inc., 462 Danbury Road, Wilton, CT 06897-2126. (800) 248-8466.

The magazine covers CD-ROM-based databases as well as dialup services. Scholarly and informative, it focuses on intelligent use of specific online services and advises on both hardware and software aspects of maintaining an effective online searching environment. It includes book and software reviews as well as summaries of product tests.

## APPENDIX B

Lyon, Lockwood and Kenniston W., Lord, Jr. *CDP Review Manual.* Fifth edition. New York: Van Nostrand Reinhold, 1991. Paper, 800 pp., $49.95.

More of a textbook than a set of practice examinations, this study guide for the Certificate in Data Processing includes material on accounting, management, systems analysis, mathematics, and statistics as well as the fundamentals of hardware and software.

Morrison, James W. *CDP Certificate in Data Processing Examination.* New York: Arco Publishing, 1980. Paper, 348 pp., $12.00.

As is typical with Arco publications, emphasis is on test taking rather than on memorization of facts. Lengthy examinations, along with solved problems, are presented to cover the five areas tested on the CDP examination.

# Index